"Even politically hostile readers will have a hard time contesting the conclusions in Rafael Medoff's extensively researched, methodical, data-driven, and accessible volume. It should be read by everyone who wants to understand October 7 in historical context."

—EUNICE G. POLLACK, coeditor of the *Encyclopedia of American Jewish History*

"I cannot imagine a more important book for the Jewish community and indeed all human rights advocates. This brilliant and much-needed volume has the great virtue of telling the truth about the October 7 attacks and the often deeply unsatisfactory reactions of western governments, universities, and mass media."

—NEIL J. KRESSEL, author of *Mass Hate: The Global Rise of Genocide and Terror*

THE ROAD TO OCTOBER 7

The Jewish Publication Society expresses its gratitude for the generosity of the sponsor of this book.

Wendy Fein Cooper, in loving memory of Leonard J. Cooper

University of Nebraska Press | Lincoln

THE ROAD TO OCTOBER 7

Hamas, the Holocaust, and the Eternal War against the Jews

RAFAEL MEDOFF

The Jewish Publication Society | Philadelphia

Manufactured in the United States of America.

For customers in the EU with safety/GPSR concerns, contact:
gpsr@mare-nostrum.co.uk
Mare Nostrum Group BV
Mauritskade 21D
1091 GC Amsterdam
The Netherlands

Library of Congress Control Number: 2025015417

Set in Minion Pro by A. Shahan.

Contents

Acknowledgments

I am fortunate to once again have the opportunity to work with The Jewish Publication Society (JPS, the nation's oldest Jewish publisher), under director and editor-in-chief Dr. Malka Z. Simkovich and her colleagues. Her two predecessors, Dr. Elias Sacks and Rabbi Barry L. Schwartz, were especially helpful in guiding this manuscript in its early stages. I am grateful for their confidence in this project. Joy Weinberg, JPS managing editor, applied her peerless skills to this undertaking, and the manuscript benefited enormously as a result; any discernible flaws remaining are solely my responsibility. I am also deeply grateful to my co-publisher, the University of Nebraska Press, and UNP's superb copyeditor Amy Wagner. I am thankful, as well, to the many individuals who supplied helpful information or insights, or assisted in other ways, in particular David Suissa, Itamar Marcus, Monty N. Penkower, Sonja P. Wentling, Yisrael Medad, and the late Stephen H. Norwood, and the numerous colleagues, friends, and family members who lent a patient ear during the writing and revising process. In addition, I am grateful to staff members at the American Jewish Historical Society, the Central Zionist Archives, and the Franklin D. Roosevelt Library and Archives for facilitating my research.

THE ROAD TO OCTOBER 7

Introduction

When Neta Stahl speaks of Kibbutz Kfar Aza, the Israeli community near the Gaza Strip where she was born and raised, she prefers to speak in English, because "in Hebrew, the words are too painful, a reminder of what we lost." In Hebrew, "the words have the sound, the smell, the images of the green lawns after the first rain that promised a stroll in red boots with colorful umbrellas in what we called 'the wadi,' a winter stream that we crossed on our way from the children's house to our parents' homes."[1]

Kfar Aza, in the 1970s and early 1980s, was where Neta and the other children tended their own vegetable garden, and on harvesting day marched excitedly through the kibbutz dining hall—as "the adults in their work clothes stopped their lunches to cheer us"—to deliver the freshly picked produce to the kitchen head. Kfar Aza was where hours of storytelling and joking once left the children laughing so hard that they broke the sofa on which they sat. And Kfar Aza was where Neta and her friend Aviv edited a children's newspaper, *Tzabariko*, chronicling thoughts and experiences that Aviv, the kibbutz archivist, would one day collect and preserve. Aviv was so passionate a kite enthusiast that the kibbutz's annual autumn kite-flying festival would come to be nicknamed the *Avivonyada*. In 2023, the event was scheduled to take place on the holiday of Simḥat Torah. That was the day Palestinian Arab terrorists murdered Aviv, his wife, and their three children. That was the day Hamas and its partners in terror turned Kfar Aza into "ruins, a political spectacle, a museum of death."[2]

Understanding what has vanished is as important as understanding how and why it was torn away. In recent years, there has been a proliferation of accounts of pre-Holocaust European Jewish life in books, museums, films, and public programs. Lucy Dawidowicz's 1989 memoir, *From That Time and Place*, described the world of secular Jewish intellectuals and Yiddish culture in interwar Europe: "You could live a full life in Vilna, as many Vilna Jews did, speaking only Yiddish, without knowing much Polish or knowing it well." But for all its lively culture, publications, and events, Dawidowicz actually experienced "a feverish flowering in the shadow of death," she later realized. "Everything I loved in Vilna rested upon a rotten crumbling foundation." As one book reviewer noted, "History was moving in wholly other directions."[3]

In Dawidowicz's best-known book, *The War Against the Jews*, she described the Holocaust not as a crime of opportunity conducted in the shadow of a world war, but as the culmination of an ideologically driven strategy hatched by Adolf Hitler decades before he was in a position to implement it. For Dawidowicz, the story of the Holocaust began with Hitler's experiences in World War I. For *The Road to October 7*, it is a story one thousand years in the making—in effect, an eternal war against the Jews.

This volume places October 7 and its aftermath within the context of the history of persecutions of the Jews. It presents a timeline of events which, despite some variations and differences, bear too many similarities to be understood as anything but parts of a single tragic history. It analyzes the perpetrators and victims of the Hamas invasion, the responses on America's streets and college campuses, and the debate over antisemitism that has taken a new turn as a result. Most of all, it shows the historical continuity of the war against the Jewish people that has raged from medieval Europe to Czarist Russia, from Hebron in 1929 to Warsaw in 1943 to Kibbutz Kfar Aza in 2023. Past violence against Jews throughout history is connected to more recent incarnations of the phenomenon in the similarity of beliefs, methods, and goals across the centuries. Moreover, many perpetrators in the modern era have been inspired and educated by those who preceded them in the war against the Jews. For the October 7 massacre, the killers drew on 1,300-year-old Islamist teachings, contemporary terrorist role models, and in some cases even the writings of Hitler. Teachers, religious authorities, and political leaders focused the younger generation's attention on ancient Quranic verses and Islamist legends that would inspire them to hate Jews and embrace the religious imperative to wage war in pursuit of worldwide Muslim sovereignty. Any attempt by Jews to rise above third-class, or *dhimmi*, status required violent opposition. Contemporary massacres of Jews in the Holy Land in turn became sources of inspiration for those who followed them, in the form of streets and schools named after mass murderers, and television and radio shows glorifying heinous acts as heroic martyrdom.

The mechanisms through which ancient hatreds helped fuel violent antisemitism in our own time pertain to Christian Europe as well. The same New Testament verses and medieval antisemitic legends known to the perpetrators of Crusader massacres of Jews and the horrors of the Inquisition also provided ideological support for anti-Jewish pogroms in seventeenth-century Ukraine and nineteenth-century Russia. Extreme nationalism, paranoia about Jews and Communism, and longstanding theological antisemitism proved a potent combination for fomenting anti-Jewish violence among pogromists in post–World War I Ukraine as well as among the perpetrators and collaborators in the Holocaust. In each era, there were unique circumstances that helped facilitate persecution—whether fear of revolution in Russia, the scapegoating of Jews for Germany's economic crises, or the prospect of Jews reestablishing their ancient homeland—but behind them all was a continuity of extremist ideology anchored in classic religious and nationalist beliefs.

Some readers may be particularly unsettled by parts of chapter 1, which includes many details of the October 7 atrocities, and chapter 6, which chronicles harrowing incidents of anti-Jewish violence around the world in earlier times. They were unsettling for me to compile. It is certainly feasible to skim over some of those parts without missing the major points of this study. But as difficult as they are to read, the actual words of those who were there, whether in thirteenth-century France or southern Israel eight centuries later, are necessary to spotlight the tragic continuity between past and present, in the hope that lessons may be learned that will ensure a better future.

Part 1. The Present

Understanding October 7 and Its Aftermath

1. In the Cities of Slaughter

Three thousand Palestinian Arab terrorists, trained by Iran and financed by Iran and Qatar, invaded southern Israel early on the morning of October 7, 2023, on Simḥat Torah, the Jewish holiday of rejoicing with the Torah. Attackers shot out security cameras along the border, then sliced through the border fence at dozens of points with bulldozers, explosives, and wire-cutting gear. Heavily armed gangs surged forward on motorcycles, vans, and, soon, in automobiles commandeered from Israeli drivers whom they shot. Some terrorists reached Israel on motorized paragliders. Israeli guard posts near the border and army bases nearby were lightly guarded, with many soldiers on leave for the holiday.

About 1,200 people, from three months to eighty-five years old, would be murdered, and thousands more injured. The vast majority were civilians; three hundred and seventy-six were soldiers and security personnel killed while retaking the invaded towns or during Hamas attacks on army bases. Seventy-one foreign nationals and several dozen Israeli Arabs employed in the besieged communities were also killed. Another 251 men, women, and children were abducted into Gaza. Forty-three of those murdered, and twelve of those kidnapped, were American citizens.[1]

THE IDEOLOGY BEHIND OCTOBER 7

Most of the terrorists were members of Hamas or its smaller partner, Palestinian Islamic Jihad.[2] Hamas named the assault "Operation Al-Aqsa Flood," a reference to the Al-Aqsa Mosque in Jerusalem. Regarded by Muslims as their third holiest site, Al-Aqsa is situated on the elevated Temple Mount, atop the ruins of the centers of ancient Jewish religious life, the First and Second Temples, which stood in biblical times. No recent events had precipitated the October 7 attack, which Hamas had been preparing for years (see chapter 2). The apocalyptic "flood" reference was intended as a jihadist rallying cry for the masses, in conjunction with false allegations of Jews secretly conspiring to attack the mosque. Similar propaganda had accompanied the Palestinian Arab pogrom against Jewish residents of Hebron in 1929 (see chapter 6).[3]

The October 7 attack represented the overwhelming power of ideology, a blend of Islamist fundamentalism and Arab nationalism. For Hamas, this was a jihad, a religious war—an existential battle between Islam and Judaism (see chapter 2).

Because its driving force was ideological, Hamas launched the October 7 attack even though its premise ran counter to conventional military doctrine and common sense. Since Israel possessed overwhelming military superiority, Hamas leaders must have expected they were sending thousands of their best-trained men to certain death. As soon as Israel employed tanks, planes, and helicopters, which Hamas did not have, the attackers would be wiped out, and a massive Israeli counterattack into Gaza would surely follow. In some of the videos the terrorists took, they expressed surprise that they managed to penetrate Israeli territory as far as they did; they assumed they would be killed long before they reached any Israeli towns.[4] They willingly and proudly proceeded on their mission of murder; educated in schools and mosques where war against the Jews was taught as a supreme value, they were eager to put their principles into practice (see chapter 3).[5]

Western military commanders largely operate according to rational considerations of advantages and disadvantages, risks versus gains. The actions of terrorists and dictators, by contrast, often are dictated by ideology. From the standpoint of military strategy, Nazi Germany's decision to divert significant resources away from its war effort in order to organize the mass murder of Jews was irrational. U.S. Secretary of State Dean Rusk assured Israeli ambassador Abba Eban on the eve of the 1967 war that Arab aggression was unlikely since it would be "irrational" for Egyptian leader Gamal Abdel Nasser to attack under the prevailing circumstances, but the attack made perfect sense to a dictator consumed by extremist ideology.[6] Likewise, Hamas leader Yahya

Sinwar asserted that the prospect of "even 100,000" innocent Gazans dying was no deterrent to invading Israel. He valued the death of Jews more than the lives of his countrymen. The prospect of an apocalyptic bloodbath was worth any price.[7]

ATTACK ON THE MUSIC FESTIVAL

Hamas's first target on October 7 was the large crowd attending the outdoor Supernova music festival just four miles from the border. Terrorists fired thousands of rockets from Gaza as cover for the arriving ground forces. Several thousand concertgoers began exiting the site, assuming the explosions were just the latest wave of Hamas rockets that had been fired across the border off and on for more than a decade. Soon, though, drivers near the front of the long line of cars realized "the first few vehicles in the traffic jam were not driving—all the people inside were dead."[8] Terrorists in trucks and on motorcycles were spraying the cars with automatic gunfire.[9] The Israeli drivers made wild U-turns, attempting to flee back toward the campgrounds. Many abandoned their cars and ran across the adjacent fields. Without any trees or other cover, "we were ducks on a shooting range," one recalled.[10] All around them was "hysteria, fear, explosions, screams." People were "running in different directions," chased by terrorists who "eliminated anyone who didn't run fast enough."[11] Outside each of the neighboring Israeli villages was a migunit, a small, doorless, concrete shelter. But the structures were designed for protection against missiles, not close-range gunfire. Many who reached the shelters were killed by hand grenades thrown into the entranceways. A handful of escapees survived because, after falling wounded, they were shielded by the dead bodies of those killed seconds later. Holocaust memoirs describe many similar scenes.

One small group of refugees managed to reach an abandoned factory near the concert site. They huddled in a tiny room there for the next twelve hours. "Every little sound that someone made by mistake and we all went crazy—'Don't move! Don't move!,'" one of the survivors recounted. "I don't want to compare, but that was the closest to Nazis looking for Jews inside people's homes. . . . You feel that you are like sheep being taken to slaughter, you are waiting for them to come and murder you. And if not murder you, then kidnap you."[12] Others hid in the woods, under hastily arranged piles of leaves or in ditches and hillside crevices that offered at least brief refuge. Hour after hour they remained perfectly still, in the scorching heat and without water, all the while hearing the terrorists' jubilant cries of "Jew! There's a Jew! Kill him!" Most of those who hid were eventually discovered and executed by roaming gangs of terrorists in the hours before Israeli troops arrived.[13] Eighty years earlier, the Nazis undertook similar *Judenjagden*, or Jew hunts, to round up individual escapees from massacres in the German-occupied Polish countryside.[14]

The terrifying experience of knowing their hiding places could be discovered at any moment inevitably evoked scenes from the history of Jewish victimization. May H., camouflaged in a pit, told the young man next to her, "You know the stories from the Holocaust where people pretended to be dead, and that's how they went unnoticed? That's what's going to happen to us."[15] Maya E. later described those hours with a similar analogy: "We became silent, a silence which wouldn't shame Anne Frank in the attic. No one breathed, we were dead silent."[16]

In all, 364 of the festival goers were murdered. Many more were wounded, and dozens were abducted and taken to Gaza.

DEVASTATION OF TOWNS AND KIBBUTZIM

Residents of the Israeli towns and kibbutzim in the region near Gaza heard the same sirens as the Supernova attendees a few miles away. They, too, assumed the alarm was nothing out of the ordinary, just another brief rocket barrage that Israel's Iron Dome antimissile system would intercept.

Each community had its own local security force, lightly armed and small in number, mostly volunteers. Their counterterrorism training had focused on defense against a lone infiltrator or a small group—not an entire army of heavily armed terrorists implementing a strategic attack with intimate knowledge of the town's layout and a large crew of civilian assistants.

Moving methodically from house to house, the terrorists shot residents to death at close range or killed them by hurling grenades through the windows, often while shouting "*Itbach al Yahud*" (Kill the Jews), a cry often heard in Palestinian Arab terror attacks and mob assaults over the years.[17] They systematically set fire to homes, sometimes as the final blow after slaughtering the residents, sometimes as a means of forcing residents to exit so they could be kidnapped or murdered. Likewise, the Nazis used flamethrowers to compel Jews in the Warsaw Ghetto and elsewhere to emerge from their hiding places.[18]

In Kibbutz Kfar Aza, Rotem C., her husband, Yakir, and their two children sheltered in their house's safe room. Amidst the sounds of "nonstop shooting, explosions, and red alert sirens," they heard terrorists "breaking into our house, getting closer to the safe room, [then] shouting in Arabic to open the [reinforced] door." For forty minutes, they wrestled with the doorknob as Yakir held fast to the handle. Rotem held the iron window shut; at one point a grenade exploded the window, but still she held on. "At that point, the terrorists stopped fighting the safe room and we heard them breaking things," she remembered. "They looted everything they could, and then one of the terrorists shouted in Hebrew, 'Today you won't have an afternoon.'" Within minutes, smoke was seeping into their hiding spot. "We realized that they wanted to burn us alive. . . . The walls of the safe room were insanely hot, as if we were in an oven with the heat turned all the way up. The kids started to throw up and we were helpless." Just before the flames and smoke engulfed them, the family escaped through the safe room window. Their home was completely destroyed.[19]

Thirty-one-year-old Nirel Zini and his partner, Niv Raviv, twenty-seven, had been living in Kfar Aza for just six months. Years earlier Nirel had been injured in an incident during his army service, and every October 10 he and Niv enjoyed a festive meal to celebrate the anniversary of his survival. Unbeknownst to her, Nirel had purchased an engagement ring and was planning to propose to her on October 10, 2023. Instead, on the morning of October 7, they were in their safe room, with Nirel holding the door with one hand and grasping a knife in the other. His final text message to his family, at 10:04 a.m., read: "I'll update, they're here. I'm putting the phone down, pray." The charred engagement ring was found among the ruins of the burned house, near their bodies.[20]

In community after community, it was the same horrible story, with a few varying details. In her safe room in Kibbutz Re'im, Katy L. received a text "from a woman who just had her firstborn child a week earlier, saying that they burned her house down and that they were suffocating in the safe room." She and her husband received voice messages from neighbors, "and we could hear them suffocating." Two-and-a-half hours into the attack, she and her husband, Shai, heard glass shattering inside their house. "The kids were hiding under the bed, and I asked them to cover their ears," she recounted later. "If we stay alive, they don't need to remember what they heard. The monsters were inside my home, arguing in Arabic, going into room after room, looking for us." They soon reached the safe room but were unable to pry it open as Shai held fast to the door handle. "We could then hear them going crazy inside our home, knocked off closets, lifted beds, shattered tvs." Israeli soldiers eventually ousted the terrorists and led the family from their destroyed house. Katy recalled that the soldiers "asked us not to look to the right and to the left while passing the kibbutz paths because there were dead bodies there."[21]

The victims included people with disabilities. One was seventeen-year-old Ruth Peretz, who was wheelchair bound and severely handicapped from cerebral palsy and muscular dystrophy. She was murdered at the festival grounds; her wheelchair was found discarded near the Gaza border.[22] One of the most infamous episodes in the history of Palestinian Arab terrorism likewise involved a disabled person, when the hijackers of the *Achille Lauro* cruise ship in the Mediterranean Sea in 1985 shot the elderly, wheelchair-bound Leon Klinghoffer in the head and dumped him overboard.[23]

HOW THEY DIED

"The plan was to go from home to home, from room to room, to throw grenades and kill everyone, including women and children," a captured terrorist later explained in a videotaped confession. "Hamas ordered us to crush their heads and cut them off, [and] to cut [off] their legs."[24]

Written instructions found on the body of a killed terrorist asserted: "You must sharpen the blades of your swords and be pure in your intentions before Allah. Know that the enemy is a disease that has no cure, except beheading and removing the hearts and livers. Attack them!"[25]

Israeli forensic pathologists found soot in the throats of many of the victims, indicating they were burned alive. Many also had their hands bound behind their backs. Dr. Ricardo Nachman, head of Israel's National Center of Forensic Medicine, described encountering "an adult and a child stuck together and burned with a metal wire around them."[26] Pathologists reported at a press conference two weeks after the invasion that "many bodies, including those of babies, were without heads."[27] Col. (Res) Golan Vach, commander of the army's National Rescue Unit, told reporters: "I found some babies with their heads cut, which I personally evacuated, I found butchered women with no hands, soldiers with their heads cut, and found dozens of burnt young people."[28]

Decapitations have been a common feature of atrocities against Jews, from the Crusades to Russian and Arab pogroms, to the Holocaust. R. M. Graves, a British official who was present during Israel's War of Independence in 1948, noted in his diary that following one Arab attack, "Some heads were cut off the bodies of the fallen Jews and have been carried round Jerusalem as trophies of victory" (see chapter 6).[29]

Captured terrorists described to Israeli police interrogators after the October 7 attack how they "cut off organs and took them to Gaza in order to trade with them in future hostage negotiations."[30] Israeli morgue volunteer Shari Mendes examined the body of a young woman "whose arm was broken in so many places it was difficult for us to lay her arm in the burial shroud, her leg too." There were women who were "shot in the crotch, in the genitals, in the breast." She saw "bodies that were beheaded or had limbs cut off, mutilated." The body of one young woman arrived "with no legs; they had been cut off. We saw several severed heads, one with a large kitchen knife still embedded in the neck." Many bodies "were burned beyond recognition, often without arms or legs; they did not resemble anything human," she said. "Sometimes we sifted through piles of ash that disintegrated as we touched them. These soldiers were burnt alive at very high temperatures." In addition, "heads and faces were covered in blood, they were shot in the eyes, face, and skull—it was often impossible for families to be shown faces, and it seems as if mutilation of these women's faces was an objective in their murders." Sometimes "heads were bashed in so badly that their brains were spilling out. Some were shot in the head so many times at close range that their heads were almost blown off."[31]

Rabbi Moshe Dickstein, a commander of the army's casualty identification unit, said "the first body we came across" when his unit reached a recaptured area was in "an overturned stroller. Inside the stroller was a baby, and his head was thrown aside with a knife in it. The woman we found, presumably the mother, was lying on the couch with blood flowing from her private area."[32] For Tal Hayun, director of nursing at Soroka Hospital's Surgery and Recovery Room, the image most deeply ingrained in her mind was "the sight of a cart packed full of arms and legs" delivered to the hospital's morgue. Accounts of the 1146 pogrom in Wolkenburg (present-day Germany) during the Second Crusade tell of wagons filled with severed limbs being carted to the local Jewish cemetery.[33]

THE COLLABORATORS

Some Palestinian Arab day laborers from Gaza who had been employed in Israeli towns gave Hamas layouts of the targeted communities and personal schedules of the residents. Data found on cellphones, notebooks, maps, and other documents carried by captured or killed terrorists showed they had inside information that could not have been obtained otherwise. "They knew who lived in which house," said senior Israeli police superintendent Micky Rosenfeld. "They knew exactly how many people were in those houses, and all of that information they transferred to the Hamas terrorists."[34]

Sabine Tasa and her family were victims of those collaborators. Sabine's husband and one of their sons were murdered, and their other two sons badly wounded, in the village of Netiv Asara on October 7. Israeli army officials told her that a Gazan named Khalil who had worked in her town as a handyman had provided information to Hamas. "They had charts, with my family name and address, the Tasa family, the age of each family member, 'Sabine Tasa, four boys, no dogs, [husband] Avraham Tasa,'" Tasa said. "He worked for us for thirty years. He painted the house, plumbing, consulted on this problem and that problem. At this person's house and that person's house. We brought him food, water. Khalil worked for everyone in Netiv. He was treated like a member of our household. We saw him as the man of peace, a bridge between us and Gaza."[35]

Batia Holin, age seventy, of Kibbutz Kfar Aza, befriended Mahmoud, a fellow photographer living in the Gaza village of al-Jiyya. They exchanged photographs of each other's towns, co-curated an online exhibit viewed by more than ten thousand people, and made plans to jointly exhibit their work at a San Diego gallery. But on the morning of October 7, in the midst of the Hamas invasion, Mahmoud telephoned Batia to ask how many soldiers were in the kibbutz and where they were stationed. That, she said later, was when she realized Mahmoud was working with Hamas and had been passing them her photos of the kibbutz to help plan the attack.[36]

During the year preceding October 7, an average of ten to fifteen thousand Gazan laborers were allowed to enter Israel daily. Some critics had urged Israel to significantly increase the number of authorized day laborers. That, however, was a risky proposition, because it had become harder for Israel to screen out potential terrorists among visiting workers after losing intelligence sources in the aftermath of the 2005 withdrawal from Gaza (see chapter 2). The involvement of some laborers in terrorist attacks underlined the security risks of the visiting worker policy. One such episode in 1994 particularly shook the Israeli public. Two axe-wielding Gazan day workers butchered sixty-seven-year-old Isaac Rotenberg, an escapee from the Nazis' Sobibor death camp, while he was repairing floor tiles in a Petah Tikvah building.[37]

Several thousand Arab civilians accompanied the October 7 terrorists from Gaza into Israel, in order to loot the homes of Israeli victims and assist the attackers. One widely publicized video showed a Hamas bulldozer tearing down part of the Israel-Gaza border fence as hundreds of civilians "wearing T-shirts, baseball caps, sneakers, and flip-flops" crossed through the opening. Some were on foot; others traveled on bicycles, scooters, motorcycles, or donkeys. Videos posted by Hamas and security footage from Nir Oz, Be'eri, and other border communities showed large numbers of Gazan civilians participating in murders as well as the kidnapping of women and children. Jacqueline Glicksman, eighty-one, a resident of Kibbutz Ein HaShlosha, said, "[T]hree teenage boys from Gaza broke through the window of [our] safe room and demanded money." When she said she had none, they burned her house down. Glicksman escaped, but her eighty-year-old next door neighbor, Silvia Mirensky, was burned to death.[38]

"The second wave of Arabs who came into the country were just as cruel as the terrorists of the first wave," said Gadi Yarkoni, head of the area's Eshkol Regional Council, referring to the Gazan civilians who followed the terrorists into Israel. "I saw a scene where a Gazan civilian chopped off a man's head. It took him several attempts to detach the head from the body. We saw that it was not only Hamas who came to slaughter us. It was [also] residents of Gaza, including people who worked in our kibbutzim."[39] Civilian looters, who sometimes also participated in atrocities, have been a common feature in anti-Jewish pogroms going all the way back to the Middle Ages.

Some of the Gazan civilians were teenagers or even preteens. Music festival survivor Raziel Tamil, who was hiding in a citrus grove, said he saw terrorists hand rifles to a group of children in Hamas garb—whom he estimated to be between six and ten years old—"and directed them to execute hostages, which they did." Amotz Bazer, barricaded with his family in their safe room at Kibbutz Nir Oz, "heard . . . gunmen push two young boys through a window [in the house]. The boys then opened the front door for the armed terrorists." Comparing the boys' voices to those of his own children, Bazer believed they were about ten years old. A security camera video of a twelve-year-old Israeli boy being kidnapped from Nir Oz showed a Gazan boy, about the same age, among the abductors.[40] Hamas's indoctrination and exploitation of children to join in the persecution of Jews was not a new phenomenon. Members of the Hitler Youth movement enthusiastically participated in numerous atrocities during the Holocaust (see chapter 6).

Kibbutz Nir Oz security official Eran Smilansky estimated that 550 of the 700 Palestinians who attacked the kibbutz were civilians. Eyal

Barad, hiding in his safe room in the kibbutz with his autistic six-year-old daughter, saw on his security camera's live feed a civilian Arab woman pointing out the home of Barad's neighbor to a uniformed terrorist, after which a resident was dragged onto a motorcycle. Video of the attack on Kibbutz Be'eri showed an elderly Palestinian Arab man on walking sticks making his way along with the mob. A Gazan civilian decapitated a Thai farm worker.[41] Two civilian photojournalists, Mohammed Fayq Abu Mostafa and Ashraf Amra, posted a video of themselves on Instagram boasting about taking part in atrocities, and laughing as an Israeli soldier was dragged out of a tank and lynched. They livestreamed the murder.[42]

From her vantage point at Kibbutz Nir Oz, Nili Margalit saw "a mob, thousands of people," pouring across the border into Israel. Some were obviously civilians—there were "women and children." Nili's abductors were "civilians, regular people—a boy [who was] 17, maybe 18 years old" and an "older man with the knife," who smashed in the door of her home and dragged her to a stolen golf cart. She saw two boys, one "no more than 4 or 5 years old" and two others, fifteen or sixteen, riding an ATV that belonged to her father, a farmer, who was murdered. Nili was driven in the golf cart to the Gaza city of Khan Younis, where her captors "negotiated with Hamas to sell me."[43]

Civilians were the perpetrators of the atrocities witnessed by Supernova festivalgoer Raz Cohen, twenty-four, as he hid with friends in bushes for almost seven hours. Cohen saw "a gang of Gazan civilians—men wearing Adidas [sneakers] and armed only with knives and axes"—assaulting a Jewish woman. "While they were raping and killing, they always laughed. I can't forget how they laughed." Several of his friends who decided to make a run for it "were caught by the same gang of Gazans." He heard his friends' screams "as they were tortured and stabbed to death."[44]

Security camera footage of the abduction of festival attendees Avinatan Or and Noa Argamani showed them being hustled away by a dozen unarmed young men in civilian clothes, including teenagers. Just before the kidnapping, Or texted friends that "there is a group of 20 people here who find those who are hiding and lynch them."[45]

From his vantage point atop one of Kibbutz Nirim's grain towers, kibbutz security chief Daniel Meir saw "about fifty Hamas terrorists" who "wore green camouflage or black uniforms and were armed with automatic rifles, rocket-propelled grenades, and hand grenades," along with "dozens of ordinary Gazans," who "wore everyday clothing and came unarmed or carrying only knives" (some would take weapons from their Israeli victims). Meir observed "complete cooperation" between the two groups: Hamas did most of the fighting, while "the civilians went into houses and turned them upside down. They took phones, computers, jewelry, whatever they could find. From what I know, they also took most of the hostages."[46]

Natali Yohanan, thirty-eight, hiding with her husband and their two small children in their safe room in Kibbutz Nir Oz, heard a Gazan woman, accompanied by armed terrorists, entering their house and shutting off the electricity to the safe room. For the next twelve hours, the Yohanans suffered in the sweltering heat, with the children "begging us for water." Meanwhile, the intruder "turned on Netflix, changed it to Arabic," and made herself at home. "She watched tv. She opened the fridge and heated up food. She drank Coke, and she talked to [the terrorists]: 'Do you want Coke? Do you want coffee?' They spent like five hours in my house, sitting on the sofa and just relaxing." The terrorists also pounded on the door to the safe room and occasionally shot at it but could not get through. When the Yohanans finally emerged from hiding, Natali's jewelry, makeup, underwear, shoes, sunglasses, and passports were missing. So were the children's clothing and toys. The family's dog had been killed. Before this experience, "I really believed that Hamas kidnapped Gaza," Yohanan said. "I never thought the common people . . . would participate in things like that. It broke my faith in the goodness of people, especially people from Gaza."[47]

Gazan civilians also guarded hostages. Four-year-old Avigail Idan, an American-Israeli whose parents were murdered, was held captive in civilian homes. Chen Goldstein-Almog, forty-eight, and three of her children spent periods in civilian homes, a grocery store, a mosque, and tunnels. Noa Argamani, who was rescued by Israeli troops in Gaza, had been held by civilians in private homes.[48] Israeli hostage

Ron Krivoi managed to escape his captors in the chaos following an Israeli air strike, but after four days on the run, Gazan civilians caught up to him and brought him back to Hamas.[49] A Gaza pediatrician held Israeli children hostage in his home, and family members helped guard them. Ahmad Al Jamal, seventy-three, a prominent physician and imam "known for his beautiful Quran recitations," and his son, the journalist Abdullah Al Jamal, held three Israelis captive in their home. The elder Jamal "went about his regular routine of work and worship" while his son and daughter-in-law guarded the Israelis in a darkened room for six months.[50] A teacher who worked for the United Nations Relief and Works Agency (UNRWA) kept an Israeli hostage in his attic, with his children guarding the door.[51] Romi Gonen, Emily Damari, and Doron Steinbrecher, who were released in a January 2025 hostages-for-terrorists exchange, said they were held in an UNRWA refugee camp for a portion of their 477 days in captivity.[52]

During the Holocaust, too, civilians collaborated in notorious atrocities against Jews. The best-known study of the infamous Jedwabne pogrom in Poland in July 1941 is titled *Neighbors* because the Polish neighbors, friends, and coworkers of the victims, not the German occupation forces, were responsible for the slaughter of many hundreds, perhaps as many as 1,600 of the town's Jewish residents. A 2018 study of the fate of the more than one million Polish Jews who went into hiding to elude the Germans found that two-thirds were murdered, and in most cases it was because they were betrayed by their non-Jewish neighbors.[53]

SEXUAL VIOLENCE

Within hours of the Hamas invasion, there was credible eyewitness testimony that the terrorists committed widespread sexual assaults. Liel Leibovitz, editor at large for *Tablet*, reported the first evidence on October 8, after spending twelve hours speaking to survivors of the Supernova massacre. One told him: "Women have been raped at the area of the rave next to their friends' bodies, dead bodies." Leibovitz noted that "several of these rape victims appear to have been later executed," while "others were taken to Gaza." Another survivor described seeing the corpses of "young women, lying cold and mutilated." Leibovitz also pointed out: "In photographs released online, you can see several paraded through the city's streets, blood gushing from between their legs."[54]

In the days and weeks following October 7, police officials reported finding evidence of "systematic sexual abuse," including "gang rape, genital mutilation, and necrophilia." Numerous survivors witnessed Hamas terrorists sexually assaulting Jewish women. Israeli coroners reported finding women victims with shattered pelvises and other evidence of sexual violence. One Israeli emergency medical technician described seeing such severe wounds to a woman's genital area that it was "as if someone tore her apart." Some terrorists circulated their own "trophy videos" of their sexual assaults on social media.[55]

The U.S. government soon confirmed that sexual violence was part of the Hamas assault. Upon his arrival in Israel on October 18, President Joe Biden described the atrocities: "Children slaughtered. Babies slaughtered. Entire families massacred. Rape, beheadings, bodies burned alive."[56]

By November 27, Shelly Harush, the Israeli police commander leading the investigation into October 7 sexual violence, would testify to a Knesset committee that the police had already collected more than 1,500 testimonials of rape or evidence of rape.[57]

Five months after the attack, a United Nations report, based on UN representatives' direct examinations of corpses as well as interviews with survivors and eyewitnesses of sexual violence, affirmed there had been numerous instances of "rape and gang rape" and other "forms of sexual violence," including "genital mutilation," on October 7. Women's bodies, naked from the waist down, were "tied to structures such as trees or poles." Many victims were "killed while being raped." Some suffered "sexualized torture" and "sexualized cruel, inhuman and degrading treatment." There was widespread "mutilation of corpses, including decapitation." However, the UN report did not identify the perpetrators as Hamas or its partners, only as "armed elements," a rhetorical anomaly that would soon be echoed by other observers whose political bias conflicted with their assessments of October 7 (see chapter 4).[58]

Escapees hiding in the woods on the perimeter of the festival grounds saw groups of Hamas terrorists gang-raping women. Yoni Saadon, thirty-nine, told the London *Sunday Times* he saw an Israeli woman surrounded by "eight or ten fighters beating and raping her" before they shot her to death. "When they finished, they were laughing." Survivor Ron Freger told the Associated Press that as he hid in a pit, "I heard a woman screaming for help, yelling: 'They're raping me, they're raping me!' and then 'Stop it—already I'm going to die anyway from what you are doing, just kill me!' When they finished, they were laughing and the last one shot her in the head."[59]

The AP published an eyewitness description of another gang rape: "The men then stood her up as blood trickled from her back, yanked her hair and sliced her breast, playing with it as they assaulted her. The last man shot her in the head while he was still inside her."[60]

Along the roads leading out from the festival grounds, numerous escapees witnessed sexual assaults. A woman hiding in a roadside bomb shelter told the police she saw terrorists "forcing [another escapee] to bend forward and then someone raped her. They were dressed in olive-toned fatigues, she was alive, and then she fell silent. She was raped and then killed."[61]

A survivor named Sapir, hiding near Highway 232, saw a large group of terrorists in Hamas uniforms, passing injured women between them. Five women were being raped. One, who had visible back injuries, her pants pulled down below her knees, was held by a terrorist by her hair while another raped her. Each time the woman resisted, the terrorist stabbed her in the back. Sapir also witnessed another terrorist raping a woman while cutting her and mutilating her body at the same time. Another rapist "shot [the woman] in the head while he was raping her, he didn't even pull up his pants."[62]

Shoham Gueta and Raz Cohen, hiding near another part of Highway 232, watched terrorists raping a young woman and stabbing her repeatedly, "literally butchering her," Gueta said. At one point, he saw "the girl wasn't moving anymore. But the terrorist continued raping her." The attackers were "giggling and shouting" as they assaulted her.[63] Cohen saw five men in civilian clothes, "all carrying knives and one carrying a hammer, dragging a woman across the ground." She was "young, naked, and screaming. They all gather around her. She's standing up. They start raping her. I saw the men standing in a half circle around her. One penetrates her. She screams, I still remember her voice, screams without words. Then one of them raises a knife and they just slaughtered her."[64]

Festival survivors who initially fled but then returned to the site in search of friends, encountered bodies of numerous sexual assault victims. "There were horrible scenes—hundreds of bodies, bodies of people half-in and half-out of cars, body parts scattered along the road," Eden Wessely said later. "We looked for my friend, but to my chagrin, there were only corpses along the highway." Then, "I spotted the bodies of a man and a woman. . . . It looked as though she had been raped, murdered, and set afire. They shot her and burned her body. Her hand was covering her face, she had a gunshot wound on the cheek and she had no underpants on. They had lifted her dress, raped her, and afterward torched her. It is not a sight that human eyes can bear."[65] Another Supernova survivor described it as an "apocalypse of bodies, girls without clothes, some missing their upper, some their lower parts."[66]

There were multiple instances of couples being abused together. Rami Davidian, a local resident who helped hundreds of people escape from the festival, told the Association of Rape Crisis Centers in Israel that he found the bodies of "a boyfriend and girlfriend, they stripped them, [as if] they were told to hug and they died hugging. There were beatings on their bodies. They abused them." Davidian also saw five bodies of women "tied to trees, each one three, five meters from the other, naked . . . tied with clothes or blankets around the tree with their hands, or standing leaning tied to the tree." Escapees from the festival who made it to Kibbutz Re'im were later found dead, "together in the same space, in a way that shows that the abuse was committed together," the rape crisis center analysis concluded.[67]

Captured Hamas terrorists said their commanders explicitly authorized sexual attacks.[68] Hussein Ahmad Rafi and his son Abdallah confessed that they took turns raping, and then murdering, women in five houses they invaded at Kibbutz Nir Oz. In some cases, a cousin of theirs joined in.[69] One terrorist described rape as part of Hamas's war strategy: "To have our way with them, to dirty them, to rape them."[70] A terrorist revealed that they were authorized to sexually assault their victims even after the women were dead.[71] An Arabic-language Hamas pamphlet carried by the terrorists included detailed instructions on how to pronounce phrases in Hebrew such as "raise your hands and open your legs" and "take off your pants."[72]

A morgue worker preparing the bodies of female victims for burial said, "Opening the body bags was scary as we didn't know what we would see. They were all young women. Most in little clothing or shredded clothing and their bodies bloodied particularly around their underwear and some women shot many times in the face as if to mutilate them." A morgue staff member said the pattern of abuse indicated "a systematic attempt at genital mutilation." Some young women's "pelvises were broken, they had been raped so much." In some instances, terrorists mutilated the genitalia of their victims, often shooting both male and female victims repeatedly in the groin. Some of the female victims had their breasts cut off. Some were sexually mutilated with scissors.[73]

Morgue volunteer Shari Mendes revealed at a New York City news conference that many women's corpses arrived "in bloody shredded rags or just in underwear—and their underwear was often very bloody." There were "several female soldiers who were shot in the [groin] or the breast. This seemed to be a systematic genital mutilation of a group of victims." In a videotaped testimonial played at the conference, an October 7 survivor said she watched a terrorist rape a woman and then cut off her breasts and play with them.[74]

Men, too, were sexually victimized. Rescue workers interviewed by the Association of Rape Crisis Centers in Israel said that when they collected the bodies from the festival area and the houses in nearby towns, they discovered "some of the men who were found were also sexually abused, [and] their intimate organs were mutilated." A Supernova survivor witnessed "bodies of men whose genitals had been cut off." A paramedic reported seeing injuries to men in which "shooting was targeted at sexual organs," adding, "We saw that a lot. They had a thing with sexual organs." First responder Rami Davidian encountered the body of a man who had been directly shot in the genitalia. Rescuers reported finding "bodies of men were found with their genitalia severed or mutilated" and others who had been sexually assaulted as well as mutilated. There were instances of sexual abuse of men in which the victim's private parts were so severely mutilated "it was hard to tell if it was a man or a woman." The medical teams treating the hostages who were released in the November 2023 hostages-for-terrorists exchange also reported that men were sexually assaulted in captivity.[75]

A male rape victim identified only as "D," who escaped his attackers when Israeli soldiers arrived, described his experience in a television interview. A circle of terrorists surrounded him. "You try to resist, and they take off your clothes, laugh at you, humiliate you, spit on you, touch your body parts, and rape you . . . a very brutal rape." It was "as if your blood is permissible—they were in a crazy state of ecstasy, celebrating, laughing with their guns, with their knives. You kind of disconnect from the situation, but on the other hand, you experience it very strongly. It's very hard." Afterward D "shut down" and engaged in compulsive behaviors common to sexual assault victims, "obsessive cleanliness, lots of showers." He tried to suppress his memories, but eventually "you have conversations with people, and suddenly, everything surfaces."[76] The Israeli branch of Physicians for Human Rights likewise concluded there was ample evidence that men were among the victims of sexual assaults.[77]

Nearly three months after the October 7 attack, the *New York Times* finally published an extensive article on Hamas's sexual violence. The report opened with a description of a video taken on October 8 by a survivor searching for a missing friend that included imagery of the corpse of a woman, sprawled half-naked on a road, who obviously had been brutally raped. This and other evidence confirmed "the attacks against women were not isolated events but part of a broader pattern of gender-based violence on Oct. 7," the *Times* reported. Meni Binyamin, head of the International Crime Investigations Unit of the Israeli police, told the *Times* that "dozens" of women and some men were raped. "There were violent rape incidents, the most extreme sexual abuses we have seen, of both women and men," he said. The *Times* documented thirty instances in which bodies of women and girls found in and around the music festival site and two of the kibbutzim had their "legs spread, clothes torn off, [and] signs of abuse in their genital areas." Some were shot in the groin area; at least two of the terrorists had made videos of themselves shooting them. One had "dozens of nails driven into her thighs and groin."[78] An accountant who survived the music festival massacre told the *Times* she witnessed about one hundred terrorists, most in military fatigues and combat boots, assembled along a road, passing "badly wounded women" to each other. She watched one terrorist rape and repeatedly stab a woman in the back simultaneously, and another mutilate his victim with a box cutter as he raped her. She also saw terrorists carrying the severed heads of three women. Rabbi Dickstein, of the casualty identification unit, testified to a Knesset committee: "We found women with severed breasts. A pregnant woman with her belly opened up to reveal the umbilical cord and the baby with a knife in its body."[79]

At least twenty-four bodies of violated women and girls were found in six different houses in the kibbutzim of Be'eri and Kfar Aza. The underwear of many of the rape victims was "soaked in blood." There was one "whose fingernails had been pulled out"—such a time-consuming act of torture that the terrorist was risking his own life to perpetrate it, knowing that at any moment, Israeli soldiers could burst in. Yet committing the torture was such a high priority that he was willing to risk his life to do it. This was not a deviation from the terrorists' mission, but a central part of it.[80]

Volunteer rescuer Nachman Dyksztejna reported finding "the bodies of two women tied by their hands and feet to a bed, one having been sexually abused and found with a knife in her genitals." Rescue unit officer Chaim Otzmagin and another responder, Simcha Greenman, testified to finding numerous similar scenes involving foreign objects.[81] Otzmazgin stated that "many of the bodies were found partially clothed or unclothed, with severe bleeding from the pelvis and destruction of sexual organs, indicating that even when there was no time to complete the rape, there was an intentional attempt to destroy the sexual organs."

One of the festival attendees had her chest cut open. "It's not easy to cut a body," he noted. "This is someone who did it and didn't stop. . . . There's almost no body they were satisfied with [only] shooting." His conclusion: "It was clear they were trying to spread as much horror as they could—to kill, to burn alive, to rape. It seemed their mission was to rape as many [people] as possible."[82] Morgue volunteer Shari Mendes found that many of the women's mouths "were in grimaces and their hands were clenched, if they had hands." The mutilation of the women was so extensive, and so severe, that "not one" of the hundreds of bodies she examined could be shown to the victims' parents.[83]

Some of the rape victims were Israeli women soldiers. Mendes saw "four bodies of female soldiers with signs of sexual violence, some with extensive bleeding in the pelvic area." A dentist and military officer named Ma'ayan testified she saw "at least ten bodies of female soldiers with clear signs of sexual violence." The *New York Times* report on sexual abuse cited a video, filmed by the Hamas terrorists themselves, showing two soldiers being shot in their genitals.[84]

The total number of sexual assault victims will never be known. Many victims were burned or mutilated beyond recognition.[85] Hazardous and chaotic battle conditions made it next to impossible for the Israeli police unit investigating the sexual assaults, Lahav 443, to collect rape kit evidence from victims' bodies. Most were buried speedily in accordance with Jewish tradition, without autopsies. In many cases, those who survived sexual assaults—usually because they were rescued by advancing Israeli soldiers—were too traumatized to discuss what happened to them.[86]

Raping women is "the quintessential act by which a male demonstrates to a female that she is conquered—vanquished—by his superior strength and power," feminist author Susan Brownmiller wrote in her book *Against Our Will: Men, Women and Rape*. In the context of the Holocaust, she noted, "It was perfectly logical within the framework of fascism that rape would be employed by the German soldier as he strove to prove himself a worthy Superman." For the Islamist fundamentalists who invaded Israel on October 7, raping Jewish women was a way of vanquishing and humiliating the Jewish state.[87]

Comparing the pattern of sexual assaults on October 7 to other instances of sexual victimization in wartime, and reviewing them in the context of studies of the phenomenon by professionals in the field, the Association of Rape Crisis Centers in Israel concluded that the features of the sexual violence and degradation inflicted by the terrorists constituted a deliberate and systematic part of their attack on Israel. The victims were "effectively under a double attack: sexual assault and armed assault simultaneously." Gang rape "is intended to prove masculinity to others and to meet the social expectations of the other fighters/perpetrators present." In many instances, there were indications that terrorists forced spouses, family members, or friends to watch as their loved ones were raped at gunpoint.[88] Compelling spouses, parents, or siblings to watch an assault "aims to undermine the dignity and masculinity of men who fail to protect their women, as well as to instill fear and to deepen oppression and degradation. . . . [It] is a practice of torture. . . . In many cases, family members are killed when they try to protect their family from sexual assault." As for "the brutal practices of mutilating intimate organs of girls, women, and men, as well as cutting of women's breasts," that was "intended to signify permanent injury" and "to reinforce the victim's own degradation and symbolically, also that of the state that failed to protect them." Other types of physical violation, such as dragging women by their hair as they screamed and tying victims together, likewise were "intended to convey a symbolic message of the perpetrator's overwhelming power and ability to reach anywhere."[89]

Similar atrocities were perpetrated in many anti-Jewish attacks throughout the previous centuries (see chapter 6), although the goriest details often were shrouded by the reluctance of those who were reporting the acts to spell out horrors that were considered insulting to the personal honor of the victims.

PARADING THE HOSTAGES

The Hamas attackers carried a manual containing detailed instructions on how to kidnap Jews. Prisoners were to be bound, blindfolded, and assembled at a single site by each unit when it "completes the cleansing of the area of its activity," a euphemism for mass murder that was also utilized by the Nazis. The prisoners would be "controlled" through "shooting, sound/stun grenades, threats, electric shocks, violence, and inducing terror." The manual authorized "killing of any person who may constitute a threat or a distraction/disturbance." Some of the captives were to be "used as artillery fodder provided they are seen clearly"—in other words, so that their deaths would serve to terrorize the others.[90]

Hostages were shocked by what they experienced as their captors led them into Gaza. Yarden Roman-Gat, thirty-five, was driven through what she called "celebratory crowds," with her kidnappers "showing me off as a trophy and showing my face as an object—I was not a person."[91] Mia Regev, twenty-one, was "paraded" through the streets of Gaza as crowds shouted "Allahu akbar!" ("Allah is great!"). "I'm with my head down," she said. "Someone pulls me backward by the hair, holding me like that so people could see my face." Sapir Cohen, twenty-nine, said "civilians who supported the terrorists kicked and punched me mercilessly, without stopping." Yaffa Adar, an eighty-five-year-old Holocaust survivor kidnapped by civilians, was surrounded by "people all around, lots of them, spitting, yelling." Shani Louk, a twenty-three-year-old German-born Israeli citizen, was displayed, bleeding and nearly naked, in the back of a pickup truck, while crowds cheered, spit, struck her body, and shouted, "Allahu akbar!"[92] Hagar Brodutch, of Kibbutz Kfar Aza, said the captors' "barbaric act of parading [my daughter and me] through the streets like trophies will forever haunt me. The cheers of the crowd as we passed through the streets were chilling. It felt like we were being paraded as prizes in a sick game."[93]

The annals of history are filled with instances of antisemitic tormentors delighting in the public humiliation of Jews. Parading cowed and injured Jews through the streets with signs bearing derogatory slogans about Jews or Judaism was a common occurrence in Nazi Germany. Another infamous episode dates back to the first century CE, when the Romans destroyed the state of Judea and proceeded to parade their Jewish captives along with looted artifacts from their ancient Temple. They commemorated the event by building the fifty-foot-tall Arch of Titus, in the center of Rome, decorated with an intricate bas relief of the degrading Roman celebration.

ABUSE OF THE HOSTAGES

Two hundred and fifty-one Israelis, including pregnant women, babies, and elderly people, many of them badly injured, were forced at gunpoint into automobiles or onto motorcycles, and driven across the border into Gaza. Some were imprisoned in private homes or in rooms inside hospitals, but most were taken into the vast labyrinth of tunnels—350 to 450 miles in total length, with 5,700 separate entrances—that Hamas had built underneath Gaza. Fully equipped with electricity, communications systems, and provisions, the tunnels were the site of Hamas command centers and weapons storage facilities, as well as barred cells built to hold Israelis captive. Many tunnels were situated under hospitals, schools, and mosques.[94] Some were wide enough to drive a car through; one tunnel, hidden under a hospital, "stretched nearly three football fields long." Others were so narrow that people had to walk single file.[95]

Videos posted by Hamas on its Telegram channel soon after October 7 showed some of the child hostages in cages. Yarden Bibas and Ofer Kalderon, who were exchanged for terrorists in February 2025, reported that they were held in cages for a number of weeks.[96] Other freed hostages reported that some women were also kept in cages and were transported from place to place in cages. Israeli troops pursuing Hamas in Gaza located some of those makeshift prisons.[97]

Former hostage Mia Regev reported that her captors "tore off [her] clothes" and deliberately struck her leg when they saw she had an injury there, laughing as they hit her.[98] Hostage Aviva Siegel said that four Hamas guards handcuffed and repeatedly beat a young woman captive with a stick.[99] Many other hostages reported undergoing "severe beatings" as well as physical and psychological torture, including compelling them to watch the mistreatment of fellow-captives and forcing them to engage in various types of degrading behavior.[100]

Hostages were kept in complete darkness for prolonged periods of time, often in extremely overcrowded conditions. "It was a tiny room, its width no larger than two meters [about six feet] from end to end," Danielle Aloni recalled. "Sixteen people were crammed next to one another on mattresses. We couldn't breathe, there was no air."[101] Aviva Siegel and other captives were taken into a tunnel more than one hundred feet below ground and kept there for four days "with almost no water and no food." The air was of such poor quality that "we got to the point where we were not able to even say a word because there was no oxygen to breathe," she said. "The terrorists just left us there because it was not comfortable for them because there was no oxygen." She and her husband were often left "gasping for air."[102]

Six Israeli hostages who were executed by Hamas in August 2024 were held in a tunnel that was "not tall enough to stand in without bending over." They were compelled to use a bucket and bottles as toilets. The tunnel entrance was a child's room in a private house, the walls decorated with brightly colored illustrations of Snow White and Mickey Mouse.[103]

The hostages were provided a near-starvation diet of one pita and small quantities of rice daily, with only filthy water to drink. Mia Schem, who nearly bled to death from gunshot wounds at the festival and was held captive by a civilian family in their home for most of the next two months, received no medicine and often went for days without food. Ofelia Roitman, seventy-seven, was held for forty-six days in the home of a Gaza technician and his wife, a nurse, who fed Ofelia nothing but small amounts of rice and pita bread.[104] Some were given so little rice that they rationed it grain by grain.[105] One hostage reported eating toilet paper when food ran out. Four hostages rescued by Israeli troops in June 2024 were found to be in a state of "severe malnutrition." One hostage's hands were tied behind his back for his first two months in captivity, compelling him to contort his body in order to eat the few scraps he was given. Yarden Roman-Gat was so traumatized that she refused to discuss the topic of food with interviewers after her release.[106] Some of the prisoners lost as much as 20 percent of their body weight. Eden Yerushalmi, who weighed over one hundred pounds before October 7 and was murdered in captivity, was later found to have weighed seventy-nine pounds at the time of her death. Ex-hostage Sharon Alony-Cunio said the prisoners rationed their tiny quantities of food. "You don't know if in the evening there will be a pita, so in the morning you save some for the evening. Everything is very calculated, a quarter of a pita, half a pita to keep for the next morning. . . . It's a Russian roulette. You don't know whether tomorrow morning they'll keep you alive or kill you."[107] The hostage's food rationing regimen calls to mind the Passover seder ritual of setting aside a piece of matzah, known as the afikomen, as a reminder that Jewish slaves in ancient Egypt saved a portion of each night's dinner because they never knew whether, given their precarious existence, there would be food available the next day.

Civilian residents of Rafah imprisoned Fernando Marman and Luis Har, two elderly Argentinian Jewish hostages, and forced them into slave labor as the family's cooks. Marman and Har subsisted on small amounts of pita bread and cheese, and sometimes went "for days" without being given food.[108] Released hostages told the family of Liri Elbag, nineteen, that she was traded from house to house, and in each case she and other prisoners "had to cook for the family . . . take care of their children, and clean their house . . . [and] prepare food, but they themselves could not eat."[109] Romi Gonen, Emily Damari, and Doron Steinbrecher were kept as "domestic slaves" in the homes of civilians, forced to clean toilets and cook meals—but likewise never allowed to eat any of the food they cooked. They were also denied elementary hygiene, such as access to showers, for months at a time.[110]

Dr. Yael Mozer-Glassberg of Schneider Children's Medical Center, who evaluated the child hostages released in November 2023, said they not only lost extreme amounts of weight, but long after their release, they still hesitated to eat the food at the medical center, because, they said, "We have to keep it for later." The terrorists "would inflict psychological terrorism on them by forcing them to eat everything given to them after their stomachs had shrunk and hunger pains diminished after having eaten nearly nothing for days." They further tortured the children by "telling them over and over again that nobody cared about them, [nobody] was looking for them or fighting for their release." The children also "had to knock on the door and wait for who knows how long for someone to come ask what they needed. They needed permission to go to the bathroom."[111] Many children were forced to view videos of Hamas terrorists committing atrocities and threatened at gunpoint if they cried out.[112] They were also required to write notes saying they were treated like royalty.[113]

Dr. Itai Pesach of the Sheba Medical Center said after examining the released hostages that every one of them had "a significant physical injury or medical problem."[114] Former hostage Nili Margalit, a nurse, said some of the older captives were suffering from heart problems, renal failure, and Parkinson's disease.[115] Gadi Mozes, age eighty, was given a bowl of water once every five days with which to "shower."[116] Many hostages were permitted to bathe only a few times during their entire captivity "and thus suffered from rashes, lice, and unhealed infections." Some of the captives were never allowed to bathe at all.[117]

Child hostages were subjected to a range of cruelties. Some were sexually abused by their captors.[118] Twelve-year-old Eitan Yahalomi was kept in solitary confinement for the first sixteen days of his captivity and repeatedly told by his captors that his mother was being held hostage (she was not) and that the State of Israel had been destroyed.[119] On the rare occasions the children were allowed to shower, young girls were compelled to do so in full view of their captors.[120] Yagil Yaakov, twelve, and Or Yaakov, sixteen, were branded on their legs with a hot metal device so they could be identified if they managed to escape, and two other former child hostages had burn marks on their legs that were consistent with branding.[121] Many of the child hostages were compelled to remain silent for weeks at a time—something that became so ingrained that in the days following their release, "most of [the children] talk about needing to be very quiet. At all times. Not to stand up. Not to talk. Of course, not to cry. Not to laugh. Just to be very, very quiet," said Dr. Efrat Bron-Harlev of Schneider Children's Medical Center.[122]

Several dozen hostages were held at the Nasser Hospital in southern Gaza. Sharon Alony-Cunio described how they slept on blood-stained bedding, were permitted to use the bathroom only at intervals of many hours, and allowed to shower only a handful of times during her two months in captivity. The hostages were "barely fed" and the little food they were given was moldy.[123] American-Israeli hostage Judith Ne'eman said that "[t]he minute [my teenage daughter and I] came in" to a Gaza hospital, "all the nurses were standing there and going like this [cheering]. They were all so happy that [Hamas] came back with prey."[124] Other hostages were held periodically at the Kamal Adwan Hospital, in northern Gaza.[125]

Hostages with life-threatening conditions were refused access to their medicine, and at least one hostage died from untreated medical issues.[126] Daniella Gilboa spent her entire fifteen months in captivity with a bullet in her leg, which her captors refused to have removed.[127] Two of Emily Damari's fingers were shot off by Hamas terrorists as they kidnapped her; she received no medical treatment during nearly sixteen months in captivity.[128] Israeli troops scouring a Gaza hospital found unopened packages of medicine that Israel had given to the Red Cross to provide to specific hostages.[129] Margalit Moses, seventy-seven, was denied access to the oxygen concentrator machine she needed for normal sleep during her forty-nine days in captivity.[130] Some of the older hostages developed deep vein thrombosis, a potentially life threatening condition, because of their forced immobility during captivity.[131] Upon her release, Elma Avrahama, eighty-four, had to be airlifted to a hospital for emergency medical treatment. Yocheved Lifshitz, eighty-five, was "ripped from her oxygen machine" when abducted, and both she and her husband Oded, eighty-three, were deprived of their medicines. Lifelong peace activists, the two had frequently driven ailing Palestinian Arabs from Gaza to Israeli hospitals for free medical treatment.[132]

UN investigators found that sexual violence was perpetrated "against some women and children during their time in captivity," and there were "reasonable grounds to believe that such violence may be ongoing."[133] One doctor who treated many of the 105 Israelis and foreign nationals released in November 2023 said at least ten of the Israelis had been sexually assaulted during their captivity.[134] Former hostage Chen Goldstein-Almog said that three young women hostages told her they were subjected to "terrifying and grotesque sexual abuse, often at gunpoint."[135] A fellow hostage told Goldstein-Almog's teenage daughter, Agam, that she had been sexually assaulted for half an hour with a gun held to her head.[136] Some hostages who were raped were reluctant to be publicly identified. The first to come forward was Amit Soussana, an attorney, who told the *New York Times* in March 2024 that she was held prisoner in several different private civilian homes, where her captors sexually assaulted her repeatedly. Sometimes "a group of captors suspended her across the gap between two couches and beat her." Upon her release, Israeli doctors discovered "fractures to her right eye socket" from multiple "punches to her right eye." A Hamas spokesman responded that "the level of detail" in Soussana's account "makes it difficult to believe the story."[137] When Soussana went public, the Qatari-funded, pro-Hamas media agency Al Jazeera countered it by publishing a claim by Gazan resident Jamila Al-Hessi that Israeli soldiers were "raping women, then killing them and burning entire families alive" in Al-Shifa Hospital; the next day, Al Jazeera deleted the story and its columnist and former director Yasser Abuhilalah tweeted that the story was fabricated.[138]

The ideological underpinning of Hamas's sexual abuse of Jewish hostages was the Islamist supremacist concept of *sabaya*, meaning "sex slave." A deeply rooted concept in militant Islam, going back to medieval times, *sabaya* presents the sexual conquest of non-Muslims as a means of degrading them and asserting the physical superiority of Islam. An infamous 2024 Islamic State video showed is commanders using the phrase *sabaya* as they chatted about the price they could fetch for a group of women they had kidnapped from the Yazidis, an ethnic minority in Iraq and Kurdistan. According to 2015 and 2016 UN reports and a 2017 European Parliament report, Yazidi women are "deemed property of ISIS and are openly termed *sabaya* or slaves" and "systematically subjected to rape." In one post-October 7 conversation intercepted by Israeli intelligence, a Hamas captor could be heard describing an Israeli woman abductee as a *sabaya*.[139] Hamas also used the word *sabaya* to characterize a group of beaten and bloodied Israeli women soldiers displayed in a May 2024 video.[140]

Consistent with Islamist supremacist thought, some of the October 7 hostages were compelled to adopt Muslim modes of behavior or pressed to convert to Islam. Agam Goldstein-Almog, seventeen, said her captors forced her to "recite Islamic prayers and wear a *hijab* [Muslim head covering]." Fellow-abductee Moran Stella Yanai likewise was forced to don a hijab and recite Quranic verses. Her captors told her, "If you would convert to Islam, we will release you sooner."[141]

Dr. Renana Eitan, director of the psychiatric division of the Tel Aviv Sourasky Medical Center—Ichilov, who treated fourteen of the released hostages, said "the physical, sexual, mental, [and] psychological abuse of these hostages who came back is just terrible—we have to rewrite the textbook." Among other things, some of the hostages were drugged with benzodiazepines, a sedative similar to Valium. "Sometimes it's difficult to control young children, adolescents. And they know that if they drug them, they will be quiet. . . . One of the girls was given ketamine [an anesthetic that creates a sense of detachment from the surrounding environment] for a few weeks." Many hostages "became psychotic, they had hallucinations," and some continued to experience dissociative states after their release. "One minute they know that they are here at Ichilov medical center, and the next they think they are back with Hamas."[142] She said Israel would need to build a treatment center solely to deal with the post-traumatic stress disorder (PTSD) suffered by victims of October 7. The trauma endured by victims of earlier anti-Jewish outrages through the centuries usually went undiagnosed and untreated. The lifelong psychological damage suffered by Holocaust survivors has come to be appreciated only in recent decades, after studies of Vietnam War veterans led to greater understanding of PTSD and after the American Psychiatric Association recognized it as a medical condition in 1980.

"IN THE CITY OF SLAUGHTER"

"Arise and go now to the city of slaughter" read the opening words of one of the most heart-rending Jewish poems of the twentieth century, written by Chaim Nachman Bialik following the 1903 Kishinev pogrom in Czarist Russia. Forty-nine Jews were massacred in a three-day rampage of murder, maiming, rape, and destruction of homes that shocked the Jewish world. "In the City of Slaughter" memorialized the gruesome violence and sheer helplessness of the victims.

October 7 was Kishinev thirty times over. In the scale of the assaults, the savagery of the attackers, and the level of depravity, Hamas managed to far surpass Kishinev's horrors. How, more than a century later, were Jewish communities once again transformed into cities of slaughter?

2. The Rise and Strategy of Hamas

Gaza, the birthplace of Hamas, has been an exclusively Arab territory in recent decades, but much of its demographic history has been multiethnic.

JEWS AND MUSLIMS IN GAZA

A center of the Philistines in biblical times, Gaza was then ruled intermittently by the Egyptians, Assyrians, Babylonians, Jews, and Romans. Ever since Muslim armies from the Arabian Peninsula conquered Gaza in 637 CE, its population has been predominantly Muslim. Yet there is ample archaeological evidence of a substantial Jewish community in Gaza both before and after the Muslim conquest, including ancient Jewish engravings that were visible for many years along the upper pillars of Gaza's largest mosque, al-Omari.[1] Numerous literary references and archaeological findings testify to the stature and longevity of the Gaza Jewish community, including its emergence in the seventeenth century CE as one of the world's most important centers of Jewish mysticism. The Jewish residents of Gaza held on until they were expelled en masse during the 1929 Palestinian Arab pogroms (see chapter 6).

After the British captured Palestine from the Turks in World War I, the League of Nations—precursor to the UN—awarded Great Britain the mandate to rule the territory until it was deemed ready for independence. Its boundaries included Gaza City and its surrounding neighborhoods, a strip of land twenty-five miles long and six to twelve miles wide at Palestine's southwestern most edge, along the Mediterranean Coast.

The British promised, in the 1917 Balfour Declaration, to "facilitate" the reestablishment "of a national home for the Jewish people" in Palestine, while also safeguarding "the civil and religious rights of existing non-Jewish communities" there.[2] But the Jewish homeland pledge began to waver after the first major eruption of Arab anti-Jewish violence in the Holy Land, in 1920. Two years later, England allotted the eastern three-fourths of the country to exclusive Arab rule (it renamed the territory Transjordan, later Jordan). In 1937, faced with continued Palestinian Arab violence, the British proposed dividing western Palestine into a tiny Jewish state and a much larger Arab one, including Gaza, but Palestinian Arab leaders rejected the idea of a Jewish state of any size. In 1939, on the eve of the Holocaust, Britain closed off the Holy Land to all but a trickle of Jews trying to escape the Nazis.

Unable to resolve the Arab-Jewish conflict, Britain returned the Palestine mandate to the United Nations in 1947. A UN committee proposed, and the General Assembly endorsed, partitioning the country into separate Jewish and Arab states: Gaza would have been part of the latter. The neighboring Arab regimes—Egypt, Syria, and Transjordan—joined the Palestinian Arabs in rejecting a Jewish state of any size, and in launching a full-scale military invasion to prevent its creation.

Egypt occupied the Gaza Strip during Israel's War of Independence in 1948, and remained there for the next nineteen years. The Egyptian government sponsored continual attacks on Israel by Palestinian Arab terrorists, known as fedayeen, explaining: "Egypt has decided to dispatch her heroes, the disciples of Pharaoh and the sons of Islam, and they will clean the land of Palestine."[3] Fourteen terrorist training centers dotted the Gaza Strip.[4]

TERROR FROM GAZA, THEN AND NOW

During the 1950s, the Gaza-based terrorists "came in and out of Israel every day on their missions of murder and plunder," Israeli ambassador Abba Eban told the UN in 1956. Jews were "subjected to savage and relentless hostility," and southern Israel became "an inferno of insecurity and danger."[5] Some of the terrorists murdered and raped; others stole agricultural equipment and other goods. Jewish residents rarely ventured out at night. Many Jews relocated; six entire towns were abandoned.[6]

Israeli buses traveling on the region's many remote roadways were easy prey. In one of the era's most notorious attacks, Palestinian Arab terrorists—apparently from Gaza—ambushed an Israeli passenger bus in a narrow Negev escarpment known as Scorpions Pass on March 17, 1954.[7] They murdered eleven passengers. One, Hannah Fuerstenberg, was raped before she was shot. Her nine-year-old son, Chaim, was wounded; he lingered, paralyzed and semiconscious, for thirty-two years before dying.[8]

Thirty-four years later, members of Fatah, the terrorist group led by Yasir Arafat, hijacked an Israeli civilian bus twenty miles from Scorpions Pass. It was transporting fifty workers from the Beersheba area, nearly all of them women, to nearby Dimona. "They entered the bus and fired a few shots to scare us so we wouldn't leave . . . [and] sat us down hunched up one next to the other," hostage Daisy Sorek later recalled. As she huddled in fright, wondering if she would live or die, she suddenly realized one of the terrorists pointing a gun at her head used to be her gardener. The terrorists hauled Victor Ram, a widower with two children, to the front of the bus and shot him in the head. They did the same to Miriam Ben-Yair, a mother of four, and Rina Shiratsky, a mother of two. Rachel Matza was next in line. Sorek's former gardener pressed his rifle against Matza's chest and was about to pull the trigger when Israeli troops stormed the bus.[9]

Some of the mass terror assaults in 1955–1956 could almost have been rehearsals for October 7. In August 1955, twelve squads of fedayeen from Gaza invaded multiple towns in southern Israel simultaneously. With automatic rifles, mines, and grenades, they murdered twelve Israelis and wounded fourteen. A senior UN official in the region, General E. L.M. Burns, compared the attackers to the Nazis.[10] In April 1956, two hundred Palestinian Arab fedayeen, organized in groups of four to seven, attacked a dozen Israeli towns, as well as travelers in the vicinity, with guns, explosives, mines, and grenades. In the village of Kfar Chabad, the terrorists approached the town's synagogue, which was crowded with children. One attacker cut the electricity wires, plunging the building into darkness. His comrades kicked in the main door and unleashed a torrent of gunfire. Five boys and a teacher were slaughtered, and five more were wounded. "The children . . . were lying in one huge pool of blood when rescuers arrived," according to one news report. "The blood stained their clothing, their [yarmulkes,] and the prayer books they had been reading."[11] All told, eleven Israelis were murdered and forty-nine wounded over five days.[12]

During the early and mid-1950s, Gazan terrorists murdered several hundred Jews, wounded many hundreds more, and stole or destroyed millions of dollars worth of property (in today's currency). Documents discovered by the Israeli army revealed that the Egyptian government was giving Gaza terrorists a cash bonus if they returned with the ear or finger of a Jewish victim.[13] A senior Egyptian official said bluntly: "There is no reason why the faithful fedayeen, hating their enemy, should not penetrate into Israel and transform the lives of its citizens into a hell."[14]

That is what they did, week after week, until the autumn of 1956, when Israel sent in troops to crush the fedayeen during its Sinai Campaign. There were no settlements or occupied territories at issue in 1956, or any fabricated news reports about Israel threatening the Al-Aqsa Mosque, which was then under Jordanian occupation. The Jews were guilty of only one offense, Ambassador Eban noted: "Israel had committed the dark sin of survival."[15]

But survival, as a sovereign Jewish state, was precisely the problem.

ISLAM AND THE JEWS

From its founding in the early seventh century CE, Islam has been anchored in the principle that its destiny is global supremacy and that force is justified in attaining that goal. Proclaiming himself a prophet of God, Islam's founder, Muhammad, led a series of military assaults on various tribes in the Arabian Peninsula in order to compel their adherence to the new religious faith. Muhammad's disciples composed the Quran, based on the messages Muhammad said he had received from heaven. Among the concepts set forth in the Quran and other traditional Islamic literature was the philosophy of jihad, a religious struggle often waged through warfare. The world is said to be divided into two regions permanently in conflict with one another, the Territory of Islam (*dar al-Islam*), where Muslims and Muslim law reign supreme, and the Territory of War (*dar al-Harb*), the regions that non-Muslims control but which rightfully belong under Muslim domain. The state of jihad is the normal relationship between the Territory of Islam and the Territory of War. The sphere in which infidels reside has no moral right to exist, and Muslims' use of force against those occupying the Territory of War is legitimate, even praiseworthy, in furthering the goal of conquering all such regions and establishing global Muslim sovereignty.[16]

The Jewish tribes of Arabia were among Muhammad's earliest targets for conversion. Muslim literary sources accuse those Jews of various offenses, ranging from insulting a young Muslim woman to passing military secrets to Muhammad's enemies—all charges uncorroborated by other historical sources. From Muhammad's perspective, the Jews' refusal to convert, combined with their other transgressions, provided ample reason to wage war. In short order, his armies decimated a number of Jewish communities and exiled others. His defeat of the Jewish tribe of Kurayza in 627 CE included the beheading of six hundred to nine hundred Jews.

Clashes between Muhammad and Mecca residents the following year point to the peril and promise of Muslim-Jewish relations through the ages. Muhammad agreed to a ten-year armistice with the Meccans, known as the treaty of Al-Ḥudaybiyya. Two years later, however, he proceeded with his conquest of Mecca. Yasir Arafat and other senior Palestinian Authority officials cited the Al-Ḥudaybiyya agreement as a precedent for signing the 1993 Oslo Accords with Israel.[17] For contemporary optimists, the fact that Muhammed signed a peace treaty with a bitter enemy offers hope that his latter-day followers would be inspired by his example. For more skeptical observers, the fact that the agreement was at best a temporary truce that lasted just two years is not a promising model for a durable Arab-Israeli peace.[18]

In 637 CE, Caliph Umar ibn al-Khattab, the second leader of Islam following Muhammad's death, instituted the subjugated status of dhimmi for non-Muslims in conquered territory, following his occupation of Jerusalem. Refined by successive generations of Muslim theologians, the document known as the Pact of Umar safeguards but severely limits the lives of defeated minority communities. Among other restrictions, it bars non-Muslims from building homes that are taller than Muslim homes, limits the construction of non-Muslim houses of worship, prohibits non-Muslims from holding positions of authority, mandates that non-Muslims wear distinctive clothing, imposes special taxes on them, and requires non-Muslims to surrender their seats in any public venue if Muslims want them. The prohibition against infidels assuming positions of authority holds special significance: the humiliating condition mandated for non-Muslims is considered a vindication of the truth of Islam, and therefore a non-Muslim holding a position of power constitutes an ideological blow against the religion of Muhammad.

The experience of Jews living as dhimmis in majority-Muslim countries through the ages was made more precarious by the many negative and dehumanizing stereotypes about Jews in Islamic literature, including Quaranic verses labeling Jews as "apes" and "pigs," and alleging that Jews poisoned Muhammad.[19] On the other hand, there are verses in the Quran and classic Islamic literature asserting that "Jews and Christians and Sabians" who believe in God and a Day of Judgment, and "do good," should be regarded positively.[20] Thus, while Jews could be tolerated within Muslim countries so long as they were relegated to a state of discrimination and humiliation, they found themselves at the mercy of a society that was steeped in anti-Jewish stereotypes and could, and occasionally did, explode into anti-Jewish violence.[21]

Given the existence of some favorable references to non-Muslim believers, contemporary Muslim theologians could choose to regard the negative references as pertaining only to specific groups of Jews in ancient times, and to rely on the more positive ones as the basis for modern Muslim-Jewish relations. Instead, many prominent Muslim authorities have echoed the derogatory language in their religious literature, thereby helping to fashion ideological justification for antisemitism. Palestinian Arab leaders have done likewise; spokesmen for Fatah, the PA's ruling faction, and Mahmoud Al-Abbash, senior adviser to PA chairman Mahmoud Abbas, have publicly referred to contemporary Jews as "apes and pigs," citing Quranic verses as their authority.[22]

Historically, an important exception to the tradition of subjugating and demeaning Jews occurred in Muslim-occupied Spain in the tenth century CE. Because of prevailing local circumstances, the ruling authorities there refrained from applying the dhimmi rules strictly or uniformly. As a result, some Jews enjoyed what was later characterized as a "golden age" of acceptance and advancement in a Muslim-ruled country. Jews served as advisers in the government and took part in the development of medicine, science, and literature. This era of relative tolerance came to a bloody end with the slaughter of hundreds of Jews by a Muslim mob in the Spanish city of Grenada in 1066 CE.[23]

Islam, like every major religion, contains within it strains of thought and practice that differ in some modest ways from those of most of its adherents. Under what circumstances it is feasible to wage war against infidels, and when at least temporary accommodation with the non-Muslim world is preferable, is a matter for individual Muslim political and religious leaders to decide. Thus, while most majority-Muslim countries refuse to accept Israel's existence, and some remain in active warfare against the Jewish state, a handful of Muslim and Arab leaders have opted to sign peace agreements with Israel. Likewise, not every Palestinian Arab supports terrorism or jihad against the Jews, and Palestinian leaders who want to live in peace with a Jewish state—and educate their young people accordingly—could find religious justification for doing so.

At first, the Oslo Accords were widely regarded as a major turning point in Arab-Jewish relations precisely because they were anchored in the Palestinian leadership's pledges to oppose violence and undertake peace education. In the three decades since those agreements were signed, however, public opinion surveys, election results, and other indicators of Palestinian Arab sentiment continued to find overwhelming hostility toward Jews and support for violence against Israel, anchored in traditional Muslim beliefs. Central to that perspective is the conviction that Zionism—the existence of a sovereign Jewish state of any size in the Holy Land—constitutes an intolerable reversal of the desired world order as decreed by Islam. Jewish national sovereignty means Jews shirking their subjugated dhimmi status and assuming authority in a region of *dar al-Islam*, even though the Jewish state occupies only one-tenth of 1 percent of the Arab Middle East. Thus the Palestinian Arab war against Jews in the Holy Land, from its beginning—even before the emergence of specifically Palestinian nationalism—was constituted as a jihad to prevent the upending of 1,300 years of Islamic supremacy.

The question of Jerusalem adds another layer of emotion and rhetoric to the controversy, although it does not alter the essence of Muslim objections to Israel's existence. Contemporary Muslims view the Al-Aqsa Mosque and its Dome of the Rock shrine as the third holiest site in Islam. The Quran does not mention the city or site by name, but according to a later *hadith* (a traditional Islamic saying attributed to Muhammad), an unnamed "farthest place" mentioned in the Quran refers to Al-Aqsa and the dome (even though Al-Aqsa was built seventy to eighty years after the Quran was written). Muhammad is said to have undertaken a magical "night journey" from the Arabian Peninsula to that "farthest place," tethered his winged horse, Buraq, at the adjoining Western Wall, and then ascended to heaven from there. The Palestinian position that the wall is exclusively Muslim territory is based on that legend. After Great Britain's 1917 Balfour Declaration and the modest Jewish immigration that followed, Palestinian Arab leaders incited anti-Jewish violence, including the 1929 Hebron massacre (see chapter 6), by promulgating the lie that Jews were plotting to seize Al-Aqsa. Hamas's decision to name its October 7 invasion "Al-Aqsa Flood" continued this tradition.

THE BIRTH OF PALESTINIAN NATIONALISM

Palestinian nationalism is a relatively recent phenomenon. When Jews began resettling the Holy Land in the late 1800s, Arabs there identified according to local clans, or as residents of the southern part of Syria, which had been under Turkish occupation since the early sixteenth century CE. They did not consider themselves members of a distinctly Palestinian nation. Nor did they consider Palestine a distinct territory, since there had never been a state of Palestine previously in history. The name itself was a foreign invention; after crushing and exiling the Jews in 70 CE, the Romans imposed the name "Palestine" upon the vanquished country of Judea, alluding to the Jews' biblical enemy, the Philistines, in an effort to erase the country's Jewish identity.[24]

The European Jewish immigrants planting crops and draining malarial swamps in Turkish-occupied Palestine in the late 1800s and early 1900s faced sporadic Arab assaults, but not because of Palestinian nationalism.[25] Although Arab advocates began using the term "Palestine" more frequently after World War I, they did not employ it in the sense of representing a separate or unique national identity. Thus the first resolution adopted by the inaugural Palestine Arab Congress, held in 1919, began, "We consider Palestine nothing but part of Arab Syria and it has never been separated from it at any stage."[26] Ironically, Jews in Palestine were commonly described as "Palestinians" during those years, right up until Israel's creation in 1948, while the Arab residents were almost always characterized simply as Arabs.

Arab nationalist sentiment, anchored in traditional Islam, spread among Palestinian Arabs in the 1920s and 1930s as a kind of anti-nationalism, an identity based on hatred of others (Jews) rather than an embrace of their own unique religious or ethnic culture. Palestinian Arab political movements established during this period, such as the Youth Congress Party and the Independence Party (both est. 1932), the National Defence Party (1934), the National Bloc and the Reform Party (both 1935), were centered around tribal clans or geographic areas; they did not even include the word "Palestine" in their names. The umbrella group for these factions, established in 1936, called itself the Arab Higher Committee, not the Palestine Higher Committee. Their goal was not the creation of a Palestinian state, but rather the unification of Palestine, which they called southern Syria, with the rest of Syria. In their view, the Jewish residents needed to be expelled from Palestine, or at least relegated to dhimmi status. For this reason, Palestinian Arab leaders, along with leaders of neighboring Arab countries, rejected offers of Palestinian statehood made to them in 1937 by the British, and 1947 by the UN.[27]

Specifically Palestinian nationalism began to develop in earnest in the 1960s. Its goal was never the creation of a Palestinian state alongside Israel, but rather one that would replace Israel. The Palestine Liberation

Organization was established in 1964, at a time when Egypt occupied Gaza and Jordan occupied the areas that would come to be known as the West Bank; the "Palestine" they sought to "liberate" was the entire State of Israel. Palestinian Arabs living under their rule did not initiate a movement for political self-determination in those territories. This silence reflects the dearth of distinctly Palestinian national identity at the time. There were few historical, religious, cultural, or linguistic differences between the Arabs who lived in Syria, Jordan, or Egypt and those who lived within the State of Israel. After Israel's victory in the 1967 Six-Day War, however, affirming specifically "Palestinian" identity became a common way of expressing opposition to Israel. In Gaza and other Israeli-administered territories, schools and religious institutions increasingly added assertions of Palestinian identity to traditional teachings that impressed upon young Arabs the importance of Islamic supremacy and hatred of Jews. Hate education ensured a steady supply of recruits for Palestinian Arab terrorist groups, and, ultimately (see chapter 3), for Hamas's October 7 invasion.

NEW AUDIENCES FOR *MEIN KAMPF*

On December 5, 1956, Israeli foreign minister Golda Meir explained to the UN General Assembly why Israel had launched a preemptive strike against Egypt five weeks earlier. "For eight years [ever since Israel's War of Independence]," she said, "Israel has had no respite from hostile acts," relentless attacks by Palestinian Arab terrorists based in Egyptian-occupied Gaza, economic warfare, "and loudly proclaimed threats of destruction." Given the recent announcement of major Soviet weapons shipments to Egypt, "the Egyptians left Israel with the choice of striking first or facing annihilation." Meir then pointed to the ideological connection between Nazism and Egypt's aggression. "The concept of annihilating Israel is a legacy of Hitler's war against the Jewish people. It is no mere coincidence that the soldiers of [Egyptian dictator Gamal Abdel] Nasser had an Arabic translation of *Mein Kampf* in their knapsacks." Nasser's dream of destroying Israel and establishing Egyptian domination of the Middle East echoed Hitler's blend of anti-Jewish hatred and dreams of German military expansion, Meir argued. Evidently the Egyptian leader viewed the tract as an inspiration for his own foot soldiers.[28]

Hitler had written *Mein Kampf* (My Struggle), his manifesto of antisemitism, racial supremacy, and militarism, while in prison after his failed coup in 1923. Following his rise to power in 1933, *Mein Kampf*'s extreme antisemitism and advocacy of German territorial expansion attracted sympathetic interest in the Arab world. Extracts appeared in the Iraqi and Lebanese press in 1934. Arabic translations also were published in Egypt in 1937 and British Mandatory Palestine in 1938. The editor of the Palestinian edition "carefully purged the passage in which the Arabs are graded fourteenth on the racial scale," one news report noted.[29]

Hitler's manifesto remained popular in the Arab world in the decades to follow. In 1982, Arabic-language copies of *Mein Kampf* were found in PLO strongholds that Israeli troops overran in Lebanon. In 1999, the French news agency AFP reported that it was a bestseller in the Palestinian Authority–controlled territories, according to sales figures compiled by the most popular bookstore in Ramallah (the PA's capital). Israeli troops in Gaza in late 2023 discovered Arabic-language copies of *Mein Kampf* in apartments used by Hamas terrorists. "This is the real war we are facing," President Isaac Herzog remarked, noting that in one of the copies of the book, a terrorist "wrote notes, marked the sections, and studied again and again the ideology of Adolf Hitler to hate the Jews, to kill the Jews, to burn and slaughter Jews wherever they are."[30]

The PA's monthly educational magazine for youth, *Zayzafuna* (a Tilia tree), has featured a list of "Hitler's sayings" and a tenth grader's essay describing Hitler appearing to her in a dream. The Nazi leader explained to her that he "killed [the Jews] so you would all know that they are a nation which spreads destruction all over the world," she wrote.[31] Students at PA high schools in Tulkarm and Anabta have posted photos of Hitler and Nazi general Erwin Rommel, with adulatory texts, on their schools' Facebook pages.[32]

The popularity of Hitler and the Nazis in Palestinian Arab society might seem contradictory, given the frequent accusation by Palestinian

Arab spokesmen (as well as article 20 of the official Hamas Charter) that Israeli behavior resembles that of the Nazis. Longtime PA chairman Mahmoud Abbas is one among many who have promulgated Holocaust denial while simultaneously accusing Israel of perpetrating a Holocaust. In Abbas's 1982 PhD dissertation, published as a book (which he never retracted), he claimed only a few hundred thousand European Jews died under Nazi rule—and in the same breath accused Israel's prime minister-to-be, David Ben-Gurion, of collaborating with the Nazis to murder Europe's Jews in order to attract international sympathy for the creation of a Jewish state after the war. This peculiar approach dovetails with the broader Islamist view of Jews. As dhimmis, their natural condition is supposed to be weak and degraded, a physical inferiority that attests to the superiority of Islam. How, then, to explain the Jews' ability to repeatedly triumph over multiple Arab armies? By viewing Israeli victories as the product of an international conspiracy which achieved what the Jews themselves could not. "The imperialists" brought about "the Palestine downfall," Nasser insisted after the 1948 war. To explain their defeat in 1967, Egypt, Syria, and Jordan alleged that U.S. and British forces fought against the Arab armies. According to the common worldview in Palestinian Arab society, international sympathy for the Jews because of the Holocaust is what created Israel, and international intervention is what has enabled Israel's military victories.[33]

THE BIRTH OF HAMAS

Hamas as an organization was thirty-six years old at the time of its October 7 invasion. But Hamas as part of the violent Palestinian Arab opposition to any Jewish sovereignty in the Holy Land is more than a century old. And Hamas as an idea draws its inspiration from the fundamentalist theological principles and territorial expansionism that have characterized militant Islam since the religion's founding in the seventh century CE.

Hamas's predecessor, the Muslim Brotherhood, was founded by schoolteacher Hassan al-Banna in Egypt in 1928. Combining fundamentalist Islam and extreme nationalism, it aspired to the creation of a single Islamic regime, or caliphate, ruling over the entire world, according to sharia religious law. The caliphate would be realized through jihad, holy war.

Educational and social initiatives enabled the Muslim Brotherhood to gradually attract a substantial grassroots following. Then it moved into violence. By the 1930s, the Brotherhood was inciting hatred of Egypt's Jews as a gesture of solidarity with Palestinian Arabs' anti-Jewish campaigns. The following decade, an estimated 1,500 Egyptian Muslim Brotherhood members joined the pan-Arab invasion intended to prevent the creation of Israel.[34]

A clear ideological line runs from the Muslim Brotherhood and the Palestinian Arab mobs of the 1920s, through the Egyptian-sponsored fedayeen in Gaza in the 1950s, to the founding of the PLO in 1964—and, twenty-three years later, the founding of Hamas. With modest but inconsequential differences in tone and strategy, all have drawn motivation from the same sources, aspired to the same goal, and, when feasible, employed similar tactics in pursuit of that aim. Medieval theological sources advocating global Islamic supremacy shaped their view of the world as a divinely designated battleground. Stereotypes of Jews as treacherous, rooted in ancient religious literature, informed their view of Israel. The issue at stake was not disputed territory, or Israeli policy, or the absence of a Palestinian state alongside Israel, but the very existence of a Jewish state in the Muslim-majority *dar al-Islam*, which violated the desired order of the world. Violence was the appropriate and religiously mandated means of dealing with infidels who had broken free of their obligatory dhimmi status. Palestinian Arab society was already steeped in violence on many levels, from corporal punishment of misbehaving students to beating of wives deemed insubordinate to the settling of political and religious scores through assault or murder. Violence likewise was widely perceived as an appropriate means of addressing offenses against Islamic supremacy.

Gaza-based Muslim Brotherhood activists established Hamas in late 1987. An acronym for the Islamic Resistance Movement, Hamas distinguished itself from the PLO and other Palestinian Arab terrorist groups by virtue of its more overt emphasis on Muslim fundamentalist ideology and practice. The PLO's National Covenant emphasizes

Arab nationalism, pan-Arab unity, the illegitimacy of Israel's creation and existence, and the need to destroy Israel through "armed struggle," but makes no mention of Islam or the Quran, even though the group's founders, leaders, and vast majority of members are devout Muslims.[35]

The Hamas Charter, issued in 1988, articulates similar beliefs and goals, but is laced with Quranic verses, reminders about the importance of a traditional Muslim religious lifestyle, and allusions to ancient Muslim battles against infidels. Like the PLO Covenant, Hamas calls for the complete eradication of Israel and dates its opposition to Zionism back to the British liberation of the Holy Land from the Muslim Turks in 1917, and England's expressed support for creating a Jewish national home there. The charter pledges to "raise high the banner of Jihad" (article 3). It also characterizes Hamas as the ideological successor to the twelfth-century CE Muslim conqueror Saladin and the Islamic Caliphate he established after defeating the Crusaders (article 15), thus centering the movement around conquest and subjugation. Underlining its deeply antisemitic nature, the charter cites a Quranic verse urging Muslims to "fight the Jews" (article 7) and another warning that "the Jews will not be pleased" until they lure Muslims away from their religion (article 13). It also accuses Jews of instigating both world wars and plotting to "rule the world" (article 22) and quotes as its authority *The Protocols of the Elders of Zion* (article 32), the nineteenth-century antisemitic Russian screed alleging global Jewish conspiracies.[36]

Hamas reiterated its historical conception in an eighteen-page English-language document it issued to explain the October 7 attack. The first sentence situated the assault in a broader context: "The battle of the Palestinian people against occupation and colonialism did not start on Oct. 7, but started 105 years ago, including 30 years of British colonialism [the Mandate period] and 75 years of Zionist occupation [the period of Israel's existence]."[37]

HAMAS TERROR

Hamas pioneered terrorist methods that would become mainstays of the Palestinian cause. Its first suicide bombing in Israel, in April 1993, killed one and wounded nine. Subsequent waves of suicide bombers, with explosives strapped to their bodies, struck crowded civilian buses, including in Tel Aviv in October 1994 (twenty-two dead, fifty-six wounded), the Beit Lid Junction in January 1995 (twenty-one dead, sixty-nine wounded), and Jerusalem in February 1996 (twenty-six dead, eighty wounded). Soon there were imitators: Palestinian Islamic Jihad, similar to Hamas in ideology but much smaller in numbers, began staging suicide attacks throughout Israel. So did the Al-Aqsa Martyrs Brigade, a division of Fatah, the ruling faction of the PLO and the PA, beginning in late 2001.

As a result of the 1993 Oslo Accords between Israel and the Palestinian Arab leadership, the PA had assumed control of all of Gaza except a small area where Israeli communities were situated. In 2005, going beyond its Oslo obligations, Israel withdrew all of its soldiers and civilians from the remainder of Gaza—an undertaking that included expelling more than nine thousand Israeli residents and dismantling twenty-five towns. Prime Minister Ariel Sharon believed that doing so would demonstrate Israel's interest in peace, remove Israeli targets from close proximity to Gaza-based terrorists, and test the PA's intentions and abilities by granting it near-sovereignty in the Gaza Strip. Hamas responded with a steadily escalating series of rocket attacks into towns in southern Israel. There were nearly one thousand such attacks in 2006, over two thousand in 2008, and more than four thousand in 2014, causing significant Israeli casualties. In response, Israel undertook pinpoint attacks on specific Hamas targets. It refrained from striking terrorist leaders in circumstances liable to result in civilian casualties. Israeli policy was the opposite of what a country bent on "genocide" would have done, but extreme critics of Israel nonetheless circulated that allegation both then and later.[38]

In December 1992, after Hamas terrorists murdered five Israelis in several attacks, Prime Minister Yitzhak Rabin ordered the deportation of 415 leading Hamas activists from Israeli-administered territories to Lebanon. It would prove to be a turning point in the movement's history.[39] Officials of the incoming Clinton administration challenged Rabin's view that crippling the terrorist group would be good for peace;

they insisted that deporting the terrorists would "complicate" the prospects for a Middle East peace process.[40] A team of State Department officials, headed by Aaron Miller and Dennis Ross, successfully pressured Rabin to permit the terrorists to return over several months in exchange for American opposition to UN sanctions against Israel. That effectively squandered the opportunity to eliminate much of the up-and-coming leadership of Hamas.[41] Many of the returning deportees subsequently emerged as major figures in Hamas and played key roles in its expansion. Abdel Aziz al-Rantisi became Hamas's political leader and spokesman in Gaza. Mahmoud Zahar was named foreign minister of the Hamas government in Gaza. Sheikh Hassan Yousef rose to the head of Hamas in the PA-governed territories. Ismail Haniyeh served as prime minister of the Hamas regime in Gaza and then became its leader abroad, based in Qatar.

In 2003, Israel located Haniyeh and seven other senior Hamas figures in a house in Gaza and began preparing an air strike. In the face of U.S. pressure to avoid casualties among civilians with whom the Hamas leaders were embedded, Israel used a quarter-ton bomb rather than the standard one-ton bomb, which only damaged the house as all eight Hamas leaders escaped alive. Similar instances of U.S. intervention to limit Israel's actions against Hamas occurred in the years to follow.[42]

HAMAS IN POWER

A critical component of the Oslo Accords was the requirement that the PA institute democratic practices such as elections. The Israelis reasoned that democratization would improve the likelihood of peace, given that throughout modern history, democratic nations have almost never gone to war against one another. Despite Israel's concern about permitting Hamas to participate, the George W. Bush administration pressed for including the terrorist organization in the legislative elections held in PA-controlled territories in January 2006. Hamas went on to win 76 out of the 132 seats in parliament. Secretary of State Condoleezza Rice insisted afterward that despite the outcome, the United States had taken the right position, since it would have been inappropriate to "support a policy of denying the Palestinians elections that had been promised to them" just "because people were fearful of the outcome."[43] That approach was at odds with the best-known precedent in America's own experience: the Truman administration and the U.S. military governors of postwar Germany outlawed the Nazi Party and barred Nazis from running in elections, regardless of how many Germans might have wanted to vote for them.[44] Given America's role as the leading financial and diplomatic supporter of the PA, U.S. opposition to the inclusion of Hamas might have kept the terrorist organization out of political power. Eighteen years later, Rice admitted she had been wrong. "In retrospect, yes, I think you don't want armed groups to be able to run in an election," she said in an October 2024 interview. "When you think about it, it is, of course, an unfair advantage if you're armed with a militia and you run in an election."[45]

Hamas established a coalition government with Fatah, the main faction of the Palestinian Authority and runner-up in the election. However, power struggles between the two led to several weeks of armed clashes the following year, and by June 2007 Hamas had ousted Fatah and assumed sole control of the strip. Under both the old PA regime and its Hamas successor, Gazans were denied free speech and other civil rights, dissidents were jailed and tortured, and women were treated as chattel. In addition, the new Hamas regime expressed its fundamentalist zeal by instituting Islamic strictures in dress such as women's head coverings and long gowns, banning alternative personal lifestyles, and regulating other areas of daily life.[46]

The responsibilities of governance did not temper Hamas's commitment to violence against Israel. Consistent with its view that the existence of a State of Israel of any size represents an "illegal occupation of Palestine" to be fought with blood and fire, Hamas began firing rockets at towns in southern Israel, first by the dozens, then by the hundreds, and then by the thousands, testing the resolve of Israel and the international community. In December 2008 and again in July 2014, Israel undertook full-scale ground invasions of Gaza to root out the terrorists. In both instances, the Obama administration pressured Israel to halt operations after several weeks, far short of defeating Hamas or eliminating its offensive capabilities.

Israeli policy toward Hamas-ruled Gaza did not involve a blockade or siege in the sense that those terms are commonly understood. Thousands of laborers were permitted to cross from Gaza into Israel daily. Nonmilitary goods—except for dual use items that could be converted into military materials—were allowed to enter Gaza. Cement was not originally considered a risk, but importation of cement was barred after Israel's military actions in Gaza revealed a substantial network of underground tunnels built by Hamas to hide weapons and burrow into Israeli territory. U.S. Mideast envoy Dennis Ross then pressed Israel to permit Hamas to bring in concrete. He argued that it made no sense to suspect Hamas would use imported concrete for tunnels, since Gaza's residents were so desperately in need of housing. Israel, he said, "needed to allow more construction materials, including cement, into Gaza so that housing, schools, and basic infrastructure could be built."[47] Israeli officials initially resisted, arguing that "Hamas would misuse" the cement. Eventually, the Israelis acquiesced to Ross's pressure, but they would soon come to regret that concession. Many years later, Ross would acknowledge in the *Washington Post* that the Israelis "were right" to oppose his demand.[48] The cement was used to build hundreds of miles of tunnels under Gaza to cloak the October 7 preparations, stockpile weapons, and hide Israeli hostages. The tunnels also severely complicated Israel's efforts to root out terrorists in the months following the October 7 invasion.

Ross's misplaced optimism extended to Hamas's supply of armaments. In the same 2014 *Washington Post* essay in which he admitted his colossal error regarding the cement, Ross predicted: "At some point, Hamas will stop firing rockets—if for no other reason than its arsenal is depleted." But the *Post* reported that when the day arrived that Hamas's arsenal was depleted, it simply manufactured more, using parts that were smuggled into Gaza "labeled for civilian use or hidden inside shipments of food or other everyday wares."[49]

MILITARY CHALLENGES AFTER OCTOBER 7

After Israeli forces eliminated the Hamas terrorists who had infiltrated the southern towns and kibbutzim on October 7, Israeli planes struck numerous Hamas targets in Gaza. Three weeks later, Israeli ground troops entered the territory in pursuit of the rest of the Hamas forces and the hostages. The principles guiding Israel's action were comparable to those of American forces that chased after, and destroyed, those who have attacked the United States, such as Pancho Villa's terrorists attacking from Mexico in 1916, the Japanese after the 1941 bombing of Pearl Harbor, and Al Qaeda after the 9/11 attacks. But the Israelis entering Gaza discovered a number of unique obstacles that the Americans did not face in Mexico, the Pacific, or Afghanistan.

Israel knew that Hamas had constructed some underground tunnels in Gaza, but soon realized the tunnel system was far more extensive than previously understood. The tunnels reached for hundreds of miles, criss-crossed the entire Gaza Strip, and constituted a veritable underground city in which terrorists hid and hostages were held. In the southern Gaza city of Rafah, Israeli troops found that "there was almost no home without a tunnel," as one brigade commander put it. Some of the tunnels led into neighboring Egypt, through which weapons had been smuggled for years.[50]

Hamas and other terrorist groups also had stationed themselves in and around residential apartment buildings, schools, and hospitals; stored weapons there; and dug entries to the tunnels from their premises. President Joe Biden noted in one of his first comments on the October 7 massacre that Hamas "uses Palestinian civilians as human shields."[51] Likewise, Secretary of State Antony Blinken acknowledged that Israel faced "an extraordinarily complex military environment in which you have an enemy, Hamas, that committed the most atrocious terrorist attacks on Israel on October 7th and then retreats to Gaza, hides behind and underneath civilians, in hospitals, schools, mosques, apartment buildings."[52] The Israeli author Amos Oz had described the situation more vividly years earlier: "What would you do if your neighbor across the street sat down on the balcony, put his little boy on his lap and started shooting machine-gun fire into your nursery?"[53]

The answer to Oz's question is that according to international law, Israel had the right to shoot at such terrorists. Article 52(2) of the Additional Protocol to the Geneva Convention authorizes attacking military targets, even when they are situated within civilian areas, if those targets "by their nature, location, purpose or use make an effective contribution to military action," and if their "total or partial destruction, capture or neutralization, in the circumstances ruling at the time, offers a definite military advantage." The targets may include "an object which is normally dedicated to civilian purposes, such as a place of worship, a house or other dwelling, or a school," if it "is being used to make an effective contribution to military action."[54]

Israeli soldiers pursuing terrorists in the Gaza town of Salatin on November 24, 2023, discovered that "there isn't a single house here without weapons, there isn't a house without [tunnel] infrastructure," a senior army officer told reporters. "In dozens of yards of homes we found dozens of rocket launchers. We found Kalashnikovs under mattresses, inside clothes closets. It wasn't thrown there suddenly, they were hidden in the homes." Weapons were situated in "schools, a cemetery, a [medical] clinic," and they "concentrated most of their tunnel shafts there." Precisely in the places where "they thought we wouldn't strike . . . we found the enemy's significant infrastructure." At one point, a family approached their apartment building, and the Israeli troops held their fire. A terrorist armed with an automatic rifle hidden in his clothing accompanied the family, disguised as one of them. He then stationed himself in an adjoining building and opened fire on the Israeli soldiers.[55]

A journalist embedded with a brigade pursuing terrorists in the Shejaia neighborhood in early December heard similar firsthand accounts of the Israeli forces discovering "weapons in every building, terrorists in every school." An officer explained that "most of Hamas's infrastructure is based on schools, mosques, hospitals, international structures of various kinds." Soldiers found "ammunition boxes hidden under the beds of children, rocket launchers placed outside of kindergartens." Terrorists frequently "fired [at the Israelis] from kindergartens and mosques."[56]

TERROR CENTERS IN UNIVERSITIES AND HOSPITALS

Gaza's universities also served as centers of Hamas terror activity. In the first week of the war, Israel struck Islamic University, which served as a

Hamas training camp for military intelligence operatives, a site for weapons development and manufacturing, and a venue to raise funds for terrorism. The university "maintained close ties with the senior leadership of Hamas," an Israeli army spokesman noted.[57] An Israeli raid on Al-Azhar University some weeks later uncovered a half-mile-long Hamas tunnel underneath the school as well as "numerous weapons, including explosive devices, rocket parts, launchers, detonation systems, and several technological assets" within the university's buildings.[58] In January 2024, Israeli forces seized a large arsenal of weapons on the Islamic University campus, including "assault rifles and other military equipment in the classrooms" as well as "dozens of weapons depots that stored more than 100 mortars, explosive devices, grenades, and maps used by Hamas operatives" on the campus and in adjacent storage areas.[59]

Hamas also commandeered Gaza's hospitals, with doctors and patients serving as human shields, yet the international news media reported Israeli actions in or near hospitals as examples of Israel's callous disregard for the safety of medical facilities. Much of the news media depicted the Israeli capture of Gaza's largest such site, Al-Shifa Hospital, in November 2023, as a moral outrage, even as National Security Council spokesman John Kirby said on November 14, "We have information that confirms that Hamas is using that particular hospital for a command and control node." In January 2024, U.S. intelligence agencies verified that Hamas and Palestinian Islamic Jihad "used Al-Shifa Hospital . . . to exercise command control activities, store weapons" and hold some Israeli hostages. The terrorists "evacuated the complex days before the multiday [Israeli] operation, destroying documents and electronics as they left," a senior U.S. intelligence official told reporters.[60] In February, a *New York Times* investigative report, headlined "How Hamas Uses Gaza's Hospitals," concluded that "Hamas used the [Al-Shifa] hospital for cover, stored weapons inside it and maintained a hardened tunnel beneath the complex that was supplied with water, power and air-conditioning." The tunnel under Al-Shifa was "at least 700 feet long" and "it extends beyond the hospital and likely connects to Hamas's larger underground network." Israel had discovered the tunnel because "ducts that ran underground from air-conditioning units were powered by the hospital's electricity supply and mounted on one of its buildings," and "the hospital's water supply was being fed to the tunnel."[61]

The *Times* also confirmed the veracity of video footage showing that Israeli soldiers found "underground bunkers, living quarters and a room that appeared to be wired for computers and communications equipment" beneath the hospital. Inside Al-Shifa, a cache of grenades was stored near an MRI machine. Soldiers also found hostages' belongings, including a bag labeled "Kibbutz Be'eri." In the parking lot was a Toyota vehicle "identical to those used in the Oct. 7 attack and loaded with the same equipment that militants carried during the raid, including guns and rocket-propelled grenades." (It was most likely a spare vehicle not used in the invasion.) In addition, footage from the hospital's own security cameras showed two hostages being brought into Al-Shifa shortly after October 7.[62]

Not only had Hamas commandeered Al-Shifa following October 7—there was "established documentation that Hamas used Al-Shifa before the war to mask some of its activities," the *Times* reported. During Israel's counterterror action against Hamas back in 2008, "armed Hamas fighters in civilian clothing were seen roaming Al-Shifa's corridors and killing an Israeli collaborator"—that is, murdering an Arab whom they suspected of assisting Israel. During Israel's 2014 operation against Hamas, "the militants routinely held news conferences at the hospital and used it as a safe meeting place for Hamas officials to speak with journalists." At that time, the *Times* noted, Amnesty International had acknowledged Hamas's use of sections of Al-Shifa, "including the outpatients' clinic area, to detain, interrogate, torture and otherwise ill-treat suspects, even as other parts of the hospital continued to function as a medical center."[63]

The *Times*'s investigation also found evidence of terrorist connections to other Gaza hospitals. Video footage showed terrorists armed with weapons in the hallways of Kamal Adwan Hospital in December 2023, and Israeli forces subsequently captured dozens of terrorists there, the Times reported.[64] An ambulance driver at Kamal Adwan revealed that Hamas had taken over the facility. "Hamas military operatives are present; they are in the courtyards, at the gates of the buildings, in the offices of Kamal Adwan Hospital," the driver said. "They operate ambulances to transport their wounded military operatives, and to transport them for their missions, and this is instead of using the ambulances for the benefit of civilians."[65]

In the months to follow, Hamas terrorists gradually reassumed control of Kamal Adwan. Israeli troops captured 240 terrorists in the hospital in December 2024. One of them, Anas Muhammad Faiz al-Sharif, confirmed under questioning that "weapons were moved in and out of the hospital for ambushes and tunnels." Al-Sharif said Hamas and Palestinian Islamic Jihad expected Israel would refrain from taking action against the facility because patients and other civilians were there. "They believe the army can't bomb the location, like with an F-16 missile, or destroy the building," he said.[66]

Video reviewed by the *Times* showed Israeli troops also finding explosives and weapons in Al-Rantisi Hospital, as well as a room where hostages had been held. In the basement they found guns, explosives, other weapons, and in a recently vacated room, there was an Arabic-language wall chart with dates where individual terrorists signed their names to schedule when it was their turn to guard hostages. A Hamas health ministry spokesman had said the chart "was nothing more than a work schedule," the *Times* noted. And, in a manner of speaking, it was; the chart began on October 7, and the title at the top read "Al Aqsa Flood Battle, 7/10/23."[67]

Additional evidence of exploitation of hospitals came from captured terrorists. Nabeel Rajab Abed Shteiwi, who said he had been involved in "missile production" for Palestinian Islamic Jihad since 2012, told his Israeli questioners in March 2024 that he and other PIJ and Hamas terrorists had been stationed in Al-Shifa Hospital for the previous three months. "Shifa and schools and places like that are our shelter," Shteiwi explained. He said that some terrorists wore medical garb as a disguise: "You might see someone who doesn't look like a nurse but is dressed in nurse clothes and walking around."[68] Likewise, Tarek Abu Shaluf, spokesman for the political wing of Palestinian Islamic Jihad, acknowledged during questioning after his arrest that PIJ and Hamas "used all the hospitals" as bases for their activity. The terrorists expected that Israel would be pilloried by the international community for "attacking schools and hospitals" (even if though those buildings were schools and hospitals in name only).[69]

A Kurdish physician who spent more than three weeks volunteering at two hospitals in northern Gaza in April and May 2024 was disturbed to discover the terrorists were using the facility as a shield. Hamas "exploit[ed] everywhere to shelter [its forces] in their strategic positions," Dr. Baxtiyar Baram told Kurdish media. "I have seen it with my eyes that the hospitals have been used for hiding Hamas leaders—yes, yes, we saw them and even spoke with them."[70]

After its initial raid on Al-Shifa in November 2023, Israel withdrew its forces from the facility. Terrorists who had fled when Israel gave advance notice of its action there soon returned and resumed control of the complex. When Israeli forces conducted a surprise follow-up raid in March 2024, terrorists hurled grenades at them from the maternity ward; ironically, one of them was Fadi Mohammed Salaam Dewik, who in 2002 had sprayed automatic gunfire in a children's bedroom in the Israeli town of Adora, murdering five-year-old Danielle Shefi and gravely wounding her younger brothers. The Israelis found sniper rifles, handguns, and mortars hidden among the maternity ward beds and within the ceiling panels.[71]

Hamas has managed to challenge Israel in ways both old and new. Its ideology and brutality represent familiar features of the century-old Palestinian Arab war against the Jews. But its unique position as the near-sovereign ruler of Gaza created opportunities for innovative terror strategies. It commandeered university campuses and hospital facilities, forcing Israel to take military action that would be met with international vilification. It took cement intended as humanitarian aid and built tunnels in which to imprison and torture defenseless captives, including children. All of this required an army of fanatical foot soldiers who were prepared both to engage in atrocities and to risk the lives of their own people in order to advance their cause. How did Hamas and other terrorist groups acquire those recruits? How did they find willing executioners to fill their ranks and carry out the most horrific slaughter of Jews since the Holocaust?

3. Killers Are Made, Not Born

Israeli soldiers pursuing terrorists house to house in Gaza's Daraj Tuffah neighborhood in December 2023 discovered, in one home, four family photographs that offered an unusually revealing glimpse of how Palestinian Arab society helped pave the road to the horrors of October 7.

In each of the first three pictures, a young teenage boy is posing together with five- to seven-year-old boys, likely his siblings, flanked by a rocket launcher and several rockets. In one image, a shoulder-fired rocket, standing on its end, is taller than the young boy next to it. In another, the eldest boy is wearing a military-style vest, and his little brother is dressed in full battle fatigues. In each of the three scenes, all of the children are holding automatic weapons.

In two photos, the children are standing in front of an enormous Hamas flag; in the third, they are on a beach at sunset. The varied background scenes and garb indicate the children were taken to a portrait studio—a popular family activity throughout the world that has taken on new meaning in Gaza.

The fourth photo shows a woman in traditional Muslim garb, most likely the boys' mother (judging from her apparent age), kneeling as if in battle position and aiming an automatic rifle at some off-camera target. This mother's idea of a parental role model, the poses chosen for her children's portraits, and the very existence of a photo studio devoted to encouraging terrorism, all point to how children who are inculcated with dreams of violence—at home, in schools, in summer camps, and elsewhere, as described below—eventually filled the ranks of Hamas's willing executioners.[1]

JIHAD EDUCATION IN SCHOOLS

From their earliest years, children in the Palestinian Authority (PA) educational system use schoolbooks and participate in class activities that teach them to hate Israel, and to glorify terrorists who murder Jews.

At the Al-Tofula Kindergarten, in the PA town of Bayt Awwa, in 2023, students participated in a military drill, marching with toy guns, pretending to shoot Israelis, and holding a mock funeral procession with one kindergartner dressed as a "martyred" terrorist.[2] A second kindergarten in the town is named after Dalal Mughrabi, leader of the massacre of thirty-seven Israelis on the Coastal Road in 1978.[3] Kindergarteners in the PA town of Tubas who joined their school's Girl Scouts branch in 2022 were welcomed with a ceremony in which children held signs reading "We are all Ahmad Mansarah," a reference to a young terrorist imprisoned for stabbing two Israelis.[4] Children from the Quarters of Jerusalem Kindergarten in the PA village of Hares held what organizers called "a solidarity rally with the heroic prisoners in the occupation prisons"—that is, convicted terrorists jailed in Israel.[5] Students at the Farah Kindergarten in Deir Ghassaneh also marched "in solidarity with the prisoners" jailed in Israel, clasping little homemade placards, as they were led by teachers and cheered on by adults in cartoon character costumes.[6] "I am scared of the Jews" because "they kill worshippers at the Al-Aqsa Mosque" and "imprison small children," a little girl declared at a rally of kindergarteners organized by the PA's Red Crescent branch near Tulkarm and broadcast on PA Television.[7]

Palestinian kindergarten graduation ceremonies likewise feature militaristic messages. The 2017 commencement at Islamic Jihad's Al-Huda kindergarten in Gaza included a children's skit in which uniformed jihadists murder Israelis (dressed in stereotypical Orthodox Jewish garb) and abduct the corpses. In the background, a song begins, "O I have prepared all sorts of rockets for my Zionist enemy that will reach where he lives."[8] The 2011 graduation party at the "Bird of Paradise" kindergarten featured children performing two plays in which they "depicted the reality of roadblocks, children, occupation soldiers, and the children's death as Martyrs," the official PA daily newspaper *Al-Hayat Al-Jadida* reported. Their "charming" acting "caused the audience to cry, as the children's performance was accompanied by the playing of nationalistic songs."[9]

One Hamas recruitment video for its kindergartens shows a graduation ceremony in which schoolchildren don Hamas headbands and, brandishing toy rifles and swords, march in formation and jump over obstacles while chanting, "Jihad! Allahu Akbar! Your role model? The Prophet [Muhammad]. Your path? Jihad! Your aspiration? Death for Allah. Your movement? Hamas! Your movement? Hamas!"[10]

In primary or elementary school, students in grades 1 through 4 are guided by textbooks steeped in anti-Israel and pro-violence messages. *Our Beautiful Language, Vol. 2* teaches first graders to identify words beginning with the letter "ya" by viewing images of a little girl playing the flute, a boy playing basketball, and—much larger than the rest—a uniformed man with a rifle and a huge PLO flag. A reading exercise explaining the letter "ha" highlights the words *shahid* (martyr) and *hujum* (attack).[11]

National and Life Education, Vol. 1 directs second graders to color a map showing all of Israel, labeled "Palestine," with human figures comprising its borders. The map is flanked by the caption, "We will draw the map of our country with our bodies." *Our Beautiful Language* for second grade features a large illustration of children wearing the uniform of the terrorist Fatah group's youth movement, next to a poem vowing to "carry the revolution's flame" to the Al-Aqsa Mosque and to Haifa and Jaffa, two cities within Israel's pre-1967 borders.[12]

Mathematics, Vol. 1 teaches addition to third graders by having them count the number of "martyrs"—Arabs killed while murdering, or attempting to murder, Israelis, or during Israeli counterterror operations—in the First and Second Intifadas and the 2014 Gaza War. Another exercise in the book has students count the number of "prisoners in the Occupation prisons."[13]

In *Our Beautiful Language, Vol. 1* fourth graders study the colorfully illustrated adventures of Palestinian Arab refugee children victimized by "the many explosions made by the Zionist gangs." Grade 4's edition of *Mathematics, Vol. 1* explains a mathematical concept by comparing the number of "martyrs" who died in various attacks on Israelis.[14]

These themes continue for middle school students, which in the Palestinian educational system comprises grades 5 through 10. Among the mandatory texts for fifth graders is *Arabic Language, Vol. 2*, which extols the massacre leader Dalal Mughrabi as a "hero" and a "moon that never sets but illuminates the darkness of our dark night." Such individuals "have an important position in every nation. . . . We are proud of them, sing their praise, learn the history of their lives, name our children after them, and name streets, squares, and prominent cultural sites after them. . . . Every one of us wishes to be like them. . . . These heroes are the crown of their nation, they are a symbol of its glory, they are the best of the best, the best of the noble people."[15] *Islamic Education, Vol. 2* teaches fifth graders that "the Jews" in Muhammad's time made "repeated attempts to kill the Prophet." The lesson also includes a "topic for discussion": "The Zionist Occupation desecrating the graves of the Companions of the Prophet and the Righteous Ones, shoveling them away and removing them from Muslim cemeteries."[16]

Social Studies, Vol. 1 explains the borders of "Palestine" to sixth graders, "from the Mediterranean Sea in the west, to the Jordan River in the East, and from Lebanon and Syria in the north to the Gulf of Aqaba and Egypt in the south," with an accompanying map clarifying that this means all of Israel. As evidence of humans as a factor in harming buildings, *Science and Life, Vol. 2* for sixth graders shows cracks in a wall of the Al-Aqsa Mosque and blames them on "the Israeli Occupation."[17]

In seventh grade, *Islamic Education, Vol. 2* relates as fact the Muslim legend of a Jew in Muhammad's time harassing a Muslim woman. *Science and Life, Vol. 2* teaches a biology lesson about the importance of a person's spine through an anecdote about a child named Ali who suffered "an injury to his spine, which led to his paralysis," caused by "a suspicious object—one of the remnants of the Zionist aggression."[18]

Eighth graders learn reading comprehension from a story in *Arabic Language, Vol. 2* about brave Palestinian fighters who "cut the necks" of Israelis and "turn their bodies into fire, burning the Zionist tank."[19] *Arabic Text and Reader* teaches eighth graders that Arabs need "to exterminate the Zionist germ and thrust this evil out of the Arab homeland" and that "the time has come for jihad and martyrdom" against "the oppressor."[20]

In ninth grade, *Social Studies, Vol. 1* hails the Palestinian Arab massacres of Jews in 1929 as "armed resistance" and "resistance operations." *Islamic Education, Vol. 1* explains how Allah offers believers opportunities for "fighting against infidels" to "honor them by martyrdom, to forgive their sins and raise their class in Paradise."[21]

In *Arabic Language* for tenth graders, students are taught that the Jews who have occupied Jerusalem with their "despicable lewdness" are no match for "the thousands of martyrs who have beautified her pure soil with their innocent blood," so the city will surely "spit out the scum of foreigners." *General Sciences* explains Newton's laws of physics through the example of "a young girl using a slingshot towards a specific target," with a photo of a child whipping a rock with a homemade sling, a weapon often used by Palestinian Arab mobs attacking Israelis. The calculation uses variations in the length of the sling and the rock's release speed to determine its rate of acceleration.[22]

Secondary education, or high school, encompasses grades 11 and 12. Palestinian eleventh graders read in *History, Vol. 2* that the 1972 Munich Olympics massacre was legitimate "Palestinian resistance" against "Zionist interests abroad," and that "the blood of each martyr is the fuel that fed the Intifada and gave it the power to go on." *Arabic Language* for grade 11 includes a poem glorifying the "falcons in their Intifadas" who "climb ever higher on their ladder of gushing blood." Additionally, *History, Vol. 1* promotes antisemitic conspiracy theories with a large cartoon depiction of an arm with a Star of David holding the planet Earth in its grip.[23]

In the twelfth grade, *Islamic Education* presents an especially detailed treatise on "the virtue of jihad in Islam," especially "if the enemy occupied a Muslim land"; and on the importance of jihad both as "one of the gates to achieving martyrdom" and as Allah's way to achieve "rescue from the fire of Hell and the attainment of pardon and Paradise." A poem in *Arabic Language* instructs twelfth graders that Haifa, a city in pre-1967 Israel, is "longing [for] you to come to her . . . with the weapon in your hand."[24]

By the time they finish their senior year of high school, Palestinian Arab teens have been nurtured for more than a decade on a diet of antisemitism, virulent hatred of Israel, and glorification of *jihad.* "The textbooks used in the Palestinian Authority school system, from elementary through high school, are replete with strong expressions of hatred towards Israel, negation of its right to exist and praise for the struggle against it, as well as antisemitic expressions against the Jews," a 2001 Israeli government study concluded. Palestinian Arabs "are educated from birth in an atmosphere of religious and nationalist incitement, with no trace of anything positive regarding Israel, which results in a deepening of their hatred towards Israel, a fanning of the flames of violence and encouragement and justification of terrorism against the State of Israel and against Jews."[25] Two years later, an analysis by the Institute for Monitoring Peace and Cultural Tolerance in School Education (IMPACT-se) of thirty-five PA schoolbooks likewise found "a systematic effort in the textbooks to demonize Israel and the Israelis." Among other examples, "Israel's name does not appear on any map" and "jihad and martyrdom are . . . praised and encouraged."[26] Studies by the U.S. State Department, the UN Committee on the Elimination of Racial Discrimination, the European Parliament, and the European Union reached nearly identical conclusions regarding PA school curriculum materials.[27]

In 2006, the PA announced the introduction of all new textbooks for grade 12. A Palestinian Media Watch (PMW) review of the new geography, history, language, math, and science texts found that they "make no attempt to educate for peace and coexistence with Israel." Instead, "[t]he teachings repeatedly reject Israel's right to exist, present the conflict as a religious battle for Islam, teach Israel's founding as imperialism, and actively portray a picture of the Middle East, both verbally and visually, in which Israel does not exist at all."[28]

PMW's findings alarmed U.S. Senator Hillary Clinton. "These textbooks do not give Palestinian children an education; they give them an indoctrination," she said at a 2007 press conference. Palestinian Arab children are "encouraged to see martyrdom and armed struggle and the murder of innocent people as ideals to strive for." The PA "profoundly poisons the minds of these children. . . . [It is] a clear example of child abuse." Evoking the themes in her book *It Takes a Village*, on how communal influences shape children's lives, Sen. Clinton warned that Palestinian Arab hate education would have "dire consequences for prospects of peace for generations to come." Sixteen years later, some of the children raised on these teachings carried out the October 7 atrocities.[29]

UNRWA'S HATE EDUCATION

In addition to the thousands of schools operated by the PA or Hamas, there are 370 schools, serving more than 320,000 students in Gaza and PA-governed territory, that are financed and run by the United Nations Relief and Works Agency (UNRWA), which was established to assist Palestinian Arab refugees from the 1948 Arab-Israeli war. While the UN is officially committed to nonviolence and interfaith coexistence, UNRWA schools have consistently echoed the extremist views of the PA and Hamas governing regimes.

UNRWA schools use the same textbooks as PA and Hamas schools, and also develop their own supplementary educational materials, including teacher's guides. An UNRWA booklet on Arabic language comprehension urges fifth grade students to savor "the smell of the ground mixed with the blood of martyrs." A teacher's guide for Grade 6 Arabic language instructs teachers to explain to students that "[t]he Zionists are the terrorists of the modern age, and they are fated to disappear." A language comprehension edition for ninth graders characterizes a firebombing attack on an Israeli bus as "a barbecue party" and asks students to "explain the beauty of the metaphor" in the sentence, "The Zionist gangs sank their fangs of hatred into her pure body." A teacher's guide for Grade 10 history and geography instructs teachers to deduct points from students who fail to "tie the perpetration of Zionist massacres to Jewish religious thought."[30]

These examples are not isolated instances. A study by UN Watch and IMPACT-se of supplementary materials introduced in the UNRWA school curricula in 2021–22 found "a systematic insertion of violence, martyrdom, overt antisemitism, and jihad across all grades and subjects with the proliferation of extreme nationalism and Islamist ideologies throughout the curriculum; rejection of the possibility of peace with Israel; and the complete omission of any historical Jewish presence in the modern-day territories of Israel and the PA."[31]

Reactions to October 7 by Palestinian Arab teachers employed by UNRWA reflected their affinity for the school system's focus on hate education. In their Telegram chat group, one UNRWA teacher posted a photo of a suicide bomb vest accompanied by the text, "Wait, sons of Judaism." He also heaped praise on Akran Abu Hasanen, an October 7 perpetrator, as a "martyr," "friend," and "brother" whom the teacher hoped would be "admitted to Paradise." A second teacher appealed to Gaza civilians to ignore Israeli warnings to leave danger zones, urging them to serve as human shields for Hamas. A third wrote of the attackers, "They breastfed Jihad with their mother's milk. May Allah grant them victory." Such expressions were typical, not aberrations.[32]

In early 2024, Israel revealed that nineteen UNRWA employees were among the October 7 perpetrators. One was Muhammad Abu Attawi, leader of a squad that sprayed automatic gunfire and hurled grenades into a roadside bomb shelter where refugees from the music festival were hiding. Sixteen were killed and four were kidnapped. (Seven wounded victims survived because the terrorists thought they were dead.)[33] Some UNRWA employees also held abducted Israelis in their homes. In January 2024, Israel identified 440 UNRWA employees in Gaza who were "active in Hamas's military operations," two thousand more who were "registered Hamas operatives," and another seven thousand who had an immediate family member who was a terrorist. Seven months later, UNRWA announced that it had investigated nineteen of the names on Israel's list, and confirmed that nine of them were involved in the October 7 massacres.[34]

In the meantime, there was mounting evidence that Hamas used many UNRWA-administered buildings in Gaza for terror operations.[35] On the first day of Israel's ground offensive, October 27, 2023, Israeli forces discovered Hamas rocket launching sites in an UNRWA warehouse in Southern Gaza, adjacent to an UNRWA school.[36] Footage from an Israeli surveillance drone showed Hamas terrorists shooting from an UNRWA warehouse in eastern Rafah.[37] A Hamas command center and arms depot filled with rockets, machine guns, grenades, and drones armed with bombs was found directly underneath UNRWA's headquarters in Gaza City.[38] Israeli troops discovered that an UNRWA medical clinic in northern Gaza served as a major weapons storage facility after terrorists stationed there opened fire on them. A senior Israeli military commander reported, "There is not an UNRWA site, school, mosque, or kindergarten in which we didn't find weapons. None." Two of the Hamas members employed by UNRWA were principals of schools under which Hamas tunnels had been built.[39] Fateh Sherif Abu el-Amin, the head of Hamas in Lebanon, was a school principal and former head of the UNRWA teachers' union in that country.[40]

In December 2024, a year after Israel's revelations about UNRWA, the *New York Times* reported that it was "an open secret" that Hamas terrorists were employed by UNRWA schools. The *Times* found dozens of UNRWA principals or teachers were serving in Hamas terror units. When UNRWA was alerted by Israel or journalists to its employees' terrorist activities, it typically responded that it would "investigate" but then claimed there was insufficient evidence—even in the case of a principal who posted a photo of himself posing with a Hamas banner on Facebook. In one instance, a tunnel shaft was discovered adjacent to an UNRWA school whose principal was a Hamas deputy squad commander; the shaft led into a half-mile-long tunnel, filled with weapons, underneath the school. An UNRWA spokesman said, "[T]he mere existence of an adjacent shaft did not necessarily implicate the principal." The *Times* also confirmed that Hamas considered the schools "the best obstacles to protect the resistance" and stashed weapons there in the expectation that Israel would be reluctant to target them. The *Times* was able to verify all this information because Hamas kept meticulous records, "tracking the weapons [its members] were issued and regularly evaluating everything from their fitness to their loyalty." They are not the first mass killers of Jews whose scrupulous record keeping ultimately helped demonstrate their own war crimes.[41]

MATRICULATION AND MARTYRDOM

Anti-Jewish and anti-Israel material riddles the PA's General Certificate of High School Examination in Palestine, the *Tawjihi*. It is arguably the most important test taken by Palestinian Arab high school students, since a good mark on the exam is necessary to apply for university study. In the 2018–19 exam, a geography question, titled "The Greediness of the Zionist Occupation," asked which countries "share the Jordan River basin"; none of the four possible answers included Israel. In the Islamic Studies section of the exam, a question about "the jihad regulations in Islam" included text explaining how Muslims confronting infidels should first "give the choice of [adopting] Islam, paying the *jizya* [a heavy tax] or war," and if there is war, Muslims may attack those who are "carrying a weapon" and anybody who is "helping against the Muslims in any way." The Arabic Language segment highlighted a poem that the accompanying text characterized as "a lamp that illuminates the paths of the armed struggle" and asked students to identify the meaning of the term "night" in the poem; the correct answer was that it means Israel, "the brute Occupation."[42] In a similar vein, a preparatory matriculation test in PA schools asks:

—*Punctuate the underlined phrase: "We shall die in order that our land may live"*
—*Add the verb "to be," or a verb that follows the same form, to the following sentence, and punctuate accordingly: "Palestinian women are fighters."*
—*Punctuate the underlined phrase: "Do not view the occupier as human."*[43]

At the same time, PA officials promote the message that murdering Jews is more important than passing the *Tawjihi* exam. Speaking at the PA Ministry of Education's 2017 end-of-year ceremony for students in Ramallah who passed their matriculation exam, the PA's governor for the Ramallah-El Bireh district, Laila Ghannam, singled out the mothers of "Martyr Muhammad Hattab" and "Martyr Laith Al-Khaledi," two teenagers who had recently been killed while attempting to burn Jews to death with Molotov cocktails. She noted that Al-Khaledi's mother "received the news of her son's death as a Martyr on the same day that they announced the results of the matriculation exams," when she was thinking of her son's future, and yet her response to the news was, "There is nothing better than sons who have died as Martyrs." This, Governor Ghannam said, "is an example of a Palestinian woman who stands firm, as the occupation wants to kill our dreams of freedom and independence, but it will not succeed in doing so as long as there are mothers like them, and the list is growing."[44]

The governor's message was consistent with the theme of a feature story in the PA daily *Al-Hayat Al-Jadida* the previous year, about sixteen teenagers who missed the exam because they were killed or arrested while trying to stab or burn Jews to death. Most students view their test scores as "the start of their path in life, work and building," the article noted. But "the families of the Martyrs and their relatives find themselves proud of the Martyrdom that their children achieved with the Creator and in the homeland." Listing all sixteen of the young terrorists' names, the article explained that "sixteen succeeded [in achieving] the Martyrdom of the homeland and withstanding its difficult tests, for death as a Martyr is the path to excellence and greatness, and the path of those who know how to reach the great victory."[45]

Another student who famously missed his exam because he was serving what was deemed a higher purpose was Muhammad Halabi. The nineteen-year-old Al-Quds University law student brutally attacked a young Israeli family on their way to the Western Wall in October 2015—stabbing the father (a rabbi) to death with a butcher knife, slashing the rabbi's wife and two-year-old son, fatally stabbing a passerby who tried to intervene, and then shooting at onlookers before Israeli police killed him. Speakers at the next Al-Quds commencement ceremony heaped praise on Halabi, and university leaders presented his family with his diploma, even though he had not completed the graduation requirements. The PA Bar Association also awarded him a posthumous law degree.[46]

PA RESPONSES TO CURRICULA CRITICISM

How do Palestinian Arab officials and their supporters respond to criticism of their school curricula? In three ways:

One is defiance. PA Prime Minister Mohammad Shtayyeh asserted in 2019 that "the occupation" (that is, Israel and its supporters) was "waging a war against us regarding the curriculum," and vowed that "despite this we will remain loyal to the curriculum."[47] The PA curriculum cannot "deviate from the identity of the Palestinian struggle," PA Minister of Education Sabri Saidam explained in 2017. "We are the sons of Martyrs, prisoners, [and the] injured, and are proud of our path of struggle. This is our liberation project."[48] Ayed Abu Qteish, a senior official of the Ramallah-based advocacy group Defense for Children International—Palestine, justified the curricula on PA Television in 2020: "The Israeli attack [on PA curricula] said that in the Palestinians' curricula there are [lessons on] Islamic battles that took place—that encourage resistance," he said. "And this is [indeed] the role of the curriculum: The Palestinian children need to know that Palestine is not only Ramallah and Bethlehem. They need to know that Palestine is Haifa and Acre [cities in pre-1967 Israel] and that there is a historical oppression that is being imposed on the Palestinian children."[49]

A second response is to attribute the critics' accusations to a Jewish forgery scheme. Minister of Education Saidam claimed, "The occupation is forging and distorting the Palestinian schoolbooks" by having "Israeli bodies" reprint "all of the Palestinian books that are published by the PA Ministry of Education" but "removing the Palestinian flag from all of the book covers." He vowed the PA would sue the (nonexistent) forgers; it never did.[50] Minister Saidam also asserted that the criticism of the curricula was nothing more than "some Zionist websites fabricating some unfounded statements."[51] The PA's governor for the Jerusalem district, Adnan Ghaith, deemed the objections an attempt "to manipulate the Palestinian schoolbooks" as part of "a systematic plan to erase the characteristics of the Islamic and Christian Arab culture and brainwash the new generations."[52]

The PA's third approach is to deny that the curriculum's content constitutes "incitement." Addressing the United Nations in 2019, PA ambassador Riyad Mansour urged the assembled to "compare the Israeli and Palestinian schoolbooks, as it will not find any incitement by Palestine." The reason the PA does not halt publication of inciting statements is because from the PA's perspective, citing a verse from Islam's most sacred text—even a verse calling Jews apes or pigs—by definition cannot constitute incitement; and calling for violence against Israelis is not incitement, but a legitimate appeal for action against the illegal occupiers of Palestine.[53]

SCHOOLS NAMED AFTER KILLERS

Many PA schools are named after terrorists or bear other symbols paying tribute to them. Six schools are named after Dalal Mughrabi, aforementioned leader of the Coastal Road massacre of thirty-seven Israelis. When students at one such school were interviewed on PA Television, they made it clear they knew whom their school's name honors. "My life's ambition is to reach the level of the Martyr fighter Dalal Mughrabi," one commented. Another called Mughrabi "a great leader" and said she was "proud to attend the Dalal Mughrabi school."[54] There are also numerous sports tournaments named after Mughrabi, including in table tennis, women's karate, and basketball, as well as a multisport festival.[55]

Five schools in PA territory are named after Khalil al-Wazir, better known as Abu Jihad, a PLO leader who organized attacks in which at least 125 Israelis were murdered.[56] In addition, al-Wazir's name adorns tournaments in chess, boxing and martial arts, table tennis, and indoor soccer (futsal).[57]

Two schools in Gaza are named in honor of Popular Front for the Liberation of Palestine (PFLP) member Shadia Abu Ghazaleh, who was one of the first female Palestinian Arab terrorists. A large painting of Abu Ghazaleh, accompanied by text about her, adorns a wall at one of the schools. Asked on PA Television in 2013, "What do you know about Shadia Abu Ghazaleh, you study in a school named after her?," students replied: "She was a model of the wonderful female Palestinian fighter. We follow her path in this school"; "The school is named after her to commemorate her . . . and encourage people to be like her"; and "Shadia was a model for us and will remain a model for us and we will follow her path."[58]

Terrorists connected to the 1972 Munich Olympics massacre are likewise honored. Two schools in Gaza are named after Salah Khalaf (also known as Abu Iyad), a PLO leader who masterminded the Munich assault and the murder of American diplomats in Sudan in 1973, among many other attacks. The PA has two Salah Khalaf schools, and also emblazoned his name on a youth sports center and a volleyball championship.[59] The names of Munich Olympics terrorists Mahmoud Al-Hamshari, Ali Hassan Salameh, Kamal Nasser, and Kamal Adwan also appear on schools, a volleyball championship, and a horse obstacle jumping championship (and, in Adwan's case, the aforementioned Gaza hospital used by Hamas).[60]

Other PA schools are named after Hamas founder Ahmed Yassin; Al Qaeda co-founder Abdullah Azzam, Hamas suicide bombing mastermind Nash'at Abu Jabara, longtime PFLP leader Abu Ali Mustafa, 1950s terrorism organizer Mustafa Hafez, 1930s terror leader Izz ad-Din al-Qassam (who is also the namesake of the Hamas terrorist operations wing), and Al-Aqsa Martyrs Brigade leader Osama Al-Najjar, who directed suicide bombings during the Second Intifada.[61] In addition, at least forty-one PA school names honor "martyrs" of various battles or individuals from Muslim history associated with violence, such as mothers who are famous for sending all their sons to war.[62]

In Gaza, there are Samir Kuntar Championships for multiple sports, honoring one of the most notorious terrorists in recent Israeli history, whose actions in some ways foreshadowed the October 7 assault. In 1979, at age sixteen, Kuntar led a four-man terror squad that reached Israel from Lebanon on a motorized rubber boat. After murdering an Israeli policeman who happened to cross their path, the terrorists broke into an apartment at random. The mother, Smadar Haran, managed to hide in a crawlspace with her two-year-old daughter, Yael. The child screamed at the sound of the terrorists shooting, so her mother "grabbed Yael and covered her mouth," she later explained. "I knew as soon as they discovered us they would throw a grenade inside. . . . I had to keep her quiet because the footsteps below—they were walking, searching. At that moment I felt as if I were going through the Holocaust with the children. . . . We are all alone. There is no one to care for us." In trying to keep Yael quiet in order to save their lives, Mrs. Haran accidentally smothered her daughter to death. Kuntar and his comrades abducted the father, Danny Haran, and his four-year-old daughter, Einat, and led them to the nearby beach, whereupon Kuntar shot Danny point-blank in front of his daughter and then held his head under water to ensure his death. Kuntar then murdered the four-year-old by smashing her head on a large rock and with the butt of his rifle.[63]

Two episodes involving PA schools named after terrorists illustrate both the promise and pitfalls of using international pressure as leverage for change. In 2002, the directors of Haj Issa, a girls high school in the PA town of Al-Shuyukh, near Hebron, renamed the school in honor of Dalal Mughrabi. In response, the U.S. State Department threatened to cut off "thousands of dollars" in aid scheduled to be received from the U.S. Agency for International Development. The school informed U.S. officials it would return to its original name, and the State Department rescinded its threat. The vice president of American Near East Refugee Aid, the nongovernmental agency channeling the funds, publicly confirmed that "they changed the name back" to Haj Issa. However, to this day the school's name on its Facebook page bears Mughrabi's name; evidently the school quietly resumed using the Mughrabi name after the funds were delivered.[64]

The PA also sidestepped the Belgian government's 2018 threat to cut off aid to the Martyr Dalal Mughrabi Elementary Mixed School in Beit Awwa, near Hebron. School authorities renamed it "Belgian Elementary Mixed School," but the PA then announced that it had merely "transferred the name [of the Mughrabi School]" to the town's other elementary school; it then held a cornerstone-laying ceremony for yet another school in Beit Awwa named after Mughrabi. Meanwhile, the new logo of the renamed school featured a PLO flag covering all of Israel.[65]

The PA employed similar smoke-and-mirrors tactics to retain the name of a public square in Ramallah named after Mughrabi. When the United States criticized the PA's plans to hold a public naming ceremony in 2010, PA officials waited several months and then held the event in the name of Fatah. Five years later, long after U.S. officials lost interest in the matter, the PA dedicated a large monument to Mughrabi in the square, complete with her likeness and a map showing all of Israel as "Palestine."[66] In the absence of sustained follow-up by the donor countries, Palestinian leaders felt no real pressure to institute meaningful change.

HATEFUL TV AND VIDEOS

Children's programs on PA and Hamas television and radio stations convey similar messages. On the PA's TV program *The Best Home*, children are interviewed or invited to read their poetry before an audience of other children. In a typical episode in 2017, a young girl replied to the host's request to explain the term "martyr": "A Martyr [*shahid*] is a person who has sacrificed his life in order to elevate the Word of Allah. A person becomes a Martyr when he defends his homeland or honor, or fights those who don't believe in Allah Almighty. Martyrdom-death [*shahada*] is a high and supreme level, according to Allah." In another episode, a Palestinian Arab boy recited a poem pledging "For you, Yasir Arafat, for you we shall die. . . . [O]ur blood is food for the revolution," and a young girl proclaimed, "O Palestinian carrying a rifle—shoot, shoot, in the name of Allah!"[67]

Televised poetry readings are commonly used for teaching hateful ideology. To mark World Children's Day in 2015, PA Television featured a young girl reciting: "Sons of Zion / . . . Jerusalem vomits from within it your impurity."[68] On the Hamas children's show *Pioneers of Tomorrow*, shown on its official television channel, Al-Aqsa TV, Nassur the host, clad in a bear costume, vowed to join the military division of Hamas, the Izz ad-Din al-Qassam Brigades. "I will be a Jihad fighter with them and I will carry a rifle," he declared in one episode. Then he asked a young girl, "Do you know why, Saraa? To defend the children of Palestine . . . I declare war on the criminal Zionists. Not only me, me and you. You are ready, right, Saraa?" Saraa replied, "We are all ready to sacrifice ourselves for our homeland!"[69]

In another episode, a host in a rabbit costume explained why his name is "Assud," the Arabic word for lion: "I, Assud, will finish off the Jews and eat them, Allah willing." When another host, Nahoul, clad in a bee costume, was dying—because of Israeli actions—a child host assured him, "Today we say congratulations, O Nahoul. This is your wedding, Nahoul. We don't see it as your death, Nahoul, but as your wedding, Nahoul." The "wedding" idea is an outgrowth of Quranic verses and Islamist literature frequently cited by Palestinian leaders concerning a male who dies as a *shahid*, a religious martyr, defined by Hamas and the PA as someone who was killed while carrying out a terrorist attack against Israel, or by Israeli forces responding to terrorism. The *shahid* is said to be rewarded in Paradise with seventy-two dark-eyed, "high-bosomed" virgins, or *houris*. Many parents of dead terrorists have proclaimed their son's death to be the "wedding" preceding their unification with their "brides" in the afterlife.[70]

Ru'a Tamimi, a young girl from the town of Nabi Saleh known for her precise and dramatic poetry readings, recited on PA Radio (and later, in a video posted on the Fatah Facebook page) a story she composed featuring a boy whose mother "promised him a gift if he finished his food." Instead of a toy, his mother presented him with a rifle, explaining, "My son, we were not created for happiness. In my eyes, you are meant for Martyrdom." The narrator then briefly digressed to explain that "the Jews killed his father for no reason other than that he prayed for too long." The mother continued: "Jerusalem is ours, our weapon is Islam, and our ammunition is our children. And you, O my son, are meant for Martyrdom." At first, the boy was disappointed—he had expected a toy—but that night he dreamed that the city of Jerusalem appeared to him in the form of a handcuffed bride and begged him to come rescue her from "the Jews." The boy awakened "in order to live the remainder of his day, saying, 'What was taken by force will only be returned by force,' while carrying in one hand the rifle, and in his other hand—a sad poem."[71]

Until faced with international criticism and the prospect of legal action, both Hamas and the PA utilized iconic American cartoon characters to promote anti-Jewish hatred and violence. Hamas TV used a

Mickey Mouse lookalike, whom it eventually wrote off by having him beaten to death by an Israeli soldier. Fatah TV used Mickey Mouse, Minnie Mouse, Winnie the Pooh, and Piglet as the backdrop of a children's quiz that described mass murderer Dalal Mughrabi as a "beloved bride, daughter of Jaffa, jasmine flower" who was "escorted [in death] with your friends and the flag of Palestine."[72]

An oft-cited hero featured on PA Television's programming for children in recent years was Faris Ouda, a fourteen-year-old who was killed while participating in a mob attack on Israelis in 2000. According to the PA daily *Al-Hayat Al-Jadida*, Ouda created a wreath with the words "Heroic Martyr Faris Ouda" and placed it around a photo of himself in his room before carrying out the attack, telling his mother, "Don't be afraid, Mother, Martyrdom is sweet, and I'm an atonement for the Al-Aqsa Mosque." A PA Television show host asked a child to solve a riddle, with the clues, "The national hero, a small child; A knight riding the 'Martyrdom' horse; Martyrdom is bliss. Paradise is yours, the hero of Palestine, who carried a stone to confront a tank." The prize for correctly naming Faris Ouda was $200.[73]

A PA Television interview with two young Palestinian Arab girls, and a third calling in to the studio, illustrated their absorption of the regime's messaging on violence and death. Asked whether she considered martyrdom "beautiful," eleven-year-old Walla replied: "Martyrdom is a very, very beautiful thing. Everyone yearns for martyrdom. What could be sweeter than going to paradise?" Asked if she agreed, Yussra, also eleven, responded, "Of course, martyrdom is sweet. We don't want this world, we want the Afterlife. We benefit not from this life, but from the Afterlife. . . . Every Palestinian child, say someone aged twelve, says: 'O Allah, I would like to become a martyr.'" A girl named Sabrine, from Ramallah, then called in to point out that Ayyat al-Akhras, who murdered two Israelis and wounded twenty-eight in a Jerusalem suicide bombing, was just seventeen years old "when she blew herself up." The host asked: "Sabrine, are you for it or against it"; she answered: "Of course I support blowing up; it is our right." The host questioned: "Sabrine, now, is it natural that Ayyat Al-Akhras blows herself up?"; Sabrine replied: "Of course it's natural."[74]

In October 2000 a PA Television broadcast featured a rally in Gaza attended by a large number of teenage girls, in conjunction with an Arab League summit meeting in Cairo. As the girls jostled and shouted, one delivered an impassioned monologue to the camera: "We only want them to give us weapons. We on our own, young boys and girls, will kill them on our own, murder them, shoot all of them. Just give us weapons. The boys and the girls themselves will kill them all. We won't leave a single Jew. We won't leave a single Jew here." The PA amplified her threat by giving her the TV platform to reach the masses.[75]

Home videos also speak to the influence of officially promulgated attitudes about violence. In 2020, the PA Television children's show *O Children of Our Neighborhood* aired two home videos made by children about Anas Allan, who was convicted of being an accomplice to a suicide bomber who murdered four Israelis. In one video, two young girls hold a framed poster of Allan and declare, "On behalf of Allah, we send all the words of pride to the tall mountains, to the lions crouching in their dens, to the heroes of this generous people, to the heroic prisoners. You are the symbol of endurance." In another, a boy proclaims, "Our prisoner Anas Allan . . . I think of him every time I see his mother and his father, my neighbors. I see the pain of separation in the eyes of [his mother]. . . . He was sentenced to four life sentences and 25 years. . . . I send love and greetings to every male and female prisoner and to all the prisoners' families."[76]

Music videos have been another frequent vehicle for glorification of death. In one Hamas-produced music video for children, a five-year-old girl responds to the news that her mother perpetrated a suicide bombing by singing, "Now I know what was more precious than us" and vows to become a suicide bomber too. It is likely not coincidental that a music video that aired repeatedly on PA Television during the Second Intifada (2000–2003) featured a young boy singing, "Don't be afraid. Allah is with them. . . . The stone in their hand has turned into an AK-47."[77] This government-controlled TV programming seemed intended to inspire the large number of youths engaged in stoning attacks to turn to more lethal forms of terrorism—and indeed, many did.

In June 2020, PA Television repeatedly aired a video of former Palestinian UN Youth Ambassador Muhammad Assaf singing "My Blood Is Palestinian" with the lyrics, "I will sacrifice myself for my family / My blood is Palestinian, Palestinian / My head is in the heavens and proud." His singing was interspersed with images of Palestinian Arabs rioting and portraits of prominent terrorists such as Coastal Road massacre leader Dalal Mugrahbi and Munich Olympics attack organizer Salah Khalaf. That Assaf was a former ambassador lent credibility to his status as an influencer while also illustrating the popularity of glorifying anti-Jewish violence.[78]

EXTRACURRICULAR ACTIVITIES PROMOTING TERRORISM

Extracurricular activities for schoolchildren in the PA territories include participating in public events honoring terrorists. American parents take their children to participate in local parades on Halloween or July 4. By contrast, in the PA village of Al-Mazra'a Al-Qibliya, the Democratic Front for the Liberation of Palestine (DFLP) terrorist group holds an annual parade to commemorate the death of Ma'an Nasr Abu Qara, a member of its youth group who was killed while trying to stab Israelis to death in 2016. Children holding DFLP flags march at the head of the procession.[79] In the village's parade that year celebrating the anniversary of the founding of Fatah, young children marched with replica suicide bomber belts, rifles, and rocket-propelled grenade launchers.[80]

Some extracurricular activities revolve around the themes of rejecting Israel and glorifying dead or imprisoned terrorists. The campus branch of Fatah's Shabiba youth movement "organized an activity against normalization [of relations with Israel]" at the Al-A'amiriya High School for Girls in Kalkilya, the PA daily *Al-Hayat Al-Jadida* reported in 2020. With the school's principal and PA Education Ministry officials presiding, the students listened to a Shabiba leader explain why peaceful interaction with Israel "is a betrayal of the Palestinian cause, of the blood of the tens of thousands of Martyrs, and of the sacrifices of the hundreds of thousands of heroic prisoners." The principal thanked her for helping "to spread national awareness among the female students."[81] That month, photos from Fatah's Facebook page showed schoolchildren marching at the head of a procession in Ramallah to denounce the United Arab Emirates for signing a peace agreement with Israel. One held a sign reading "The UAE Is Not an Arab State." Slogans on other children's signs hailed terrorists imprisoned in Israel as "our heroic prisoners."[82]

Another popular afterschool activity is attempting to stone Jews to death. To teach its readers that there is religious authorization for stoning Jews, the PLO-PA youth magazine *Zayzafuna* published photographs of young Arab rock-throwers next to a poem instructing children to sing "by Muhammad's command" that "we carry a rock / that we will throw at the people of the Gharqad." A Muslim tradition holds that Jews will hide behind the Gharqad tree when Muslims come to slaughter them on the Day of Judgment.[83]

Fatah's X (Twitter) account includes a guide to effective rock throwing:

In order to hit the target, there are three conditions:

1. *Stand stably and balance your legs, arms, and body well.*
2. *Focus your gaze on the center of the target, and do not look at anything else.*
3. *Keep the desired balance between your body and your weapon; you are the one that controls the weapon, and not the other way around. If you do not understand this, read it again, and if you still have not understood, here is an example picture for you. . . .*[84]

From time to time, the rock-throwers succeed: sixteen Israelis have been murdered in Palestinian Arab stoning attacks since 1983; many others have been maimed.[85]

MARTYR GAMES

To promote the concept of "martyrdom" as the highest spiritual achievement in a Muslim's life, the PA and Fatah teach children The Martyr Game.[86] Illustrating how to play the game, Fatah's Facebook page displays photographs of a child pretending to be dead, wrapped in a PLO flag and being carried on a makeshift stretcher by other children. "All the children of the world play regular games, except for your children, O Palestine, who play 'The Martyr Game,'" the accompanying text explains. "A thousand blessings to your children, Palestine." Observing children preparing to play the game, a reporter for the PA newspaper *Al-Hayat Al-Jadida* recounted: "A seven-year-old girl says to her friends, 'Let's play The Martyr Game!' The children . . . argue who will play the Martyr. Fa'iz, six years old, says, 'You were the Martyr yesterday, today it's my turn! I'm younger than you. I'll be the one to die!'"[87] On October 22, 2023, two weeks after the atrocities of October 7, Al Jazeera TV aired a video clip showing four- and five-year-old Gazan girls playing The Martyr Game: "We're playing Martyr," a young girl says, "The Martyr is the beloved of Allah."[88]

A related game popular among Palestinian Arab children involves the actual body of a "martyr." *Al-Hayat Al-Jadida* reported the scene as a body was carried through a neighborhood: "A boy is hanging out the window of a room and watching the parting from the Martyr. . . . He comes out quickly and tries to touch the head of the Martyr. He wants to reach the glory in order to brag to his friends that he touched a Martyr."[89]

As a child, Palestinian Arab serial killer Raed al-Karmi "loved the game 'Jews and Arabs,' a game that children of the neighborhood would play," according to Fatah's Facebook page. "He always played the role of the Arab who, with his simple weapon, attacked the treacherous Jew who occupied his homeland and settled in it." Al-Karmi grew up to murder nine Jews in a series of attacks in 2001, until Israeli security forces finally caught up with him.[90] According to the Palestinian Arab newspaper *Al-Ayyam*, Gaza children who cannot afford plastic rifles play "Jews and Arabs" with sticks and hammers instead.[91]

American children play with dolls based on mythical creatures or superheroes. Palestinian Arab children favor a doll of a child holding a rock in his upraised arm, his face covered by a *keffiyeh* with an emblem of the Al-Aqsa Mosque. Puzzles can serve the same purpose. In January 2024 Israeli soldiers discovered, in a child's bedroom in the Gaza city of Khan Yunis, an arsenal of weapons, grenades, and ammunition alongside a large, colorful children's puzzle depicting heavily armed

Arab children converging on Israel by air, land, and sea, hurling rocks and firing guns at the Jewish state.[92]

The PA also encourages children to think of their toys as potential weapons. At a January 2025 Fatah rally celebrating the anniversary of the group's first terrorist attack, a young girl read a poem appealing to the children of Gaza to "teach us how the stone becomes a precious diamond in the hands of the children / how the child's bicycle turns into a mine and the silk ribbon turns into an ambush / how the spout of the baby bottle, when placed under arrest, turns into a knife." Her recital was broadcast on PA Television.[93]

SUMMER CAMPS OF TERROR

When school lets out, the violent antisemitic messaging continues in hundreds of summer camps operated by the PA and Hamas in their respective territories. Many of the camps are named after terror icons Dalal Mughrabi and Abu Jihad.

In the summer of 2023, 65,000 boys and girls ages thirteen to seventeen attended the PA's 648 camps. The summer's theme was "Moons and Not Numbers"—that is, glorifying dead terrorists as "moons, they are stars, they are the elite, and they were the ones who sacrificed their lives," Jibril Rajoub, head of the PLO Supreme Council for Youth and Sports, explained. "They were and will remain in our memories and in the memory of their children and their grandchildren. . . . [They] are recorded in our hearts." Activities included performing skits about Israelis cruelly persecuting Arabs and Arabs shooting or stabbing Israelis, art projects spotlighting dead or imprisoned terrorists, singalongs featuring songs about martyrdom, making maps out of paint, clay, or rocks showing all of Israel as "Palestine," and face painting with PLO flags in the shape of all of Israel.[94]

In addition to ideological indoctrination, many of the camps include significant military components. Video posted on Fatah's Facebook page shows high school age boys at a 2023 summer camp training in close combat and learning how to assemble and use Kalashnikov assault rifles.[95] Another 2023 camp video, posted on the Facebook page of Fatah's Awdah Television channel, shows boys learning how to handle rifles and practice shooting positions, with a PA security force member explaining that the forces collaborate with regional Fatah branches to run summer camps because "the occupation is always lying in ambush for us, and we need to deal with it intellectually, culturally, mentally, and in struggle, in every field."[96] A PLO youth council video of a 2022 summer camp features campers in military fatigues (and some wearing shirts bearing images of terrorists) armed with automatic rifles, in a drill simulation of moving from house to house. Campers also leap over burning trenches, navigate obstacle courses, and emerge from tunnels amidst clouds of black smoke.[97]

Photos from a Palestinian Islamic Jihad summer camp in Gaza posted by Gaza-based journalist Muthanna Najjar show teens participating in military training exercises such as maneuvering around obstacles on their stomachs and hiding in dug-out spaces. The accompanying text reads: "The culture of weapons, tunnels, first aid, religious studies, sermons about Prophet Muhammad's life, blessing and peace to him, and the laws of purity are characteristics of the Jihad camp run by the Islamic Jihad movement titled 'Resistance Campers.'"[98] Najjar also posted photographs of the Hamas-run "Liberation Pioneers Camp" in 2016, showing teenage boys in military fatigues marching in formation and lining up at attention with rifles in hand. According to Palestinian news reports, some twenty thousand campers participated in the Hamas "Liberation Pioneers" summer camps in 2015, where they were trained "to carry weapons and use them, and for additional military training."[99] On October 7, 2023, those boys would have been in their early twenties.[100]

TERRORIST ROLE MODELS FOR GIRLS

A memorable controversy erupted in September 1995, when Yasir Arafat delivered what became known as his "Abir and Dalal speech." Since Western monitoring of the Palestinian Arab news media was still in its infancy, few Americans were familiar with the content of the public addresses delivered by Arafat and other Palestinian Authority officials. Thus it was shocking to many to learn that the Palestinian Authority chairman kicked off the new school year with an address to a girls school in Gaza about the importance of following in the footsteps of famous women terrorists. He focused on two role models: the aforementioned Dalal Mughrabi and Abir al-Wahidi, a Birzeit University student who gunned down an Israeli civilian. "We are proud of the Palestinian girl, the Palestinian woman [who] participated in the Palestinian revolution," Arafat told the audience of teenage girls. "I bow in respect and admiration to the Palestinian woman who receives her martyred son with joyful cheering. The soul and blood for you, O Palestine!"[101]

Women terrorists occupy a unique position in the Palestinian Arab pantheon. A study by IMPACT-se found that thirteen PA schoolbooks used in 2023–24 "express diverse forms of contempt towards women, singularly accusing them of impeding Islamic missionary work, of propagating adultery, and of blindly imitating Western culture." Students are taught that sexual harassment results from "women not being dressed according to Islamic code." There is one exception. Women are presented as equal to men when they are "conducting jihad, becoming martyrs, and sacrificing sons and husbands," which makes them "sisters to the men in sacrifice and altruism." PA textbooks esteem women "in the context of . . . their 'nationalist struggle role' fighting against the Zionist occupation 'in all forms and ways,'" as in [the books'] "glorification of female terrorists, such as Dalal Mughrabi, as role models." Women terrorists are cited as evidence that "Islam raised the status of women, and honored them in a way no other religion had honored." As a result, "the path of violence implicitly appears to be the only option for women to demonstrate an outstanding commitment to their people and country."[102]

The Fatah Facebook page "Yasir's Girls" (*Mitqy Bnat Al-Yasr* in Arabic) highlights heroines of Palestinian Arab history. A color montage shows Mughrabi and Arafat side by side against a Jerusalem backdrop. She is also the subject of adulatory programming on official PA TV, radio, and public events held yearly on her birthday, and on the anniversary of the Coastal Road massacre. Many commentators refer to her affectionately as "the Princess of Fatah," "the Bride of Jaffa," or "the Kernel of Palestine."[103] An episode of the PA TV show *Palestine This Morning* highlighted a young schoolgirl's portrait of Mughrabi, which was featured in a children's art exhibit in Khan Younis. The youthful artist explained her reason for choosing Mughrabi as her subject: "[She was] a fighter who participated in operations [terrorist attacks], a woman who had a role in these struggles and the resolve" and "died as a Martyr."[104]

Mughrabi is also lauded in school curricula. A YouTube video shows Hebron elementary school teacher Nasser Al-Rajabi reading from the PA's 5th grade *Arabic Language* schoolbook about Mughrabi "leading her group of self-sacrificing fighters" to carry out the Coastal Road attack, during which she "watered the soil of Palestine with her pure blood." The teacher asks his students, "How old was Dalal Mughrabi when she died as a Martyr?" and "[Name] the number of heroes in the group of self-sacrificing fighters."[105] The message trickles down. A 2020 video message posted by the PA's governor for Ramallah and El-Bireh, Laila Ghannam, shows a little girl in her district proclaiming to her, "O how great you are, Laila the Palestinian. O how great you are, sister of Dalal, when you fight the [Coronavirus] epidemic and when you fight the Zionist enemy."[106]

Mughrabi also starred in a 2019 PA book series of "stories meant for boys and girls" about "the glorious deeds, the deeds of heroism and the people's sacrifices." The volume honoring her, *The Mermaid*, tells of "the heroism of self-sacrificing fighter Dalal Mughrabi and the carrying out of an operation at sea"—that is, her squad's use of small rubber boats to reach Israel's shore and carry out the Coastal Road massacre. The book covers in the series depict armed terrorists underneath the Fatah logo of crossed rifles, a hand grenade, and a map on which all of Israel is labeled "Palestine."[107]

RAISING MARTYRS

Mothers in Nazi Germany were taught by their government to believe they had an obligation to breed and raise a generation of young Nazis. Many Palestinian Arab mothers believe their role is to "nurse" their children "with the milk of heroism, pride, and sacrifice," as the mother of multiple murderer Sa'id Shtayyeh explained on PA Television's *Giants of Endurance* program in 2000. Evidently she was referring to the "heroism" of proudly sacrificing her children's lives in order to murder Jews.[108]

Two mothers interviewed on PA Television in 1998 described their response to the news that their children had been killed while attempting to kill Israelis. One said, "I hope that all my children will be martyrs." The second recalled, "I said, 'Thank Allah, thank Allah. . . . [her daughter] Intisar fell, and it is an honor for us and an honor for our children." A relative added: "Every time [Intisar] heard a bang, [she said,] 'Someone was shot, I hope that next time it will be me, I want to die as a martyr.'"[109]

Muhammad Shamasneh stabbed three Israelis near Jerusalem's central bus station in 2016; Fatah posted on its Facebook page a photograph of his mother, Rusaila Shamasneh, smiling and making a V-for-victory sign with her hand.[110] Maryam Al-Khaddour appeared on PA Television in 2016 to explain that her daughter Majd rammed her car into a hitchhiking station near the town of Kiryat Arba earlier that year because she was inspired by a Muslim legend about a woman named Al-Khansa who rejoiced when her sons were killed in battle. "We in the land of *ribat* stand firm," she said, using the Arabic term for a religiously motivated struggle to conquer territory from non-Muslims. "And we are all on this path . . . all of us, praise Allah, present our children [as sacrifices], and we do not regret a thing."[111]

Ibrahim al-Nabulsi, who at eighteen was already a commander in Fatah's Al-Aqsa Martyrs Brigade, was killed while shooting at Israelis in August 2022. His mother explained to viewers of PA Television's *Palestine This Morning*: "He told me, 'If I die as a Martyr, don't cry and don't mourn.' [H]e is with the Master of the Universe, with Allah. He is a Martyr, praise Allah, a Martyr, a Martyr, praise Allah."[112] Teenage terrorist Karam Salman was shot dead as he tried to infiltrate an Israeli town in January 2023. "Praise Allah, he asked for Martyrdom, and he received it," his mother proclaimed on the PA TV nightly news. "[He is] the most handsome groom in the world, the most handsome groom in Paradise. The angels will accompany him to his wedding. . . . Allah willing, we will accompany him as a groom to his wedding in Paradise."[113]

The death of seventeen-year-old Zaid al-Qaysiya during an attack on Israelis in 2020 inspired his mother to offer the lives of her other children. "My son is a sacrifice for the sake of the homeland," al-Qaysiya's mother declared in a Fatah Facebook interview. "I'm proud of the sons of Palestine, the young people of Palestine. . . . I'm prepared to sacrifice even more. I'm prepared to give more Martyrs for the homeland."[114]

Muntasir Al-Shawa, sixteen, was killed while attacking Israelis at the Tomb of Joseph, a Jewish religious site in Nablus (Shechem), in February 2023. Shortly afterwards, his mother appeared on PA Television to recount her conversation with him the day before the attack. "He told me, 'I want to go [to the area near the tomb] and I'll come back to you as a Martyr. I laughed at him and told him: 'Do you think being a Martyr is something trivial? Go bathe, pray, bow down to Allah, and then there might be a chance that Allah will agree to accept you [as a martyr].' The following night he came back to me as a Martyr. Praise Allah."[115]

In 2020, PA Television aired *Bus 47*, a staged nostalgic recreation of a bus ride from Jerusalem to Amman that was popular before 1967. The mothers and young daughters who volunteered as passengers entertained themselves along the way with a mother-daughter rendition of a song glorifying suicide bombers, which is often performed at PA cultural festivals and videos. The lyrics vow that "no force in the world" can "remove the weapon from my hand."[116]

Why are Palestinian women "not like any other women in the world," according to Fatah Central Committee member Abbas Zaki? Because "they view their children as insignificant compared to the homeland. . . . And all they do is make sounds of joy for the Martyrs, be proud of Martyrdom, and sing for the grooms."[117]

The sentiments expressed by fathers of dead terrorists echo those of the killers' mothers. Murad Adais, sixteen, fatally stabbed Mrs. Dafna Meir in front of her four young children in the entranceway to their home in January 2016; Adais's father declared, "I am proud of my son."[118] "I'm so amazed and happy that my son died as a Martyr," the father of fifteen-year-old Muhammad Da'das declared on PA TV after the boy was killed while participating in a mob rock and firebombing attack on Israelis. "In the name of Merciful Allah, this is a source of pride for us. This raised our heads. . . . He is going to meet the prophets, the Martyrs, and the righteous. The angels will carry him and say: 'We brought you a Martyr today.' It's incredible how good the feeling and joy of the prophets and Martyrs is."[119]

Dirar al-Kafrini, seventeen, was killed while shooting at Israelis in 2022. He would say to his father, "Dad, I want to die as a martyr," the elder al-Kafrini later recalled on Fatah's Facebook page. "And I told him, 'My son, Allah willing, may Allah designate you [for Martyrdom].'" Raed al-Dakhil, father of Muhammad al-Dakhil, who was killed while shooting at Israelis in Nablus, appealed to other young people to follow his son's fatal path on PA Television in February 2023. "The path that the Martyrs walked on—Muhammad [and two other terrorists who were killed with him]—and all the Martyrs—is the most correct path, which all the young people today need to adopt."[120]

For Yasir As'ous, one "martyred" son was not enough. In the PA daily *Al-Hayat Al-Jadida*, he recounted how he stood over the grave of his son Muhammad, who had been killed while attacking Israelis, and prayed that his other son, Wadi, who was injured in the attack, "should die as a Martyr rather than recuperate." He explained: "Allah chose my children [Muhammad and Wadi]. The second [child], Allah willing, Allah will grant him Martyrdom. Allah willing, now before I leave [the cemetery], Allah will inform me that he became a Martyr. Praise Allah, Master of the Universe, our God chose them."[121]

"Allah be praised, he wanted [martyrdom], and Allah gave it to him," the father of sixteen-year-old Muhammed Nouri stated on PA Television three weeks after his son was killed while attacking Israelis in September 2022. "Allah be praised, in place of [my son] Muhammad a million like Muhammad will rise up. Palestine gives birth to Martyrs." Nouri's mother concurred: "We'll continue to sacrifice Martyr after Martyr until Palestine is liberated. My son wanted to be a martyr his whole life and he achieved it, Allah be praised." The Nouris made their comments three weeks after Muhammad's death, enough time for them to have contemplated whether the martyrdom he chose, with parental support, truly represented the achievement of a worthy goal.[122]

ASPIRING TO MARTYRDOM

For Japanese kamikaze pilots in World War II, and for young Germans longing to give their lives for the *Reich*, the prevailing sentiment was fanatical nationalism. For Palestinian Muslims aspiring to martyrdom, extreme nationalism blends with fundamentalist religion (see chapter 2).

In the spring of 2024, PA TV's *Moons of Paradise* show ran a series featuring relatives of terrorists recently killed while carrying out attacks on Israelis. "I told him: 'Get married, let me hold your child,'" the mother of the late terrorist Uday Al-Zayyat (also known as Abu Saqr), recalled on the March 19 episode. "He said: 'Allah willing, in Paradise.' I thought he was just saying that, and every time I said: 'Get married,' he would say: 'In Paradise.' He would say: 'Mom, don't be sad, our paths are the paths of Martyrdom.'" She noted proudly that when she now asks neighborhood children, "What do you want to be?," they reply, "Like Abu Saqr [Uday]. . . . He fought and went to Paradise, and we will fight and go to Paradise." That, she said, "is pride for Palestine and for me. . . . I congratulate him on his Martyrdom, and I'm prepared to give all my children as ransom for Palestine and the Al-Aqsa Mosque."[123]

On the April 8 segment, Yanal Samhan, granddaughter of terrorist Jihad Al-Abd Rushd Samhan, gushed: "I'm very happy that he's my grandfather. I'm very proud of him. . . . I' m happy that Allah chose us to be the family of a Martyr. . . . He was a great leader, a Jihad fighter, a self-sacrificing fighter. . . . He really loved to see people doing Jihad for Allah. Given how he loved this matter and aspired to Martyrdom, Allah chose him."[124]

The next day's episode featured the mother and brother of Muhammad Fawaqa, who was killed during an attack on Israelis the previous October, which he undertook as a gesture of solidarity with the Gaza invaders. "He would always tell me: 'I want to be a Martyr. Pray for me, mom, that I will die as a Martyr,'" his mother, Um Hussein, recalled. "I would tell him: 'You're making a precious request of me'; the truth is I prayed for him [that he be granted Martyrdom]." Muhammad's brother Hussein added: "Praise Allah's name, He chose [Muhammad Fawaqa], and He chose a path for him that everyone wishes for but not everyone achieves. Ever since he was little, he always would talk about Martyrdom: 'I will die as a Martyr, and you will miss me.' . . . He wished for it, and he achieved it."[125]

"Every Martyr wants to be a Martyr. Every child wants to be a Martyr. Every young boy wants to be a Martyr," the mother of Yusuf Muhaisen, killed while attacking Israelis in January 2023, declared on the Facebook page of the Fatah Commission of Information and Culture.[126]

A PA military intelligence officer gave a similar response in a PA Television interview concerning his sixteen-year-old son Khaled Al-Uruq, who had been killed while shooting at Israelis in Ramallah just that day. Khaled "is not the first Martyr and not the last, praise Allah," the father said. "He asked for [martyrdom] and achieved it, praise Allah. He always told me: 'I want to die as a Martyr.' Praise Allah, [the conditions] were enabled and he achieved it."[127]

It does "take a village" to raise a child. An array of influences, including family, teachers, political and cultural leaders, and the broader culture, help shape a young person's outlook on life. Like many Palestinian Arab children, Muhammad Halabi, the aforementioned law school student who brutally slashed a young Israeli family and passersby in Jerusalem, was raised by parents who supported their son on his journey down the road of death. His father, Shafiq Halabi, told reporters: "Muhammad has led the way, and I feel that all those young people rising up are joining him. His attack was the wake-up call that Palestinians needed to act and break the current deadlock." His mother, Suhair Halabi, posted a photo of herself at the site of her son's attack making V-for-victory signs with both hands.[128]

Muhammad's parents were only one source of influence in the village around him. He attended schools where the curriculum incited him to hate Jews and revere violence. He was in the midst of his studies at a university law school where stabbing Jews was regarded not as a violation of the law, but as an act of sacred resistance against an evil foe; as a gesture of solidarity with Muhammad's actions, the law school administration granted him a posthumous law degree. In effect, murdering Jews became a part of the curriculum. The PA also named a park after Muhammad in his hometown, Surda-Abu Kash. "This is the least we can do for Martyr Halabi," Mayor Muhammad Hussein explained, deeming him "a pride and badge of honor for the whole village."[129]

Most Americans would not consider a terrorist who slashed defenseless women and children a source of pride or a badge of honor. The army of Muhammad Halabis who were raised to become the eager perpetrators of mass atrocities on October 7 represented the most reprehensible aspects of Palestinian Arab society, and the very opposite of the values most Americans instill in their own children. Yet some American political activists, cultural figures, and policy advocates—a minority, to be sure, but a noticeable segment nonetheless—would respond to October 7 by turning against Israel.

4. The War on the Truth

The events of October 7 triggered an unprecedented frenzy of anti-Israel and antisemitic activity in America's streets and on college campuses. Within hours of the Hamas attack, advocates of the Palestinian Arab cause were loudly defending Hamas's actions on op-ed pages, college campuses, and street corners from coast to coast.

The protesters were highly organized and relentless. Almost overnight, demonstrators appeared with the latest model bullhorns, professionally printed banners and placards, carefully crafted slogans, and detailed manifestos. The fact that the protests began within hours of the attack showed the participants were responding to the Hamas slaughter, not to the Israeli counterattack, which had not yet begun. The timing, professionalism, and similarity of the protests suggested they were well-financed and carefully organized. According to the Biden administration's director of national intelligence, the government of Iran was involved in funding the demonstrations.[1]

Many protests took place under the aegis of an impressively extensive list of sponsoring organizations, although closer inspection suggested that some of them may have been less than actual functioning entities. Consider, for example, some of the sponsors of the "National March on Washington to Free Palestine," held on November 4, 2023. The website of "Queers Undermining Israeli Terrorism!" does not list a single name of a person affiliated with it. Neither does the "Palestinian Assembly for Liberation." The "Jericho Movement" operates out of a P.O. box in Pine Lake, Georgia. "Arab Americans for Syria" has a Facebook page that likewise does not list any officers. "The Key" does not appear to have a website, a P.O. box, or a presence on Facebook.[2]

Many of the protesters were young Arab Americans, who came attired in traditional Muslim garb. They led Arabic-language chants that sometimes invoked specific historical references such as "Khaybar, Khaybar!" alluding to the massacre of Jews in that Arabian Peninsula city by Muhammad in 628 CE.[3] These fervent Arab-American activists were joined at the rallies by sympathizers from radical political groups that embrace the Palestinian cause, such as the Democratic Socialists of America and Code Pink.

In protests from Berkeley to Manhattan's Upper West Side, many women as well as men donned *keffiyehs*, head scarves popular throughout the Middle East (not uniquely among Palestinian Arabs) that first came to widespread attention in the West as the apparel of notorious Palestinian terrorists, chiefly PLO leader Yasir Arafat and Leila Khaled, the first female airplane hijacker. In the Middle East, *keffiyehs* typically are worn solely by men; devout Muslim women wear a different type of head covering. For the female demonstrators in the US, then, it was a somewhat disingenuous display; in Gaza, they would not have publicly contravened Islamic strictures against women wearing traditionally male garb. Critics of cultural appropriation did not comment on the post–October 7 *keffiyeh* craze.[4]

Whether the protests were spontaneous or long-planned was unclear. A PLO executive committee member, Osama al-Qawasmi, told the Palestinian Authority's news agency Wafa in May 2024 that "this protest movement came as a result of an effort that the Palestinian communities there have made for many years." In a similar vein, Hayel Mansour, identified as a Palestinian activist in the United States, told PA Television that the protests were "part of the fruits of the ongoing labor that has been conducted by the Arab, Palestinian, and Islamic communities and the supporters in the American arena." Neither al-Qawasmi nor Mansour elaborated.[5]

STAGED DISRUPTIONS

The protests featured false narratives that major media outlets generously amplified.

Media-savvy anti-Israel militants understood that simply by being disruptive, they could attract news media attention far beyond what their relatively small numbers would have otherwise received. In the nation's capital, hundreds of extremists demanding that Israel cease firing at Hamas were arrested after taking over the Cannon House Office Building just eleven days after the October 7 invasion. Pro-Hamas hecklers interrupted President Biden at multiple campaign events. Militants smeared red paint on the White House gates, defaced the Lincoln Memorial, and poured gallons of fake blood on the automobile and home driveway of Secretary of State Antony Blinken. Shouting about "Israeli genocide," they disrupted Christmas tree lighting ceremonies in Manhattan, the Macy's Thanksgiving Day parade, and the Rose Bowl parade in Pasadena. On Christmas Day, they dumped a pile of manure in front of the home of Secretary of Defense Lloyd Austin, burst into a Christmas party for Democratic Party officials in Detroit with cries accusing attendees of genocide, harassed passersby in major shopping malls with ear-splitting megaphones, and prevented access to major airports during the holiday travel crush. They blocked the Holland Tunnel and New York City's three largest bridges, as well as the Golden Gate Bridge and other major bridges around the country. Shouting "Intifada revolution!," they swarmed Grand Central Station and forced a California State Assembly session to adjourn. Outside the Memorial Sloan Kettering Cancer Center in Manhattan, they yelled slogans accusing the hospital of complicity in genocide because it accepted a large gift from a "Zionist" (read: Jewish) donor.[6] In Los Angeles, they blocked the entrance to Adas Israel Synagogue and harassed passersby. In New York City, a mob in a subway car demanded that "Zionists" identify themselves and exit the train. On college campuses from coast to coast, Jewish students were subjected to anti-Israel slurs and physically prevented from walking in the vicinity of protest sites, and Hillel centers were damaged or daubed with hostile slogans. In city after city, synagogues and Jewish businesses were defaced with anti-Israel graffiti, posters of Israeli abductees were destroyed, and identifiably Jewish passersby were assaulted or taunted with shouts about Gaza. In November 2023, January 2024, and June 2024, tens of thousands of extremists marched to the White House, defacing property along the way, burning American flags, blocking traffic, hurling bottles at police officers, and shaking the White House gate so violently that it was partly dislodged as they shouted solidarity with the Hamas "resistance" to Israel.[7]

Some protests were especially violent. In Berkeley, militants set a police car and construction site on fire and threw a firebomb at a University of California campus building. In Portland, they torched seventeen police cars in a single night and damaged the Portland State University library so extensively that the library had to shut down for five months for repairs. At Stanford University, they vandalized the president's office and injured a police office. In a Los Angeles suburb, a Hamas supporter assaulted an elderly pro-Israel demonstrator, resulting in his death.[8]

Not all of the anti-Israel turmoil was disruptive or violent. Some of it consisted of legal, peaceful vigils in which pro-Palestinian activists, sometimes including Jewish anti-Zionists, chanted harsh accusations against Israel and then went on their way. Many of these seemingly well-intentioned activists genuinely believed the widely circulated falsehoods about mass murder, famine, or expulsions in Gaza. Sometimes those who simply sympathized with Gaza's civilians—not with the atrocities perpetrated by Hamas—in practice lent aid to the pro-terror elements by swelling the ranks of rallies where placards about civilian casualties were hoisted side-by-side with Hamas and Hezbollah flags and banners championing "the resistance," "intifadas," and "armed struggle" against the Jewish state.

Some protests were so far removed from any connection to Israeli policies that it was impossible to see them as anything other than antisemitism. A participant in a pro-Hamas rally in New York City's Times Square in January 2025 shouted at Jewish critics of Hamas: "We're sending you back to Europe, you white bitches. Go back to Europe!"[9] At rallies in Los Angeles and Madison, Wisconsin, Hamas supporters gave the Nazi salute.[10] In Houston, an attacker broke into the "Taste of Tel Aviv" Judaica store and stole or damaged numerous religious items, but left the store's cash behind.[11] Some demonstrators outside the "Mr. Broadway" kosher restaurant in Manhattan were heard chanting "All kikes are racist!"[12] A swastika was smeared on Canter's Deli in Los Angeles. Swastikas were daubed on the Second Avenue Deli and Zizi, two prominent New York kosher restaurants, and the front windows of the Rothschild TLV restaurant were smashed.[13] Extremists in Philadelphia gathered outside Goldie's, a kosher falafel shop, chanting, "Goldie, Goldie, you can't hide, we charge you with genocide." That was a "blatant act of antisemitism, not a peaceful protest," Pennsylvania governor Josh Shapiro tweeted. "This hate and bigotry is reminiscent of a dark time in history."[14] Mobs vandalized at least fifteen kosher restaurants nationwide between October 2023 and May 2024.[15]

Such behavior was not inevitable. Supporters of the Palestinian Arab cause could have denounced the murders, rapes, and beheadings as immoral, urged a Palestinian-Israeli alliance against Hamas and Islamic Jihad, and called for the creation of a Palestinian state in some portion of the disputed territories, rather than as a replacement for all of Israel. They could have demanded changes in specific Israeli policies affecting either Israeli Arabs or the 3 percent of Palestinian Arabs who reside in the areas governed by Israel according to the Oslo agreements. Instead, the protesters voiced the most extreme positions: Israel is evil, Zionism is racist, American supporters of Israel are war criminals, violence against Israel is justified. And they articulated those positions in the most extreme ways imaginable. When they blocked a bridge, it meant impeding motorists on their way to work or school or medical appointments. When they formed a human chain across an airport access road, it meant compelling harried travelers to drag heavy suitcases some distance to reach their terminals and possibly miss their flights. They hardly could have expected such tactics to inspire sympathy for Gazans. Rather, their strategy seemed to be to make themselves such a nuisance that weary political, civic, and academic leaders would, in one way or another, surrender to their demands just so they would go away.

One disturbance that elicited the desired response occurred on November 16, 2023, when hundreds of pro-Hamas activists blocked traffic on the San Francisco Bay Bridge. Among the vehicles impeded were three trucks connected to the University of California, San Francisco (UCSF) health system, transporting organs that needed to be delivered within thirty minutes because they were due to be transplanted later that day. The four-hour traffic delay forced postponement of those operations. Instructors in UCSF's mandatory six-week unit on "Justice and Advocacy in Medicine" subsequently taught first-year medical students that the blocking of the bridge was an example of "direct action," comparable to "civil disobedience in protest of unjust laws and practices," which sought to interrupt "business as usual" in order to "pressure targeted decision-makers."[16]

At the very first public rally after October 7, in Manhattan's Times Square on Sunday, October 8, several hundred extremists chanted, "Resistance is justified," "Zionism is genocide" and "Seven hundred," a celebratory reference to the number of Israelis initially reported to have been slaughtered. In their war on truth, the protesters did not claim that Israeli *actions* were genocidal; they said that Zionism itself—the very concept that a Jewish state should exist—constituted genocide. One demonstrator at that rally waved an image of Nazi Germany's swastika flag on his cell phone over his head so all could see. Hundreds of protests, with comparable chants and placards, took place around the country in the months to follow. The signs included "Kill Hostages Now" and "Allah Is Gathering All the Zionists for the 'Final Solution,'" as well as "Free Palestine Is a Climate Justice Issue" and "Reproductive Justice Means Free Palestine."[17] At a march through Washington DC on November 4, the signs ran the gamut of extremist sentiments. Some justified the Hamas invasion, such as "Fighting Back Against Oppression Is Not Terrorism" and "Resistance Is Justified" with a large portrait of 1970s Palestinian hijacker Leila Khaled. Many placards called for the destruction of Israel, including "Death to the Colonial State of Israel" and "Down with Zionism." There were signs accusing Israel of Nazi-style genocide, such as "History Repeats Itself, Israel = Nazis," replete with swastikas. There were others denigrating Israelis and Jews, including "Zionism Is a Cancer to This Planet" and "Keep the World Clean," with a drawing of Israeli flags and a garbage can, invoking the image of Jews as dirty.[18]

Anti-American expressions were also part of many protests. Participants resented American support for Israel, and some protesters shared a worldview in which America and Israel both represent oppression and racism. Demonstrators chanted "Death to America" at a Michigan rally, burned American flags on July 4 in Manhattan's Washington Square Park, and stomped on an American flag upon which they daubed the word "Gangsters," in Massachusetts. At Stanford University, protesters daubed the words "F—Amerikkka" on a memorial plaque honoring men and women killed in the line of duty.[19]

In the months to follow, many rallies focused in part on the number of civilians killed during Israel's pursuit of Hamas in Gaza, an approach that garnered some public sympathy, as would any ostensibly humanitarian plea. Yet slogans and chants about civilian casualties were often interspersed with unabashed calls for replacing Israel with an Arab "Palestine" and applauding the Hamas massacres. Some rallies focused entirely on cheerleading for the terrorists. Following Israel's elimination of senior Hamas leader Ismail Haniye in Iran and a top Hezbollah official in Lebanon on consecutive days in July 2024, demonstrators in New York City chanted "The martyr is loved by Allah" and "Zionists are the enemy of Allah" while waving Hamas and Hezbollah flags. In Boston, the Palestinian Youth Movement announced an "emergency rally" in honor of the assassinated terror leaders (whom it called "the martyrs"), while the San Francisco chapter of the Council on American Islamic Relations tweeted, "Tonight we mourn Ismail but know his martyrdom is not in vain." After Hamas leader Yahya Sinwar was killed, Hamas supporters in New York City in November 2024 waved signs reading "Death to Zionists" and "Sinwar Lives!"[20]

OCTOBER 7 DENIAL

While Israel was still burying the victims of the October 7 atrocities, Hamas and its supporters began denying that the atrocities had even occurred. The phenomenon of 10/7 denial, a close relative of Holocaust denial, was born.

Like Holocaust deniers, the 10/7 deniers attempted to portray their position as a legitimate dispute over evidence. But as with the Holocaust, there were mountains of evidence to document the Hamas atrocities, including security camera footage, videos the killers themselves posted on social media, transcripts of the murderers' telephone calls to friends and family members, confessions by captured terrorists, and voluminous eyewitness testimony from October 7 survivors and emergency medical personnel.

The essence of both 10/7 denial and Holocaust denial is the antisemitic allegation that there is a worldwide Jewish conspiracy to control the media, rewrite historical narratives, and compel the international community to believe falsehoods. Khaled Mashal, who carries the title "Hamas Leader Abroad," told Saudi Arabian media that reports of atrocities against civilians were all "fabricated by [Israeli prime minister Benjamin] Netanyahu."[21] Salel al-Arouri, deputy chairman of the Hamas political bureau, said in an interview with *Al-Jazeera* that "our fighters do not target civilians" and it was "inconceivable that they would perpetrate the kind of crimes mentioned by the occupation, like rape, killing children, or killing civilians." The abductions, he said, were all perpetrated by "ordinary people" from Gaza who accompanied the terrorists.[22] Hamas official Hisham Qasem asserted that Hamas did not abduct foreign workers from Israeli towns, but rather "detained them for their own protection."[23] Hamas officials told the Palestinian Arab news agency Donia Al-Watan that the atrocity reports were "fabrications and lies against our Palestinian people and its resistance." Moreover, they asserted that the Hamas terrorists in southern Israel actually "made efforts to avoid civilians, and many videos from the ground are witness to this, and many settlers spoke about this in filmed testimonies in the media outlets." The latter claim was particularly ironic because the terrorists themselves filmed their atrocities and circulated the videos on social media.[24]

Soon Hamas officially went on record with its 10/7 denial. Its eighteen-page, English-language explanation of the invasion, issued to the news media in January 2024, claimed that the attackers "targeted the Israeli military sites" and "only targeted the occupation soldiers and those who carried weapons against our people." The terrorists "were keen to avoid harming civilians" because "avoiding harm to civilians, especially children, women and elderly people is a religious and moral commitment" to which Hamas is devoted. "Maybe some faults happened" amidst "the chaos caused along the border areas," but whatever those unidentified "faults" may have been, "if there was any case of targeting civilians, it happened accidentally." The Israeli hostages were all treated "in a kind manner."[25]

The Palestinian Authority joined the ranks of the 10/7 deniers. Mahmoud Al-Habbash, religious affairs adviser to PA Chairman Mahmoud Abbas, declared on his Facebook page that Israel "spread lies, falsehoods, and fabrications regarding what happened on Oct. 7, and therefore the world turned against the Palestinians."[26] Qadura Fares, the PA cabinet minister in charge of prisoners' affairs, claimed on PA Television on November 20 that Israel's military campaign against Hamas "is based on a lie, which it took Israel 24 hours to create and formulate properly. They killed their [own] civilians [on October 7], and they committed all these crimes and burned the bodies, and they made up this story and said: 'They [Hamas] raped, killed, and burned.' . . . However, this narrative fell apart quickly. . . . Israel's lie is no longer tripping anyone up."[27]

The PA's ambassador to Austria asserted—nearly a year after the attack—that it was "not clear" if Hamas deliberately killed any Israeli civilians.[28] Wasel Abu Yusuf, a member of the PLO executive committee and secretary-general of the Palestine Liberation Front (a part of the PLO and PA) declared on PA Television: "Since Oct. 7 there has been a Zionist version that [Israel] has attempted to spread worldwide out of tendentious propaganda, [claiming] that there was murder of children, rape of women, crimes, and the like."[29] Hanan Ashrawi, longtime Palestinian spokesperson to the international media, declared that the reports of "women being raped, or children being beheaded" are "nonsense, doctored pictures" produced by "the Israeli spin machine."[30] Reporters on PA Television broadcasts likewise characterized stories about Hamas atrocities as fabrications.[31]

Even as PA leaders denied the atrocities, they simultaneously defended the attack and praised the attackers—the kind of contradictory messaging that has long been part of Palestinian Arab leaders' public responses to events they endorse but which could also endanger international support for their cause. On October 7, in response to the ongoing Hamas invasion, Chairman Abbas issued a statement affirming "the Palestinian people's right to self-defense." Abu Mohammed, spokesman for the Al-Aqsa Martyrs Brigade, the militia of the PA's main faction, Fatah—which Abbas chairs—bragged that "on October 7, our heroes in the brave unit participated in the invasion of the colonies surrounding Gaza." The group also circulated a video showing some of its terrorists taking part in the attack and boasting about their participation.[32]

Abbas's religious affairs adviser, al-Habbash, posted on his Facebook page an interview with himself, in which he asked, rhetorically, "From President Mahmoud Abbas to the last of the people in the Palestinian leadership—has anyone heard from us one word against the Hamas Movement or against any Palestinian?," to which he replied, "No."[33] Al-Habbash also threatened that if Israel did not agree to the PA's various demands, "then Oct. 7 can repeat itself 100 times, and perhaps even more seriously."[34] Fatah Central Committee member Abbas Zaki told the PA's Palestine Today television channel that the October 7 attack was a "source of pride" that should be "studied in the universities and echoed widely."[35]

PA diplomats around the world posted celebratory messages and images on their social media accounts on October 7 and the days that followed. In England, Rana Abuayyash, consul at the PA's mission, circulated an image of an Israeli flag transforming into the face of Adolf Hitler. The PA ambassador to Paris, Hala Abou-Hassira, wrote: "Israel bears full responsibility." Another PA diplomat in France, Nadine Abualheija, tweeted: "A colonial state is not an innocent victim when its victims resist genocide," and her colleague Jamila Hassan Eragat declared: "Don't judge a group of people for rising up against their oppressors. . . . [V]iolence is necessary for decolonisation." The PA ambassador in Mozambique, Fayez Abduljawad, commented: "If you are silent when Israel kills Palestinians, remain silent when Palestinians defend themselves." The PA ambassador to Guinea and Sierra Leone, Thaer Abubaker, tweeted that October 7 was "heroic," and "liberation is the goal of every fighter who risks their life for the sake of freedom and jihad for God's path." A PA diplomat in Zimbabwe, Manar Alagha, posted a video on Facebook showing Israelis fleeing from the concert grounds above the slogan, "Here to victory!" At the PA's embassy in the Ivory Coast, diplomat Khattab Bayyari displayed a graphic of a paragliding terrorist above the caption "You are the soldiers of Allah in the field." The PA's ambassador to Japan and South Korea, Waleed Siam, tweeted: "Zionism is really curse on all humanity." PA diplomats to international agencies responded similarly. Khuloussi Bsaiso, a PA diplomat at the UN, circulated a map of the Middle East without Israel, above the words "Palestine as it should be." The deputy head of the PA mission to the European Union, Hassan Albalawi, hailed the Hamas massacres as "heroic." Adel Atieh, the PA ambassador to the EU, praised the perpetrators as "the people of the mighty" who are fighting for "freedom and breaking tyranny." Another PA representative to the EU, Lema Nazeeh, tweeted that the Hamas slaughter was "decolonisation in tangible terms," a day of "dignity and triumph." Adding an element of classic religious antisemitism, Salman El Herfi, a former PA ambassador to South Africa and France who is now an adviser to PA chairman Abbas, distributed an image of Mary and Jesus flanked by a photo of a mother and and child in Gaza, with the caption: "The pain of the Mother is the same as it was 2,000 years ago. The same killer."[36]

Polls indicated wide support for the PA's pro-Hamas pronouncements among the Palestinian Arab public. Seventy-nine percent of PA territory residents told the Qatar-based Arab Center for Research and Policy Studies in December 2023 and January 2024 that the October 7 attack was "a legitimate resistance operation"; another 11 percent described it as "somewhat flawed but legitimate"; and 4 percent said it was "a legitimate resistance operation" even though it "involved heinous or even criminal acts." The percentage that called it "an illegitimate operation" was zero.[37] Likewise, 91 percent of Palestinian Arabs participating in a March 2024 Palestinian Center for Policy and Survey Research survey said Hamas did not commit atrocities in the October 7 attack. When the researchers pointed to the circulation of videos (including some by Hamas) showing atrocities and asked if Hamas committed the acts seen in these videos; 93 percent said no.[38] While measuring public opinion in a dictatorship is difficult because of dissidents' reluctance to speak against the ruling regime, all previous indicators of public opinion—such as Hamas's electoral victory in 2006, pre-October 7 polls, and the absence of any dissident movements in the previous eighteen years—were consistent with the persistence of extremism, including 10/7 denial, among Gaza's general public.

Meanwhile, the PA provided direct financial support to many perpetrators. In January 2024, its prisoners affairs division announced that since October 7, an additional 3,350 individuals had been added to the official list of imprisoned terrorists to whom the PA pays salaries, and that 661 of them were Hamas members who had been arrested in Gaza. In June, it announced that another 899 terrorists captured by the Israelis in Gaza were added to the list. Each would receive a starting salary of $375 monthly, with regular increases according to their number of years in prison, up to a maximum of $3,215 monthly. Families of dead terrorists receive a one-time grant of $1600 and a monthly salary of $425 for the rest of their lives. The PA's allotment solely to the thousands of families of dead Hamas terrorists from Gaza families totaled more than $100 million in 2024.[39]

BLOOD LIBELS, OLD AND NEW

The allegation that Jews murder Christians in order to use their blood for Passover matzohs or other religious purposes first gained popularity in the twelfth century CE, when the Jewish community in Norwich, England, was accused of slaughtering a local boy named William for that reason. From then on, the "blood libel," as it became known, periodically was unleashed against various European Jewish communities, usually after a Christian child disappeared or was found dead under unclear circumstances. Sometimes the ruling authorities or church officials endorsed the blood libels. The accused faced torture, and anti-Jewish pogroms often erupted (see chapter 6).

With time, most ideas of the Middle Ages gave way to modernity. But antisemitic blood libels continued well into the twentieth century. In Russia in 1913, Jewish factory superintendent Mendel Beilis was accused of the ritual murder of a Christian child, and spent years in prison before he was finally acquitted. In the 1930s and 1940s, blood libels became a staple of Nazi Germany's antisemitic propaganda.

In the decades preceding October 7, the blood libel assumed frightening new dimensions in the Arab propaganda war against Israel and its supporters. An early instance occurred in the small Palestinian Arab village of Arrabe in the spring of 1983. A schoolgirl fainted after opening a window in her classroom. Her classmates detected a strong odor of "rotten fish or eggs," and some of them likewise fainted. Both Israeli and Arab doctors who visited the scene that day reported a strong smell of hydrogen sulfide, which commonly occurs in raw sewage. Schoolgirls in nearby towns soon complained of dizziness and headaches and were hospitalized, but then discharged when their symptoms quickly vanished. As in medieval episodes in which antisemitic agitators took advantage of a misunderstood incident (such as the disappearance of a child), PLO chairman Yasir Arafat seized the opportunity to declare that Israel was carrying out "mass poisoning" of Arab girls in order to render them sterile. He said the school incidents were evidence of "chemical warfare" and "the genocide against the Palestinian people." As in medieval times, the accusations triggered mob violence against Jews, which in this case resulted in the near-lynching of an Israeli investigator and mass rock-throwing at other Israeli Jews.[40]

Some foreign news media outlets published the story despite the absence of evidence. A front-page article in the *Los Angeles Times*, headlined "300 Arab Girls in West Bank Poisoned by Gas," stated that "a yellow dust that proved to be rich in sulfur was found on a windowsill at one of the schools" and that unnamed "investigators" were "reported to believe that the dust was a residue of the gas."[41] The yellow dust turned out to be pollen. A mysterious tin of white powder that supposedly was an Israeli gas actually was evaporated milk. A bottle of strong-smelling liquid that Palestinians found "suspicious" was revealed as a common household disinfectant. Israeli authorities discovered that a Palestinian Arab activist claiming symptoms of "poisoning" had himself hospitalized six times, and was caught "pressuring girls to continue to remain in hospital," the *Jerusalem Post* reported. Exploiting the news from Arrabe, masked extremists in Nablus, twenty miles to the south, announced over a local mosque's public address system that Israelis had polluted the city's water. Some doctors in Arrabe acknowledged that "they were being pressured not to release the girls from hospital," according to the *Post*. An investigation by the U.S. Centers for Disease Control and Prevention (CDC) concluded that the symptoms exhibited by the girls in Arrabe were caused either by "psychological factors" or by hydrogen sulfide (from raw sewage), not poison. Girls in the other schools had suffered from nothing more than "anxiety," to which Palestinian newspaper and radio reports "may have contributed." The CDC found "no evidence of reproductive impairment." Separate investigations by the World Health Organization and the International Red Cross likewise found no evidence of Israeli poisoning. Nonetheless, Arafat never retracted his accusations about Arrabe.[42]

Similar allegations circulated widely in the Palestinian Arab community in subsequent years, especially after the creation of the Palestinian Authority in 1994. The director of the PA's Committee for Consumer Protection accused Israel of supplying Palestinian markets with chocolates that cause mad cow disease.[43] The PA's website charged that Israeli planes drop bags of poisoned candy into Palestinian neighborhoods.[44] The Palestinian representative to the UN in Geneva claimed "the Israeli authorities infected by injection 300 Palestinian children with the HIV virus."[45] The PA's deputy minister of supplies, Abdel Hamid al-Qudsi, proclaimed: "Israel is distributing food containing material that causes cancer and hormones that harm male virility and other spoiled products in the Palestinian Authority's territories in order to poison and harm the Palestinian population. . . . It is an organized plan and conspiracy which is under the auspices of the Israel Defense Forces."[46] Abdel Aziz Shaheen, PA minister of supplies, alleged that "Israeli agents" were giving Arab schoolgirls bubble gum spiked with the hormone progesterone, which supposedly made girls sexually ravenous and then sterile, and also was "completely destroying the genetic system of young boys." PA officials provided gum samples to the *Washington Post* for chemical analysis; the *Post* found they did not contain progesterone or any other foreign substance.[47] In an infamous incident in 1999, Palestinian First

Lady Suha Arafat embarrassed then-U.S. Senator Hillary Clinton by claiming, with Clinton by her side, that Israel was engaged in the "daily intensive use of poisonous gases" against Palestinian Arabs in order to produce "an increase in cancer cases among women and children." After Yasir Arafat died from a stroke in 2004, PA officials claimed Israel had poisoned him—and continued spreading that blood libel long after multiple international investigations found no evidence of poisoning.[48]

Palestinian Arab leaders also circulated blood libels that hewed closely to timeworn allegations, such as accusing Jews of literally drinking blood. A skit presented on Al-Aqsa TV, the official Hamas television channel, in 2009 portrayed a Jewish father and son, dressed in stereotypical Hasidic garb, discussing Jewish attitudes toward Muslims. The father explained, "We Jews hate the Muslims, we want to kill the Muslims, we Jews want to drink the blood of Muslims" and "We have to wash our hands with the blood of Muslims."[49]

PA-controlled media and mosques have promoted similar allegations. Columnist Yahya Rabah wrote in the PA daily *Al-Hayat Al-Jadid* in 2014: "These Israeli murderers' God, 'Yahweh' . . . demands, according to the *Protocols of the Elders of Zion*, that they offer him sacrifices during Passover in the form of Matzah made from the blood of our children."[50] The following year, a PA-salaried imam at the Al-Aqsa Mosque, Sheikh Khaled Al-Mughrabi, explained to participants in his twice-weekly religious classes there that Jews believe "if you killed a human being and drank his blood in a certain way, you would attain eternal life." As a result, "on the holiday of Passover, it is forbidden for them to eat regular bread. They prepare their matzahs. These matzahs were not kneaded in the regular way, but rather with the blood of children." To obtain the blood, they "look for a small child, kidnap and steal him, bring a barrel called the barrel of nails [and] put the small child in the barrel and his body would be pierced by these nails. In the bottom of the barrel they would put a faucet and pour the blood." The sermon was broadcast on the mosque's YouTube Channel.[51]

In 2016, PA Television reported that an Israeli rabbi ordered his followers to "poison the drinking water and the natural wells in the [Palestinian] villages and towns throughout the West Bank," and Chairman Abbas repeated the accusation in a speech to the European Parliament.[52] Fatah's Facebook page has featured children's drawings of Israelis drinking the blood of Palestinian Arabs.[53] In 2017, Palestinian Arab activist Manal Tamimi tweeted: "Vampire zionist celebrating their Kebore day [she was writing on Yom Kippur] by drinking Palestinian bloods, yes our blood is pure & delicious but it will kill u at the end." When Tamimi was challenged about her tweet, she replied, "I'm not a Jew heater [*sic*], I have a very good Jew friends." A forty-five-year-old mother of four hailed by *Al Jazeera* as a "Palestinian supermom" and by the UN as a "human rights defender," Tamimi leads weekly protests that include hurling rocks at Jews in the adjacent town of Halamish.[54]

Middle Eastern incarnations of the blood libel can be found in Arab news media elsewhere, from Abu Dhabi Television broadcasting an animated skit of Israel's prime minister drinking Arab blood to a Syrian diplomat's public claims that Israeli children sing songs about drinking Arab blood. But it is in the Palestinian Arab community that the libels appear with particular frequency.[55]

In the aftermath of October 7, the PA news media presented numerous iterations of the blood libel theme. A PA Television broadcast on October 27, 2023, asserted that "the occupation [i.e., Israel] stole organs from the corpses such as the cornea of the eye, the concha of the ear, liver, kidneys and heart."[56] The PA daily *Al-Hayat Al-Jadida* reported on December 29 that "the Israeli occupation is deliberately using a new silent weapon, through a systematic and deliberate policy of creating a hothouse for the spread of lethal epidemics and infectious diseases among children in the centers of uprooted people in the Gaza Strip, in order to kill as many civilians as possible, and particularly children."[57] *Al-Hayat Al-Jadida* informed its readers on January 2, 2024, that Israel's leaders "dream of realizing their racist Talmudic prophecies about murder, permitting [the spilling of] the blood of children and women, and even cutting open the stomachs of pregnant women to kill the fetuses, and also annihilating the members of the Palestinian people to the last of them."[58] On March 20, 2024, a PA Television news correspondent asserted that Israeli rabbis "permit poisoning water wells."[59]

For all these accusations of Israel using various poisons, Palestinian Arab leaders' own interest in using poison against Jews actually has some pedigree. In 1978, five children in Holland became ill after eating oranges imported from Israel that had been injected with mercury, and Dutch police found fourteen more poisoned oranges. The PLO announced it injected the mercury in order "to damage the Israeli economy."[60]

An earlier poisoning episode occurred in 1944, when the grand mufti of Jerusalem, the political leader and senior Muslim religious authority of the Palestinian Arabs, was residing in Berlin and collaborating with the Nazis. Haj Amin el-Husseini dispatched five of his men to British Mandatory Palestine, armed with maps of Tel Aviv and canisters of "a fine white powder" that they intended to dump into Tel Aviv's water system. They were captured en route. "I remember how amazed we all were," district police commander Fayiz Bey Idrissi recalled. "The laboratory report stated that each container held enough poison to kill 25,000 people, and there were at least ten containers."[61] The Tel Aviv population at the time was approximately two hundred thousand. Consistent with the Hamas and PA policy of naming schools after individuals they consider heroes (see chapter 3), there are today two Hamas schools in Gaza named in honor of Hassan Salameh, one of the gang of five poisoners; and a school in the PA city of El Bireh is named after the mufti.[62]

On October 7, fifteen soldiers in a room at the Nahal Oz military base were murdered by toxic gas from a canister thrown through the entrance. A terrorist captured by the Israelis was found to be in possession of documents describing how to prepare "a device for dispersing cyanide agents," Israeli authorities revealed.[63]

Once Israel's counterterror operation in Gaza began in late October 2023, a new wave of blood libels appeared in the international news media and via social media. Euro-Med Human Rights Monitor, a prominent nongovernmental organization, cited unnamed "medical professionals in Gaza" who speculated that Israeli soldiers were stealing organs from the bodies of Gazan civilians. Supermodel Gigi Hadid shared with her seventy-nine million Instagram followers a video featuring that lie. Palestinian advocates on TikTok claimed that Israel maintains a "skin bank" filled with skin taken from Gaza corpses. The Council on American-Islamic Relations alleged that Israeli drones were "broadcasting sounds of babies crying to lure Gazans to kill zones." Social activist Saira Rao alerted her fifty-one thousand followers on X (Twitter) that "many American doctors and nurses are Zionists," which made her feel "genuinely terrified for Palestinian, Arab, Muslim, South Asian and Black patients—even more than usual. And usually it's bad."[64]

THE GAZA GENOCIDE BLOOD LIBEL

A frequently heard accusation in the aftermath of October 7 was that Israel was conducting a genocidal campaign of deliberately and indiscriminately murdering civilians in Gaza. The allegation was so far removed from objective reality as to constitute a contemporary variation on the ages-old blood libel against Jews.

In its pursuit of Hamas in Gaza, Israel took numerous steps to minimize civilian casualties, despite the increased risk to its own soldiers' lives. The Israeli military frequently surrendered the element of surprise—thereby endangering its soldiers—by announcing in advance where and when it would attack, so that civilians could escape. Israeli planes dropped leaflets over impending target areas, urging civilians to get out of the way. Arabic-speaking Israeli soldiers made thousands of phone calls to individual private residents, encouraging them to travel the few miles necessary to get out of the danger zone. Israel also established safe-passage corridors for fleeing residents with publicly announced four-hour periods during which there would be no military action in the vicinity. In some instances, however, Hamas terrorists physically prevented civilians from escaping.[65] The Israeli military even halted its pursuit of terrorists in various parts of Gaza in the summer of 2024, in order to permit mass vaccination against polio, even though only one actual case of the disease had been reported.[66] These steps also enabled terrorists to escape, or to make plans for attacking Israeli soldiers whom they knew would soon be approaching a particular neighborhood.

Hamas situated its terrorists, command centers, and arms depots within and underneath civilian neighborhoods (see chapter 2). This compelled Israeli forces to enter civilian areas they would have preferred to avoid. Israeli commanders reported early in the war that it "became normal" to find large quantities of munitions in civilian sites, forcing Israel to destroy many civilian buildings. Terrorists stationed themselves inside civilian apartments; one Israeli soldier told the *New York Times* how he found guns "behind a false wall in a child's bedroom," while another said he "found grenades in a woman's clothes closet." Weapons were often found "inside the lining of furniture." The hundreds of miles of underground tunnels running throughout the territory had entry points in private homes, mosques, schools, and hospitals, and weapons were stored in all such locations. Rockets were fired at Israel from densely populated neighborhoods, so that when Israel fired back, civilians would be killed. Terrorists took advantage of the Israeli military's concern about civilian casualties by donning civilian clothes to avoid detection, escaping from oncoming Israeli forces by mingling among evacuated civilians, and then going back with families once Israel permitted residents to return home. The Hamas tactic of exploiting Gazan civilians as human shields extended even to using children as rooftop lookouts to supply information about nearby Israeli soldiers to terrorists below, in effect daring the Israelis to shoot at the children.[67]

Despite these realities, Gazan civilian casualties were far fewer than those of comparable conflicts. A study in *Tablet* magazine by Abraham Wyner, professor of statistics and data science at Penn's Wharton School, found the ratio of civilian casualties to combatants in Gaza was between 1 to 1 and 1.4 to 1, which is considerably lower than other instances of concentrated urban warfare in modern times. Michael Oren, the historian and former Israeli ambassador to the United States, likewise pointed out that the Israeli figure compared favorably to the combatant-to-civilian ratio in America's military campaigns in Afghanistan, Iraq, and Syria, and NATO's action in Serbia in 1999, in each of which approximately four civilians were killed for every combatant.[68]

Nonetheless, Israel was repeatedly accused of deliberately and wantonly killing Gazan civilians. Barely three weeks into Israel's counterterror campaign, UN Secretary-General Antonio Guterres proclaimed: "We are witnessing a killing of civilians that is unparalleled and unprecedented in any conflict since I have been Secretary General," apparently forgetting the hundreds of thousands of civilians killed in Syria, Yemen, and Ethiopia during the six years since he took office.[69] As the weeks passed, news media worldwide reported constantly increasing casualty claims, quickly rising from the hundreds, to the thousands, to the tens of thousands. A study of news articles mentioning Gaza fatalities that appeared in the world's most influential media outlets from February to May 2024 found that 98 percent of them relied upon numbers provided by the Hamas Ministry of Health, and only 5 percent cited figures supplied by Israel.[70]

The unreliability of Hamas's numbers was obvious from the start to President Joe Biden and his administration. Three weeks into the war, the president remarked, "I have no notion that the Palestinians are telling the truth about how many people are killed. I'm sure innocents have been killed, and it's the price of waging a war. . . . I have no confidence in the number that the Palestinians are using."[71] After Defense Secretary Lloyd Austin mentioned a Hamas-supplied death toll in congressional testimony on February 29, 2024 (without noting the source), Pentagon spokesman Air Force Maj. Gen. Pat Ryder clarified to reporters, "I cannot verify the veracity of those figures, and we're not able to corroborate them and so we don't have a lot of confidence in the information."[72] Director of National Intelligence Avril Haines told a congressional committee in March that the United States does not "take on face value" numbers provided by Hamas.[73] A bipartisan House of Representatives resolution in June barred the State Department from using casualty statistics provided by Hamas.[74]

The first problem with the casualty numbers was their source. Although news reports frequently stated that "the Gaza Health Ministry" or "the health authorities in Gaza" provided the figures, the numbers came from the *Hamas* health ministry—that is, a division of a terrorist group with a long track record of lying about everything from the outcome of its terrorist attacks (inflating the number of Israeli victims, characterizing defenseless Israeli civilians as soldiers, and the like) to topics such as the Holocaust, which it calls a hoax, and *The Protocols of the Elders of Zion*, which it calls genuine. It also has an obviously strong interest in artificially inflating the numbers in order to increase international of criticism of Israel. Major American news media outlets did not take at face value claims made by Nazi Germany or other totalitarian regimes in past wars.

Journalists covering the Gaza war, like those covering the World War II battles, had limited access to war zones and few means of even estimating casualties, leaving them with a choice between believing the democracies or the terrorist dictators, or neither. The Israelis were honest about the difficulty in accurately calculating the death toll in the midst of raging battlefield conditions, and thus offered their estimates only infrequently. By contrast, Hamas supplied its figures to the news media daily, thereby giving them an air of authority even when they were not accompanied by corroborating evidence.

Another problem with the Hamas numbers was the blatant contradictions between the figures Hamas presented in the Gaza war of 2023–24, as compared to similar battles that took place in Gaza in 2014. In the earlier conflict, Hamas reported that 65 percent of the casualties were men, 15 percent were women, and 16 percent were children, but at the beginning of the recent war, Hamas claimed that over 25 percent of the casualties were women, and more than 40 percent were children. That significant discrepancy was bolstered by Hamas's strategic burial of men in groups of one hundred in trenches, with bulldozers, thereby obscuring the real numbers of dead men from outside scrutiny.[75] Moreover, after the first few weeks of the war Hamas stopped breaking down the numbers by gender or age. An Associated Press analysis in June 2024 found that while Hamas was continuing to claim a figure of 70 percent or more (for women and children), in fact by April the real number was 38 percent.[76]

Estimating the casualty tolls was further complicated by Hamas's refusal to distinguish between civilian and terrorist deaths. According to a 2024 Washington Institute for Near East Policy analysis, "Hamas-produced statistics [concerning the Gaza war] are inconsistent, imprecise, and appear to have been systematically manipulated to downplay the number of militants killed and to exaggerate the proportion of noncombatants confirmed as dead."[77] Israel estimated that a substantial portion of the fatalities, perhaps as many as half, were terrorists. In May 2024, the Israelis reported that approximately fourteen thousand terrorists and sixteen thousand civilians had been killed.[78] Two months later, Reuters cited Israeli security officials as saying they made their estimates "through a combination of counting bodies on the battlefield, intercepts of Hamas communications and intelligence assessments of personnel in targets that were destroyed."[79]

Another issue was the fact that the Hamas fatality count included Gazans killed by any means, including terrorist groups' own misfired rockets. According to the Israeli army, at least 11 percent of all the rockets fired by Hamas or Palestinian Islamic Jihad on October 7 and in the weeks to follow fell within Gaza, killing a number of Arab civilians.[80] Immediately following the explosion at the Al-Ahli Hospital on October 17, 2023, Hamas claimed it was a deliberate Israeli bombing of the hospital, killing exactly 471 civilians and injuring 342. In fact, the explosion happened in a parking lot near the hospital, the number of fatalities was in the dozens, and it was caused by a misfired Palestinian Islamic Jihad missile that fell short of its intended Israeli target. Six months later, senior PIJ official Tarek Abu Shaluf acknowledged that one of its rockets was responsible for the blast (although previously he had publicly claimed "the rocket belonged to the Occupation and that the target was the [hospital] building").[81]

Hamas's credibility was further undermined by the evidence that it had inflated death tolls in earlier Gaza conflicts. In 2014, the *New York Times*, citing human rights groups, reported that "people killed by Hamas as collaborators and people who died naturally, or perhaps through domestic violence, are most likely counted [as Gazans killed by Israel] as well."[82] According to recent editions of the U.S. government's *World Factbook*, fifteen to sixteen Gazans die daily from natural causes; if Hamas continued the practice that the *Times* said was "most likely," that alone would have added over five thousand "martyrs" to Hamas's death toll for the first year of the 2023–24 war.[83] Hamas also manipulated death numbers during its conflicts with Israel in 2020 and 2022, according to internal Hamas documents uncovered by Israeli forces in Gaza. In one instance, officials of Hamas's al-Qassam Brigades had pressed Palestinian Islamic Jihad to admit it was responsible for some misfired rockets, so Hamas would not be blamed; in response, the PIJ suggested that the misfirings, and the casualties they caused, be concealed from the public in order "to support the image of the resistance." Another document showed Hamas knew a misfired rocket caused the fatalities from an explosion at a Gaza mosque, yet Hamas spokespeople had publicly claimed they were victims of an Israeli air strike. In another indication that the terrorist leadership recognized the high rate of misfirings, Hamas officials also asked the PIJ to refrain from firing rockets from launchers near Hamas leaders' homes.[84]

Additional questions were raised by Hamas's failure to provide the names of ten thousand of the thirty-four thousand Gazans it claimed had been killed by the end of April 2024. On April 24, the daily chart of casualty numbers presented by Hamas to the news media acknowledged that only twenty-four thousand of the thirty-four thousand were "martyrs whose idintities [*sic*] are recognized." Despite failing to supply the names of so many alleged victims, Hamas expected international media outlets to cite the higher figure based on Hamas's say-so—which most of them did.[85]

Several UN-affiliated agencies also circulated wildly inflated numbers of women and children killed—until the UN body in charge of monitoring the situation drastically revised those figures downward. Initially both UNRWA and the UN's World Health Organization had asserted that "a child is killed every 10 minutes in the Gaza Strip," which would mean 30,240 Gaza children were killed between October and May, more than twice what Hamas itself had claimed. On May 8, however, the UN Office for Coordination of Humanitarian Affairs announced that the actual number of child fatalities was 7,796, not the 14,500 Hamas had claimed; and the number of women killed was really 4,959, not the 9,500 Hamas had alleged. The deputy spokesman for the UN Secretary-General attributed the earlier numbers to "the fog of war."[86] The real number of deaths of children in Gaza actually was even lower, because Hamas defined a "child" as anyone younger than twenty. Thus, many dead terrorists between sixteen and nineteen were classified as "children." The number of teenagers within Hamas's ranks grew steadily over the months, as it replaced members who were killed by aggressively recruiting sixteen- to nineteen-year-olds.[87]

A study published in December 2024 by a London-based think tank, the Henry M. Jackson Society, concluded that the Hamas-reported death toll—which was then about forty-five thousand—was significantly "overstated." About half the deaths were of terrorists. The number of civilian casualties had been inflated by including "natural deaths, deaths from before this conflict began, and deaths of those killed by Hamas itself," and by listing dead terrorists as civilians. Hamas also falsely increased the number of women and children it claimed were killed, by reporting some dead men as women and misrepresenting the ages of some fatalities.[88]

In April 2024, Hamas circulated a new blood libel: that "mass graves" of Palestinians had been "discovered in Gaza," indicating that Israelis had slaughtered civilians and dumped them into pits. The *New York Times* columnist Nicholas Kristof tweeted about the "disturbing reports about mass graves."[89] Amnesty International echoed the slur.[90] The European Union piled on with a similar accusation.[91] Congresswoman Alexandria Ocasio-Cortez (D-New York) urged the news media to focus more attention on this "discovery" and less on "campus protests."[92]

Two days later, however, a *New York Times* follow-up article bearing the ominous headline, "Gaza Authorities Say More Bodies Were Discovered in Mass Grave" included information that proved the accuracy of Israel's original explanation that it had exhumed the graves in search of the bodies of hostages, and then reburied the corpses. The *Times* said it had "verified" that the mass graves were dug months ago and bore Arabic-language signs reading "Unknown martyr," indicating that the digging and burials were the work of Arabs, not Israelis. The *Times* then found satellite imagery showing the graves were only later "disturbed by Israeli forces, including with a bulldozer, lending credence to the Israeli claim that they exhumed and reburied bodies." Perhaps the most serious detail of the allegation came from a UN official who, citing "local health authorities in Gaza" (i.e., Hamas), claimed that the bodies were found with "their hands tied" and "stripped of their clothes." The *Times* acknowledged that the accusation "could not be independently verified and the [UN agency] did not provide evidence for its claim"—but that statement appeared only in the nineteenth and twentieth paragraphs of the article.[93]

THE FAMINE LIE

An offshoot of the inflated claims about civilian casualties was the accusation that Israel was either deliberately, or through recklessness, causing famine in Gaza. Many of these allegations were articulated by media pundits or opinionated diplomats who claimed the situation was "approaching famine" or "close to a famine," elastic terminology that created an impression of starvation while stopping just short of the full accusation. Several dozen American volunteer doctors in Gaza claimed in open letter to President Biden in July 2024 that it was "likely" about thirty-eight thousand Gazans had died of starvation during the previous nine months; three months later, they and other doctors issued an updated letter to the president which made no claims of death by starvation and spoke only of the dangers of malnutrition in Gaza.[94]

Starting early in the war and continuing since then, Israel permitted hundreds of truckloads of food and supplies to enter Gaza daily. From October 2023 to February 2024, a total of 13,834 trucks entered—an average of more than 130 trucks daily. This equalled 3,211 calories worth of nutrition per Gazan, per day—far exceeding the World Health Organization standard for calorie consumption (2,200 for women, and 2,900 for men).[95] A study of the food delivered to Gaza between January and April 2024, conducted by Hebrew University's Institute of Biochemistry, Food Science, and Nutrition together with four other Israeli universities and the Israeli ministry of health, concluded that "the food supply contain[ed] sufficient energy and protein for the population's needs."[96]

In general, Israel made reasonable efforts to ensure the flow of the aid, as conditions in war zones permitted. On occasion, factors beyond Israel's control impeded the process. Dangerous battlefield conditions occasionally halted aid deliveries. A $320-million offshore pier constructed by the U.S. military to accelerate food deliveries quickly broke apart under high winds and had to be discarded. Hamas stole copious quantities of aid for its own use, and for resale. Ehud Yaari, an analyst for the Washington Institute for Near East Policy, estimated in May 2024 that Hamas had already stolen "no less than" $500-million worth of the aid. Tape-recorded conversations between Hamas operatives in September 2024 revealed that some Hamas storage facilities were literally overflowing with stolen goods, to the point that there were "trucks filled with goods" lined up outside warehouses that had no more space.[97]

As a result, many Gazans did face significant food insecurity, but it affected a minority of the populace, and it was not a famine, despite warnings to that effect in April 2024 by Samantha Power, head of the United States Agency for International Development (USAID), which manages U.S. humanitarian assistance projects around the world.[98] A July 2024 report conducted by the Integrated Food Security Phase Classification agency (associated with the UN's Food and Agriculture Association) concluded that 15 percent of Gazans had reached its most severe category of food insecurity, "Phase 5—Catastrophe." Additionally, the level of malnutrition among children in northern Gaza—the area at highest risk—was 1 percent, which was the same as the level before the war. The rates in other parts of Gaza were only slightly higher. Furthermore, data used in the Integrated Food Security agency's report indicated that its own earlier fears of famine were misplaced. The agency defined a famine as occurring when at least two adults or four children per ten thousand people are dying daily from starvation alone. Its report cited a Palestinian survey undertaken for the World Food Program between April and June 2024 which found 42 deaths from among a total of 5,707 citizens, from all causes, including war casualties. "Given that only 42 deaths were recorded," said Prof. Aaron Troen of Hebrew University's School of Nutrition Science, "it is safe to assume that the nonviolent death rate was close to nil."[99]

In December 2024, the outgoing U.S. ambassador to Israel took the highly unusual step of publicly reprimanding his own Biden administration colleagues over the famine issue. Ambassador Jack Lew said "outdated and inaccurate data" had been used by USAID's Famine Early Warning System Network to reach its conclusion that "acute malnutrition thresholds for famine have now been surpassed in North Gaza." Lew pointed out that USAID skewed its calculations by estimating the area's population was 65,000–75,000, when in fact the correct number "is in the range of 7,000–15,000." USAID removed the report from its website the next day.[100]

TRUTH AS CASUALTY: WORLD WAR II LESSONS

In World War II, the United States and its allies made victory the overriding goal regardless of civilian casualties. While Israel took steps to avoid harm to civilians in Gaza, even at the risk of its own soldiers' lives, the Allies frequently carried out attacks on enemy targets that they knew would result in substantial numbers of civilian fatalities. Moreover, on some occasions they deliberately attacked civilian targets in order to undermine the enemy's morale. They considered such actions justified because Germany and Japan were the aggressors in the war. The Allies did not notify the German public as to which areas they were about to attack; nor did they pause their advance across Europe in order to facilitate shipments of humanitarian aid to civilians in Nazi Germany.

Beginning in March 1944, the Americans and British carried out extensive attacks on railways across France, Belgium, and western Germany in advance of the June 6 D-Day landings. The breadth of the air strikes made civilian casualties inevitable; they were averaging about one hundred per bombing. On May 7, British prime minister Winston Churchill told President Franklin D. Roosevelt of his concern about "the number of Frenchmen killed in the raids on the railway centers in France." He estimated the total number of French civilian deaths in the operation was liable to reach ten thousand, in addition to tens of thousands of injured. Churchill feared the bombings could "leave a legacy of hate" toward the Allies among the French populace. Roosevelt responded: "However regrettable the attendant loss of civilian lives, I am not prepared to impose from this distance any restriction on military action by the responsible commanders that in their opinion might militate against the success of [the upcoming D-Day landings] or cause additional loss of life to our Allied Forces of invasion."[101]

Later that year, British planes attacked the Gestapo's Danish headquarters on the University of Aarhus campus. The target was situated in the dormitory buildings, which were flanked by civilian hospitals on both sides; nonetheless, the raid proceeded, in broad daylight, because it was militarily advantageous to do so. Most of the bombs hit their mark, but several stray bombs hit another campus building which was under construction, killing ten workers. Likewise, a British bombing raid on Gestapo headquarters in Copenhagen the following year destroyed the building, but some bombs accidentally hit a nearby school, killing an estimated 125 civilians.[102]

The United States carried out bombing strikes on German oil factories in the industrial zone of the Auschwitz death camp in occupied Poland during daylight hours, when military planners had every reason to believe the factories would be filled with Jewish slave laborers. Civilian casualties were inevitable, but the administration felt that harm to the Jewish prisoners was justified in order to achieve America's war aims. For the same reason, U.S. bombers were sent to strike the V-2 rocket factory in the Buchenwald concentration camp in broad daylight, when it could have been assumed that Jewish prisoners would be in the factory. Nearly four hundred of them were killed in the bombing.[103]

Not only was the Roosevelt administration willing to risk killing Jewish civilians in order to strike those military targets—it even was willing to endanger the lives of Allied POWs. About 1,400 British servicemen were imprisoned in Auschwitz beginning in the autumn of 1943, and six hundred remained there as of the summer of 1944, working as slave laborers in the oil factories. The U.S. and British governments were well aware that the POWs were there; the Red Cross regularly brought them food packages, and one POW, Charles Coward, had been smuggling information to the British about the mass gassings of Jews taking place in the Birkenau section of the camp. But the presence of the POWs did not deter the daylight air strikes on factories where British prisoners might be working. As a result, thirty-eight British prisoners were killed, and many others injured, in the American bombing of the camp's industrial zone on August 20.[104]

In the February 1945 battle to liberate Manila, capital of the Philippines, U.S. forces found themselves arrayed against Japanese troops who were stationed in heavily civilian areas. That did not stop the Americans from advancing, or from using weapons likely to harm civilians, such as Sherman tanks, flamethrowers, and 155-mm Howitzer field guns. In addition to the sixteen thousand Japanese soldiers who were killed in the month-long battle, more than one hundred thousand Filipino civilians lost their lives. Many of them were massacred by the Japanese, but an estimated 30 to 40 percent were killed by American artillery strikes.[105]

In some instances, the United States and its allies went further and undertook deliberate attacks on enemy civilians in order to advance the war effort. Beginning in February 1942, the British undertook what was known as "area bombing," which meant attacking civilian areas in order to undermine the German public's morale. The United States assented to this approach and participated in many of the strikes on civilian targets. The British-American bombing of Hamburg in July 1943 left forty thousand dead, and the attack on Dresden by U.S. and British bombers in February 1945 killed tens of thousands more. This approach was sometimes employed on the Pacific front as well. The Roosevelt administration's firebombing of Tokyo in March 1945 resulted in over one hundred thousand civilian fatalities. In August, the Truman administration selected two Japanese civilian centers as the targets of its nuclear bombs, leaving approximately one hundred and thirty-five thousand dead in Hiroshima and sixty-four thousand in Nagasaki.[106]

The Americans and the British were not the only Allies responsible for killing German civilians in World War II. Canadian troops fought a storied urban battle in World War II that bore similarities to the contemporary situation in Gaza, with enemy fighters hiding in underground tunnels, savage house-to-house fighting, widespread booby-traps, and substantial civilian casualties. It took place in late 1943, when Canadian troops pushing through Italy took aim at German forces situated in the quiet seaside town of Ortona. Many of the Italian town's ten thousand residents fled after the Germans took over, but some remained. The *New York Times* provided a day-by-day, blow-by-blow description of the Battle of Ortona. "Mines, demolitions and booby traps" planted by the Germans "are steadily taking [a] toll" on the Canadian troops. Holed up in "cellars and sewers," German snipers would pop up, shoot at the advancing Canadians, and then disappear underground again. "You can hardly stick your head around a corner without hearing a sniper's bullet zing by," one Canadian soldier remarked. The Nazis "have defended the town street by street and almost house by house," the *Times* explained. Utilizing the city's underground railroad tunnels, the Nazis had turned Ortona into "a veritable underground fortress." The Canadians responded with a new tactic called "mouse-holing." To avoid venturing into the streets, they used explosives to blast their way through the interior walls of adjoining houses, moving from house to house through the rubble. The Canadian officer in charge of the massive bombing operation "never gave a thought to the destruction he was wreaking on Ortona with his explosives," Canadian military historian Mark Zuehlke noted in his detailed chronicle of the battle. "There was a job to do, so he did it." When the battle was over, "[h]ardly a building was left intact" in "the once pleasant coastal resort," the *Times* noted. An estimated 1,375 Canadian soldiers were killed. So were more than 1,300 innocent Italian civilians. Canada regarded this as an acceptable price to pay for the devastating liberation of Ortona. The precise number of Germans killed is unknown, but it appears to have been in the low to mid-hundreds—meaning that the ratio of civilians to combatants killed by the Canadians was three or four to one, far higher than the ratio of civilians to combatants killed in Israeli counter terror operations in Gaza.[107]

FEMINISTS EXCUSING HAMAS RAPES

The systematic use of sexual violence as a weapon on October 7 should have shocked and outraged the many women's rights advocates who speak out when such acts are committed elsewhere around the world, and who emphasize the need to believe the victims. But when it came to Hamas and their Israeli victims, many of those voices fell silent—or worse.

An early example was Congresswoman Pramila Jayapal (D-Washington), chair of the Congressional Progressive Caucus, representing ninety-five strongly liberal Democrats in the House of Representatives. An outspoken advocate for rape victims, Jayapal's legislative achievements include a 2021 bill eliminating forced arbitration for sexual assault victims. Yet when it came to the amply documented mass rape of Israeli women, Jayapal expressed doubt that those rapes had occurred. In a December 4, 2023, interview on CNN, correspondent Dana Bash asked Jayapal why "a lot of progressive women," who were "quick to defend women's rights and speak out against using rape as a weapon of war," were "downright silent on what we saw on October 7 and what might be happening inside Gaza right now to these hostages." She responded, "I mean, I don't know that that's true." Bash asked Rep. Jayapal if she had "talked about it since October 7"; the congresswoman replied, "Oh, absolutely. And I have condemned what Hamas has done. I have condemned all of the actions," even though her condemnation had not mentioned the sexual assaults. When Bash persisted, "Specifically against women?," Jayapal pivoted to charging that Israel "do[es] not comply with international law," and "Frankly, morally, I think we cannot say that one war crime deserves another." Bash tried one more time: "OK, with respect, I was just asking about the women, and you turned it back to Israel. I'm asking you about Hamas, in fact," to which Jayapal responded, "I think that rape is horrific. Sexual assault is horrific. I think that it happens in war situations. Terrorist organizations like Hamas obviously are using these as tools—however, I think we must be balanced about bringing in the outrages against Palestinians."[108] She then recited statistics (circulated by Hamas) about civilian casualties in Gaza. Responding to a storm of criticism later that day, Jayapal issued a new statement, but it differed only marginally from her original remarks on CNN. Once again, she failed to say explicitly that Hamas committed sexual violence against Israeli women. She bemoaned the "pain and trauma of so many—Israelis, Palestinians and their diaspora communities." She devoted much of her "clarification" to denouncing her critics for their "outrageous insinuations" and for "deeply hurting" her ability to facilitate Mideast peace.[109]

Many leading women's organizations likewise responded to the Hamas rapes with silence, evasion, or distortions. UN Women, an organization representing all 193 member countries in the United Nations on women's concerns, has made the plight of sexual assault victims around the world a top priority. One of its signature publications, a pamphlet titled "Rape as a Tactic of War," defines "wartime sexual violence" as "one of history's greatest silences and one of today's most extreme atrocities" and refers to rape in numerous conflicts in recent decades, including Rwanda, the Balkans, Sierre Leone, and Congo.[110] But when Palestinian Arab terrorists were the rapists, and Israeli women the victims, UN Women joined the silence. Six days after the Hamas invasion, UN Women issued a brief statement "condemning the attacks on civilians in Israel and the Occupied Palestinian Territories," but without mentioning Hamas or the rape victims. For the next seven weeks, all of UN Women's public remarks about the war referred to Palestinian Arabs, with one brief mention of the hostages. The UN group also depicted Hamas in a positive light: on November 8, it tweeted, "Hamas appoints woman spokeswoman, 23 year old Isra al-Modallal," atop a photograph of al-Modallal smiling broadly, as if the appointment of a woman as a senior official of a gang of rapists represented an achievement for women.[111] An improved statement about the invasion—but not the rapes—was issued on November 24. It read, "We condemn the brutal attacks by Hamas on October 7 and continue to call for the immediate and unconditional release of all hostages." But it was quickly deleted and replaced with a statement omitting any condemnation of Hamas and simply calling for the release of the hostages.[112] On December 1, in response to widespread criticism of its earlier pronouncements, UN Women finally mentioned sexual violence in Israel. However, instead of accepting the ample forensic evidence and eyewitnesses testimony, the new statement merely acknowledged that there were "numerous accounts of gender-based atrocities and sexual violence" which should be "duly investigated." The statement also asserted that "all women, Israeli women, Palestinian women, as well as others, are entitled to a life lived in safety and free from violence," thereby implying that Palestinian women were equally victims of sexual violence, and that Israeli soldiers were sexual predators comparable to the Hamas rapists.[113]

The response of #MeToo International, the international movement against sexual violence, followed a similar trajectory. It was not until November 13, five weeks after the attack, that #MeToo commented on October 7. Its general, 335-word statement noted that sexual violence in any war is "abhorrent," "horrific," and a "war crime," but did not mention either that the victims were Jewish Israelis or that the perpetrators were Hamas and other Palestinian Arab terrorists. Its main focus was the humanitarian situation in Gaza.[114]

Two days later, after a barrage of protests, #MeToo International issued an "updated" statement acknowledging that "Israeli women have given horrific accounts of gender-based violence in the last month." Speaking about "accounts" and not affirming their credibility was inconsistent with the movement's principle of "believe the women." As in the original statement, the updated version did not identify the perpetrators as Palestinian terrorists from Gaza. It also noted that there had been "acts of gender-based violence" in "places like Israel, Palestine, Sudan, Congo, and Tigray," with the implication that both Israelis and Palestinians had engaged in such attacks. But that was false.[115]

The National Women's Studies Association (NWSA), the leading professional association of American scholars focused on women and gender, trod a similar path. Although its primary focus is academic, the NWSA periodically issues statements on current events, both at home and abroad. Its first statement about Gaza, issued four days after October 7, referred to "the dramatic escalation of violence in Palestine and Israel" without mentioning the Hamas sexual assaults and killings. It then implicitly condoned the Hamas invasion by accusing Israel of "apartheid, occupation, [and] oppression." It also condemned U.S. aid to Israel and reiterated its earlier endorsement of the Boycott-Divestment-Sanctions (BDS) campaign against Israel. The NWSA's only reference to gender was this sentence: "As feminists, we recognize that violence and war often inflict gendered and sexualized harms on women and queer, trans and non-binary people."[116] The statement promised that at the annual NWSA annual conference later that month, there would be "spaces to support one another and to share feminist resources on the recent violence and its implications," but there were no sessions or panels about rape in warfare at the event. The conference did discuss "the systemic violence in Palestine" and adopted a resolution accusing Israel of waging "a genocidal war," characterizing Gaza's residents as "a caged population," opposing U.S. aid to Israel, and declaring the association's "support for Students for Justice in Palestine."[117]

Statements by other prominent women's groups were equally slow and problematic. The National Organization for Women, which focuses on domestic issues but occasionally comments on foreign affairs, issued a 115-word statement on November 30, more than seven weeks after the Hamas attack. It referred to "the continued devastating use of rape as a weapon of war," without acknowledgment of Hamas, Israel, or the mass rape perpetrated in the war against the Jews.[118] A week later, V-day, which defines itself as "a global activist movement to end violence against all women," issued a statement condemning the use of "rape and sexual assault as a weapon of war" around the world. It cited seven countries where rape had taken place, but did not mention the mass violence against women in Israel on October 7 or its perpetrators. A lone sentence noted the need "to protect the bodies and lives of all Israeli and Palestinian women," implying that Palestinian Arab women were being equally victimized.[119]

In February 2024, several hundred self-identified feminists, most of them American (including former Black Panther militant Angela Davis and some members of the anti-Zionist group Jewish Voice for Peace) signed a letter denouncing efforts by Israeli and American Jewish feminists to draw attention to the Hamas rapes. Publicizing the rapes constituted "weaponizing the issue of sexual violence for political outcome" and was part of a conspiracy to "undermine our demands that Israel cease its genocidal massacre of Palestinians," the letter asserted.[120]

The League of Women Voters, which almost never comments on foreign affairs, made an exception for what it called "the violence in Israel and Gaza," issuing a statement on October 11 in conjunction with the International Day of the Girl Child. Even if the evidence of mass rape was only beginning to emerge by then, there was ample evidence that many girls in Israel had been massacred. Yet the League's vague statement, which made no mention of Hamas or even that Israel had been invaded, asserted only that both sides were suffering "human rights violations." The subsequent documentation of the mass sexual violence perpetrated by Hamas did not prompt the League to revisit the issue.[121]

The International Young Women's Christian Association (YWCA), for its part, took a strong interest in the issue—and came down on Hamas's side each time. A lengthy statement on October 9, 2023, refrained from acknowledging the Hamas invasion; it declared that "the root cause of the unending situation and suffering" was "the Israeli Occupation" and the "physical and psychological harassment" Palestinian Arab women "face constantly." One month later—fewer than two weeks after Israeli ground troops entered Gaza—the YWCA said Israel was "conducting genocide against Gaza" and that Gazan women were experiencing "a severe lack of menstrual hygiene products in shelters." The second statement, like the first, made no mention of the mass rape of Israeli women. The U.S. branch of the YWCA, which lists "preventing gender-based violence" as its top concern, issued its own statement on the one-year anniversary of October 7. It asserted that "many of our sisters have experienced the daily horrors" of "the Israel-Hamas war," without mentioning the mass sexual violence or any of the other atrocities perpetrated by Hamas, or even that Hamas had attacked Israel.[122]

Only a few major women's groups strongly and explicitly condemned the Hamas rapes. Planned Parenthood "unequivocally condemned the atrocities committed by Hamas" in its "brutal attack, killing over one thousand civilians, sexually assaulting women and girls and kidnapping over 200 people." Still, three-quarters of the statement was about health care in general and the humanitarian situation in Gaza; and the statement was not issued until December, two months after the attack. The Women's Media Center likewise issued an explicit condemnation of the Hamas rapes in December, but it too devoted most of its statement to general comments about sexual violence around the world.[123]

HUMAN WRONGS BY HUMAN RIGHTS ADVOCATES

Many leading human rights advocates likewise exhibited a blind spot when it came to the right of Israeli Jewish women not to be raped, tortured, and killed by Palestinian Arab terrorists.

Amnesty International excused Hamas atrocities from the start. On the day of the Hamas invasion—which Amnesty called "an operation," not an attack—it issued a statement emphasizing what it called "the root causes of these repeated cycles of violence," namely the "system of apartheid" which Amnesty falsely accused Israel of imposing. Even before Israel's ground troops had entered Gaza, Amnesty claimed, on October 20, that Israeli bombing attacks on Hamas targets were "evidence of war crimes," because Israel "failed to take feasible precautions to spare civilians." It did not offer any suggestion as to what such precautions might look like, short of refraining from bombing terrorists who embedded themselves in civilian neighborhoods.[124] Amnesty even asserted, on October 25, that Israel's attempts to save the lives of civilians in north Gaza by dropping leaflets urging them to move out of the way of impending hostilities "may amount to war crimes," because encouraging their relocation constituted "collective punishment."[125] By March, it was asserting that it was "reasonable" to accuse Israel of "genocide." It was not until July 2024 that Amnesty acknowledged that some of the Israeli hostages released the previous November reported being sexually assaulted. Of the sixty-two press releases about Gaza issued during the first year following the invasion, including those summarizing the war on its one-year anniversary, not one Amnesty statement acknowledged the mass gang-rapes of October 7. Nor did Amnesty undertake an investigation of the sexual violence.[126]

In December 2024, Amnesty issued a report in which it for the first time definitively accused Israel of committing genocide in Gaza. It did so by changing the definition of genocide. To qualify as genocidal according to international law, the acts in question must be intended to annihilate the targeted minority group. Amnesty's report declared that existing international jurisprudence on the matter depended upon "an overly cramped interpretation" of intent.[127] Therefore Amnesty decided to employ "a holistic approach," in which it looked at factors other than intent on the grounds that they provide "context" in which intent is the "only reasonable inference." Thus Amnesty charged there had been "racist and derogatory" statements by Israelis that "reflected a deeply ingrained and escalating racism towards Palestinians within Israeli society" and therefore must have paved the way to genocide.[128] Its lead example of such a statement was President Isaac Herzog saying "it's not true" that civilians from Gaza were "not aware, not involved." According to Amnesty, the fact that many buildings were destroyed in Israeli operations could "lead to Palestinians' slow death," and since

Israel must have known that could happen, it meant Israel "intended to inflict conditions of life on Palestinians in Gaza calculated to bring about their destruction." Further evidence of genocidal intent, according to Amnesty, was Israel's awareness of Gazans' "pre-existing vulnerability" due to Israel's "57- year-old occupation."[129] The report did not acknowledge that the Israeli occupation, which began in 1967, actually ended in 2005; Gaza was governed by the Palestinian Authority and Hamas for the past twenty years. When Amnesty's Israel branch publicly disagreed with the genocide accusation, its international leadership ordered the branch to shut down for the next two years.[130] By coincidence, just a few weeks earlier, the UN declined to renew the contract of its Special Advisor on the Prevention of Genocide, Alice Wairimu Nderitu, after she concluded that Israel was not committing genocide in Gaza.[131] That was the price Amnesty-Israel and Nderitu paid for speaking the truth.

Human Rights Watch was even more prolific than Amnesty International in its response to October 7. It issued fifty-one press releases about Gaza in the first eight weeks following the Hamas invasion. Their theme was moral equivalency: HRW acknowledged Hamas committed "horrific" attacks, but claimed that Israel did too. None of the news releases mentioned the Hamas gang rapes. An October 24 statement by HRW's Women's Rights Division warned about the "risk of sexual violence in Gaza" as a result of Israeli counterterror actions. Eventually, on December 12, HRW said in a statement that the "harrowing reports of sexual violence" by "Hamas-led gunmen" on October 7 "demand urgent, careful, independent, and credible investigation." Finally, in July 2024, more than nine months after the Hamas attack, Human Rights Watch acknowledged in a report that Hamas committed "deliberate and indiscriminate attacks against civilians" on October 7, including "sexual and gender-based violence." HRW claimed it was "not able to gather verifiable information through interviews with survivors of or witnesses to rape," even though many such individuals had been interviewed by the news media. It did, however, accept UN investigators' belated conclusion—based on their interviews with survivors and witnesses—that there were "multiple" instances of rape during the Hamas attack.[132]

HRW's bias against Israel in the wake of October 7 drove one of its senior officials, Danielle Haas, to resign. Haas served as editor of HRW's most prestigious publication, its annual *World Report*, from 2010 to 2023. Each year, she would ask her colleagues why the section on Israel was consistently longer than more than 90 percent of the entries, "including those highlighting corrupt dictatorships sans free speech, repressive regimes in which women are second-class citizens, and countries that practice generational forced labor," but "there never was a clear explanation" about the imbalance. After October 7, HRW's decision to pay minimal attention to the massacres demonstrated to Haas that HRW's outrage "depends not on human-rights principles, but on who is being abused and who is being accused." When at one point HRW staffers circulated a draft of a mild press release about the Gaza hostages, more than one hundred HRW researchers signed an internal petition demanding that the press release include references to "Israeli apartheid."[133]

Haas recalled, as an example of her colleagues' slant against Israel, that when HRW's senior military analyst was exposed, in 2009, as an avid collector of Nazi memorabilia, HRW denounced criticism of him as "a distraction from the real issue, which is the Israeli government's behavior." HRW staff members who tried to raise questions about "antisemitism and methodological problems related to [the group's] Israel work" in recent years were met by "hostility at worst, inaction and indifference at best" from the organization's leaders, according to Haas. After October 7, those who were uncomfortable with "the toxic climate" at HRW were so intimidated that they could express themselves "only by resorting to encrypted apps and other platforms outside internal communication systems."[134]

In explaining what brought Human Rights Watch to this state, Haas noted reports of the group accepting money from Saudi and Qatari sources. But she concluded that the root of the problem was ideological, not financial. "The political and ideological creep in many NGOs has become so pervasive and deep-rooted," she wrote, "that Israel has become their watchword of outrage, the focus of disproportionate attention, and the note to sound for signaling fealty to a human-rights movement that is increasingly hijacked by politics and dominated by groupthink."[135]

This inconsistency was epitomized in the response to October 7 by Biden administration official Samantha Power. A journalist prior to entering government service, in 2002 she had authored *A Problem from Hell: America and the Age of Genocide*, which criticized the United States and the international community for ignoring instances of mass murder. It also included multiple references to the use of rape as a weapon of genocide. She reported on Turkish forces raping Armenian women in 1915, Serbian forces imprisoning Bosnia Muslim women in "rape camps" during the ethnic cleansing atrocities in the Balkans in the 1990s, and an international war crimes tribunal's conviction of a Rwandan mayor for genocide specifically because he was responsible for systematic rape against the Tutsi minority in 1994.[136] The book led to her appointment as U.S. ambassador to the United Nations (in the Obama administration), and then director of USAID under President Biden.

Power's prolific X (Twitter) feed following October 7 included dozens of posts about Arab civilians suffering in Gaza, but not one tweet about the numerous Israeli Jewish women gang-raped by Hamas terrorists. She did tweet about sexual attacks on women in the Democratic Republic of the Congo, and, on another occasion, about "horrific sexual violence" against women in Sudan, urging her followers to check out the "important reporting by Reuters" on that subject.[137]

Power's recommendation to read the Reuters articles about rape in Sudan was ironic, since she did not mention to her followers the important reporting Reuters had also done on Hamas rapes of Israeli women. As early as October 15, Reuters had reported that Israeli forensic experts "found multiple signs of torture, rape and other atrocities" among the victims of Hamas.[138] Two days later, Reuters quoted Israeli first responders describing evidence of rape on some of the corpses they found.[139] Subsequent Reuters dispatches cited a senior Israeli police official describing "eyewitness testimony and forensics" that documented sexual assaults (Nov. 14) and noting that "Reuters has seen photos corroborating some of those accounts" (Nov. 28 and Nov. 30).[140] Yet Power did not share those Reuters reports with her readers.

BELIEVING DISINFORMATION

Previous Palestinian Arab terrorist attacks had never triggered such reactions abroad. Nor had previous Arab-Israeli wars. The vehemence, and in many instances sheer irrationality, of the reactions to October 7 raised important questions. How could so many people accept as fact assertions about Israel and Gaza that were unsupported by evidence? What caused people who are sincerely concerned about sexual violence to consciously look away from sexual violence against Israeli Jewish women? What was it about this particular terrorist attack that induced such a uniquely massive and extreme response?

THE DIFFICULTY OF ADMITTING A MISTAKE

One the most significant factors was psychological: the unwillingness of most supporters of the Palestinian cause to admit they had been fundamentally mistaken in their beliefs. Support for the Palestinian Arab agenda had always been based on the premise that Israel was primarily at fault for the Arab-Israeli conflict and that the Palestinian Arabs were innocent victims of Israel's unjust policies. This paradigm required perceiving Palestinian terrorists as over the top in their actions—but not as monsters. Then October 7 revealed them to be monsters. It also revealed (to those who paid attention) how little difference there was between Hamas and other Palestinian factions that were widely presumed to be more moderate. The logical consequence of acknowledging the barbarism would have been to spurn the barbarians' cause. Yet human reluctance to acknowledge a significant error and then deal with the consequences is a common psychological frailty. The consequence in this instance would have been giving up on a cause that has become so central to the worldview of many American champions of "Palestine" that it sometimes approaches the status of a religion.

Learning the truth about the leaders of a cherished political or social cause can be shattering, akin to members of a religious cult discovering their leader is not a prophet but a fraud. In 1954, the social scientists Leon Festinger, Henry W. Riecken, and Stanley Schachter infiltrated and studied a small Chicago-based doomsday cult known as The Seekers.

Its leader predicted a global apocalypse on December 21 of that year, from which she and her followers would be rescued by a spaceship from another planet. When the prediction failed to come true, most of the group's members manufactured rationalizations and redoubled their devotion to the cult. Rather than concede that their core belief was false, they clung to their faith, "firm, unshaken, and lasting." To do otherwise would have been too painful.[141]

Many supporters of the Palestinian Arab cause likewise opted for a dishonest reckoning after October 7. Rather than have their perception of the world turned upside down, they embraced the most upside down of theories and explanations emanating from the Hamas camp, such as that there were no rapes or beheadings on October 7; that the attackers were freedom fighters understandably provoked by Israeli occupation policies, akin to black slaves in America who rebelled against slaveowners; or that American support of Israel or unfavorable media reports about Hamas must be the result of "Zionist" control. The widespread public distrust of mainstream news media and elected officials in recent years, and the instant dissemination of far-fetched claims on social media, have made it easier for true believers to embrace such disinformation.

MAKING EVERYTHING FIT THE PARADIGM

Another factor explaining the responses to October 7 was the political and ideological lens through which many Gaza protesters viewed current events. In recent decades, some influential academics, journalists, and political partisans have promulgated the concept of intersectionality, according to which all forms of oppression and racism are interconnected.

The prevalence of this perspective in college classrooms, much of the news media, and elsewhere has created an intellectual framework through which many radicals view October 7. They do not divorce their perception of the Middle East from other issues around the world; it is part of a broader view which sees the world divided between white oppressors—including Israel and America—and oppressed nations of color. Their vision of a just world is one in which Israel has been replaced by an Arab "Palestine" and the United States has been severely humbled. When everything must fit this paradigm, then all Jews and all Israelis are seen as white oppressors—despite the fact the majority of Israelis today are of Middle Eastern or African origin, making them just as much "people of color" as everyone else in that region of the world. Included among the "oppressed" people are Palestinian Arab terrorists, who are perceived as having no choice but to use violence against their evil foe.

ECHO CHAMBERS

Some months after the signing of the 2015 Iran nuclear agreement, a *New York Times* interviewer asked President Obama's deputy national security adviser, Ben Rhodes, "to explain the onslaught of freshly minted experts cheerleading for the deal" in the months leading up to the congressional vote on it. "We created an echo chamber," Rhodes replied. The administration arranged for large numbers of arms-control experts to weigh in on social media and at think tanks, and they "became key sources for hundreds of often-clueless reporters," as the *Times* put it. "They were saying things that validated what we had given them to say," Rhodes bluntly recalled.[142]

There is a tendency among some people to sequester themselves in a cocoon of likeminded thinkers. Prior inclinations are then reinforced by the repetition of one viewpoint, especially if it is coming from someone with seemingly verified expertise, such as an academic. For some journalists covering the Iran agreement but not really understanding its details or ramifications, the most comfortable approach was to repeatedly quote ostensibly authoritative sources furnished by an administration with which they generally sympathized anyway. The more the "experts" were cited, the more other journalists turned to them, thus creating, as Rhodes put it, a veritable echo chamber for the administration's agenda.

Similarly, academics, think tank fellows, and ex-diplomats harshly critical of Israel played a significant role in influencing public opinion on the war in Gaza. Appearing frequently in the mainstream news media, at public events, and on social media as experts on the Gaza situation, they hammered away at a handful of common themes: Israel was not trying to avoid harming civilians; Israel was not permitting the entry of enough humanitarian aid; Israel was to blame for the failure of ceasefire and hostage negotiations; and since it was impossible to defeat Hamas, Israel should withdraw from Gaza and agree to creating a sovereign Palestinian Arab state in the disputed territories. The blame-Israel themes promulgated by the presumed experts created an echo chamber which made anti-Israel demonstrators feel more comfortable taking similar, albeit slightly harsher, positions.

ANTISEMITISM

Antisemitism was an additional factor driving some of the extreme reactions to October 7. Criticism of Israeli policy sometimes descended into the rank bigotry of swastika daubings, slogans invoking a "final solution," the use of "Zionist" as a pejorative for "Jew," and accusations that nonpolitical Jewish institutions such as synagogues and kosher restaurants were accomplices to genocide. Shouting "Go back to Poland!" at Jews on a New York City street had nothing to do with Israeli policies and everything to do with old-fashioned antisemitism. Just how significant a factor antisemitism was depends in part on how one defines antisemitism (see chapter 8).

FEAR OF HAMAS LOSING

Fear may also have been a factor in shaping how some Americans sympathetic to the Palestinian cause responded to October 7. If Israel was successful in its declared objective of destroying Hamas, that would preclude Hamas's own long-term objective of destroying the State of Israel. Hamas supporters in the United States had good reason to fear that the longer the Israeli operation continued, the more Hamas terrorists would be killed, and the more tunnels and other terror infrastructure would be eliminated. Calls for a "ceasefire" became, in practice, calls for Israel to cease firing Hamas. There were no rallies by ceasefire advocates urging Hamas to cease firing at Israel.

An unsavory melange of blood libels, atrocity-denials, hypocritical finger-pointing and tortured evasions characterized the response to

October 7 by anti-Israel activists and their sympathizers in the media and the community of advocacy groups. All these troubling trends would converge in the tinderbox of America's college campuses, where a war of words—and sometimes worse—would erupt with a ferocity that few had expected.

5. The War on Campus

In the aftermath of October 7, America's universities became the major battlegrounds for controversies and conflicts over Gaza, Israel, and antisemitism.

STUDENTS FOR JUSTICE IN PALESTINE

On campuses from coast to coast, chapters of Students for Justice in Palestine (SJP) organized marches, rallies, and sit-ins in support of the October 7 attack. There is evidence that at least some SJP campus leaders had prior knowledge of the attack. Just three minutes before the invasion began, SJP's Columbia University chapter posted on its previously dormant Instagram account: "We are back!" That message suggested they were returning to public activity in coordination with the Hamas attack. In addition, Shlomi Ziv, who was kidnapped from the Supernova music festival and held by Hamas for 246 days, said his captors boasted of the close relationship between Hamas and student groups at Columbia and other American universities.[1] Certainly, SJP was well prepared for what it did next, with substantial financial backing and organizational support from a Chicago-based extremist group called American Muslims for Palestine (AMP) and a left-of-center philanthropic agency, the Westchester (NY) People's Action Committee Foundation. The extent of their funding is unknown because SJP is not registered as a 501(c)(3) charity and therefore does not have to disclose its internal financial information. Numerous AMP officials had worked for, or with, groups connected to Hamas, such as the Texas-based Holy Land Foundation, identified by the U.S. Treasury Department as a Hamas front group in 2001 (Holy Land sent $12.4-million to the terrorist group between 1995 and 2001); the Islamic Association for Palestine, which in 2004 was found civilly liable in a federal district court for assisting Hamas; and the ironically named KindHearts for Charitable Development, which the U.S. Treasury Department forced to disband in 2011 after determining that it, too, was a Hamas support group.[2] In effect, Students for Justice in Palestine was tapping into the Hamas support network for both financial and organizational connections.[3]

SJP's affinity for Hamas was evident from members' private responses to October 7 as well as their public activities. A slew of private text messages exchanged by members of Boston University's SJP chapter on the day of the attack were leaked to the news media. One cheered on "the freedom fighters [who] have pushed the occupation forces back. They're so close to Tel Aviv." A student named James shared his hopes for "the State of Israel to collapse." The students' enthusiasm for anti-Israel violence long predated October 7, 2023, as demonstrated by the fact that the message thread reached back to 2021, with earlier posts lauding the violent Palestinian "resistance" and sharing outbursts of "Long live the Intifada!"[4]

The SJP's torrent of public activities defending the Hamas attack matched its members' private sentiments. Almost immediately upon the news of the Hamas invasion, the SJP national office posted an electronic "toolkit" for its campus representatives, explaining how to organize local demonstrations, design leaflets, craft petitions, and "respond to common Zionist arguments." [5] The kit included suggested hashtags and graphic templates, with one showing Gazans standing triumphantly atop a burning Israeli tank, and another depicting a terrorist paraglider above a surging mob. Much of the toolkit read like an ideological manifesto, with talking points explaining which themes and slogans the protesters should highlight.

The manifesto began by describing how "the resistance in Gaza launched a surprise operation against the Zionist enemy which disrupted the very foundation of Zionist settler society." It was "a historic win for the Palestinian resistance"—the attackers "re-entered 1948 Palestine," "gained control over illegal Israeli settlements," and "have taken occupation soldiers hostage" (actually the vast majority of the hostages were defenseless civilians). "National liberation is near," the document proclaimed. "Glory to our resistance, to our martyrs, and to our steadfast people." Now what was needed was "mass mobilization" by "the student movement for Palestine liberation on college campuses across occupied Turtle Island (so-called US and Canada) and beyond." The toolkit emphasized that student supporters of the October 7 attack were not mere onlookers or cheerleaders: "We as Palestinian students in exile are part of this movement, not in solidarity with this movement. All of our efforts continue the work and resistance of Palestinians on the ground." The way to "struggle alongside our people back home" and participate in "directly dismantling Zionism," the toolkit advised, is to "wield the political power that our organizations hold on our campuses and in our communities," and promote "a narrative which centers the legitimacy of resistance" (that is, the legitimacy of killing Israeli Jews) and "the necessity of complete liberation" (that is, "liberating" all of Israel and replacing it with "Palestine.")[6]

The toolkit then presented specific talking points and slogans, which became the themes of the protests, expressed in the demonstrators' chants and on their placards and banners, on campuses nationwide throughout the months to follow:

—*"When people are occupied, resistance is justified."* The toolkit argued that the invaders' actions were "morally just" because they were "provoked" by "75 years of settler colonialism"—that is, seventy-five years of Israel's existence.

—*All of Israel is "occupied Palestine."* Gaza had not been occupied by Israel since 2005; the "resistance" thus was against what the toolkit called " '48 Palestine," the Jewish state that had been established in 1948. This concept was encapsulated in slogans defining "Palestine" as the land "from the river to the sea"—that is, the Jordan River and the Mediterranean Sea, between which is the State of Israel.

—*Israel is committing "genocide."* How could a document written within hours of the Hamas invasion, before the Israelis had even begun striking Hamas targets, claim "genocide"? Because, the toolkit asserted, "Zionists are telling Gazans to leave"—

> meaning urging them to stay away from Hamas-controlled parts of Gaza that were likely to become battle zones—and "this is a call for genocide of Palestinians." Thus, the twisted "genocide" accusation was baked into protesters' plans even before there was a single casualty in Gaza. It became a major part of their rhetorical arsenal as soon as casualties began to mount.[7]

Among the most frequently heard chants at campus demonstrations were those involving the term Intifada, especially "Globalize the Intifada" and "There is only one solution, Intifada revolution!" The Arabic-speaking students who made up the core of the protests undoubtedly understood the meaning and context of the term, even if some of the other demonstrators may not have. The two Palestinian Arab intifadas against Israel, one lasting from 1987 to 1991 and the other from 2000 to 2005, consisted of more than one hundred suicide bombings (many on Israeli buses) as well as the machine-gun massacre of attendees at a Passover seder (thirty dead), the bombing of the Hebrew University cafeteria (nine dead, including five American students), and thousands of other bombings, shootings, stabbings, and firebombings, all of which left several thousand Israelis dead and thousands more seriously injured. To call for more intifadas was to call for a repetition of these horrors.

A number of commonly heard campus chants explicitly endorsed October 7, including "Red, black, green, and white, we support Hamas's fight!" and "Resistance by any means necessary!" In case it was not clear that those means included the mass murder of Jewish civilians, another chant clarified: "We say justice. You say how? Burn Tel Aviv to the ground!"[8]

SJP extremists also railed against Israel's very existence. They did not call for two states, the creation of a "Palestine" next to Israel; they echoed the Hamas position of one state, Palestine instead of Israel. Their campus chants made this clear: "We don't want no two states, we want all of '48"; "One, two, three, four, Israel will be no more! Five, six, seven, eight, Israel we'll eliminate!"; and "Hitler, Hitler, go back home! Palestine is ours alone!"[9]

They did not chant for mutual compromise. When they called for a "ceasefire," they were calling on Israel to cease firing at Hamas; they never urged Hamas to cease firing at Israel. They never demanded that Hamas release the hostages; on the contrary, on numerous occasions student militants tore down posters bearing photos of the hostages. They never condemned the gang rapes or beheadings; instead, they graffitied or projected "Glory to Our Martyrs," often in gigantic letters, on the side of campus buildings.[10] The possessive term "our" in "Our Martyrs" indicated a degree of intimacy resembling adulation, the same tone as the SJP toolkit. The protesters did not wear or share peace symbols; they circulated emojis of terrorist paragliders, and wore T-shirts with the images of prominent Palestinian terrorists.[11]

Flags were ubiquitous at campus protests—as well as at pro-Hamas rallies in general—and frequently became a point of contention. Although media outlets commonly refer to the red, green, black, and white banner as "the Palestinian flag," there never has been a sovereign state called Palestine, and the flag's origins reflect this. The flag began as the emblem of one of the groups promoting Arab culture or nationalism in the Ottoman Turkish Empire in the early 1900s. When the Palestine Liberation Organization was established in 1964 to pursue Israel's destruction, its committee on symbols adopted the old Ottoman era banner as the official PLO flag. It continues to represent a specific terrorist organization, the PLO, to this day.

In the spring of 2024, students on various campuses tore down the American flag that customarily flies on university property and replaced it with the PLO flag. On the George Washington University campus, they draped a PLO flag over the statue of George Washington.[12] At Harvard, they hoisted the PLO flag in a spot customarily reserved for the American flag, and shouted "Shame!" at the campus security officials who removed it.[13] American flags were burned at pro-Hamas marches in Manhattan, Brooklyn, and Chicago, as well as at the protest encampments at Columbia University and the University of Washington.[14] The official flags of Hamas and Hezbollah (the Lebanon-based Islamist terror group) were unfurled at some of these events.[15]

Hours after Jewish students at Northwestern University set up 1,200 American and Israeli flags as a memorial to the October 7 victims, the flags were torn to pieces and smeared with red paint.[16] A City University of New York law professor who waved an American flag near one rally was confronted by protesters who denounced it as "a Nazi flag" and "a fascist symbol."[17] At the University of North Carolina at Chapel Hill, radical students replaced the American flag with a PLO flag, and after local police removed it and restored the American one, dozens of fraternity members set up a round-the-clock human chain to physically guard it from further attacks. An outpouring of public support generated more than $500,000 to a GoFundMe campaign to maintain the guard.[18]

SJP national headquarters encouraged expressions of anti-American hatred by circulating, on social media, a message from anti-Israel activists at Columbia University that characterized the Gaza protests as part of a broader struggle against America. "Divestment [against Israel] is not an incremental goal," the message declared. "True divestment necessitates nothing short of the total collapse of the university structure and the American empire itself. To divest from this is to undermine and eradicate America as we know it." The message was authored by Palestine Action US, which also boasted of vandalizing AIPAC's offices, property at Columbia University, and various banks and factories. It also publicly urged setting "pigs" (police officers) on fire. Palestine Action US later changed its name to "Unity of Friends," a Palestinian Islamic Jihad phrase that encouraged terror factions to unite.[19]

JEWISH STUDENTS ASSAULTED

Many Jewish students were subjected to physical assaults, vandalism, and acts of harassment and intimidation following October 7. A Hillel-ADL poll one month later found 73 percent of Jewish college students experienced or witnessed antisemitism during the prior month.[20] By February 2024, the number of antisemitic incidents on campuses had surpassed one thousand, an increase of more than 700 percent compared to the same period a year earlier. At least forty-four of the reported incidents were physical attacks. Hillel International reported a total of 1,854 antisemitic incidents on college campuses for the entire academic year of 2023–24, and another 1,039 during the first semester of 2024–25.[21]

At the University of Massachusetts-Amherst on November 3, 2023, a Jewish student was setting up a symbolic Shabbat table at a vigil to call attention to the Israeli hostages when a student in a nearby building "charged out of the building and punched me in the head several times," the victim recounted. "I put my hands up to protect my face and he grabbed the flag and kicked me in the chest several times and shoved me." The attacker then produced a foot-long knife and "kept stabbing the Israeli flag until it was completely destroyed."[22]

At Yale, *keffiyeh*-garbed extremists surrounded a visibly religious Jewish student who was observing their protest. For long minutes, they screamed anti-Israel vulgarities, shoved a boombox blaring a profane anti-Israel rap song in her face, and then jabbed her in the eye with the pole on which they had hoisted a PLO flag. "Ask yourself if this would happen to a student who did not look visibly Jewish," she wrote afterwards. The terrifying experience reminded her of what it must have been like for her mother, growing up as a Jewish girl in Iran. "Her neighbors threw rocks at her for being a Jew," she noted. "She has a scar on her eyelid to this day."[23]

At Tulane University, some of the students attending an October 26 rally sponsored by Tulane4Palestine, held partly on campus and partly nearby, yelled "Gas the Jews!" and "Get in the shower!" They also assaulted three Jewish students, leaving one with severe head injuries and another with a broken nose. One hundred Tulane students subsequently signed a letter to the administration documenting the antisemitic activities of another student organization, Tulane Students for a Democratic Society (TSDS), which served as a stand-in for SJP since SJP was not a recognized campus organization. The TSDS "has instigated fights, doxxed and physically threatened Jewish students, and recently falsely accused one of Tulane's top Jewish professors . . . of assaulting a student," the letter revealed.[24]

The situation was similar at Columbia University. About one-fourth of the fifty-four Jewish students at Columbia interviewed by the campus newspaper in late October said they had been harassed or attacked, and more than half said they felt unsafe on campus. At one point, the campus Hillel went into lockdown in response to indications of an imminent mob attack. Jewish students organized a system of escorts so that none of them would have to walk across the Columbia campus alone.[25] By early December, many were saying that antisemitism had become "the new normal" on their campus.[26]

At Ohio State University, radicals punched two Jewish students while calling them "kike Zionists." Student extremists blocked an entrance to the City College of New York library and shoved a cell phone into the face of a Jewish student who tried to walk by, to record her despite her objections. A rally on that campus included placards bearing the threatening slogan "Zionists Are Among Us."[27] Two Jewish students at DePaul University who held a sign inviting passersby to talk to them about Israel were assaulted by masked extremists, leaving one with a concussion and the other a broken wrist.[28] At the University of California at Berkeley, militants grabbed a Jewish student by the neck and tried to steal his Israeli flag. At a George Mason University fraternity house, they assaulted a Jewish student and ripped his Star of David necklace from his neck. They surrounded and taunted a Jewish student at the New School, in Manhattan, and shoved and accosted a Jewish student outside the Harvard Business School. A bandana-masked extremist shouting "F—all of you prick crackers!" assaulted and injured a Columbia student posting a leaflet about the hostages; a dean advised the victim to leave campus because the university could not ensure his safety.[29] There were other known incidents, and likely a great many that went unreported, because some victims feared reprisals or doubted authorities would take appropriate action.

In November 2023, a Hillel-ADL poll of 3,084 college students nationwide found that 46 percent of Jewish students felt physically safe on campus (as opposed to 67 percent before October 7); that only 33 percent (down from 66 percent) felt emotionally safe; that just 39 percent (as opposed to 64 percent before) felt comfortable with others knowing they were Jewish; and that 44 percent (previously 64 percent) viewed their university as "welcoming and supportive of Jewish students." In a related poll, 37 percent said they had needed to hide their Jewish identity on campus.[30] Poll results also pointed to problems with the Diversity-Equity-Inclusion (DEI) programs established on many campuses. Only 18 percent of the Jewish students who had completed DEI training reported that their trainers had acknowledged the problem of antisemitism.[31]

Another study, conducted in November and December 2023, divided the nearly two thousand respondents at fifty-one American universities and colleges into groups by levels of anti-Jewish hostility on campus, and found that from 39 percent to 58 percent of the Jewish students were "very concerned about antisemitism from the left," and 12 percent to 16 percent were "very concerned" about antisemitism from the right.[32] The responses reflected key trends in antisemitism on contemporary campuses. The major sources of antisemitism on campuses in the aftermath of October 7 are pro-Palestinian groups on the political far left that despise Israel and, by extension, Jewish students. They are supplemented by socialist or Marxist students who attribute the world's evils to racism and capitalism and see all "liberation struggles" as connected; in their view, Israel and Jews are part of the white privileged class, and therefore represent the enemy of both the Palestinian Arab cause and justice generally. By contrast, there do not appear to be any chapters of the KKK or other white supremacist groups on college campuses, although small pockets of such extremists undoubtedly exist at various schools, and some of them may be responsible for incidents such as the daubing of swastikas.

HOW UNIVERSITIES RESPONDED

From the start, many pro-Hamas protests ran afoul of internal university regulations. Some rallies violated rules against trespassing since the organizers did not request official permission to hold them. Many participants wore masks as a way to express their fanatical sentiments without consequence, violating various universities' code of conduct. Rallies often involved extreme levels of noise—shouting, banging on drums and other objects, and loud music that disrupted fellow students' studies. Jewish passersby were also frequently harassed. Yet many universities were reluctant to take disciplinary action against students.

Many university administrations likewise failed to hold extremist faculty members to account, despite the fact that neither the principle of free speech nor a tenured position necessarily prevented the university from disciplining or even firing faculty whose expressions were deemed in violation of the school's code of conduct. In 2016, for example, Oberlin College fired a professor for posting anti-America and anti-Israel conspiracy theories on her Facebook page; in 2017, Rutgers University disciplined a professor for posting antisemitic cartoons on his Facebook page; and in 2020, Babson College fired a professor for writing on his Facebook page that Iran should announce sites in the United States that it would bomb.[33] Cornell history professor Russell Rickford hailed October 7 as "exhilarating" and "energizing"; he took a leave of absence for one semester, during which he spoke at pro-Hamas rallies on campus, and then resumed his regular teaching duties without having faced any disciplinary action.[34] Another Cornell history professor, Eric Cheyfitz, organized an anti-Israel "teach-in" on "settler colonialism" as part of the campus protests; the university then invited him to teach a course called "Gaza, Indigeneity, Resistance."[35]

Four days after the Hamas invasion, Egyptian scholar-activist Mohamed Abdou tweeted, "I'm with Hamas & Hezbollah & Islamic Jihad"; Columbia nonetheless hired him to teach "Decolonial-Queerness and Abolition" in the Spring 2024 semester. Under questioning by a congressional committee, Columbia president Minouche Shafik said Abdou had been "terminated," but he apparently continued teaching until the end of the semester as planned.[36] Joseph Massad, professor of Arab politics at Columbia, praised what he called "the Palestinian resistance" of October 7 as "awesome" in an article he authored.[37] President Shafik told Congress that Massad had been removed as chair of an academic review committee because of his statements; Massad clarified that he was not removed, but his one-year term was due to conclude in a few weeks.[38]

Ambereen Dadabhoy, associate professor of literature at Harvey Mudd College, tweeted that October 7 was "real heroism and resistance." Osman Umarji, lecturer in education at the University of California-Irvine, told his students that October 7 was "a gift from Allah to the world." The October 7 attackers were "merely defending themselves," tweeted Rabab Abdulhadi, director of the Arab and Muslim studies program at San Francisco State University. Danny Shaw, a lecturer in Race, Ethnicity, Class, and Gender at the City University of New York, addressed himself to the Jewish community at a pro-Hamas rally, shouting, "Go back to Yiddish land!" A lecturer at the University of California at Berkeley offered extra credit for any student who participated in protests "against the settler colonial occupation of Gaza" or watched a "short documentary on Palestine" that she recommended; the university's response was to broaden the criteria for the extra credit to include any Middle East-related activity or film.[39] A guest lecturer in a mandatory course on "structural racism" at the UCLA Medical School demanded that students bow down to "mama earth" while chanting "Free, Free Palestine"; at least half complied, according to eyewitnesses.[40] A lecturer in global and civic studies at Stanford University compelled Jewish students in his class to stand in a corner of the room so that they could see "what Israel does to the Palestinians." He then belittled the Holocaust, saying "colonizers like Israel killed more than six million." He was temporarily suspended, not fired.[41]

At the University of California-Berkeley, several hundred extremists besieged an event where an Israeli speaker was scheduled to appear. Shouting "Intifida! Intifada!," and in at least one case calling a Jewish student "a dirty Jew," the rioters shattered a glass door, assaulted three Jewish students, and forced police to evacuate the audience. The administration responded with a statement that did not even mention Jews or antisemitism, only the importance of "an inclusive civil society."[42] University administrators at Middlebury College ordered Jewish students planning a vigil for victims of Hamas to remove the word "Jewish" from all literature associated with the event, and to refrain from displaying Israeli flags at the vigil, lest anti-Israel activists find them provocative.[43]

A study of the public activity of faculty members at branches of the University of California between October 7, 2023, and March 15, 2024, found an 1,100 percent increase in anti-Zionist advocacy.[44] In February 2024, anti-Israel academics established a new organization, Faculty for Justice in Palestine (FJP), for the declared purpose of "supporting and amplifying the work of Students for Justice in Palestine." Like SJP, FJP's mission statement asserted that its goal is to fight "the 75+ years of Israel's violent, repressive occupation," another way of saying that it regards Israel's very creation, in 1948, as an illegal occupation. Also like SJP, FJP did not register as a tax-deductible organization and therefore is not required to disclose its sources of funding. As of November 2024, FJP's website listed 125 universities and colleges where the organization has chapters. A study by the campus monitoring group Amcha Initiative, covering the period October 2023 through May 2024, found that campuses with FJP chapters had more than seven times the number of physical attacks on Jewish students than campuses without FJP chapters. Pro-Hamas demonstrations on those campuses on average lasted two and a half times longer, and tent encampment protests lasted almost five times as long. Students at those schools were almost eleven times more likely to demand divestment from Israel, and the divestment resolutions were five times more likely to pass.[45]

HARVARD

On the evening of October 7, before the Israelis had buried their dead, thirty-three student groups at Harvard issued a statement accusing Israel of being "entirely responsible" for the "unfolding violence," because of "the ongoing annihilation of Palestinians."[46] Internal Harvard emails released by a congressional committee in 2024 revealed the discussions between President Claudine Gay and the members of the Harvard Corporation, the university's governing board, over the language to be included in their response to the Hamas assault. An early draft included the sentence, "We denounce this act of terror," but that was deleted. Medical school dean George Q. Daley objected to calling the attack "violent" because "it sound[s] like assigning blame when it's best we express horror at the carnage that is unfolding." The word "violent" was dropped. Provost (later president) Alan Garber initially supported describing the attack as "violent," but backed down after President Gay asked him to change his position for the sake of "getting to yes." A reference to the Israeli hostages in an early draft was dropped after law school dean (later provost) John Manning protested that it would create an impression that Harvard did not care about those "who may be hurt in the escalation of the conflict." Vice president Marc Goodheart hoped there "might still be a way to dissociate" the university from the statement by the thirty-three student groups, but he was overruled by his colleagues. The final statement, signed by Gay and seventeen other administrators, said they were "heartbroken by the death and destruction unleashed by the attack by Hamas," but did not mention the anti-Israel declaration by the student groups.[47]

The next day, in response to criticism from Jewish alumni and students, Gay issued a second statement, in her name only, which condemned "the terrorist atrocities perpetrated by Hamas." She alluded to the statement by the thirty-three student groups but did not denounce it, saying only that its authors did not speak for the university.[48] Two days after that, President Gay issued yet another statement, again condemning Hamas but not its supporters at Harvard.[49] Meanwhile, the campus was erupting. In the days following October 7, a number of Harvard students posted pro-terror or antisemitic comments on social media. One post asserted, "I proudly accept the label of terrorist." Another, referring to Hamas burning Jews alive, declared "let em cook" next to a PLO flag emoji. Another responded to an Israeli flag emoji with an image of a baby's head severed from the rest of its body.[50] On campus, a mob of Harvard students surrounded and harassed a Jewish student who was trying to navigate past crowds of pro-Hamas demonstrators who were spread out across a campus lawn and pavement in a "die-in." Protesters shoved kefiyyehs in his face as they followed him, shouting "Shame! Shame! Shame!" Among the mob leaders was Ibrahim Bharmal, editor of the *Harvard Law Review*.[51] During the third week of October alone, there were five separate anti-Israel protests on campus featuring chants of "From the river to the sea."[52]

Appeals by Jewish students and alumni to President Gay to denounce that chant prompted a vigorous discussion within the university leadership. Board member Penny Pritzker wrote President Gay that a "river to the sea" placard at a recent protest was "clearly an antisemitic sign which calls for the annihilation of the Jewish state and Jews." Pritzker added that she was "being asked by some why we would tolerate that and not signage calling for lynchings by the K.K.K." Gay consulted with Provost Garber, who commented that the slogan's "genocidal implications when used by Hamas supporters seem clear enough to me, but that's not the same as saying that there is a consensus that the phrase itself is always antisemitic." Gay, for her part, worried that calling the phrase antisemitic would "prompt [people to ask] what we're doing about it, i.e., discipline."[53]

In the face of mounting criticism over her administration's response to these developments, President Gay announced, on October 27, the creation of an Antisemitism Advisory Group, consisting of seven faculty members and alumni, and one student representative. She pledged that the group would work with her "to develop a robust strategy for confronting antisemitism on campus." Gay turned over the "river to the sea" question to her Antisemitism Advisory Group and issued a long statement, on November 9, listing the names of the group's members, topics it hoped to examine, and counseling services the university offered to students victimized by antisemitism. Near the end, she briefly noted that "a great many people" believe the slogan "'From the river to the sea' . . . implies the eradication of Jews from Israel," but she declined to endorse that view.[54]

Nonetheless, more than one hundred Harvard faculty members, from eight different schools, denounced Gay's statement as "imprudent" and "dangerously one-sided."[55] Subsequently it emerged that hundreds of Harvard faculty members, including History Department chairman Sidney Chalhoub, belonged to a group called "Harvard Faculty and Staff for Justice in Palestine." The group would later come to public attention in February 2024, when its Instagram account showcased an antisemitic cartoon showing a hand with a Star of David lynching two men, one Arab and one black. Afterwards, the Harvard administration condemned "social media posts containing deeply offensive antisemitic tropes," but did not criticize, or even name, the group responsible.[56]

In December, Gay's Antisemitism Advisory Group presented her with its recommendations, including holding student organizations accountable for abiding by the university's rules; countering antisemitic speech; reviewing the failure of Harvard's Office of Equity, Diversity, Inclusion, and Belonging to address antisemitism; and investigating the potential influence of "dark money" from Iran, Qatar, and terrorist-affiliated groups on campus. When Gay failed to act on any of the recommendations, committee member Rabbi David Wolpe, a visiting scholar at Harvard's Divinity School, resigned in protest. "The things that I felt needed to happen, almost immediately, didn't happen," Wolpe explained, and he did not want to "give [the committee] legitimacy when nothing is happening."[57] The rest of the committee dissolved itself shortly afterwards.[58] Several weeks later, the administration reconstituted the advisory group and appointed as its co-chair Prof. Derek Penslar, a historian who had accused Israel of "apartheid" and "ethnic cleansing," and who had claimed that "outsiders took a very real problem" of antisemitism at Harvard "and proceeded to exaggerate its scope."[59] A subsequent Congressional investigation concluded that despite "an unprecedented explosion of virulent antisemitism on its campus," Harvard's leaders "failed to implement the recommendations" made by the antisemitism advisory group; the Harvard administration essentially used the group's existence "for show," to give the appearance of concern about the problem while not taking any concrete steps to address it.[60]

Meanwhile, the Harvard administration sought to "balance" its creation of an antisemitism task force by also establishing a Presidential Task Force on Combating Anti-Muslim and Anti-Arab Bias, although there had not been any rallies at Harvard calling for the mass murder of Arabs. The co-chair of the new task force, Middle Eastern Studies professor Ali Asani, was revealed to have signed a letter embracing the "Palestinian liberation struggle," accusing Israel of "ethnonationalist violence," and demanding that the United States halt all aid to the Jewish state. Asani also signed a letter opposing any disciplinary action against pro-Hamas protesters on campus.[61]

All the while, in Harvard classrooms, professors teaching about the Middle East were branding Israel as "racist" and "genocidal," portraying Palestinian Arabs as "innocent victims of Jewish (white) oppression," and depicting terrorist groups as legitimate "political movements," according to a May 2024 report by the Harvard Jewish Alumni Alliance based on conversations with dozens of Jewish students and faculty. Such courses were "indoctrination, not education" and "a 12-week hate fest." Visiting speakers and department-organized events on campus reinforced these themes. Jewish students in such classes largely remained silent, fearing grade reprisals.[62]

COLUMBIA

The responses to October 7 at Columbia University followed a trajectory similar to Harvard's: an extreme pro-Hamas declaration by student groups, a series of pro-Hamas rallies on campus, harassment and assaults against Jewish students, and a weak stance by the university administration.

Two days after the Hamas invasion, fifteen Columbia student groups released a statement denouncing "Israeli aggression" and condemning the Jewish state for fighting back. "Israel does not have the right to defend its occupation," the students declared, by which they meant defend its existence. The Columbia administration did not comment on the declaration. Dozens of other student groups announced that in response to the Hamas attack, they were joining an anti-Israel campus coalition called "Columbia University Apartheid Divest."[63]

Three days later, the campus chapters of Students for Justice in Palestine and the anti-Zionist Jewish Voice for Peace (JVP) organized the first in a series of raucous gatherings on campus. According to the *Columbia Spectator*, the participants shouted "Free, free Palestine" and "From the river to the sea." In conjunction with the rally, the two groups issued an open letter declaring they "stand in full solidarity with Palestinian resistance against over 75 years of Israeli settler-colonialism and apartheid" (meaning since Israel's creation seventy-five years earlier). Some protesters tore down posters of Israeli hostages, and one assaulted an Israeli student with a stick. Jewish students reported incidents in which pro-Hamas students shouted antisemitic slurs, ripped off their jewelry while going to and from synagogue, berated them for showing support for Zionism, and burned Israeli flags.[64] Complaints they filed about such harassment were "treated as evidence that they had mental health problems" and they were "directed to counseling services," according to Columbia's Task Force on Antisemitism.[65]

The dean of the Columbia Law School, Gillian Lester, issued a statement bemoaning the "violence that erupted in Israel and Gaza" without saying who was responsible for that eruption.[66] After a storm of criticism, Lester issued a second statement acknowledging that Hamas carried out "atrocious terrorist attacks," and added that students were feeling "trauma, fear and despair" as a result of both the Hamas attack "and Israel's subsequent declaration of war."[67] Several weeks later, Lester resigned.[68]

On November 10, the Columbia administration announced it was suspending both SJP and JVP because their events had "included threatening rhetoric and intimidation." The suspension was effective until the end of the semester, which was just a few weeks away. In practice, the suspension did not last even that long. Within days, both groups were holding protests on campus, sometimes under their own names, sometimes under different ones. At some of the events, they chanted "From the river to the sea, Palestine will be free" and "Intifada, intifada, long live the intifada," the very activities that had led to their suspension. According to Jewish students monitoring the situation, the groups were even more active than before, holding events "almost on a daily basis." The very next month, Columbia's Barnard College invited SJP founder Hatem Bazian to speak on campus.[69]

Another recently formed group, Columbia Social Workers 4 Palestine (CSWP)—which praised SJP but was technically not associated with it—ramped up its activities following the other groups' suspension. At a December 6 CSWP "teach-in" on the subject of "Significance of the October 7th Palestinian Counteroffensive," a speaker praised the Hamas killers for "their refusal to be dominated . . . through creativity, determination, and combined strength, the masses can accomplish great feats." The university took no action.[70]

A campus incident in January 2024 echoed the 1983 Arrabe "poisoning" libel (see chapter 4). Two students sprayed an unknown odorous substance at participants in an anti-Israel rally outside Columbia's main library. Two dozen self-described "victims" claimed they were targeted in "a chemical attack" by "IDF veterans" that inflicted "burning eyes, headaches, and nausea." Palestinian Arab student Layla Saliba told reporters she was in "severe pain." Some pundits alleged that the Israeli army had developed the toxic substance for use against Arab demonstrators. The episode was widely cited as proof that pro-Israel activists were just as raucous, if not more so, than pro-Hamas protesters. Emails released by the congressional committee a year later revealed that at the time, Vice President of Public Safety Gerald Lewis wrote to his colleagues about the "chemical attack" allegation, saying, "I was in the thick of the rally with my personnel and to my knowledge this is untrue," and "We also have not had any reports of such actions from our personnel." Columbia officials' account of the incident as sent to the FBI expressed doubt about the claims made by the anti-Israel protesters. In public, however, Columbia asserted that the perpetrators had carried out "serious crimes, possible hate crimes." Even after determining that the substance was a "non-toxic, legal, novelty spray" with a mildly unpleasant odor, a fact confirmed by viewing the students' purchase receipt from Amazon, Columbia immediately banned the two student perpetrators from campus "while the law enforcement investigation proceeds," then revealed in April that they had been formally suspended.[71] When one of the students sued, Columbia paid him $395,000 in an out-of-court settlement, belatedly acknowledged that the substance was "not any bio-chemical weapon, illicit substance or personal protective spray," and retroactively canceled the suspensions.[72]

Three weeks after the October 7 invasion, Columbia president Minouche Shafik had announced the establishment of a Task Force on Antisemitism. Four months later, the group issued a twenty-four-page analysis of the situation on campus and a list of recommendations. While acknowledging that "there have been repeated violations of the rules on protests," the task force warned against any "overly aggressive response" such as "forcible removal of protesters." Instead, it recommended that security officers inform trespassers that "they are violating the rules, offer a card with the relevant rules, and ask them to disperse within a specified period of time." As if protesters did not already know that trespassing is a crime and a violation of their university's rules of conduct, task force members predicted that with a card in hand, "most protesters will choose to comply with the rules." The task force also urged the university to seek "informal resolutions" and avoid formal disciplinary processes for violators. Since, "unfortunately, a number of students have not participated in informal proceedings in recent months," the university should tell them that if they "attend an informal meeting," they will "not be required to agree to an informal resolution."[73]

On the specific question of pro-genocide chants at Columbia, the task force noted that the Rules of University Conduct define "discriminatory harassment" to "subjecting an individual to unwelcome conduct . . . that creates an intimidating, hostile, or abusive working, learning or campus living environment," such as "verbal abuse, epithets, or slurs; negative stereotyping; [and] threatening, intimidating, and hostile acts." The task force named three phrases that would qualify: "F*** the Jews," "gas the Jews" and "Hitler was right"—"but fortunately no one at Columbia has been shouting these phrases," the task force reported. The task force equivocated on the meaning of "chants at protests like 'Globalize the Intifada' and 'Death to the Zionist State.'" While "many have heard these . . . as calls for violence against them and their families," "others feel strongly that they are not." To say that calling for an intifada is not a call for violence against Jews belies the historical fact that the intifadas consisted of mass violence resulting in the murder of thousands of Jews.[74]

MIT

> The MIT Jewish community huddled together in Hillel, supporting one another, as a swelling crowd loudly called for the extermination of our friends and family. Outside, the crowd was chanting "one solution, intifada revolution," using a term which connotes violent uprising against Jews.

Those were the opening words of a Jewish student's chilling description of a post-October 7 eruption on the Massachusetts Institute of Technology campus. "To say that I felt unsafe," he continued, "would be a gross understatement of the fear and horror I experienced as a group of students from the university which I have chosen to call my home supported violent, indiscriminate attacks against the home of my people."[75] This was America in 2023, not Kiev in 1903 or Warsaw in 1943; nobody at MIT was murdered or deported. But the spirit of terrorizing Jews was not unprecedented—and therefore the potential for a repeat of past tragedies felt very real. So did the feeling of abandonment. The student's "sense of belonging" to the MIT community "came crashing down as I observed the Institute's passivity and complacence in the face of violent speech." While the MIT administration might feel compelled to permit such speech, at least it should condemn it, he said. "MIT has failed to fulfill this responsibility."[76]

MIT students were among the first to cheer the Hamas slaughter. On October 8, while 1,200 dead bodies still lay strewn throughout towns in southern Israel, the MIT Coalition Against Apartheid (CAA) endorsed the killers' right "to resist oppression" and asserted that "the Israeli regime" was "responsible for all unfolding violence." Two days later, President Sally Kornbluth posted a video message. "The brutality perpetrated on innocent civilians in Israel by terrorists from Hamas . . . can never be justified," she said. "And now we are bracing for a prolonged conflict that will also gravely harm or kill many innocent Palestinians in Gaza." While many innocent Gazans would indeed be harmed, her juxtaposition implied that both sides ultimately would be equally guilty of taking innocent lives. Yet it was never Israel's objective to slaughter Gazan civilians, but to eradicate Hamas, and the deaths of innocents would be the result of Hamas inciting a war and using civilians as human shields (see chapter 4). President Kornbluth also failed to mention CAA's pro-violence rhetoric. She emphasized that MIT "cherish[es] free expression," while expressing hope that "the rhetoric on our own campus does not escalate to the point of personal attacks, harassment or violence." The implication was that the Coalition would be free to chant genocidal slogans so long as they did not turn into physical violence.[77]

In the weeks to follow, pro-Hamas students "harassed MIT staff members in their offices for being Jewish" and "interrupted classes" without any meaningful administrative response, to the point that "many Jewish students fear leaving their dorm rooms and have stated that they feel MIT is not safe for Jews," the MIT Israel Alliance reported. On November 9 (the anniversary of the 1938 Kristallnacht pogrom in Nazi Germany), CAA staged a protest in the lobby of the main building on campus. Administration officials and faculty members warned Jewish students to use a rear entrance or stay away from the building entirely that day and avoid the Hillel House. Afterwards, President Kornbluth wrote that "the protesters became disruptive, loud and sustained," forcing the administration to tell them (the group was not named) to leave the scene or face "suspension." Some left. As it turned out, those who did not leave were not suspended; Kornbluth said she was concerned about "collateral consequences for the students, such as visa issues," meaning that some of the pro-Hamas students were foreigners who might be deported for violating the conditions of their visas. Therefore, she announced, an unspecified number of protesters would only be "suspended from non-academic campus activities."[78]

Finally, three months later, after the CAA held yet another disruptive takeover of a campus building, President Kornbluth announced that the group would be temporarily suspended. At the same time, she emphasized that her action was "not related to the content of their speech"—such as calling for the mass murder of Jews—and "we shouldn't feel it's ok to vilify everyone who advocates for the Palestinian people as 'supporting Hamas,'" although the CAA's actions and statements would support that interpretation of its position.[79]

Meanwhile, Kornbluth's declared intention after October 7 to combat campus antisemitism met an untimely fate. She had called on a group of Jewish faculty members to advise her on the initiative. In January 2024, however, MIT chancellor Melissa Nobles announced that the planned advisory group would be diversified into a broader undertaking called "Standing Together Against Hate," which would consist of four public panels, on "antisemitism," "anti-Palestinian racism," "Islamophobia," and "campus freedom of expression." One of the speakers chosen for the Islamophobia program was Dalia Mogahed, who had defended the October 7 attack as an expression of "the right to resist" and called Israelis "savages" who "kill babies" and "bomb hospitals." In February, the Jewish faculty members on the advisory committee announced they were disbanding the group, since President Kornbluth had not consulted them regarding the selection of speakers, or anything else. The faculty members warned that the scheduled panels would "only continue to marginalize Jewish members of the MIT community who are already traumatized by the antisemitic incidents on MIT's campus from the fall, and leave them vulnerable to further harassment and discrimination, none of which has yet to be properly addressed by the MIT senior leadership."[80]

YALE

Among those murdered in southern Israel on October 7 was Eitan Neeman, a clinical fellow at Yale's School of Medicine who was a reserve combat medic. Despite that connection, the statements issued by Yale University leaders in response to the Hamas invasion were weak and vague, and contrasted sharply with how Yale had responded to other events, such as the George Floyd killing. Two days after the Hamas attack, the vice president for university life, Kimberly Goff-Crews, issued a "Statement on the Violent Events in Israel and Gaza" that "mourned" the "violence taking place in Israel and Gaza." There was no reference to Hamas, terrorism, or Jews, nor any condemnation. Two-thirds of the vice president's 319 words consisted of contact information for campus mental health support groups.[81]

By contrast, Yale's response to the death of George Floyd was strong and direct, and came from the top. President Peter Salovey's statement, "Yale Leadership Addresses the Murder of George Floyd and the Legacy of Racist Violence," characterized the loss of human life as "a national emergency" and part of a pattern of "racism, nativism, and bigotry too pervasive in society today and throughout our country's history." The 783-word statement, more than twice as long as the October 7 statement, was followed by separate and in many cases equally lengthy letters of condemnation from the deans of Yale's schools of law, medicine, art, drama, public health, and eight other schools, followed by separate letters from four Yale cultural centers. The eighteen letters showed that the university administration knew how to make its feelings known when it wanted to.[82]

On October 10, after an outpouring of criticism over President Salovey's silence and Vice President Goff-Crews's flawed statement, Salovey issued his own statement. It named Hamas, called the attack "terrorism," and condemned it "in the strongest possible terms." But it also conflated the deaths of Israeli victims and Hamas terrorists, describing the casualties as "over 1,700 individuals in the region," and did not mention Jews or antisemitism.[83] Four weeks later, Salovey finally acknowledged the increased antisemitism in the United States, but he did so by bracketing it within what he claimed were the "waves of hatred toward members of Jewish, Muslim, Israeli, Palestinian and Arab communities at home, across the nation, and worldwide." His implication was that the levels of victimization of those groups were similar, an assertion not supported by hate crimes statistics.[84]

The Yale administration responded very differently to statements by anti-Israel and pro-Israel faculty members. Zareena Grewal, a professor of ethnic studies, tweeted about October 7: "My heart is in my throat. . . . [I]t's been such an extraordinary day. . . . Palestinians have every right to resist through armed struggle." She defended the murder of Israeli civilians by saying "settlers are not civilians." Since the attacks took place in areas of pre-1967 Israel, she was effectively saying that all Israelis were "settlers" and therefore deserved to be raped and murdered. The Yale administration defended Prof. Grewal on the grounds of free speech.[85] At the same time, the administration continued its year-long investigation of a Jewish professor, Evan Morris, over his op-ed (in an off-campus Jewish newspaper) about antisemitism at Yale, in which he mentioned that a researcher at Yale's medical school had "blocked an Israeli postdoc from speaking" on campus. The university formally "rebuked" Morris because it said it could not confirm the accuracy of the term "blocked" in that sentence.[86]

The Yale administration's double standard also was evident in its response to Israel-related events on campus. Just a few days after October 7, the main pro-Hamas group on campus, Yalies4Palestine, mobilized students for a rally at New Haven city hall in support of "Palestinian resistance against violent settler colonial oppression." A spokesman said that "the Israeli Zionist regime" alone was "responsible for the unfolding violence." The featured chant at the rally was "From the river to the sea, Palestine will be free." The group's post about the event declared: "Breaking out of a prison requires force, not desperate appeals to the colonizer."[87] Similar rallies took place on the Yale campus in the weeks to follow. In a faculty-sponsored seminar in November, two extreme critics of Israel, Nadia Abu El Haj (of Barnard) and Amaahi Bishara (of Tufts), praised the October 7 perpetrators as "a resistance group" and alleged that Israel was "trying to inflict as much harm, damage, and death as possible." Pressed by questioners to denounce Hamas unequivocally, both speakers declined.[88] A statement by the Yale administration lauded the event as enabling "community members of all backgrounds to engage intellectually and respectfully," and dismissed reports that pro-Israel students had been denied admission.[89] The administration responded very differently when a truck appeared on campus displaying the photos and names of six Yale students, whom it labeled "Yale's leading antisemites" because they signed statements blaming Israel for the Hamas attack. The administration issued a statement denouncing "this cowardly act of harassment and attempted intimidation." It did not acknowledge the students' actions that had triggered the antisemitism charge.[90]

GEORGE WASHINGTON UNIVERSITY

Students for Justice in Palestine activists at George Washington University pioneered a protest tactic that would soon be mimicked on campuses nationwide. On October 25, they projected "Free Palestine from the River to the Sea" and "Glory to Our Martyrs" in huge letters on the side of the Estelle and Melvin Gelman Library (which, as it happens, had been built with funding from Jewish philanthropists). The projections continued for more than two hours until university authorities finally intervened. The administration's subsequent statement about the incident did not condemn the contents of the pro-terrorism slogans, but said merely that they caused "distress, hurt, and pain" for "many members of our community" and "in no way reflect the views of the university." It also referred to the instigators of the projections merely as unnamed "individuals" rather than as SJP members.[91]

Two days after the Hamas invasion, President Ellen Granberg issued her first public statement about it. She did not mention Hamas or characterize the attack as terrorism; she merely expressed sadness over "the recent attack on Israel and the continued violence in the region."[92] President Granberg's second statement, three days later, was stronger, condemning Hamas by name and criticizing "the celebration of terrorism." She made no reference to the celebrations that had taken place on her own campus, such as the October 10 SJP campus vigil at which speakers "hailed the attackers," according to the campus newspaper. SJP members at the event chanted "From the river to the sea, Palestine will be free"; a protest organizer praised the Hamas "resistance fighters" for making the "ultimate sacrifice for liberation"; and other speakers defended the slaughter as "a response to 75 years of Israeli occupation . . . and genocide."[93]

GW stood out in the anti-Israel campus movement not only for the light projection tactic, but also for a sign bearing the words "Final Solution" displayed alongside a large PLO flag at an anti-Israel rally on campus some months later. Whether the point of the sign was to accuse Israel of perpetrating genocide in Gaza, or to call for a Hitler-style "solution" to Israel's existence, the use of that infamous Nazi phrase underlined many Jews' worst fears about the protesters' intentions.[94]

UNIVERSITY OF PENNSYLVANIA

Disputes over antisemitism and Israel at the University of Pennsylvania actually began several weeks before October 7. In late September 2023 four university departments co-sponsored a two-day literary festival on campus called "Palestine Writes," featuring several speakers who had compared Israel to Nazi Germany, accused "Zionists" of controlling the media, and blamed European Jews for their own persecution during the Holocaust. Festival organizer Susan Abulhawa, an author and BDS activist, had tweeted that she "takes comfort in knowing" that Israel eventually will be "wiped off the map." Her denunciation of Ukrainian president Volodymyr Zelenskyy as a "Nazi-promoting Zionist" who was dragging "the whole world into the inferno of WWIII" also raised eyebrows.[95] Penn President M. Elizabeth Magill acknowledged that some of the speakers had made antisemitic remarks, but rejected a petition against the festival by more than four thousand alumni on the grounds of free speech.[96] In the days preceding the conference, a swastika was daubed on a campus wall and the Penn Hillel center was vandalized by a man shouting antisemitic slurs. The event itself passed without incident; there were harsh denunciations of Israel and calls to boycott the Jewish state, but nothing that crossed into explicit antisemitism.[97]

President Magill's first statement following October 7 was vaguely titled "Supporting Our Community" in one version, and "War in the Middle East" in another. In it, Magill and her colleagues said they were "devastated" but did not condemn the invasion or characterize it as a terrorist attack. It also made no reference to antisemitism. Five days later, following widespread criticism, Magill issued a second statement that used the terms "condemn," "terrorism," and "antisemitism." Three days after that, Magill issued yet another statement, asserting that "hateful speech has no place at Penn" while affirming students' right to engage in "peaceful protests." There was no indication that genocidal chants would be prohibited.[98]

In the meantime, at a rally outside Penn's main library on October 16, a speaker explained why all Israeli Jews deserved to be murdered: "Anyone who forms a settler colony is putting forward an act of war against a collective population; therefore, all settlers and all settlements are legitimate military targets and they will be targeted." Shortly afterwards, that speaker assaulted a Jewish student and was arrested. According to an observer's account, another speaker at the rally assured Jewish students that "while he would never be satisfied so long as the Jewish state exists, [Jews] would be welcomed in a secular, socialist Palestinian state." Chants of "There is only one solution, Intifada Revolution" and "From the river to the sea, Palestine will be free" rang out across campus.[99] Two days later, the words "The Jews R Nazis" were painted on a site next door to the campus Jewish fraternity.[100]

Penn students, together with likeminded students from other area universities, held a rally outside Philadelphia city hall on October 28. Among the speakers was an exhilarated Penn junior named Tara Tarawneh. She declared:

> Do you guys remember the photo of the kids and men laughing and smiling as they sat on the top of the Israeli military jeep captured by our freedom fighters? . . . How about the photos of the bulldozer breaking through the border? Do you remember that picture? And the several other joyful and powerful images which came from the glorious October 7!
>
> I remember feeling so empowered and happy, so confident that victory was near and so tangible. I want all of you to hold that feeling in your hearts. Never let go of it. Channel it through every action you take. Bring it to the streets! Go down to the streets every day! And don't ever let them feel that you quietly accept this genocide! . . . The blood of the martyrs asks my blood! How could you accept the path of peaceful soluction?

Tarawneh then hailed Hamas as "a resistance movement fighting for liberation," implored her listeners to "continue to fight for the complete liberation of Palestinian land from the river to the sea!," and then led the crowd in chants of "From the river to the sea, Palestine will be free!"[101]

Additional eruptions on campus in the days to follow met with minimal administrative response. On November 8, Penn Against the Occupation and the Philly Palestine Coalition projected "From the river to the sea" and other extremist slogans onto campus buildings. President Magill called the projections "vile" and "antisemitic," but did not name the sponsoring groups or punish the students involved.[102] A few days later, a group of pro-Hamas students took over the ground floor of a major campus building and harassed Jewish passersby. At the end of the day, campus security officials informed them that they were trespassing but allowed them to stay overnight. Weeks later, they were still there.[103] Shortly after that, Hamas supporters on campus announced a screening of the anti-Israel film "Israelism." Administration officials urged them to postpone the event until the subsequent semester, but the students went ahead with the showing and the administration did not intervene. In addition, hundreds of posters mocking the Israeli hostages, by showing cows instead of human prisoners, were plastered across campus.[104]

During a pro-Hamas march from Penn across the city on December 3, participants chanted "From the river to the sea, Palestine will be free" and spray-painted "Intifada," "Free Palestine," and obscenities about Israel on public and private property along the route. The protesters paused outside Goldie's, a kosher restaurant, and chanted slogans accusing its Jewish owners of genocide. The march culminated in a rally at which speakers denounced the Pennsylvania legislature for passing a resolution affirming Israel's right to exist.[105] President Magill did not comment on the protest. Eyal Yakoby, a Penn senior, offered his perspective at a press conference in Washington with several members of Congress: "I, along with most [Jewish students on] campus, sought refuge in our rooms as classmates and professors chanted proudly for the genocide of Jews, while igniting smoke bombs and defacing school property." He characterized the Penn environment as a "chilling landscape of hatred and hostility" toward Jews. Yakoby himself had been targeted by fellow students, and even professors, with comments such as "You're a dirty little Jew, you deserve to die" and references to "the glorious October 7." The words "90% of Pigs Are Gas Chambered" and other antisemitic slurs were scrawled in chalk across a main walkway. Yakoby strongly criticized Penn administration officials for ignoring such outrages and for advising Jewish students to "not wear clothing or accessories associated with Judaism."[106]

In early 2024 Dwayne Booth, a lecturer at Penn's Annenberg School of Communications, drew two antisemitic cartoons and circulated them on the internet. One showed Zionists drinking the blood of Gazans from wine glasses; the other depicted Jews in a Nazi death camp holding placards reading "Stop the Holocaust in Gaza" and "Gaza, the World's Biggest Concentration Camp." The administration said it would not take action against Booth because of its "bedrock commitment to open expression." Soon afterwards, it announced that it was hiring Booth to teach in the 2024–25 academic year as well.[107]

SHOWDOWN IN CONGRESS

With campus events spiraling out of control, members of Congress invited the presidents of Harvard, Penn, and MIT to testify about the situation before the Education and Workforce subcommittee of the U.S. House of Representatives. Columbia's president was also invited, but could not participate because of a scheduling conflict. The hearing took place on December 5, 2023.

Harvard President Claudine Gay was asked twice by Congresswoman Elise Stefanik (R-NY), "[Do] you understand that the use of the term 'intifada' in the context of the Israeli-Arab conflict is indeed a call for violent armed resistance against the state of Israel, including violence against civilians and the genocide of Jews[?]" Gay replied that such language was "personally abhorrent to me," but did not address whether she considered it genocidal. Asked whether disciplinary action would be taken against students "who say 'from the river to the sea' or 'intifada' advocating for the murder of Jews," the Harvard president again said only that it was "personally abhorrent." The congresswoman then asked whether that language violated the Harvard student code of conduct. That "depended on the context," Gay said. It would be a violation only if it "crosses into conduct" or if it "targeted an individual" and was "severe, pervasive."[108]

Asked the same questions, MIT President Sally Kornbluth said "chants for intifada" might or might not be antisemitic, "depending on the context." She said "calling for the genocide of Jews" on the MIT campus would be "investigated" only if the calls were "pervasive and severe" and "targeted at individuals, not making public statements."[109]

University of Pennsylvania President M. Elizabeth Magill likewise responded that "calling for the genocide of Jews" would violate Penn's code of conduct only if such speech "turns into conduct," and if that conduct was "directed and severe or pervasive." Determining whether such speech should be restricted was, Magill said, "a context dependent decision."[110]

The three presidents were widely criticized for their cold, formulaic responses and apparent reliance on coaching and stock phrases, likely drafted by attorneys. But most importantly, the heads of Harvard, MIT, and Penn failed to understand that in the wake of October 7, the real-life consequences of incendiary language had become a crucial factor in assessing whether that language qualified as antisemitism.

Extremist slogans on campus were not uttered in the context of a calm academic discussion; they were being used to rile up angry crowds. In many instances, the language appeared to be helping to incite militants to physically harass Jewish passersby. Incendiary utterances were becoming antisemitic in practice, whether or not university presidents believed they were antisemitic in principle.

One way to judge whether the pro-Hamas slogans were potentially dangerous and actionable would be to consider how universities would judge similar rhetoric targeting a different minority group. If white supremacists in a foreign country massacred, tortured, raped, and beheaded 1,200 black men, women, and children; and white supremacist students on American college campuses chanted slogans endorsing that violence, would universities protect it as free speech, or would they take action to prevent it?

That was one of the pointed questions repeatedly raised at the December 5 congressional hearings. Congressman Donald Norcross (D-NJ) asked Penn's Magill about her decision to permit a conference on campus involving twenty-five pro-Palestinian organizations, some of whose representatives the Penn administration itself had identified as antisemitic. In response, Magill reiterated that canceling the conference "would have been very inconsistent with academic freedom and free expression." Norcross then asked: "Would you permit your academic departments to sponsor a conference if [it included] twenty-five speakers that the NAACP would identify as racist?" Magill avoided giving a direct answer: "Congressman, we follow our policies always, and our policies are guided by the United States Constitution and a commitment to academic freedom and free expression." Norcross asked, "So is that a yes or no answer?," and Magill replied, "The answer is, that we follow our policies."[111]

California Republican congressman Keven Kiley raised the same point, but in the context of admitting white supremacist students to Harvard: "Would you say that a person who is an avowed neo-Nazi is someone that you would want to be part of the Harvard community?" Gay answered: "Those are not consistent with Harvard's values, but at the same time we allow a wide berth for free expression on a variety of views." Kiley: "The question was, would you want such a person, who was an avowed neo-Nazi, to be part of the Harvard community, yes or no?" Gay: "Those are not consistent with Harvard values." He asked again; she replied with the same evasive language.[112] She would not say either that both antisemitic rhetoric and racist rhetoric would be prohibited on campus, or that both types of bigotry should be considered protected free speech.

Within days of the congressional hearing, Penn's board of directors compelled Magill to resign. Gay, too, came under strong pressure to step down, but resisted until the exposure of a pattern of plagiarism in her academic work compelled her resignation. Only Kornbluth managed to hang on.

THE SECOND EXPLOSION

After the wave of pro-Hamas campus demonstrations following October 7, the fever pitch briefly waned, especially during winter break, from mid-December to mid-January. Movement leaders began planning for a major new round in the spring.

Prominent activists from Columbia and other schools undertook "months of training, planning and encouragement by longtime activists and left-wing groups" in preparation for a second major wave of priests in the spring of 2024, the *Wall Street Journal* reported. Among the consultants were former members of the Black Panthers movement and officials of Samidoun, a Canada-based organization that calls itself a "Palestinian Prisoner Solidarity Network." Samidoun has been outlawed in both Israel and Germany because of its terrorist connections, and was sanctioned by the U.S. Treasury Department for providing material support to Palestinian Arab terrorists.[113] "We took notes from our elders, engaged in dialogue with them and analyzed how the university responded to previous protests," one of the Columbia organizers, graduate student Sueda Polat, told the *Journal*. She also said that some of the pro-Hamas activists had been involved in Black Lives Matter protests and patterned some of their efforts on those experiences.[114]

Preparation and coordination also explained how students on more than sixty campuses nationwide suddenly had brand-new Coleman pop-up tents (which retail for $89.99), professionally printed placards, identical slogans, and similar lists of "demands." They waited for a moment when a prominent university president would be in the national spotlight and could be targeted as the focal point for the protests. Columbia president Minouche Shafik unwittingly played that role.[115]

Unable to participate in the December 2023 congressional hearing, Shafik appeared the following April before the House subcommittee on Education and Workforce. Unlike her predecessors, who had refused to say that calls for genocide against Jews should be prohibited on campus, Shafik agreed with her congressional questioners that, in principle, calling for genocide should not be permitted at Columbia. But she eluded the question of whether any of the slogans chanted on her campus qualified as calls for genocide. When Congresswoman Elise Stefanik asked Shafik whether she considered "From the river to the sea, Palestine will be free" a call for genocide, she responded, "That language is hurtful, and we would prefer not to hear it on our campus." Rep. Stefanik then asked whether any students who had used those words had been disciplined; Shafik replied: "We have some disciplinary cases ongoing around that language. We have specified that those kinds of chants should be restricted in terms of where they happen. We are looking at it. We are looking at it."[116] Rep. Ilhan Omar (D-MN) asked Shafik if she had "seen a protest [at Columbia] saying 'We are against Jewish people'?," implying that in Omar's view, a student literally would have to say the words "We are against Jewish people" for the language to qualify as antisemitic. Shafik responded, "No, I have not." The Columbia president in effect let stand criteria for measuring antisemitism that is not used when measuring bigotry against other ethnic, religious, or racial groups.[117]

Rep. Tim Walberg (R-MI) asked Shafik what, if any, disciplinary action was taken against Prof. Joseph Massad for praising October 7 as "awesome." She replied that "he's been spoken to." She also said that while Massad had chaired the academic review committee for Columbia's school of arts and sciences, he "does not have a leadership role" any longer and was "under investigation" for his public comments. When Rep. Stefanik pointed out that Massad was still listed as committee chair on the Columbia website, President Shafik responded that she "wasn't sure" about his status. Meanwhile, Massad told CNN that he was continuing as chair until his one-year term expired the following month, and that far from investigating him, the chair and deans of his school had expressed their "solidarity" with him.[118]

The Columbia president returned to New York City to find dozens of students setting up anti-Israel "protest tents" in the central grassy area on campus known as the Quad. The hundred or so student participants constituted less than one-third of 1 percent of Columbia's approximately thirty-seven thousand students, but media coverage amplified their message before a national audience. One result of the media spotlight was the revelation that protest leader Khymani James had spoken frankly about his desire to "murder Zionists" during a university disciplinary hearing, back in January (to which he had been summoned because of previously threatening remarks he had made on social media about "Zionists"). In that private hearing before university officials, James had felt comfortable asserting that "Zionists don't deserve to live," and that he felt "very comfortable, very comfortable, calling for those people to die." He added that the public should "be grateful that I'm not just going out and murdering Zionists." James's menacing words were important because they confirmed previous concerns about the violent intentions of some of the protesters—in this case, a protest leader—and underlined the genocidal nature of many protesters' rhetoric. It also was significant that the university knew about James's threats of violence for at least three months, yet took no action against him. Following a torrent of negative publicity in April, the university announced he was "barred from campus," but did not explain whether James, a junior, had been expelled or merely suspended, and if the latter, for how long; moreover, the penalty was mitigated by the fact that the academic year was just days from its conclusion. The day after the "barring," Congresswoman Ilhan Omar visited Columbia; her daughter had been among those arrested in an illegal pro-Hamas protest. The Omars were photographed embracing. It was during her encounter with James that Rep. Omar made her infamous remark to reporters that she opposed "antisemitism or bigotry for all Jewish students, whether they are pro-genocide or anti-genocide."[119]

Columbia University faculty members spearheaded what soon became a nationwide trend of faculty becoming directly involved in pro-Hamas protests. Professors from various Columbia departments moved their classes to the encampment. In an address to the protesters, Derecka Purnell, a scholar-in-residence at the Columbia Law School, spoke about "the connections between the gentrification of Harlem and what's happening in Palestine right now."[120] Other faculty members took up positions to physically shield the trespassers from being arrested. No action was taken against the faculty members. Rebecca Jordan-Young, a gender studies professor who was active in the campus chapter of Faculty for Justice in Palestine and served as one of those human shields for the protesters, was subsequently promoted to director of the Center for Research on Women at Columbia's Barnard College.[121]

Similar turmoil involving faculty took place on other campuses as well. Professors at Northeastern University formed a human barrier to block police from dismantling an illegal encampment. At Emory University, economics professor Caroline Fohlin physically intervened to prevent the arrest of a pro-Hamas student by repeatedly shouting, "I'm a professor!"[122] At Dartmouth, Jewish studies professor Annelise Orleck tried to prevent campus police from arresting pro-Hamas trespassers, then grabbed her phone from an officer who had confiscated it, triggering a skirmish in which Orleck ended up on the ground. She alleged "police brutality"; a colleague charged she "intended to be arrested" by putting herself "in the place where everyone was told, 'if you are in this place, we will arrest you.'"[123] At the University of Texas-Dallas, gender studies professor Anne Gray Fischer said she "experienced violence" at the hands of the police at a pro-Hamas rally on campus, although nobody else there said violence occurred; when questioned later, she claimed she had meant "carceral violence"—that is, the atmosphere felt like violence to her even though it was not violence, according to the common understanding of that word.[124]

IGNORANT PROTESTERS

Former Secretary of State Hillary Clinton, a visiting professor in public affairs at Columbia, spoke of the ignorance of the pro-Hamas protesters concerning the issues they were protesting. "I have had many conversations with a lot of young people over the last many months," Clinton said. "They don't know very much at all about the history of the Middle East or frankly about history in many areas of the world, including in our own country." She bemoaned the fact that much of the protesters' knowledge of the conflict came from "willfully false . . . incredibly slanted, pro-Hamas, anti-Israel" sources. "Remember, there was a ceasefire on October 6, that Hamas broke by their barbaric assault on peaceful civilians," she noted. "There was a ceasefire. It did not hold because Hamas chose to break it."[125] Clinton's assessment of the student protesters was supported by a November 2023 poll that found only 47 percent of the pro-Hamas protesters could identify the "river" and the "sea" in their chant. When eighty of the respondents were shown a map of the Middle East, and told that establishing a Palestinian state from the Jordan River to the Mediterranean Sea would leave "no room for Israel," 75 percent of them said they "probably would not" chant that slogan any longer.[126]

Chief among the sources of information to which students turned, according to the *New York Times*, was Al Jazeera, the Qatar government-financed media outlet. "Many student protesters" and faculty interviewed by the *Times* in May 2024 said they relied on Al Jazeera's English-language website for their information about Gaza. Al Jazeera is "a major exporter of hateful content against the Jewish people, Israel, and the United States," the Anti-Defamation League reported, with "a troubling record of providing a platform to all manner of virulent anti-Israel and even anti-Semitic extremists and of serving as a propaganda tool against the State of Israel." That has included repeatedly publishing antisemitic cartoons featuring hook-nosed Jews in religious garb massacring Arabs and boasting about their control of America's elections.[127] As of May 2024, Al Jazeera had 1.9-million followers on TikTok, up from 750,000 in October 2023, and its mobile apps had been downloaded in the United States 295,000 times since October, a 200 percent increase.[128]

TENT ENCAMPMENTS AND STUDENT DEMANDS

Returning to the Columbia campus on Thursday, April 18 after her congressional testimony, President Shafik initially ordered the police to intervene against the tent encampments. One hundred and eight protesters who refused to vacate the scene were arrested.

Within hours, the tents began returning. As the onset of the Sabbath approached on Friday afternoon, protesters displayed a large sign with Shafik's face and the words "Shabbat Shalom, Moth——-er."[129] Other banners proclaimed, "Revolution Until Victory," "By Any Means Necessary," and, as always, "From the River to the Sea, Palestine Will be Free." A demonstrator waving a PLO flag repeatedly shouted at Jewish students, "Go back to Poland! Go back to Belarus!"[130] One speaker, the anti-Zionist ex-academic Norman Finkelstein, heaped praise on the protesters, but also tried to persuade them it would be preferable to say "Palestinians will be free" rather than "Palestine will be free," since the latter could be "misunderstood." When Finkelstein concluded his remarks, "protesters continued to chant, 'From the river to the sea, Palestine will be free,'" the *Columbia Spectator* reported. Apparently the chanters knew exactly what message they wanted to convey, and how they wanted to convey it.[131]

President Shafik chose to initiate negotiations with the tentees. Congressional email disclosures later revealed that Shafik offered significant concessions, including giving serious consideration to divesting from some companies doing business with Israel and creating a scholarship fund for students from Gaza or Palestinian Authority–governed areas. The protesters rejected the university's offers.[132]

While the negotiations dragged on, the protesters and their allies made plans for escalation. On the evening of April 29, more than one hundred militants from various New York City college campuses gathered at the Manhattan offices of the extremist People's Forum group. Its leader exhorted them to "give Joe Biden a hot summer" and "make it untenable for the politics of usual to take place in this country."

He praised the Columbia student representatives at the meeting for "decid[ing] that resistance is more important than negotiations."[133] Hours later, dozens of students smashed the windows of Columbia's Hamilton Hall, occupied the building, and physically prevented its three sanitation workers from leaving. Holding the janitors against their will was particularly ironic, since the protests were aimed at bolstering those who were holding Americans and Israelis hostage at that very moment in Gaza. "We don't expect to go to work and get swarmed by an angry mob with rope and duct tape and masks and gloves," one of the victims, maintenance worker Mario Torres, told *The Free Press*. "They came from both sides of the staircases. They came through the elevators, and they were just rushing. It was just like, they had a plan." The attackers "just multiplied and multiplied." At one point, Torres recalled, he was "looking up and I noticed the cameras are covered." The cameras were twenty feet from the ground. It seemed obvious to him that "this was definitely planned." The students "pushed and shoved him" as they grabbed furniture to block all the exits. They pulled the elevator's fire alarm, then filled the elevator with chairs and tables to prevent it from being used. At the same time, they threw furniture, and even vending machines, down the stairwells to physically block the exits. They also used zip ties to prevent the doors from being opened. With considerable effort, Torres and his colleagues managed to climb over the piles of furniture, cut away the zip ties, and escape. When they emerged from the building, Torres said he was shocked that "there wasn't even one public safety officer" anywhere in the vicinity. "What's that about? Were they told to stay in place or something? . . . We had to fight our way out." Torres said he "felt abandoned" by the Columbia administration. A photo later leaked to the news media showed Torres grappling with a protester, who, it turned out, was forty-year-old James Carlson, a veteran radical activist and owner of a $2.3-million townhouse in a posh Brooklyn neighborhood.[134]

The supplies that the Hamilton Hall attackers brought with them were not "pencils, books, laptops . . . the tools of students and what you expect to find on a college campus," the New York City Police Department's deputy commissioner for operations, Kaz Daughtry, wrote later. "But here's what the nypd found in Hamilton Hall at Columbia University" when President Shafik belatedly asked them to intervene on May 2: "Gas masks, ear plugs, helmets, goggles, tape, hammers, knives, ropes," and pamphlets urging the public "from New York to Gaza and across the Turtle Island" (radicals' name for North America) to "disrupt/reclaim/destroy [Z]ionist business interests everywhere." The pamphlet covers bore slogans such as "Death to America!" and "Long live the Intifada!"[135]

Within hours, the police cleared out both Hamilton Hall and the nearby tents, arresting 112 protesters. Despite supporters' claims of "police brutality," there were no injuries.[136] Of the twenty-two students who occupied Hamilton, only four were penalized; the other eighteen remained in good standing and resumed classes in the fall. Thirty-one of the tent protesters were suspended, but had their suspensions reversed by the time the fall semester began; only three were temporarily barred from campus, and a fourth was put on probation.[137] Photographs of the Columbia tent encampment revealed that two faculty members on the disciplinary committee participated in the pro-Hamas protests.[138] One of the two, English professor Joseph Slaughter, was subsequently videotaped giving a lecture in which he praised airplane hijackings by the Popular Front for the Liberation of Palestine as "spectacular," "remarkable," and "a national liberation imaginary."[139] By August, only two of the forty students arrested or disciplined for the April unrest remained suspended.[140] "If you had a group of white supremacists camped out and yelling racial slurs every day, that would be met with a different response than antisemites camped out, yelling antisemitic tropes," Pennsylvania governor Josh Shapiro commented.[141]

The hammers, ropes, wrenches, wire cutters and other tools used in the takeover were displayed, along with photos of the assault and other mementoes, in a multiday exhibit staged at a Columbia University literary society in November 2024. Attendees at the exhibit could also take part in classes in "Protest Skills Training" and "Direct Action Training" and listen to speakers such as Nerdeen Kiswani, leader of the pro-Hamas group Within Our Lifetime. A video showed her thanking a roomful of *keffiyeh*-clad activists for occupying Hamilton, which she hoped would inspire others to “take over the city block by block.” The goal, Kiswani explained, is “a Zionist-free NYC.” She was followed on stage by three students who recited a poem that they said “borrowed from the will of Yayha Sinwar,” mastermind of the October 7 atrocities.[142]

Identical tent encampments simultaneously appeared on campuses from coast to coast, accompanied by extreme rhetoric, including advocacy of violence, and sometimes actual violence. At MIT a dozen *keffiyeh*-clad students banged on drums and tambourines as they chanted, “From the river to the sea, death to Zionists,” “From the river to the sea, Israel—destroyed,” and “We don’t want to see Zionists here.”[143] The tent protests at George Washington University featured signs and chants with slogans such as “Zionists Are Not Welcome Here” and “Go Back to Poland.”[144] At DePaul University, more than one thousand students and faculty filed official complaints about the pro-Hamas tentists, ranging from their antisemitic posters (including a huge banner of guidelines instructing the protesters, “No engaging with Zionists”) to damaging university property (when protesters periodically ventured outside the tents) to assault. “My son and I watched a group of five masked men carrying Palestinian flags push a Jewish man to the ground and then steal his Israeli flag,” one complainant reported. “I was called a baby killer, a murderer, a genocide supporter. My friends had paint thrown on them, were pushed and verbally assaulted.” It could have been worse: police officers who dismantled the tents at DePaul found knives, a pellet gun, and a wooden board with protruding nails that had been erected to serve as a trap, a university spokesman said.[145]

Some protesters at the tent encampments paid tribute to their heroes through their fashion choices. Students at Stanford and at Washington University sported Hamas headbands.[146] The image of senior Hamas leader Abu Obeida appeared on hoodies at Northwestern, in oil paintings sold at the Ohio State University encampment, and on a banner at University of Wisconsin-Madison.[147] At Baruch College (CUNY), an image of airplane hijacker Leila Khaled appeared on shirts at a campus rally, alongside a swastika banner held by a student shouting, “Synagogue of Satan!” and another banner telling the campus Hillel to “go to hell.”[148]

From their tents, pro-Hamas students issued lists of demands that ranged from the menacing to the comical. The UCLA students' list included rope, zip ties, wood, helmets, shields, flashlights ("w/strobe"), as well as food prepared according to special dietary requirements.[149] A similar list of "supply needs" demanded by University of Chicago students added sexual devices and hiv tests.[150] Tentees at Claremont Graduate University objected that "all the donations they'd been receiving were healthy snacks, such as granola bars, fruit and nuts"; Eve Oishi, professor of culture studies, promptly brought them some "unhealthy snacks."[151] At Columbia, protest spokeswoman Johannah King-Slutsky appealed for "basic humanitarian aid," as if conditions in the encampment were comparable to wartime Gaza. She said the protesters might "die of dehydration and starvation, or get severely ill" unless the university swiftly came to their rescue.[152]

Some students' demands ranged far beyond supplies. University of Arizona protesters demanded, among other things, defunding of the university's police department, non-enforcement of a ban on student groups that support foreign terrorist organizations, and divestment from companies connected to what it called the Biden administration's "militarization of the US/Mexico borderlands." Cornell's protesters called on the university to "return all mineral interests" and "provide restitution" to the indigenous tribes of upstate New York; permanently replace all campus police with "healthcare workers"; and establish a "Palestinian Studies Program" with hiring decisions to be made by a committee comprised of SJP officials.[153] UCLA tent protesters insisted on divestment from Israel. But that was just for starters, a spokesman made clear: "Given that the University of California is founded on colonialism, it's inherently a violent institution." It may not be a coincidence that ucla has more than eighty courses dealing with colonialism, including one on colonialism and Zionism.[154] UCLA encampment organizers also set up what was effectively a "Jew Exclusion Zone," by blocking off the section of campus they occupied and refusing to let Jewish students cross through it. Congressional email disclosures revealed that the UCLA administration had instructed the campus police to "hold off" on taking action against the illegal encampment.[155] A federal judge subsequently ruled that it was illegal for the administration to permit the protesters to block Jewish students' access to any part of the campus.[156]

Militant students at Drexel University demanded that the school "terminate" the campus chapters of Hillel and Chabad. "These organizations must be replaced by non-Zionist Jewish ones that in no way support the ongoing genocide, occupation, or apartheid in Palestine," the Drexel Palestine Coalition proclaimed. Protesters at UC-Santa Cruz, the School of Visual Arts (in Manhattan), and Georgia Tech had previously demanded their universities disallow Hillel; Drexel's expansion to include Chabad was new, and came on the heels of a wave of incidents that included the vandalizing of the university's Center for Jewish Life, the daubing of antisemitic graffiti on campus property, and the ripping of mezuzahs from the doorposts of Jewish students' rooms. The Palestine Coalition also demanded abolition of the Drexel police force and a 60 percent reduction in the president's salary.[157] The situation at Drexel attracted additional attention when a public health professor was arrested for stealing pro-Israel signs from the front lawns of a synagogue and a Jewish family in the area.[158]

Other notable demands by student protest groups included free tuition (University at Albany); "rejection of colonial feminism" (Evergreen State); "no Zionists on Denver streets" (University of Colorado); "removal of Zionists" from the board of trustees (DePaul); "remove any Israeli faculty member" (University of Maryland-Baltimore County); and "an end" to "the ignorance" that "maintains Zionism at our university" (Fordham).[159] University of Chicago tentees called for ending "fossil fuel production," canceling "property ownership on the South Side [of the city]," and paying "reparations" to unidentified city residents.[160] Columbia students added a demand for "no land grabs in Lenapehoking," the Native American name for a vast region including New Jersey, much of Connecticut, southern New York State, eastern Pennsylvania, and northern Delaware.[161]

APPEASING EXTREMISM

A number of universities capitulated to all or some of the Hamas supporters' demands. Sonoma State University, in northern California, agreed to divest from all companies doing business with Israel; refrain from any exchange programs with Israeli universities; create a Palestine Studies curriculum; and install Students for Justice in Palestine as an "advisory council" that will "ensure that the university administration is held accountable for meeting the demands." University president Mike Lee also declared that Israel should cease firing at Hamas.[162] "SSU demands met," the SJP's Sonoma chapter boasted on Instagram.[163] As it turned out, Lee had agreed to the protesters' demands without the required consultations with the chancellor and other university leaders; as a result, he was placed on administrative leave.[164] Lee then announced his retirement, and the university removed the terms of the agreement with the students from its website, although five months later, the interim administration still had not officially said whether it canceled the deal. In the meantime, the university announced that protesters would no longer be permitted to erect tents, wear face coverings, or brandish poles.[165]

Other institutions made substantial concessions. The New School promised to have its board hold a vote on divestment, and granted amnesty to all protesters in exchange for taking down their tents.[166] Brown University agreed, after six days of tent protests, to permit students to present their proposal for an anti-Israel boycott before a meeting of the university leadership, and President Christina Paxson promised to ask her colleagues to "fast track" the proposal.[167] At Johns Hopkins, the students ended their protest after thirteen days in exchange for the university accelerating, by five months, the process of consid ering their divestment demand; they also secured amnesty for the protesters.[168] Rutgers, the University of Minnesota, the University of California-Riverside and Middlebury College similarly granted hearings on Israel divestment.[169] Militants at the University of Wisconsin-Milwaukee dismantled their tents after chancellor Mark Mone promised to publicly call on Israel to cease firing at Hamas; to accuse the Israelis of destroying Gaza universities; and to meet with the protesters to discuss divesting from Israel.[170] The Union Theological Seminary, which trains liberal Protestant clergy and partners with Columbia, did not even wait for student protesters to set up camp on its grounds; it voted in May to divest from what it called "companies benefiting from the war in Palestine."[171]

Northwestern University president Michael Schill made especially sweeping concessions. In exchange for removing the illegal encampment, Schill pledged to "support visiting Palestinian faculty and students at risk (funding two faculty per year for two years; and providing full cost of attendance for five Palestinian undergraduates to attend Northwestern for the duration of their undergraduate careers)" and "fundraise to sustain this program beyond this current commitment"; to provide "a house for MENA [Middle Eastern and North African] Muslim students"; and to "advise" prospective employers not to rescind job offers made to "students engaging in speech protected by the First Amendment."[172]

The university did not offer to fund any visiting Israeli faculty or students harmed by the October 7 attack, provide housing to Israeli refugees, or urge employers to refrain from discriminating against anti-Hamas students. The double standard was particularly egregious because Jewish students at Northwestern had endured frequent harassment, and campus rallies had called for the mass murder of Israeli Jews. Northwestern students who met with members of Congress on May 1 described "really shocking and scary" antisemitic incidents on campus. A freshman civil engineering student named Mia said that when she walked past the tent encampment, "I was told to go back to Germany and get gassed." She also "overheard in my dorm people talking about the white Jewish power on campus, and what we have to do to address this Jewish power." Jaime, a senior, said graffiti at the tent site included "a Jewish star with an 'X' on it." Lauren, a freshman, said a number of her professors were active in the protests, including one who expressed "pride in our university for forming the [anti-Israel] encampment and for the students' conduct. He urged us to attend, canceling class."[173] Other Northwestern professors encouraged students to skip classes in order to participate in pro-Hamas rallies on campus, and some moved their classes to the Deering Meadow protest site. Journalism professor Steven Thrasher scuffled with police trying to enter the encampment, and posted afterwards on social media, "We locked arms and kept the police at bay. They retreated. 24 hours later the camp is still up. We will put our bodies on the line to protect our students." Evidently he meant that the professors would put their bodies on the line solely to protect pro-Hamas students, since there was no similar physical demonstration of their concern for Jewish students who were then being harassed on campus.[174] The Anti-Defamation League and other major Jewish organizations called for Schill's resignation.[175]

If President Schill expected his concessions to augur harmony with the Hamas supporters, he was mistaken. Following the signing of the agreement, more than one thousand Northwestern faculty, administrators, and students signed a five-page manifesto accusing the university of "the targeted harassment of students" and "intimidating students and educators" through "the disproportionate censorship of pro-Palestine speech," a surprising accusation given the unhindered proliferation of such speech on the campus. The manifesto also included such oddities as charging supporters of Israel with "removalism" (that is, secretly hoping to remove Arabs from Israeli controlled territory), calling all criticism of the slogan "From the river to the sea, Palestine will be free" racist, and condemning Schill's creation of an Advisory Committee on Preventing Antisemitism and Hate as an act of "asymmetric silencing." They objected to the very concept of such a committee, not its actual membership, since Schill's appointees included a professor who publicly defended the "From the river to the sea" chant, another who was a prominent advocate of boycotting Israel, and a student who endorsed the October 7 massacres. Ironically, if the signatories on the petition had examined that committee's activities since its establishment in November 2023, they might have liked what they saw: in the six months since its creation, Schill had never consulted it, even when he was negotiating with the tent protesters, prompting the committee's seven Jewish members to resign in protest in May 2024.[176]

The University of California-Berkeley likewise made concessions to the protesters, only to be immediately slapped in the face by them. Chancellor Judith Christ announced on May 14 that in exchange for dismantling the tents, the school would consider divesting from Israel and would review its academic partnerships to ensure they do not discriminate against Palestinians, which the protesters hailed as "a pathway to boycott of Israeli university programs on grounds of anti-Palestinian and anti-Arab discrimination." The next day, the tents came down. The day after that, however, dozens of militant students occupied a nearby university-owned site, Anna Head Alumnae Hall. In front of the building, they set up tents and wooden barricades. Inside, they hung a "Jihad of Victory or Martyrdom" banner and graffitied the walls with a Star of David equated to a swastika and the slogans "Zionism = Nazism" and "Martyrs Never Die." The latter appeared to allude to the fundamentalist Muslim concept that the reward for "martyrdom" is eternal life in paradise. The police quickly cleared the site.[177]

At Brown University, the aforementioned concessions made by President Christina Paxson likewise failed to buy her peace; Hamas supporters repeatedly heckled Paxson when she spoke at commencement.[178] A subsequent U.S. Department of Education investigation concluded that the university took "little or no action" in response to the harassment of Jewish students at Brown.[179]

Although many universities did not formally capitulate to the Hamas supporters, they gave in to them in other ways. Most tent encampments were allowed to remain in place for days, even weeks, although they were in violation of the law. Columbia made all of its classes remote for the final weeks of the semester in order to avoid confronting the protesters. Some institutions, including Columbia and USC, canceled their commencement ceremonies, in effect punishing the vast majority of their students. USC had canceled the valedictorian's planned address when it was revealed that she had publicized antisemitic videos through social media; then the university announced it was canceling commencement altogether rather than address "substantial risks relating to security and disruption at commencement."[180] At other schools, such as Bryn Mawr College and Penn, commencement ceremonies were moved from their usual campus sites, where pro-Hamas tents were pitched, to less desirable locales.[181] Penn likewise changed the locale of its "Hey Day" event, a century-old annual gathering on the green outside College Hall.[182]

At least two university presidents experienced buyer's remorse after cutting deals. University of Minnesota president Jeff Ettinger claimed he had agreed to include the Arabic word *thwabet* in the university's announcement of the deal without understanding that it refers to the right of Arabs to fight until Israel is destroyed.[183] University of Wisconsin-Milwaukee chancellor Mark Mone apologized to the local Jewish community for the deal he signed two weeks earlier: "UWM should not have weighed in on deeply complex geopolitical and historical issues," Mone conceded.[184]

FIZZLED PROTESTS

What began with a bang, ended in some instances with a whimper. With the conclusion of the academic year in early May 2024, Harvard's tent site was "foundering," the *New York Times* noted. Harvard Out of Occupied Palestine, organizer of the protest, acknowledged that "when students finished moving out of the Yard, police became the dominant presence." In exchange for the last few students folding up their tents prior to Harvard's May 23 commencement, Interim President Alan M. Garber agreed to reinstate all suspended students; to arrange for the protesters to present their divestment demand to the Harvard official overseeing "shareholder responsibility"; and to "meet with students to hear their perspectives" regarding "longstanding conflicts in the Middle East." The featured speaker at commencement was the journalist Maria Ressa, who had published an editorial comparing Israel to Hitler.[185]

At Cornell, Students for Justice in Palestine announced on May 14 that it was voluntarily disbanding its encampment, without explanation; spokeswoman Sivan Gordon-Buxbaum said only, "This is us being like, this is our choice." Tufts University administrators had warned students they might be suspended, or banned from graduation, if they did not stop trespassing, but did not give them a deadline; they voluntarily disbanded shortly before the semester ended. After seventeen days of encampments at DePaul University, President Robert Manuel told the protesters to leave or be arrested; they all voluntarily departed.[186]

Lost amidst the media coverage of the tents was any sense of the actual magnitude of the pro-Hamas campus protests. After three weeks of encampments erected and dismantled on more than sixty campuses nationwide, a total of about three thousand Hamas supporters were arrested, and some thousands more participated but were not arrested. That might seem like a substantial number in the context of the extremely low level of political activity on campuses prior to October 7, when very few protesters were ever arrested for anything. However, compared to the size of the national college student body, the number of anti-Israel protesters, including arrestees, was minuscule. There are more than eighteen million students at American colleges and universities; thus, the number of participants in the pro-Hamas encampments was less than one-tenth of 1 percent of that total.[187]

THE FIRST ANNIVERSARY

By the first anniversary of October 7, the anti-Israel protest movement, both on and off campus, had diminished dramatically. The protests did not disappear entirely, but they took place less frequently, attracted fewer participants, and in some cases were compelled to move off campus and thus no longer disrupted day-to-day university life. Some students switched their focus to other issues, such as the 2024 U.S. presidential race. For others, the increased willingness of university administrations to arrest participants in illegal protests became a deterrent to participation.

Additionally, the aspect of the previous protests that had attracted the most public sympathy, the mounting casualty toll in Gaza, lost considerable momentum by the late spring of 2024, as Israel's counterterror campaign in Gaza became essentially a mopping-up operation and casualty numbers dropped significantly from what they had been earlier in the war. In May, Israel took action in the last major bastion of Hamas activity, the city of Rafah. For many weeks, the international community had strongly pressed Israel to stay out of Rafah and predicted there would be massive casualties if it entered. The Israelis proved them wrong by arranging for nearly the entire civilian population to relocate a few miles away, and then proceeding to eliminate Hamas strongholds in and beneath the city with minimal civilian casualties.

The passions of the hardline core of the protesters were unaffected by the changing facts on the ground, since their devotion was not based on the number of casualties but on their affinity for Hamas and its dream of destroying Israel. Thus, the first anniversary became an occasion for extremists to vent in frustration at Israel's success in decimating the terrorists, including eliminating Hamas's most prominent leaders.

Columbia University Apartheid Divest, the major anti-Israel group on that campus, marked October 7 by issuing a statement of solidarity with Khymani James, the protest leader who had announced his aspiration to "murder Zionists." CUAD announced it was retracting the apology for James's bloodlust that it had issued in his name six months earlier. The original apology was now said to be the work of rogue individuals who failed "to maintain our political line," contributed to James's "ostracization," and undermined "our movement for Palestinian liberation." A second CUAD statement hailed the October 7 as "Palestinian resistance" against "the Zionist genocidal entity" and vowed "Revolution until victory."[188]

The Harvard University Palestine Solidarity Committee celebrated the first anniversary of the Hamas invasion as the day when "Gaza broke through Israel's blockade, showing the world that the ongoing Nakba and apartheid cannot stand."[189] Yalies4Palestine sponsored a rally celebrating October 7 as the occasion when "Palestinians stood tall against Zionism, as they have for nearly 100 years" (i.e., since the 1920s); the Hamas attack "showed the world that the colonized can fight against their colonizer and win."[190] Protesters at a march organized by the SJP chapter at Penn chanted "From Beirut to Jenin, burn the settler colony [Israel]"; banners read "Resistance is Just"; and speakers openly declared their support for Hamas's Al-Qassam Brigades and the "al-Aqsa Flood"—that is, the October 7 massacres.[191] One hundred SJP activists at Northwestern marked October 7 by marching out of their classes in the middle of the day, shouting on a megaphone about "genocidal escalation by the Zionist occupation," and holding signs proclaiming "Right to Resist." University officials said the protesters would be disciplined for violating recently adopted regulations prohibiting rallies and amplified sound at that time of day.[192] At a UC-Berkeley rally celebrating the anniversary, some speakers "expressed support for Hamas, which they described as resistance fighters combating imperialism," according to reporters covering the event. A leaflet distributed at the rally praised the Hamas attack and concluded with the words "Long Live Al-Aqsa Flood," a slogan that also appeared on a sign held by two protesters.[193] Members of Brown University's SJP chapter marched through downtown Providence on October 5 with banners declaring "Resistance Is Justified When People Are Occupied" and "From the River to the Sea."[194] Extremists smashed windows and splashed red paint on a City University of New York building. Additionally, several hundred Hamas supporters marched through lower Manhattan with signs reading "Israel Has a Right to Go to Hell" and "Israel, Eat S—t."[195]

Campus protests diminished significantly during the 2024–25 school year, although there were some notable, and particularly ugly, exceptions to that general trend. At the University of Michigan in December 2024, pro-Hamas protesters hurled urine-filled jars through the windows at the home of a Jewish member of the school's governing board of regents and painted "Free Palestine" on his car.[196] Student extremists at Columbia marked International Holocaust Remembrance Day in January 2025 by issuing a statement comparing Auschwitz to "Zionist dungeons and torture camps" in Gaza.[197] Other Hamas supporters poured concrete into the toilets of a Columbia building and spray-painted anti-Israel slogans nearby.[198] Police officers who raided the apartment of the leaders of the Students for Justice in Palestine chapter at George Mason University in November 2024 found guns, ammunition, foreign passports, Hamas and Hezbollah flags, and signs reading "Death to America" and "Death to Jews." The two were also charged with having painted "intifada" slogans on the student center. The following month, another George Mason student was arrested for conspiring to bomb the Israeli Consulate in New York City. He told his co-conspirator that building would be an appropriate target because it represented "the Yahud," the Arabic word for Jews.[199]

ADDRESSING THE PROBLEM

For many years, most American college campuses had experienced minimal politically motivated protests. After October 7, university presidents facing the mass eruption of demonstrations found themselves in largely uncharted waters.

A handful of university administrations, most notably Dartmouth and the University of Arizona, quickly brought in law enforcement to stymie pro-Hamas takeovers of campus spaces.[200] But in keeping with the academic world's self-perception as a bastion of untrammeled free speech, administrators at Columbia, Yale, and many other universities treated the protests as peaceful expressions of opinion and turned a blind eye when they descended into illegality and antisemitism. Expressions of hatred for Jews (sometimes through the euphemism "Zionists") often escalated into violence, vandalism, and harassment of Jewish students. Mass gatherings frequently involved violations both of university regulations and local laws. Many university officials feared that cracking down on lawbreakers would lead to unpleasant accusations of violating free speech and perhaps fuel greater unrest, so schools such as Harvard and Northwestern tried appeasement, from tolerating illegal encampments for lengthy periods of time to capitulating to protesters' demands. But that kind of appeasement seldom achieves its aims. Political bullies tend to regard concessions as signs of weakness and an invitation to push further, as exemplified by UC-Berkeley, where the protesters' evacuation of their encampment in exchange for various concessions was followed the next day by the erection of new tents, and at Northwestern, where administrative concessions were greeted with vicious new declarations by the extremists. Some university presidents, including at Harvard, Columbia, and Penn, ultimately chose to resign rather than shoulder the burden of preventing mobs from overwhelming campus life.

On the other hand, some institutions changed course to address the chaos. Harvard students and faculty who held sit-ins in campus libraries in 2024 were temporarily banned from those libraries, a step the administration did not take when similar protests were staged a year earlier. When pro-Hamas students at the University of Minnesota took over campus buildings in 2023–24, the administration let them stay overnight, sometimes for days on end; when eleven militants took over a campus building in October 2024, they were promptly arrested. When extremists at Pomona College set up a tent encampment in May 2024, the university let it stand for eight days and even relocated commencement ceremonies; when eighteen students took over a campus building to mark the anniversary of October 7, the school's president invoked a little-used "extraordinary authority" to immediately suspend and discipline them without the university's usual judicial process.[201]

Curfews on demonstrations were adopted to prevent overnight protests at universities such as Northwestern (3:00 p.m. on weekdays), Rutgers (4:00 p.m.), and Ohio State (10:00 p.m.). Student protesters who violated Indiana University's 11:00 p.m. curfew were disciplined. At Case Western, Rutgers, and Carnegie Mellon, students were required to apply for a rally permit several days in advance. Encampments were banned altogether at schools that are part of the University of California and California State University systems, as well as at Emory and the University of Virginia. Tufts, Brown, Temple, Rutgers, the University of Michigan, the University of Georgia, and other schools banned Students for Justice in Palestine from campus for periods of varying lengths, although only Brandeis did so permanently. Some universities, including Princeton and James Madison, declared specific common areas off-limits to demonstrations. Harvard, Penn, Yale, and others announced they would no longer take positions on public policy issues not related directly to their universities. One school, New York University, announced that expressions using the word "Zionist" as code for "Jew" might qualify as a violation of its nondiscrimination regulations.[202]

The result was a significant decrease in pro-Hamas agitation on college campuses. There were about 950 demonstrations on campuses nationwide in the fall 2024 semester, compared to some three thousand the previous semester. The number of students arrested at such protests dropped from more than three thousand in the spring 2024 semester to about fifty in the fall.[203]

In some instances, outside pressure was necessary to stimulate change. Congressional inquiries that forced some university presidents to face tough questions about their handling of protesters also helped facilitate the beginnings of a national reckoning over the situation. At Columbia, a journalist's exposure of deans exchanging snide and in some cases antisemitic messages during a May 31 campus panel on antisemitism resulted in three of them resigning.[204]

At the same time, the legal system offered some recourse for Jews on campus. A judge ruled against UCLA for permitting protesters to maintain a "Jew exclusion zone." A lawsuit by Jewish students accusing Columbia of allowing protesters to create an "unsafe environment" for Jews on campus resulted in the university's agreement to provide escorts for Jewish students and to ensure greater student access during campus protests.[205] The out-of-court settlements of lawsuits by Jewish students at Harvard, New York University, and Occidental College were especially significant. All three schools promised to take greater steps to combat antisemitism on campus and pledged to be guided by the International Holocaust Remembrance Alliance's definition of antisemitism. Since that definition classifies Israel-Nazis comparisons and opposition to Israel's existence as examples of antisemitism, fulfillment of the settlement terms would mean, in practice, an end to the pro-Hamas demonstrations on those campuses.[206]

For America's universities and colleges, 2023–24 was a year of unprecedented challenges, which few of them met in a prompt or effective manner. Only a handful of college presidents acknowledged their mistakes. City College of New York president Vincent Boudreau was one. He said at an online town hall meeting with faculty in May 2024 that he "rejects the [idea] that we have to allow demonstrators free run of the campus" and that his "one regret" was "allowing the [protest] site to harden." It took until day five of the CCNY tent protest, when the anti-Israel extremists physically pushed all the campus police officers out of their encampment area, that Boudreau "realized how volatile the protest was potentially" and belatedly asked the New York City police to intervene.[207]

A national soul-searching by university administrators is yet to come—and is made all the more urgent by the dark shadow that hangs over the history of many of America's elite institutions of higher education. Their tragic record of abdicating moral responsibility, especially when Jews are the victims, will be explored in chapter 7. Before that, a broader review of historical parallels to October 7, from the Crusades to the Holocaust, will follow in chapter 6.

Part 2. The Past

Tracing the Echoes of History

6. Historical Parallels to October 7

October 7 was not only part and parcel of the century-long Palestinian Arab war against the Jews, it was an integral component of a much older war. A veritable conveyor belt of hateful ideas connects antisemitic mob violence in medieval Europe and the Middle East across the centuries, not only in similarity of methods, but in providing ideological underpinnings for anti-Jewish violence.

THE CRUSADERS

In 1095 CE, eight hundred years before Muslim zealots began their contemporary *jihad* to "liberate" the Holy Land from Jews, Christian zealots from the regions today comprising France and Germany set out on what became known as the First Crusade. Their ostensible aim was to reconquer the Holy Land from the Muslim armies of the Arabian Peninsula that had vanquished and occupied it in 632 CE. The Crusaders stopped along the way to target local infidels—their Jewish neighbors, a closer and more vulnerable group. Three Hebrew chroniclers of the period described atrocities all too similar to what Israelis suffered on October 7.

The First Crusade was driven by a combination of antisemitic incitement and religious extremism. In some instances, the mere existence of possible descendants of those whom the church blamed for killing Jesus was sufficient reason for mass torture and murder. On other occasions, a local pretext was manufactured. *Mainz Anonymous*, one of the contemporaneous Hebrew chronicles of the period, reported on how anti-Jewish agitators in Worms stirred up local support for the Crusaders: they "took a corpse of theirs, a trodden one that had been buried thirty days previously, and carried it through the city, saying 'See what the Jews did to our neighbor! They took a Gentile, boiled him in water, and poured the water in our wells, in order to kill us.'"[1] A common practice in Palestinian Arab society is for crowds to hoist and parade the body of a dead terrorist through the streets as evidence of "what the Jews did to our neighbor," which therefore requires avenging.

The Crusaders' attacks on local Jews rested on the conviction that since Jews killed Jesus and rejected Christianity, "anyone who kills a Jew has his sins forgiven."[2] Likewise, contemporary Islamist murders of Jews are infused with a profoundly religious spirit, in their case the belief that someone who dies while trying to murder Jews or other infidels qualifies as a martyr, and male martyrs will be rewarded with entry to heaven and seventy-two virgins. Both Hamas and the Palestinian Authority present martyrdom as the highest possible achievement in life in their media, schools, and other institutions (see chapter 3).

The attacking Crusaders were, according to a second chronicler, "a raging mob" composed of "mercenaries and Crusaders and villagers," a description calling to mind the crowds of Gazan civilians who followed the Hamas gangs into southern Israel. A third chronicler reported that "their ranks swelled so that the number of men, women, and children exceeded a locust horde," an allusion similar to Israeli soldiers' descriptions of the terrorists swarming across the Gaza border on October 7.[3]

When the Crusaders arrived in Worms, the Hebrew chronicler continued, "We were fearful of stepping beyond our thresholds"—in other words, they hid in their equivalent of safe rooms—because Crusaders lay in wait outside, and "when they saw one of us, they ran after him and pierced him with their spears." Others "shot the Jews with arrows." Then the attackers "came and smote those remaining in their homes. . . . They were killed like oxen and were dragged through the streets and markets like sheep to the slaughter; they lay naked, for the Crusaders had stripped them and left them naked." The mobs "attacked those who had remained in their houses and exterminated them—men, women, and children, young and old; they hurled them down the stairs and hacked down the houses and plundered and looted; they stole the scrolls of the Torah and stamped them into the mud and plundered and burned them and left death and horror behind them where the children of Israel had dwelled."[4]

The Jews in Mainz likewise were subjected to unimaginable horrors. The attackers "did not pity the old, the bachelors or maidens, the children or sucklings, even the sick." They "ripped open the bellies of our women who were with child." They "broke the doors" of Jewish homes, "took the Jews' money, stripped them naked, and smote the remaining ones, not leaving any remnant. . . . The corpses were still twitching and becoming stained in their own blood as they were stripping them. . . . Then they tossed them, naked, from the room through the windows."[5] One victim was "subjected to great torture, defiling him against his will, as he was unable to resist, being senseless from their beatings." After another man and his sons were murdered, "they defiled their bodies by dragging them through the muddy streets and trampling them." The chroniclers also hinted at widespread sexual abuse, noting that in Mainz, "they left only a few alive and had their way with them," and in Mehr, "they slew some of them and forcibly defiled those whom they permitted to live, and they had their way with them."[6]

The Second Crusade hardly differed in its impact on the Jews. Details of one small part of the horror were preserved by a teenage eyewitness in the village of Wolkenburg when crusaders arrived from France in 1146. His account describes Jews being crushed in winepresses, decapitated, and burned. Entire wagons full of severed limbs were carted to the Jewish cemetery. A Jewish woman was beaten nearly to death in a church "with stone and fist," because "they do not bring swords" into their houses of worship. Crusaders "ripped up a Torah scroll" in the face of a Jewish captive, upon whom they inflicted wounds according to "the way you inflicted five wounds on our god."[7]

MEDIEVAL BLOOD LIBELS

The innovation of blood libel accusations, with attendant anti-Jewish violence, began around the same time. Often the disappearance or death of a Christian child stirred up accusations that local Jews killed him to use his blood for a ritual purpose, such as baking his blood into their Passover matzot. The earliest such episode occurred in Norwich,

England, in 1144 (see chapter 4). There were similar libels in 1168, in Gloucester; in 1181, in Edmunds; and in 1183, in Bristol. The accusations typically led to the extraction by torture of "confessions" from local Jews, followed by massacres of their coreligionists as punishment for the admitted crime. Past accusations in those cities inflamed the slaughter of hundreds of Jews in York and London in 1190. Among the best known of these outrages occurred in the town of Lincoln in 1255, when the body of a nine-year-old boy named Hugh was found in a well, and the local Jewish community was accused of murdering him for ritual purposes. False confessions were obtained through torture supervised by the brother of the local bishop, following which King Henry III intervened directly and ordered the execution of nineteen Jewish suspects. His son and successor, King Edward I, decreed the expulsion of all Jews from England, and the construction of a shrine to Hugh in Lincoln. It became a focal point of Christian religious pilgrimages.[8]

In 1215, the Church formally adopted the doctrine of transubstantiation, in which the wafers and wine used in the ritual of communion were considered to be transformed into the actual body and blood of Jesus. Soon thereafter, stories began to circulate in central and western Europe about Jews desecrating the Christian sacramental wafers, also known as hosts, by stabbing, stomping, or boiling the wafers. Traditional religious-based hatred of Jews and the new theological doctrine made for a combustible combination. A wafer-desecration allegation in the German town of Rottingen in 1298 led to massacres of thousands of Jews throughout the region, especially in Rothenburg, Wurzburg, and Nuremberg, and the decimation of nearly 150 Jewish communities. Contemporaneous clerical accounts, such as those of the Dominican monk Rudolph and Abbot Peter of Zittau, heaped praise upon one Lord Rintfleisch for leading crowds of peasants from town to town in search of Jews to victimize. One of many such incidents involved Rintfleisch's followers locking seventy-six Jews in a house and then setting fire to it, a method of destruction to be repeated on multiple occasions in the centuries to follow, including during the Holocaust and on October 7.[9]

A more extensive wave of pogroms erupted in the same area around 1332, continuing until 1339 and spreading into the Austrian region of

Styria. One monastic chronicle of the events claimed the violence was provoked by a Jew's insult concerning a church wafer. Mobs led by Arnold of Uissigheim, reportedly acting with Pope Boniface's authorization, armed themselves with "hatchets, rakes, swords, hammers, threshing sledges, knives, axes, battle-axes, hunting spears, bows, missiles and lances," with which they "miserably and cruelly" killed Jews in town after town. (These came to be known as the *Armleder* massacres because of the leather [*leder*] the killers strapped to their arms.) After Arnold's death, his tomb became a religious shrine; numerous visitors to the site claimed to experience visions of him or other supernatural occurrences. In the German city of Konstanz in 1333, Christians avenging a supposed host-desecration "slaughtered [the Jews] like cows," in some cases "pressing them to death."[10]

In 1421, host desecration charges, amplified by local authorities, led to massacres and the expulsion of all Jews from Vienna and other Austrian cities. The carnage was almost a foreshadowing of October 7. In the Austrian town of Pulkau, for example, "[m]any Jews, their wives and their children in cribs were killed. . . . They were drowned, burnt, beheaded, eviscerated and punished miserably." Like fervent imams in modern-day Gaza, theologians at the University of Vienna had prepared the ideological groundwork for the Austrian pogrom by inveighing against "the multitude of Jews, about their luxurious life and their despicable books, which they keep as an insult to the Creator, and in blasphemy of Christ and all the saints, and to the greatest injury of all Christians."[11]

In many instances, a synagogue or Jewish home in which a wafer allegedly had been mistreated was burned to the ground, and a commemorative chapel was constructed on the site, complete with a shrine showcasing a tattered cloth or blood-stained napkin in which the injured host was said to have been wrapped. "Behold the wonder!," the fourteenth-century Viennese theologian Peter of Pulkau proclaimed. "The synagogue of the Old Law is miraculously transformed into the school of virtue of the New Law." The practice of building a Christian religious site precisely where a Jewish edifice previously stood finds its parallel in the longstanding tradition of Muslim conquerors to build mosques atop the ruins of churches or synagogues as a demonstration of Islamic religious supremacy. The Al-Aqsa Mosque, constructed in the late 600s or early 700s CE on the site of Jerusalem's biblical temples, is perhaps the best-known example. Likewise, the decree preventing non-Muslim homes from being taller than Muslim homes, enforced by Muslim regimes throughout the ages, also promulgated the notion of physical superiority as a means of asserting spiritual domination.[12]

The Black Death, a bubonic plague pandemic that killed tens of millions of people in fourteenth-century Europe, was widely blamed on the Jews. Fear of the advancing plague as it spread across the continent generated the libel that Jews caused the plague by poisoning wells. Hundreds of pogroms erupted in central and western Europe between 1349 and 1351, often with explicit permission from governmental authorities. Torture was employed to produce confessions, and the confessions then became the basis for mass murder. Sometimes the killings were carried out not through chaotic mob violence but in a highly organized manner all too familiar to modern ears. The fourteenth-century chronicler Matthias von Neuenburg described the Jewish population of Strasbourg being stripped of their clothes and marched naked to a cemetery where they were burned en masse in a wooden house built for that purpose. Another source from that time period reports that the slaughter took place over the course of six days.[13]

The pogromists sometimes actively encouraged their compatriots in nearby areas to do likewise. Jacob von Konigshofen, a near-contemporaneous chronicler who likely derived his account from eyewitness testimony, described how after a number of Jews confessed under torture in Berne and Zofingen, Switzerland, "thereupon they burnt the Jews in many towns and wrote of this affair to Strasbourg, Freiburg, and Basel in order that they too should burn their Jews." It was indicative of the force of antisemitic public opinion at the time that when some municipal officials in Basel hesitated to enlist in the genocidal project, "the citizens marched to the city-hall and compelled the council to take an oath that they would burn the Jews, and that they would allow no Jew to enter the city for the next two hundred years." Basel's Jews were then rounded up and a conference of religious and civic leaders was held in the French town of Benfeld-Alsace to determine their fate, six centuries before the Nazi leadership convened at Wannsee in January 1942 to plot the disposition of Europe's Jews, and another quarter-century before Arab leaders met in Khartoum in August 1967 to vow continuation of their own genocidal campaign against the Jews. "The Bishop and the lords and the Imperial Cities agreed to do away with the Jews," Von Konigshofen reported. "The result was that they were burnt in many cities, and wherever they were expelled they were caught by the peasants and stabbed to death or drowned." A brief attempt to forestall mass murder in Strasbourg was quickly overridden: municipal officials who opposed annihilating Jews were hastily deposed and replaced with successors who voted for mass murder.[14]

In Basel, the killers constructed a unique kind of primitive death chamber for the Jews, according to von Neuenburg. The entire Jewish community of Basel, "without a legal sentence and because of the clamor of the people, were burned on an island in the Rhine River in a new house." The perpetrators carried out the mass murder on a Friday, a day of spiritual significance in Christianity because that was the day Jesus died. Selecting that day for the slaughter underlined the religious dimension of the massacres in the killers' minds.[15]

The Austrian crusade of 1421 provided an additional occasion for an inventive new way to murder Jews: some were "put on a rudderless ship and sent to their death" on the Danube River.[16] Five centuries later, the Nazis employed a similar tactic. In the town of Jelsk in occupied Ukraine in the summer of 1942, the Germans forced five hundred Jews aboard a barge which they anchored in the middle of a river and then sank. Similar mass drownings were undertaken in the city of Mozyr, near Minsk, and elsewhere.[17]

GLORIFICATION OF HORROR

Those who endorsed, and sought to encourage, violent persecution of the Jews in the Middle Ages employed various means to publicly glorify the killings and the killers.

Sermons were one. The Italian Dominican monk Giordano da Rivalto, the preeminent Christian preacher of his time, railed against the Jews, "this wicked people," inculcating his audiences with the vilest antisemitic beliefs. The hero of one well-known Giordano sermon, in 1304, was an unnamed "spiritual person, possessing zeal for the faith," who led a crowd "shouting 'death to the Jews'" as they passed through the province, "and all the Jews were killed so that it was impossible to find one in the whole province, and it was a blessed thing that he could kill them." He also described personally witnessing an appearance by the boy Jesus, who, he asserted, led Christians in an unnamed town in massacring twenty-four thousand Jews as appropriate punishment for their heresy.[18]

Another means of incitement was the *passio*, a text in which contemporary events were told in the language and style of New Testament verses about the passion of Jesus, the final events of his life. The host desecration libel in Prague in 1389 and its attendant violence were commemorated in a *passio* featuring a celebratory account of the townspeople attacking all their Jewish neighbors and amputating their limbs, one by one.[19]

Naming public sites after those deemed worthy of emulation is another time-honored way of drawing positive attention to their actions. In the German village of Uissigheim, for example, the main street to this day is named Ritter Arnold Strasse, in honor of the fourteenth-century pogrom leader. Today's residents may not know the bloody history behind the street's name, but those who originally singled out Arnold for this public accolade likely knew of his deeds and wished to pay tribute to them.[20]

On the stage, too, commemorating anti-Jewish violence was a popular medieval pastime. In the fifteenth-century Italian drama *Un Miracolo del Corpo di Cristo*, a wicked Jewish pawnbroker tricks a vulnerable Christian woman into "bringing to him the body of her living God" (that is, a Eucharist wafer), which he cooks and stabs. The evildoer is exposed and executed, after which a chapel is built atop his demolished house. At the end of each performance, local Jewish residents were dragged onto the stage and beaten.[21]

The advent of the printing press in the mid-1400s facilitated a wider dissemination of writings celebrating the killing of Jews. In the German town of Passau in 1478, for example, Jews were tortured into confessing that the bleeding wafer they stabbed in their synagogue miraculously transformed into a little boy. As punishment for their sacrilege, the "culprits" were beheaded, the rest of the town's Jewish residents were expelled, the synagogue was destroyed, and the Chapel of the Holy Saviour was built atop its rubble. The events at Passau were soon celebrated in an illustrated pamphlet exposing the evildoings of the Jews, followed by explicit depictions of their just rewards: burning of their feet, torture with glowing tongs, and decapitations.[22]

A host-desecration allegation in 1492 resulted in twenty-seven Jews being burned alive on a hill in Mecklenberg, with the chief victim's home destroyed and replaced by a Chapel of the Holy Blood. The new church showcased a pot and other relics of the supposed desecration and a tablet bearing the engraved confessions of the Jews. The town's remaining 265 Jews were stripped of their property and expelled en masse. Text celebrating the episode appeared soon afterward in pamphlets, woodcuts, a lengthy poem, and an early encyclopedia entry with an illustration depicting a mass burning of Jews as local dukes look on approvingly.[23]

The mass murder of Jews in Degenberg in 1337 was celebrated more than 150 years later with a series of paintings in the local church and a widely circulated, four-page illustrated poem. The artwork and text portrayed Jews as committing a variety of offenses ranging from host-desecration to well-poisoning, after which the town elders welcomed the arrival of fifty pious men "to kill the Jews, men and women, and burn down their houses." The abused wafer managed to escape the flames and proceeded to heal the blind and the lame throughout the countryside. Two chapels erected in Bavaria to commemorate the events, one in Deggendorf and the other at the Holy Saviour of Bettbrunn, became major pilgrimage destinations.[24]

The mass burning of Jews in Brussels and the expulsion of others from the region, following a wafer-desecration episode in 1369, likewise was celebrated in a series of stained-glass windows in the city's main church as well as various poems and pamphlets. Under Pope Eugenius IV, a papal delegate encouraged the glorification of the mass burning by offering an indulgence (the reduction of divine punishment for a sin) to those who participated in an annual procession to the church in St. Gudule, where the damaged wafers were kept on display.[25]

Primarily religious antisemitism could sometimes take on racialist overtones, as in the case of the Inquisition. From the late 1400s through the mid-1500s (and sporadically for many years afterward), the inquisitors of the Catholic Church in Spain and elsewhere tortured and murdered suspected heretics, especially Jewish converts to Christianity and descendants of converts. They were persecuted not because they were insufficiently devout, but simply because they were suspected of having "Jewish blood" in their veins that was leading them to corrupt "pure" Christians by "Judaizing" them—in other words, a racial flaw that could not be remedied through religious conversion. They were said to lack *limpeza de sangre*, or purity of blood, a concept more commonly associated with Germany in the 1930s but which was enshrined in law in Toledo, Spain, beginning in 1449. Scholars' estimates of the number of people tortured to death by inquisitors range from the tens of thousands to the hundreds of thousands.[26]

Although there were many differences between the medieval horrors and the October 7 atrocities, there were also noteworthy similarities. Then as now, religious authorities incited the masses to hate Jews. Irrational antisemitic conspiracy theories were widely believed. The Middle Ages had their own version of "fake news"—false confessions extracted from Jews through torture. Then, too, extreme violence was used even against individuals who were physically incapable of committing the imagined offenses, such as the elderly, the handicapped, and small children. All were judged culpable and deserving of a violent death not because of any actual wrongdoing, but by virtue of the fact that they were Jews.[27]

The history of Jews in medieval Europe did not consist solely, or even primarily, of mass assaults and the extinction of entire communities. In Jewish communities throughout the continent, daily life proceeded. Despite the confines of severe economic and social restrictions, Jewish men and women found meaning in personal accomplishments, family bonds, religious devotion, and communal celebrations. Rabbinic sages produced erudite works of religious scholarship. Students pored over timeless works of Jewish literature that infused daily life with spiritual significance. The Jewish calendar was filled with occasions that focused Jewish existence on a higher purpose than the drudgery and struggle for survival that typified the Middle Ages. Moreover, individual Jews made significant contributions to the early development of the sciences, mathematics, medicine, philosophy, and literature. Nonetheless, for Jewish communities dark clouds of danger always hovered nearby.

COSSACK MASSACRES

There were many cultural and other differences between Spain, on the western edge of Europe, and Ukraine, on the continent's eastern frontier, but the two nations found common ground in hatred of Jews and periodic bursts of anti-Jewish violence.

In Ukraine, the Cossack forces of Bogdan Chmielnicki carried out massive pogroms against hundreds of Jewish communities during an uprising they staged in 1648 against Polish rule. Historians estimate the total number of deaths in the tens of thousands. Rabbi Nathan Hanover, a witness to some of the pogroms and collector of oral testimonies about others, reported on gruesome details that were all too reminiscent of October 7: "Some were skinned alive and their flesh was thrown to the dogs; some had their hands and limbs chopped off, and their bodies thrown on the highway only to be trampled by wagons and crushed by horses; some had wounds inflicted upon them, and thrown on the street to die a slow death; they writhed in their blood until they breathed their last; others were buried alive."[28]

The Cossacks' mistreatment of children and pregnant women was recounted in excruciating detail:

> They slashed the bellies of pregnant women, removed their infants and tossed them in their faces. Some women had their bellies torn open and live cats placed in them. The bellies were then sewed up with the live cats remaining within. They chopped off the hands of

> the victims so that they would not be able to remove the cats from the bellies.[29]

Sexual abuse and enslavement were also rampant: "Many were taken . . . into captivity, and women and virgins were ravished, and they lay with the women in the presence of their husbands. They seized comely women as handservants and bakers and to be wives and concubines."[30]

Chemielnicki's Cossacks also undertook wanton desecration of Jewish sacred objects: "Scrolls of the Law were torn to pieces, and turned into boots and shoes for their feet; the straps of the phylacteries served as laces around their feet. The leather boxes of the phylacteries were cast into the streets. Other sacred books served to pave the streets. Some were used for kindling purposes, and others to stuff the barrels of their guns."[31]

Although not identical, the reference to paving streets has a contemporary corollary. During the Jordanian occupation of eastern Jerusalem from 1949 to 1967, the authorities destroyed an estimated forty thousand Jewish graves on the Mount of Olives, the oldest Jewish cemetery in the world. Tombstones carted away from the graveyard were used to construct roads, Arab homes, a hotel, and latrines in Jordanian Army barracks nearby.

Such violence against sites representing Judaism undermines the view that Arab belligerence toward Israel reflects opposition to specific Israeli policies. In a similar spirit, a synagogue and study center at the Tomb of Joseph, the burial site of the Jewish biblical patriarch in the city of Nablus (Shechem), has been the target of frequent Palestinian Arab attacks. A particularly notorious mob assault occurred on October 7, 2000. "Hundreds of Palestinians overran the site," the *New York Times* reported. "The Palestinians burned the compound and tore it apart with pick-axes, sledgehammers and their bare hands." Photos of the scene showed the attackers stomping on a Jewish religious scroll and destroying prayer books. "Torn pages of Hebrew religious books were strewn on the ground," and the entire structure was set on fire, which "largely reduced the site to charred rubble." Then "Palestinian flags and a large green banner of the militant Hamas movement were hoisted over the compound as Fatah gunmen fired celebratory shots in the air." The desecration and destruction of a Jewish religious site was cause for celebration on October 7, 2000, just as the mass murder, gang rapes, and beheadings unleashed on October 7, 2023, would likewise be considered a crowning achievement.[32]

TERROR IN RUSSIA

Anti-Jewish pogroms erupted throughout western Russia following the assassination of Czar Alexander II in 1881, and continued for years. Harrowing descriptions of some of those pogroms may be found in a 192-page report compiled by Phillip Cowen, an immigration inspector sent by the U.S. government to Russia in 1906 to investigate the causes of Jewish emigration from that country. What Cowen reported and what transpired on October 7 are similar both in scope and savagery.

Cowen focused on 637 pogroms that took place in late 1905 and early 1906. The official combined death toll was 856, although "my investigation satisfies me that the death list herein given is far below the actual facts," Cowen noted at the outset. In Odessa, the official number of reported deaths was 237, but Cowen estimated the real toll was "450 as a minimum," because "many bodies were thrown by the soldiers and police into the Black Sea" or buried in unmarked locations to obscure the extent of the killing. More than 1,100 Jews were injured. The total property damage was calculated at nearly 51 million rubles, about $1.4 billion in 2025 dollars.[33]

The pogromists, some of whom were soldiers or police officers, were driven by a mixture of motives, Cowen concluded. Some harbored a religious-like fealty to the Czar, whom they understood wanted them "to punish the Jew." Others sought an opportunity "where their bloodthirsty nature may have its fill without danger of punishment." Still others "are glad of a chance to replenish their stock" of various goods—that is, by taking them from the Jews. The perpetrators had three aims: "to make it appear to the Czar and his ministers that the great body of the Russian people are antagonistic to the Jews," "to drive the Jews from the country by thus terrorizing them," and "to permit the rabble to participate in and profit by these pogroms and thus have at hand a workable element to carry out any terroristic program they may decide on."[34] Substitute "some Gazan civilians" for "the rabble" (see chapter 1) and the contemporary similarities become apparent.

Propaganda played an important role in indoctrinating the populace in Czarist Russia with antisemitic beliefs, as it did in Gaza a century later. Cowen cited the influence of *Ruskaia Retsch*, the daily newspaper produced by the League of True Russian People, which was closely associated with the Cossack gangs known as the Black Hundreds. "Its columns seem to have the distinct purpose of arousing the orthodox Russian people against the Jews, the Armenians, the Poles, and other dissident peoples."[35]

After interviewing survivors, speaking with government officials, and adding his own observations, Cowen wrote a detailed account of three pogroms that typified hundreds of others. One attack took place in Bialystok in June 1906 on a religious occasion, "when the fanatical mob is usually very much excited." As residents were viewing a "Greek-Catholic procession," an explosion was heard in the neighborhood, and a rumor spread that Jews had thrown a bomb at a priest. "The crowd waited for no proof—there was no father killed or injured—and turned on the Jews to shoot them, and the Jewish houses to loot them." Soldiers on hand ordered Jews out of their houses so they could be more easily targeted. "The killing was barbarous. . . . Nails were driven into the heads of the people, their bones were broken in their hands and bodies, and then they were clubbed to death with rifles. This went on all day." One victim's head "was smashed in and he was disemboweled." A father of eight young children had his tongue torn out; "then they tied a rope around his neck and pulled him along till the blood streamed from his eyes and nose." A woman whose husband had been wounded three times in the Russo-Japanese war found that his service to his country was of no avail; when she and her five-year-old son tried to flee their hiding place, a policeman gunned down the child. There was "a continuous fusillade" of gunfire. "If a Christian walked through the street, nobody assailed him, but as soon as a Jew appeared, bullets flew at him from all sides." It was not "a struggle between two adversaries; it was a hunt by armed [men] on unarmed people." Police agents "fired and attributed the firing to Jews" in order to "supply a fresh pretext for further attacks upon the Jews." The pogromists set fire to a large wooden building to which many had fled for safety, "and here they were burned to death." The death toll in that instance was at least ninety.[36]

Cowen arrived in the town of Siedice, in Russian-occupied Poland, in October 1905, one month after a three-day pogrom. He "found a community still terrorized, business paralyzed, and all the signs of a city that had been besieged." In addition to thirty-two known fatalities, "20 persons were so severely wounded as to be unfitted for work hereafter." The homes of the Jews "looked as though an enemy had gone through the town, its way fought step by step. Scarcely a house occupied by a Jew escaped riddling [with bullets], and in houses partly occupied by them only those portions were shot at." Broken windows and bullet holes were everywhere, including the synagogue, the Jewish hospital, and "the rabbi's home, which was a shining mark" for attack, with at least sixty bullet holes. Cowen was told "of a woman's dishonor by soldiery too horrible to repeat, and that the fire was set to cover the crime." A wounded man brought to the Jewish hospital "was bayoneted by a soldier and then mashed to death with the butt of his rifle." At least five people "became insane" because of what they experienced.[37]

"Some of the horrors the people endured are nigh unmentionable," Cowen wrote. Like the Jews barricaded in safe rooms as Hamas rampaged through their houses on October 7, the Jews in Sidice were "confined in cellars for two or three days, [where] no food or drink could be had." In one instance, "on the second day a man ventured forth to the town pumps—the only place for water, and nine times brought a pail for his thirsty children in the cellar and every time but the last, a soldier spilled it out before he got home. The ninth time he washed his dirty boots in it and they let him take it in."[38]

TERROR IN UKRAINE

War raged in Ukraine from 1917 to 1921 between the Soviet Red Army, the Russian anticommunist White Army, and Ukrainian loyalists. Amidst the strife, various groups, especially the Army of the Ukrainian Republic, led by Simon Petlura, simultaneously turned their fury on

Ukraine's Jews.[39] Between 150,000 and 200,000 Jews were slaughtered.[40] As in the preceding pogroms in Czarist Russia, the attackers in Ukraine were inspired by a combination of traditional Christian religious sentiment, extreme nationalism, resentment that some Jews (albeit a small number) were Communists, and a desire to loot. Much of what the Jews experienced in Ukraine was echoed in descriptions of October 7.

In Kamenetz-Podolsk and Bratzlav, Jews "were hanged by their hands while their tormentors chopped off various limbs." Some were "roasted alive over bonfires or had lit cigarettes applied to their wounds." In Brailov, "tongues were plucked out, their eyes gouged, and their noses cut off."[41] In many locales, hundreds of Jews were driven into a river and shot if they tried to escape from drowning. In Uman, the barbarism included "the cutting off of hands and fingers (to obtain gold wedding bands) . . . mutilation of feet, ears, noses, breasts. Naked and half-naked bodies lay where they had fallen. . . . One old Jew was shot down as he attempted to flee across an open field. He did not die immediately. His cries attracted Ukrainian schoolchildren who proceeded to stone him to death. A compatriot was shot by soldiers who then tied his body to a tree and used it for target practice."[42]

When they murdered families, the pogromists "first killed the children, torturing them in the sight of their parents, whom they slew afterward." They "ripped open the bellies of pregnant women" and beheaded infants or smashed them against stone walls.[43] In Kopai-Gorod, "a father was knocked to the pavement and forced to gag on the blood of his dead son." In Kitai-Gorod, "a young woman, carrying her child, was grabbed by the hair, tied to a horse and dragged through the streets before she and her child were shot dead."[44]

In the towns of Berdichev, Radomyshul, Fastov, Koziatyn, and Zhitomir, a popular "game" was to line Jews up and see how many could be killed with a single bullet. ("Six or seven was the record.") In Dubovo, eight hundred Jews were murdered one by one by being led to the doors of a basement between two Cossacks with swords, who beheaded them as they passed. "Within a short time, the cellar was filled with fragments of corpses." Jews who congregated together for safety were easy prey. In Trostianetz, hundreds found brief haven in a community house. But soon, a survivor recalled, "A bloody dance of death began. Knives flashed, axes whizzed, special weapons were improvised for the occasion, pickaxes and boot heels were employed. A river of blood was formed with the victims swimming in it. There were tortures and abuses such as the world never knew."[45]

In Tetiev, two thousand Jews took refuge in the town synagogue. The pogromists burned it down. Seventy more Jews were found hiding in a cellar. Soon "the children wandered about blind, their eyes put out. . . . Infants were tossed up into the air and their bodies dashing against the pavement squirted blood on the murderers." Many pogromists posed for photos with the corpses of their victims, much as the killers from Gaza would do a century later.[46]

As on October 7, these early twentieth-century Ukrainian pogromists "utilized the systematic rape of Jewish women as a strategic weapon to convey that they were superior and to dehumanize the Jewish victims," according to the authoritative study of the subject. "Vast numbers of women . . . were raped by groups of assailants, often publicly."[47] In her account of the sexual assaults, derived from contemporaneous Red Cross reports, *Against Our Will* author Susan Brownmiller described how, in a "typical" pogrom, "the gang breaks into the township, spreads all over the streets, separate groups break into the Jewish houses, killing without distinction or age and sex everybody they meet, with the exception of women, who are bestially violated before they are murdered." A Red Cross report on a pogrom in another village, Kremenchug, referred to "three hundred and fifty cases of rape . . . neither children of 12 nor old women of 60 were spared. After they had been ravished, the little girls were thrown down the water-closets."[48]

The *New York Times*, employing the guarded language of the day, reported that in many of the pogroms, "Jewish women were subjected to shameful treatment." In the town of Stepantzy, fifty Jewish women were raped on a single day, and nine were assaulted so violently that they died. In Smotrich, Jewish girls were gang-raped by ten or more Cossacks at a time. In Potoapovichi and Vaskilkov, teenage girls who resisted sexual attackers "were beaten until their faces were bloody pulps." In Kyiv, rape victims brought to the Jewish hospital were "terribly mutilated" and "suffering from venereal diseases contracted from their violators." Many Jewish women and girls "jumped out of windows in order not to fall into the hands of the murderers."[49]

A staff member at the Belgian Consulate in Kyev described what he saw in one Jewish home: "In one of the rooms, a whole family, father, mother, and little girl were lying in a pool of blood, their bodies terribly mutilated, their hands torn and cut away from the bodies by sword cuts. The faces of those martyrs were covered with wounds. Is it necessary to add that the poor little girl had been violated before she was killed?"[50]

In the town of Fastov, where six hundred Jews were massacred, the pogromists "threw themselves upon the girls under age with a perfect brutal fury and ravished them before the very eyes of their parents, powerless to interfere." Some "particularly atrocious scenes took place in the courtyard of the synagogue where the Jews had sought refuge." The courtyard was "covered with the bodies of women, children, old men, and young girls who had been ravished. Many people became insane."[51]

ARAB TERROR, THEN AND NOW

The extent of the Hamas assault set it apart from its predecessors; prior to October 7, no single day's Arab terrorist attack in the past century had claimed more than 133 lives. But the savage depravity of October 7 was consistent with longstanding patterns of Arab terrorist methodology. Strikingly similar Palestinian Arab waves of violence, including sexual assaults, were perpetrated against Jews in the Holy Land since the early 1900s. In its motivation and its execution, the Hamas attack was a continuation of the century-long Palestinian Arab terrorist war against Israel (see chapter 2).

TERROR IN THE EARLY 1900S

Attacks on the fledgling Jewish communities in Turkish-ruled Palestine began in the early 1900s. These included assaults on remote Jewish settlements in the Galilee and elsewhere, as well as attacks on Jews in or near cities such as Jaffa (1908) and Haifa (1912). Some resulted in fatalities.[52]

At the time, Palestine was very sparsely populated. By the turn of the century, approximately five hundred thousand Arabs and fifty thousand Jews lived in the area that soon became the Palestine Mandate under Great Britain—about twelve people per square mile, the same population density as modern-day South Dakota.[53] After World War I, Jewish immigration increased from 3,815 in 1919 to 8,223 in 1920.[54] The annual total was still small, and Jews remained a small minority in the country, but Palestinian Arab militants noticed the increase, especially in view of Great Britain's promise, in its 1917 Balfour Declaration, to facilitate the creation of a Jewish national home.

The Jewish newcomers brought demonstrable economic benefits to the country, including employment opportunities that attracted a significant number of illegal Arab immigrants. Yet the new economic reality did not suffice to counteract a widespread Arab perception that Jews were conspiring to take over what Muslims viewed as an exclusively Islamic domain, alongside the other five million square miles of Muslim-dominated territory in the region.

THE POGROM OF 1920

Months of antisemitic incitement in early 1920 preceded the first mass Palestinian Arab attack on Jews. In January of that year, a Muslim religious leader delivered a sermon asserting, with unintended irony, that the Jews were conspiring to sexually violate Arab women and therefore Arabs should begin preparing to unleash "days of revenge." In March, Jewish security officials in Palestine warned in an internal intelligence report that "the extremists [among the Arabs] are sure that a great revolution could be brought forth" in conjunction with the upcoming Muslim religious procession in Jerusalem known as Nebi Moussa. British investigators likewise later concluded that the Palestinian Arab violence that would erupt in the spring was long in the planning: "It seems to have been evident to everybody that a storm was heating up and might burst at any moment."[55]

It burst on April 4, 1920. Haj Amin el-Husseini, a Muslim preacher who would soon be named Grand Mufti, delivered a fiery anti-Jewish speech that incited crowds of Arabs who came to Jerusalem for Nebi

Moussa. Mobs of Arabs set out across the city, stabbing and beating Jewish passersby over the course of the next three days. Five Jews were murdered and about two hundred wounded. Many Jewish women were raped. About one hundred Jewish shops were looted and damaged, and a yeshiva was burned to the ground.[56] An American Zionist activist volunteering at Jerusalem's Rothschild Hospital described the arrival of some of the victims:

> For three days, the silent procession came in, one by one. On the first day, old men and women, little boys, stabbed in the back, beaten on the head. . . . On the second and third days, young men, dead and dying, verily cut to pieces, wrecks of human bodies bandaged and bloody on the stretchers. . . . An old woman with her ear cut off. A girl of fifteen violated. . . . [Her] little brother of twelve cut up with swords; we still hope he may live. One hundred and seventy-five wounded Jews and a half dozen dead.[57]

THE POGROM OF 1921

The following year, Palestinian Arab rioters focused on Jews in the city of Jaffa. Beginning on the first of May 1921 and continuing for a week, mobs of Arabs undertook what a later British commission of inquiry characterized as "a general hunting of the Jews." The attackers invaded Jewish shops and homes, and stabbed, beat, and raped their occupants. Arab looters followed closely in their wake. Arab policemen led a mob to slaughter fourteen Jews in an immigrant hostel; some of the Jews escaped into the street, where they were beaten to death with wooden boards and sticks. On the nearby outskirts of Tel Aviv, the peace activist Yosef Haim Brenner and four friends were massacred, their bodies mutilated. All told, forty-seven Jews were murdered in Jaffa and beyond, and 146 were wounded.[58]

THE POGROM OF 1929

In the summer of 1929, the Mufti delivered a series of incendiary sermons claiming (much like Hamas and the PA today) that the Jews were secretly planning to conquer the Al-Aqsa Mosque. Crowds streaming from Friday services at Al-Aqsa on August 30 stormed the city's Jewish neighborhoods, shooting, beating, looting, and burning. In the city's Georgian Jewish Quarter, "the mob broke into houses and slaughtered the inhabitants," the *Palestine Bulletin* (later *Post*) reported. Institutions housing the most vulnerable, such as the Misgav Ladach Hospital and the Diskin Orphanage, were singled out for attack. The private libraries of two of the era's most renowned Jewish scholars, Prof. Joseph Klausner and S. Y. Agnon, were ransacked and burned, with thousands of precious books and documents destroyed. In the suburb of Motza, a mob burst into a Jewish home "and slaughtered the whole family and burnt the house. . . . The women were raped and mutilated before the murder."[59]

The *Bulletin* reported that in Hebron, local pogromists were joined by "Arabs from the neighboring villages, Dura, Halhoul, and Yatta," which previously had been "said to be friendly to the Jews." In addition, "a number of Bedouins" took part. The first Jewish house they reached was that of Rabbi Hanoch Hassoun. "They murdered him and his wife," then they "entered another flat, that of a one-legged Jew, raped his daughter, mutilated and butchered her to death, and poked out the father's eyes in answer to his screams." The mob then "passed through the whole city, raping and butchering women, murdering men and mutilating and cutting the bodies to pieces, looting the houses and burning them."[60]

A British policeman who happened upon an atrocity in the making later described a scene not unlike those of October 2023: "On hearing screams in a room, I went up a sort of tunnel passage and saw an Arab in the act of cutting off a child's head with a sword. He had already hit him and was having another cut, but on seeing me he tried to aim the stroke at me but missed. . . . Behind him was a Jewish woman smothered in blood, with a man I recognized as a[n Arab] police constable named Issa Sherif from Jaffa in [disguise]. He was standing over the woman with a dagger in his hand."[61]

The French journalist Albert Londres interviewed survivors who tried to hide in the Hebron branch of the Anglo-Palestine Bank. An Arab mob smashed through the doors. "They cut off hands, they cut off fingers, they held heads over a stove, they gouged out eyes," Londres reported. "A rabbi stood immobile, commending the souls of his Jews to God—they scalped him. They made off with his brains." They sat yeshiva students, one after the other, on a woman's lap "and, with her still alive, slit their throats." They "mutilated the men," then "they shoved thirteen-year-old girls, mothers, and grandmothers into the blood and raped them in unison."[62] The savagery was eerily similar to October 7

Lt. Col. Frederick Kisch, head of the Zionist Executive's Political Department, reported that half of the forty-two wounded Hebron Jews hospitalized in Jerusalem had suffered multiple wounds ("in some cases from eleven to eighteen") inflicted "on various parts of the body in the most brutal way by rough and blunt instruments"; and a large majority had head injuries. Most of the victims were women, the elderly, or children.[63] Helen Bentwich, wife of the attorney-general of the British administration, visited some of the hospitalized victims and observed: "Most of the children had fractured skulls from being beaten with clubs, and other ghastly wounds. One woman whose husband had been killed put her arm round her children to protect them, and the Arabs deliberately slashed each child's head, and cut her so badly that she died. Another woman, whose fingers were cut off, lay so long under a pile of dead bodies with her baby that she has since gone out of her mind."[64]

A report by a journalist who visited one of the Hebron victims' homes in the aftermath of the carnage pointed to the peculiar intersection of antisemitism, Islamist fervor, and sexual violence: "The 12 foot-high ceiling [was] splashed with blood. The rooms looked like a slaughterhouse . . . the severed sexual organs and the cut-off women's breasts . . . lying scattered over the floor and in the beds. . . . [N]ot a single item had been left intact except a large black-and-white photograph of Dr. Theodor Herzl, the founder of political Zionism. Around the picture frame the murderers had draped the blood-drenched underwear of a woman."[65]

In all, sixty-seven Jews in Hebron were murdered, often with rapes, beheadings, eye-gougings, castrations, and other forms of mutilation.[66] The attackers also pillaged the local synagogue and burned hundreds of holy books. The Hebron victims were not Zionist settlers, but members of a centuries-old community of unassuming Talmudic scholars, and in some instances the assailants were personal friends or neighbors of their victims. But those relationships were of no avail, because the victims were Jews, and in the eyes of their attackers, that was sufficient.[67]

In the city of Safed, Arab mobs went from house to house in the Jewish neighborhood, butchering residents with axes and then setting the buildings on fire. "As the fire raged, the mob murdered and looted," the *Palestine Bulletin* reported. "Terrible mutilations were committed." Twenty-two Jews were killed, some of them tortured before being burned alive. A Jewish orphanage was also singled out for assault.[68]

One survivor described how dozens of armed Arabs smashed down the front door of his house with axes, "stabbed my father eleven times with a dagger," then pillaged the house and set it on fire. Many of the attackers had been family friends. Another survivor, Habib David Aprit, the son of a local teacher, said that "three of [my] father's former pupils entered his house, killed [my] father, killed [my] mother, and cut off the fingers of [my] sister who pretended to be dead as she lay over [our] mother." A few months earlier, the journalist Albert Londres met the city's elderly chief rabbi, Ismael Cohen. After the pogrom, he returned to the rabbi's apartment. "They slit his throat, too!" Londres wrote. "On the sofa, where he had sat and welcomed me not long ago, lay bloody remnants of clothing. A pool of dry blood stained the tiled floor . . . on the wall, the imprints of his bloodstained hands."[69]

TERROR IN THE 1930S

Palestinian Arab violence intensified in the late 1930s. With growing numbers of Jews fleeing Nazi Germany, the Mufti and his allies organized a wide-ranging effort to pressure the British to prevent those Jews from reaching the Holy Land. Their campaign included a general strike, non-payment of taxes, and violence against both Jews and the British. Between 1936 and 1939, Arabs murdered about three hundred Jews, sometimes as savagely as on October 7. In August 1936, for example, Arab terrorists burst into a home in Safed and massacred a rabbi and his three young children.[70] In March 1938, terrorists ambushed a taxi on the Safed-Haifa road, killing six passengers and mutilating their bodies. One victim, a teenage girl, reportedly was raped before being hacked to death; her body was found some distance from the shooting site.[71]

TERROR IN 1948

Arab massacres of Jews during Israel's 1948 War of Independence frequently included mutilations of victims' bodies.

Investigative journalist John Roy Carlson (Arthur Derounian), who worked undercover in Arab areas in and next to Israel during the war, wrote of the aftermath of one Arab attack near Jerusalem: "The next day on sale everywhere in the Holy City were gruesome photographs of the battle: the burnt and mutilated bodies of Haganah men . . . had been stripped of clothing and photographed in the nude. . . . Arabs carried them in their wallets and displayed them frequently."[72]

R. M. Graves, who served the British administration in Palestine at the beginning of the war, wrote in his diary that "the mutilation of the Jewish dead" was "a common practice" among the Arab forces. In one case, he noted, "a British member of my staff met a younger [Arab] in the German Colony yesterday, who showed him a handful of severed fingers."[73] Hamas assailants perpetrated similar mutilations and "trophy" displays on October 7. For example, the remains of one Israeli victim, Adir Tahar, were returned to his family without his head. A captured terrorist subsequently admitted that he and his comrades had severed Tahar's head from his body in order to sell it for $10,000 as a trophy. Before they could find a buyer, though, Israeli soldiers operating in Gaza found Tahar's head among one of the killers' belongings.[74]

Histories of the 1948 Arab invasion of newborn Israel cite numerous actions by the Arab forces that sound as if they were taken from October 7 reports. A Jewish truck from Kibbutz Negba was ambushed on the Kiryat Gat-Ashkelon road on December 6, 1947. The driver and passenger fled but were caught; their dead bodies showed "signs of abuse." On December 9, a patrol from Kibbutz Gvulot encountered Jordanian troops near the village of Shu'ot; "British troops later brought the mutilated corpses of the dead to Kibbutz Gvulot." Arab forces ambushed a Jewish convoy from Jerusalem to Gush Etzion on December 11. Medic Yaffa Mundlak, who survived, recounted: "When our bullets ran out, the Arabs went down to the road and slaughtered the [Jews] one by one. . . . The Arabs mutilated the corpses and burned the truck."[75] Jewish fighters were briefly driven from the Bir Tamila Outpost on December 26, with several of their wounded trapped under a bridge; when they recaptured the site half an hour later, they found the mutilated corpses of their comrades, their severed penises in their mouths and their eyes blinded by burning cigarettes.[76]

The new year brought more of the same. Thirty-five Haganah fighters trying to reach the besieged community of Kfar Etzion in January 1948 were ambushed; their bodies were "mutilated" so savagely, *Time* reported, that they were "reminiscent of the terrible black and white mass of photographs that had illustrated [the Holocaust] and the [Nazi] war crimes-trials." Another account put it this way: "Chunks of mutilated flesh—testicles stuffed into eye sockets, penises into mouths—lay piled in the truck [of corpses] in a pool of blood."[77] A Jew murdered by Arabs in Jerusalem in mid-January "was mutilated and his body was partially burned," while "an unidentified Jewish male was found near Haifa with the head severed from the body," the Jewish Telegraphic Agency reported.[78] On January 22, Arabs assaulted a convoy from Mikveh Yisrael passing by the town of Yazur. "All seven men in the pickup were killed, some instantly in the explosion, the other wounded victims beaten and stabbed to death by [the Arab attackers], who then abused the corpses." On February 2, Arabs ambushed a Jewish vehicle traveling through Jerusalem's Sheikh Jarrah neighborhood; they murdered two Jews, "burned the car and mutilated the bodies." Four Haganah members arrested by the British in Jerusalem on February 12 were handed over to a Palestinian Arab mob that murdered and castrated them.[79] Watching from beyond the burning hulk of his car, a survivor of an aid convoy ambushed by Arabs on its way to the besieged communities of Gush Etzion on March 27 "saw Arabs dancing around the mutilated bodies" of his comrades.[80]

Troops arriving in the immediate aftermath of the battle of the Kastel on April 9 found the bodies of several dozen Jewish soldiers who had been badly mutilated.[81] So were the last fifty defenders of Gush Etzion, who were murdered after they surrendered to Arab Legion forces on May 13. The bodies were stripped naked and in some cases mutilated so badly they were almost impossible to identify. At least one was decapitated. Some had their severed sexual organs in their mouths.[82] At the village of Qaqun, near Tulkarm, on June 5, Israeli forces found the bodies of sixteen soldiers. "On most of them were signs of severe mutilation: stab wounds, some had their genitals cut off, some were missing ears. One body was cut into many bits with its genitalia stuffed in its mouth."[83]

Eerily similar atrocities were committed during the 1967 war. Then–Hebrew University law professor Amnon Rubinstein (later a prominent leftwing Knesset and cabinet member) wrote that during his wartime service, his unit came upon the bodies of "three Israelis guarding their stranded tank [who] had been attacked and murdered by Egyptian soldiers." Their "mutilated bodies, the male organs cut off and and placed in their mouths, were found beside the tank."[84] Mutilation of Jews continued to be a staple of Palestinian Arab terrorism in the years to follow. For example, the terrorists who attacked Israeli athletes at the 1972 Munich Olympics castrated one of their victims.[85] The killers of three young seminary students in a Golan Heights yeshiva in 1975 used axes, intending "to cut off the Jews' heads" and bring them back to their comrades as evidence of a mission accomplished.[86]

THE ROLE OF ANTISEMITIC IDEOLOGY

The question of why some ordinary individuals are capable of committing acts of brutal murder was the centerpiece of Daniel Goldhagen's 1996 book, *Hitler's Willing Executioners*. His account of the actions of a particular German police unit, Reserve Police Battalion 101, sheds light on the mindset of Hamas's own savage executioners.

In June 1942, 502 battalion members were sent to the town of Jozefow, in German-occupied southern Poland. They were instructed to force local Jews out of their homes, take them to a nearby forest, and shoot them point-blank. Able-bodied men would be temporarily spared for slave labor; the policemen would focus on killing Jewish women, children, and the elderly.

Just before the mass murder began, unit commander Major Wilhelm Trapp gave his men a pep talk. He explained that slaughtering Jews was necessary because the Jews were to blame for Allied bombings of German cities. Trapp also informed the men that anyone who felt he could not do the job would be excused without penalty. Only a dozen policemen excused themselves.[87]

Prof. Goldhagen's analysis of the murder process emphasized the killers' close proximity to their victims. When a truck unloaded its Jewish prisoners at the edge of the Józefów forest, each of the waiting policemen would select a victim. The two would then walk together to the nearby execution site. Many of the captives were children. The walk "afforded each perpetrator an opportunity for reflection," Goldhagen noted. "It is highly likely that, back in Germany, these men had previously walked through woods with their own children by their sides. . . . In these moments, each killer had a personalized, face-to-face relationship to his victims."[88]

Goldhagen wondered if the typical policeman ever "asked himself why he was about to kill this little, delicate human being who, if seen as a little girl by him, would normally have received his compassion, protection, and nurturing." Or perhaps it was that the killer could only "see a Jew, a young one, but a Jew nonetheless," and therefore accepted "the reasonableness of the order, the necessity of nipping the believed-in Jewish blight in the bud."[89]

The killing mechanics were necessarily "a gruesome affair," Goldhagen noted. "Each of the Germans had to raise his gun to the back of the head, now face down on the ground, that had bobbed along beside him, [and] pull the trigger." They had to "remain hardened to the crying of the victims, to the crying of women, to the whimpering of children," and to the splatterings of blood and gore. The reserve police officers slaughtered defenseless Jews in this manner for hours on end.[90]

Both Goldhagen and Christoper Browning, author of *Ordinary Men: Reserve Police Battalion 101 and the Final Solution*, emphasized the formative role of antisemitic ideology in facilitating the deeds of these killers. "The men of Reserve Police Battalion 101, like the rest of German society, were immersed in a deluge of racist and anti-Semitic propaganda," Browning wrote. "Furthermore [the men received] indoctrination both in basic training and as an ongoing practice within each unit. Such incessant propagandizing must have had a considerable effect in reinforcing general notions of German racial superiority . . . as well as Jewish inferiority and otherness."[91]

Goldhagen described what he called the uniquely "eliminationist" quality of German antisemitism. Government-controlled news media and schools dehumanized Jews as rats, spiders, or lice that had to be destroyed. The only solution to the "Jewish problem" was the "final solution," death.[92] Likewise, as details began to emerge about the atrocities committed by Hamas on October 7, the instinctive response of many observers was shock that human beings could be capable of such savagery. Shooting disabled children and elderly people at close range, binding and executing entire families together, beheading infants, gang rapes and mutilations are all acts so depraved and cruel that it seems almost unfathomable anyone could commit them. But, like the rulers of Nazi Germany, Hamas and the PA spent years inculcating their young people, through the media and schools, with depictions of Jews as vermin and insects (see chapter 3). Only such dehumanization can explain how Hamas terrorists were capable of murdering the two youngest Israeli hostages, four-year-old Ariel Bibas and his nine-month-old brother, Kfir, "in cold blood, with their bare hands," as the pathologist reported.[93] Dehumanization preceded elimination.

CIVILIAN COLLABORATORS

Another historical parallel to October 7 was the voluntary participation of European civilians, particularly Poles and Lithuanians, in Nazi atrocities.

In July 1941, mobs of civilians raped, robbed, tortured, and then murdered their Jewish neighbors in Wasosz, Radzilow, and Jedwabne, three Polish towns only nominally occupied by the German army. With minimal German support, they herded many hundreds of Jews into barns that they then set afire. They tore Jewish infants from their mothers' arms and butchered them before the mothers' eyes. In Radzilow, they dumped bodies into a pit used for curdling dairy products; one eyewitness later reported that "the earth was moving" from the breath of victims who were only half-dead. In the Jedwabne synagogue, they forced Jews to sing and destroy holy books. Peasant women in Radzilow tore the dresses off Jewish women as they were being herded off at gunpoint. One housewife acknowledged stealing and ripping apart Torah scrolls because of a popular belief that money was hidden within them. In Jedwabne, the destruction was almost complete: only seven of the town's 1,600 Jewish residents survived.[94]

As in Gaza, the massacres in the three Polish towns were preceded by years of antisemitic indoctrination. Anti-Jewish rhetoric in local literature, especially in church publications, in the 1920s and 1930s was ugly, inflammatory, and pervasive. A regional newspaper, *The Catholic Cause*, reported, in 1937, "the mood of excitement" sweeping the region as "farmers refuse to sell to Jews" and "No Jews" signs appeared. In one village, "Jewish stalls [in the marketplace] are watched so carefully that no peasant can go near them, and 250 Jewish families are doomed to hunger." Parents warned children who resisted bedtime, "The Jews will turn you into matzo." Parents also frightened children who wanted to tag along to the market that they would have to "kiss the Jewish lady's beard" at the entrance. Radoslaw J. Ignatiew, a prosecutor who headed a Polish government commission investigating the Jedwabne massacre many years later, said he encountered so much antisemitism in the course of his work that he wondered "if Poles hadn't imbibed it all with their mother's milk."[95]

Civilians also perpetrated atrocities at the Lietukis Garage, in the German-occupied Lithuanian capital of Kovno, in 1941. Over the course of three days, Lithuanian civilians slaughtered more than one thousand Jews. On day three, they herded about sixty Jews into the courtyard of the garage. An onlooker named Laimonas Noreika later described how "in the middle of the yard, in broad daylight and in full view of the assembled crowd, a group of well-dressed, spruce [neat] intelligent-looking people held iron bars which they used to viciously beat another group of similarly well dressed, spruce, intelligent people." The attackers "kept hitting them until finally they lay inert," then hosed them with water "until they came round, following which the abuse would start all over again. And so it went on and on until the hapless victims lay dead. Bodies began to pile up everywhere."[96]

Postwar testimony by a Nazi colonel, Lothar Von Bischoffshausen, provided additional details. "There were women in the crowd and many of them clambered onto chairs and crates so that they and their children could get a better view of the 'spectacle' taking place in the yard below," he recalled. "At first, I thought this must be a victory celebration or some type of sporting event because of the cheering, clapping, and laughter that kept breaking out." Members of the crowd told him that a man nicknamed "the death dealer of Kovno" was punishing "traitors." The man, about twenty-five years old, "leaned on a long iron bar as thick as a human arm and around his feet lay between fifteen to twenty people who were either dying or already dead." Armed civilians guarded another group of Jews nearby. "Every few minutes he signaled with his hand and another person quietly stepped forward and had his skull shattered with one blow from the huge iron bar the killer held in his hand," each blow eliciting "another round of clapping and cheering from the enthralled crowd."[97]

The Lietukis Garage massacre is well documented because both German soldiers and Lithuanian onlookers photographed it extensively. In the photos, dozens of Jews, some alive, some dead, are sprawled across the blood-drenched ground. Lithuanians in civilian clothes are beating the prone Jews with iron bars. Spectators are lifting children onto their shoulders to get a better look. The images are reminiscent of parents bringing their children to watch the lynching of African Americans, or Palestinian Arab crowds cheering the lynching of two Israelis in Ramallah in 2000.

RAISING GERMAN YOUTH TO KILL

The Palestinian Arab leadership was not the first to prioritize training children to hate and kill. Adolf Hitler viewed Germany's schools as a breeding ground for raising an entire generation of Nazis. Following Hitler's rise to power in 1933, German school curricula and textbooks were rewritten to reflect Nazi ideas. New biology texts advocated "Aryan" racial superiority. Atlases claimed that various territories along Germany's borders with France, Poland, and Lithuania had been stolen from Germany. History books presented German militarism as necessary to defend the country from (imagined) enemies and portrayed Jews as traitors and dangerous radicals. The Nazis even created their own version of the Cinderella story, with the prince favoring a racially pure young heroine who rejects her racially alien stepmother.

President Roosevelt recognized the danger of hate education in Nazi Germany. In 1934, he relayed to reporters an anecdote, off-the-record, to illustrate French fears of Germany's militarization.[98] "The school children in Germany are now going through an educational process," he explained. An American professor who had recently visited friends in Germany told the president she had overheard her hosts' eight-year-old son saying his nightly prayers. "He kneeled down at his mother's knee and said his prayers and ended in good German, like a good German boy, and he said, 'Dear God, please permit it that I shall die with a French bullet in my heart.'" President Roosevelt then commented, "You get that sort of thing and that is what has got the French scared when ninety percent of the German people are thinking and talking that way. If I were a Frenchman, I would be scared too."[99]

During World War II, short cartoon films created by Disney to support the war effort were shown in movie theaters prior to the main feature. One nine-minute film, *Education for Death: The Making of the Nazi*, follows a German child, Hans, as the Nazi school system turns him into a Hitler worshipper. When Hans's teacher shows him a fox capturing and eating a rabbit, Hans makes the innocent mistake of expressing sympathy for "the poor rabbit." As punishment, he must put on a dunce cap and sit in a corner, while another student gives the "correct" answer: "The world belongs to the strong. . . . The rabbit is a coward and deserves to die." Finally surrendering to peer pressure, Hans agrees that the rabbit was "a weakling" who got what it deserved. The teacher then provides the moral of the story: the German people are "an unconquerable super race" who will "destroy all weak and cowardly nations." Hans's upbringing then proceeds with "marching and 'Heil'-ing, 'Heil'-ing and marching," the narrator says. He becomes almost robotic in heeding the Nazi Party's orders to "trample on the rights of others." The narrator concludes: "For now his education is complete—his education for death."[100]

CBS news correspondent Howard K. Smith was stationed in Germany in 1940–41. The following year, back in the United States, he authored a book sharing prescient insights about young Germans that are all too similar to the lives of young Palestinian Arabs today. While other segments of the German populace were starting to become demoralized over the toll of the war effort, German youth were "enthusiastic and keep crying for more of the same," Smith wrote. "For nine years now, their malleable little minds have been systematically warped. They are growing up in a mental plaster-cast." Smith declared that he was "more afraid, more terrorized, at watching a squad of these little boys, their tender faces screwed up in frowns to ape their idolized leaders," than he was at seeing "a panzer brigade of grown-up fighters." After all, when it came to Germany's soldiers, "we only have to fight," Smith explained. "But we shall have to live under the children who are being trained for their role." In a passage eerily reminiscent of what young Palestinian Arabs are taught about the priority of martyrdom (see chapter 3), Smith wrote of the members of the Hitler Youth movement: "The highest goal any of them can attain is to die in battle for the Fuehrer. And they all strive to do so."[101]

Nazi-educated German children filled the ranks of the Hitler Youth. Teenage and preteen members took part in numerous atrocities, from forcing Jews to scrub the streets of Vienna with toothbrushes in 1938 to shooting en masse Jews swimming from sinking boats in the German harbor of Lubeck in 1945 to burning alive thousands of Jewish prisoners that same year. Menachem Weinryb, an Auschwitz survivor forced to take part in a death march from Poland to Germany, recalled how when he and the other prisoners reached the Belsen area on April 13, 1945, the German guards went to a nearby town "and returned with a lot of young people from the Hitler Youth [and local policemen]. . . . They chased us all into a large barn. . . . [W]e were five to six thousand people. . . . [They] poured out petrol and set the barn on fire. Several thousand people were burned alive."[102]

Many Hitler Youth graduates went on to join the Gestapo and participate in the mass murder of European Jewry. Upon hearing battlefield reports of Hitler Youth alumni in action, Hitler reportedly praised them as "fanatical fighters . . . fight[ing] more fanatically than their older comrades."[103] Members of the Hitler Youth also remained unflinchingly loyal to their Fuhrer to the very end of the war, even as most branches of the Nazi apparatus collapsed or surrendered.

The Allies' recognition of the long-lasting dangers of hate education led, in postwar Europe, to the policy known as denazification. Defeating Nazi Germany and its partners on the battlefield was not sufficient to ensure they would not rise again. It became necessary to root out the ideas, institutions, and symbols of the Nazi regime.

One such symbol was the Hitler salute, known in German as a *Hitlergrub* (Hitler greeting), accompanied by the words "Heil Hitler" or "Sieg Heil." After the Nazis rose to power in 1933, the salute was made compulsory for all German government employees and during the singing of the German national anthem. To entrench the Hitler salute in the national culture, the government distributed to all children a three-inch-tall plastic figurine of Hitler with a movable right arm (akin to the aforementioned doll popular in Gaza, of a child holding a rock in his upraised arm, his face covered by a *keffiyeh*). Failure to give the salute could result in criminal prosecution or worse. (German Jews were prohibited from giving the salute on the grounds that this would dishonor the gesture.)

Thus, in post–World War II Germany, the Allies outlawed the Nazi salute and all other such symbols, gestures, and activities. By eliminating all traces of Nazism from the political and educational systems, and from popular culture, Hitler's followers would never again be able to play a significant role in German society.

The Allies pursued a similar policy in Japan. The American occupation authorities rewrote the Japanese Constitution to guarantee a democratic form of government, equal rights for women, reduction of the Emperor's status to a figurehead with no actual power, and civil control over the military. They also drastically reformed Japan's schools by removing militaristic and nationalist materials from textbooks and democratizing the school system through the creation of teacher unions and elected school boards. Additionally, the Allies implemented what became known as the Shinto Directive to curb the influence of the Shinto religion, because of its militaristic elements. Shinto-linked government officials were removed from office, Shinto priests and shrines were deprived of government funding, and school textbooks reflecting Shinto ideology were revised or eliminated.

In the years following World War II, many other countries implemented laws to obstruct neo-Nazi activity, even when such legislation ruffled the feathers of some civil libertarians. As of 2025, the Nazi salute is outlawed in Germany, Austria, Slovakia, the Czech Republic, and Australia. In Sweden, giving the salute is considered a hate crime. In many other European countries, it is prohibited if used to promote Nazism. Twenty-one countries also ban public display of the swastika (most recently, Australia, in late 2023). Some nations have instituted partial restrictions on the symbol, such as permitting its display only for educational or artistic purposes. Some countries, including Germany, Greece, and Finland, prevent neo-Nazis from running for office.[104]

GENOCIDE TROPHIES

Some Hamas terrorists uploaded gruesome October 7 "trophy videos" of torture and sexual assault to the victims' own social media accounts, to intensify their families' suffering. In other instances, they livestreamed the atrocities on Facebook.

Hamas's subversion of social media to promote jihad against Jews may seem like a twenty-first-century innovation. But while the technology is new, the mindset is not. Using available media to boast about genocide has a precedent in the Holocaust.

The Nazi regime prohibited individuals from photographing the killings. Only officially assigned photographers were given access to mass killings, to record them for the government's internal records. The Germans feared that leaked images of the atrocities could lead to Allied intervention to rescue Jews (which did not happen), or become unwanted evidence in future war crimes trials (which did).

Some photos leaked out. Members of the Reserve Police Battalion 101 often photographed themselves in the act. Sometimes, Daniel Goldhagen pointed out, they used Jews "as playthings for their own satisfaction," by posing for photos showing them cutting off the beards of Jews, or compelling them to don prayer shawls and cower on the ground. "The photos capture [German] men who look tranquil and happy, and others show them in poses of pride and joy as they undertake their dealings with their Jewish victims."[105]

Both the photos of the massacre process and the posed humiliations "represented the absolute mastery of the photographed German over the Jew," Goldhagen noted. It was all "done in front of the camera's recording eye, ensuring that the victim's shame would be displayed to people for years to come. . . . This simple act conveyed unequivocally—to the German, to the Jew, to all who watched, contemporaneously or later—the virtually limitless power of the [German] over his victim."[106]

Photos taken by members of Reserve Police Battalion 101 were "generously shared among the entire battalion," Goldhagen noted, citing a battalion member who said, "They were laid out hanging on the wall and anyone, as he pleased, could order copies of them." For Goldhagen, the entire spectacle was reminiscent of "travelers purchasing postcards or asking for duplicates of friends' snapshots that have captured vistas and scenes from an enjoyable and memorable trip."[107]

High-ranking officers in some Nazi death camps ordered their underlings to compile albums of photos showing scenes from the camp, mostly of smiling Nazis and their families, sometimes posing for the camera. They were intended for the personal enjoyment of the camp commandants. Prisoners who worked in the photo lab in the Mauthausen camp created such an album; one prisoner clandestinely made an extra copy and smuggled it out of the camp to document what was taking place. The album was later used in the war crimes trial of camp commander Ernst Kaltenbrunner—exactly what the Nazis feared would be done with photos of their war against the Jews. Kaltenbrunner was convicted at Nuremberg and hanged. An album belonging to Treblinka commandant Kurt Franz included photos of the camp above a caption reading "The Good Old Days." Franz was convicted of war crimes in

1965, but sentenced only to life imprisonment. He was released after serving twenty-eight years.[108]

Among the documents released by Israeli authorities after the October 7 attack was a recording of a telephone call between a Hamas terrorist and his parents. "Hi Dad! I'm talking to you from [Kibbutz] Mefalsim," he begins. "Open my WhatsApp now and you'll see all those killed. Look how many I killed with my own hands! Your son killed Jews! It's inside Mefalsim, Dad!" The father responds, "May Allah protect you." The son continues: "Dad, I'm talking to you from a Jewish woman's phone. I killed her, and I killed her husband. I killed ten with my own hands! Dad, ten with my own hands! . . . Put Mom on the phone!" His mother tells him, "Oh my son, Allah bless you!" The terrorist continues: "I swear, ten with my own hands, Mother!" She replies, "May Allah bring you home safely!," then, "I wish I was with you! Kill, kill, kill! Kill them!" In the background is the voice of a Jewish woman crying in pain, just before she became another war trophy.[109]

Mor Brayder and her family learned of her grandmother's murder in Kibbutz Nir Oz when the killer publicized it on social media. "The whole floor was covered in blood," she said. "My grandma was lying there. The terrorist just grabbed her cellphone, took a video of her, and uploaded it to her personal Facebook account. That's how we received the news." In a video posted on TikTok, Arab terrorists filmed themselves discovering an Israeli jewelry designer cowering in a pit. On camera, one of the terrorists exclaimed with delight, "Jewish dogs, we caught one!"[110]

From the psychology and methods of the killers, to the education that inspired them, to their glorification of their cruel deeds, the historical parallels to October 7 are unmistakeable. They are not the only similarities, however. How major American universities responded to Nazism in the 1930s offered a foreshadowing of academia's responses to the Hamas invasion.

7. Universities and the Nazis

America's leading universities actively cultivated friendly relationships with the Nazi regime and Nazi-controlled German universities prior to World War II. Having long admired Germany as the international center of science, culture, and learning, many American university presidents and faculty members chose to overlook Hitler's antisemitism for the prestige of close ties with German educational institutions. While there are differences between those circumstances and those of our own time, there are some troubling parallels as well.

HARVARD

The history of Harvard University and the Nazis began with Hitler's foreign spokesman, Ernst "Putzi" Hanfstaengl, a German-born graduate of Harvard (class of 1909.) Hanfstaengl subsequently returned to Germany, actively supported the Nazi Party from its earliest days, and rose to become Hitler's spokesman to the international news media.[1]

Hanfstaengl's announcement in early 1934 that he intended to attend his twenty fifth class reunion sparked a debate on campus over whether he should be welcome at Harvard. Critics held that the policies of the Nazi regime Hanfstaengl represented repudiated Harvard's own ideals of liberty and free inquiry. Hanfstaengl's supporters included the editors of the student newspaper, *The Harvard Crimson*, who argued that the Harvard administration should not only welcome Hanfstaengl but should bestow upon him "the marks of honor appropriate to his high position in the government of a friendly country, which happens to be a great world power—that is, by conferring upon him an honorary degree."[2] Ultimately Hanfstaengl was given a red-carpet welcome by Harvard president James Conant, while students participating in a rally on campus against Hanfstaengl were arrested and sentenced to six months in prison.[3] That same year, Conant welcomed Nazi Germany's consul-general in Boston, Baron Kurt von Tippelskirch, to place a swastika wreath in the university's chapel (in honor of German war veterans who were Harvard alumni).[4]

Harvard also maintained strong ties to Nazi-controlled German universities, especially the University of Heidelberg. Even long after Heidelberg had fired all its Jewish faculty members, instituted a Nazified curriculum, and hosted a mass book burning, President Conant accepted an invitation to participate in the university's 550th anniversary celebration. Conant asserted that "political conditions" (his euphemism for Germany's persecution of Jews and elimination of civil rights) should not prevent Harvard from taking part in the 1936 event. A *Crimson* editorial hailed Conant's decision as "splendid."[5]

The Harvard administration fostered friendly relations with Nazi Germany more generally as well. When a Nazi warship, the *Karlsruhe*, docked in Boston harbor in 1934, the swastika flag flying from its mast, its officers and crew were entertained on the Harvard campus, and faculty members attended a gala reception in Boston at which the ship's captain effusively praised Hitler.[6]

Conant also rejected appeals by the Emergency Committee in Aid of Displaced German Scholars to hire—and thus save the lives of—Jewish refugee scholars fleeing the Nazis. The Harvard president declined to hire one German Jewish refugee scientist on the grounds that he was "definitely of the Jewish type—very heavy." In another instance, when colleagues suggested hiring European Jewish scholars, he responded, "A deluge of medium and good men of the Jewish race in scientific positions would do a lot of harm." Conant noted that "Yale is taking exactly the same attitude as we are." Edward R. Murrow, director of the Emergency Committee, met with leaders of universities he hoped would take in refugee scholars, including Harvard, in 1934–35. He found "a general indifference of the university world and a smug complacency in the face of what has happened in Germany . . . a tendency to consider the matter a Jewish problem and a failure to realize that it represents a threat to academic freedom in this country as well as in

Europe. Part of this attitude undoubtedly has its roots in a latent anti-Semitism."[7] From 1933 to 1941, the peak period of escaping from the Nazis, the Emergency Committee received more than six thousand appeals from European refugee scholars seeking American universities to bring them over, but was able to secure faculty positions for only 335, or fewer than 6 percent, of them.[8]

While showing only minimal interest in scholars who were victims of the Nazis, Harvard and other American universities participated in student exchange programs with Nazi-controlled German universities. The Hitler regime viewed such exchanges as a way to soften the Nazis' image abroad, and made no secret of its intentions. In 1936 and again in 1937, the *New York Times* and *Newsweek* reported that all German students intending to study overseas were required to first undergo "special training in the principles of National Socialism," and every such student "will be expected to devote some of his time [abroad] to propaganda for the Nazi regime." One of the *Times* articles, appearing just weeks before Harvard and other U.S. universities took part in the "nonpolitical" University of Heidelberg celebration, reported that the German government had enlisted Heidelberg to aggressively recruit foreign students because "it has become the center of the enthusiastic National Socialism popular with Hitler Youth." The *Times* also quoted the government official in charge of sending German students to American universities bluntly describing the students in such exchanges as "political soldiers" in service of the Reich.[9]

Not every American school with ties to Nazi Germany turned a blind eye to the Nazi takeover of the country's universities. Williams College, for one, terminated its student exchanges with Germany to protest Nazi policies. But Harvard and others maintained them.[10]

COLUMBIA

Like Harvard, Columbia actively pursued friendly relations with Nazi Germany in the 1930s, including student exchange programs and extending invitations to Nazi representatives to visit the school. In December 1933, some ten months after the Nazis rose to power, Columbia president Nicholas Murray Butler invited the Nazi German ambassador to the United States, Hans Luther, to speak on campus, and also hosted a reception for him. When students protested, Butler responded that Luther represented "the government of a friendly people" and therefore was "entitled to be received . . . with the greatest courtesy and respect." (By contrast, when students invited an anti-Nazi refugee to speak on campus the following year, Butler refused to join him on the podium.) The director of Columbia's Institute of Arts and Sciences, Russell Potter, dismissed the student protesters outside Luther's speech as "ill-mannered children." Ambassador Luther's speech remarks focused on what he characterized as Hitler's "peaceful intentions."[11]

In 1936, the Columbia administration announced that, like Harvard, it would send a delegate to Germany to take part in the University of Heidelberg celebration.[12] "Academic relationships have no political implications," President Butler declared. He then conferred with the presidents of Harvard and Yale on how to deflect criticism of their decisions to send representatives to the Nazi event.[13]

More than one thousand Columbia students and faculty signed a petition opposing Butler's decision. Columbia's student newspaper, the *Spectator*, denounced it; students protested in front of Butler's mansion; and students also held a "Mock Heidelberg Festival" on campus, complete with a bonfire, mock book burning, and posters proclaiming, "Butler Diddles While the Books Burn." Butler accused a rally leader, Robert Burke, of having "delivered a speech in which he referred to the President [Butler] disrespectfully." As punishment, Burke was permanently expelled from Columbia, even though he had excellent grades, and despite the later acknowledgement by Columbia's own attorney that "the evidence that Burke himself used bad language is slight." The protests failed to persuade Butler to reverse course. Columbia's representative to the University of Heidelberg celebration, Professor Arthur Remy, reported that he had a "very enjoyable" time at a reception for foreign delegates hosted by Nazi propaganda minister Josef Goebbels. On the eve of World War II, Butler finally changed his position regarding the Nazis; but he never readmitted Robert Burke to the university.[14]

MIT

MIT's record regarding Nazi Germany was comparable to that of the Ivy League universities. In 1933, MIT president Karl Compton pressured Jewish students to refrain from sending a protest message to Hitler over the persecution of German Jews.[15] In 1937, Compton sent an MIT representative to participate in the bicentennial celebration of the Nazi-controlled University of Goettingen, despite the warning by the editors of the MIT student newspaper, *The Tech*, that he would be "placing a feather in the cap of the educational gangsters . . . who control the present German system of schooling."[16]

Compton was asked to hire a German Jewish refugee scholar for MIT's mathematics department in 1942; he refused on the grounds that there was "a tactical danger of having too large a proportion of the mathematical staff from the Jewish race," and one Jewish math professor was already on staff. "The appointment of an additional member of the Jewish race would increase the proportion of such men in the Department far beyond the proportion of [Jews in the general] population," Compton wrote.[17]

In view of the many instances in which posters of the hostages in Gaza were torn down by Hamas supporters in 2023–24, a poster-tearing incident at MIT in May 1934 is noteworthy. It was related to the aforementioned 1934 visit of the Nazi warship *Karlsruhe* to the United States. The ship's officers and crew were being entertained at both Harvard and MIT, and local Jewish organizations and other opponents of Nazism called for a mass protest. James A. Wechsler, an anti-Nazi activist at Columbia University (and, later, a prominent journalist and editor), wrote about the MIT reception: "The officialdom of M.I.T. was . . . entertaining cadets from the ship with Dean [Harold] Lobdell as their personal supervisor. The Dean was distraught. He scurried through the building tearing down posters announcing the anti-Nazi demonstration. When one student accosted him during this performance, the Dean explained that the sponsors of the protest were not a recognized group—although they had been even granted official permission by the [administration] to use the bulletin boards."[18]

YALE

Yale University likewise pursued friendly relations with Nazi Germany in the 1930s and disregarded the plight of the Jews persecuted there.

Yale president James Rowan Angell declined an invitation by the New Haven Jewish community to speak at a local rally in March 1933 against the Nazis' mistreatment of German Jewry. A delegation of Italian Fascist students was welcomed to the Yale campus in October 1934, as was a diplomat from Nazi Germany's embassy in Washington, Dr. Richard Sallet, two months later (he addressed the Germanic Club on "The New Foundations of the German Commonwealth"). Yale participated in student exchanges with Nazi-controlled universities, and sent a delegate to participate in the 1936 University of Heidelberg celebration. When pressed to save German refugee scholars, President Angell and his administration hired six—several of them non-Jews, and most on a temporary basis.[19]

In 1938, Yale students began fundraising to rescue books from the Austrian National Library that Hitler demanded be burned. The head librarian at Yale's Sterling Memorial Library, Prof. Andrew Keogh, opposed the students' campaign, asserting that purchasing "non-Aryan books" would be "a political violation" since it would contradict Germany's ban on the sale of such books. Besides, he declared, "European bonfires are never so serious as the newspapers would make them" and were little more than "students letting off steam."[20]

GEORGE WASHINGTON UNIVERSITY

In the 1930s, George Washington University maintained a junior-year student exchange program with the Nazi-controlled University of Munich, despite that school's purging of Jewish faculty, implementation of a Nazi curriculum, and mass book burning. Some of the GW exchange students offered upbeat reports about the new Germany. Mary-Anne Greenough, for one, wrote that during her year there, she attended the Nazis' celebration of the anniversary of Hitler's failed 1923 putsch and found it "worthy of admiration."[21]

Some GW faculty who visited Germany during the 1930s likewise came back with positive descriptions of the Nazi regime. Assistant professor of philosophy Christopher Garnett, returning from a 1934 visit, reported to the campus historical society: "The optimism which permeated the Germans, even those who at first opposed the present regime, is almost unbelievable."[22]

In October 1933, Gustav Struve, an official of Nazi Germany's embassy in Washington, spoke on campus under the auspices of the GW German Club.[23] In February 1934, Gerrit Von Haeften, third secretary of the German embassy, addressed the GW German Club's Valentine party.[24] In May 1937, two Nazi representatives, the wife and daughter of the German embassy's chancellor, Franz Schulz, participated in a campus event sponsored by GW's International Studies Society.[25] The visits proceeded without any reported protest.

Both the German Club and the International Studies Society also held film screenings "procured through the German Consul," according to the student newspaper, *The Hatchet*. At least one event featured displays of Nazi Germany's swastika flag.[26] This was in April 1937, four years after Hitler's rise to power, the nationwide boycott of Jewish businesses, the book burnings, the Nazi takeover of German universities, and the mass firing of Jews from most professions; and two years after mass street violence against Jews in Berlin and the enactment of the 1935 Nuremberg Laws stripping German Jews of citizenship. Yet *The Hatchet*, a university publication, was still printing advertisements from the German government's tourism department and touting upcoming summer tours to Europe that included a visit to Nazi Germany. And George Washington University itself was still sending students to the University of Munich.[27]

The phenomenon of totalitarian governments deceiving foreign visitors was not invented by the Nazis; Josef Stalin used visits by American intellectuals and cultural celebrities to the Soviet Union to his advantage, as have other dictators.[28] Hitler, however, was particularly skilled at deceiving foreigners. In addition to the U.S. exchange students and foreign faculty who participated in the 1936 Heidelberg celebration and other events, various American university officials and professors visited Germany—either on organized tours or privately, out of curiosity—where they saw only what the government wanted them to see. Columbia University dean Thomas Alexander became convinced that Hitler's forced sterilization policy was a good way of "throwing out the criminals and other undesirables." American University chancellor Joseph Gray reported that German cities were "amazingly clean" and that "everybody was working in Germany."[29] Likewise, before visitors arrived in Berlin for the 1936 Olympics, antisemitic literature was removed from Berlin's newsstands and two thousand translators were trained in how to put the best possible face on Nazism.[30] The manipulation efforts continued during the Holocaust, most notoriously in 1944, when the Nazis invited an International Red Cross delegation to visit Theresienstadt, a Jewish ghetto in Czechoslovakia that served as a transit point for Jews being shipped to the gas chambers in Auschwitz. In the days before the visitors arrived, the Nazis ordered Jewish slave laborers to build makeshift schools, stores, a bank, and a cafe, to give the appearance of a normal village. Houses were freshly painted, but only those portions that would be visible to Red Cross inspectors as they walked down the street on a preselected route. Deportations of prisoners to Auschwitz were increased so as to temporarily relieve overcrowding in the camp. The Red Cross delegates concluded that conditions in Theresienstadt were "relatively good."[31]

There is an additional disturbing episode in the history of George Washington University's relations with Nazis. In 1985, the university presented an honorary doctorate to a noted scholar of comparative religion, Mircea Eliade. But before he was a scholar, Eliade was an outspoken antisemite and a Nazi collaborator. During the 1930s, Eliade authored viciously antisemitic articles in the extremist Rumanian periodical *Cuvantul*, supporting the fascist Legion of the Archangel Michael, better known as the Iron Guard, and accusing Jews of mounting an "onslaught" against Rumanian Christians. One article honored Ion Mota, who translated the *Protocols of the Elders of Zion* into Rumanian. Eliade was among the Iron Guard activists imprisoned by the Rumanian government for some months in 1938. After the Iron Guard assumed power in 1940, Eliade was served as one of its diplomats in London. (The British called him "the most Nazi member of the legation."[32])

The Iron Guard regime actively collaborated in the mass murder of Rumania's Jews. Among its most notorious crimes was a series of atrocities in late January 1941 eerily similar to what Hamas did on October 7, 2023. An eyewitness report published by the Jewish Telegraphic Agency described the slaughter of "at least 1,000" Jews in the capital of Bucharest. "Dozens of Jews—women and children as well as men—were . . . beaten senseless on the streets, robbed, then doused with gasoline and set afire." Hundreds more "were burned to death in hundreds of buildings to which Guardists set fire, after shooting and beating the inhabitants and looting the contents of their homes." There were "numerous cases of Jewish women whose breasts were cut off, not to mention sadistic mutilations like gouged out eyes, brandings and bone-breakings." More than two hundred Jews were taken to a municipal slaughterhouse, where they were forced to undress and then "led to the chopping blocks, where [Iron Guardists] cut their throats in a horrible parody of the traditional Jewish methods of slaughtering fowls and livestock. Tiring of this sport after a few score had been thus dispatched, 40 to 50 armed legionaries, mad with hate, beheaded the rest with axes and knives. Some mangled bodies were disposed of by pouring them down manholes to the sewers usually used to carry off animal remains."[33] Yet in his postwar writings, Eliade never criticized the Iron Guard or expressed any regret for his involvement with it.[34]

It would be unusual for a major university to confer an honorary degree without vetting the potential recipient. It is conceivable GW officials neglected to read Eliade's autobiography; perhaps Yale (1966), Ripon College (1969), Loyola University of Chicago (1970), and Oberlin (1972) likewise failed to check on Eliade's past before each gave him an honorary degree. Since the 1990s, however, numerous articles mentioning Eliade's relationship with the Iron Guard have appeared in the scholarly and general press, so there are ample grounds for revocation of the degree.[35] Moreover, there are precedents for revoking degrees at these same institutions: GW, Yale, and Oberlin each gave an honorary degree to the actor Bill Cosby, then later rescinded it after he was found guilty of multiple counts of sexual assault. As of this writing, none of the universities has revoked the award bestowed upon Eliade.[36]

ISOLATIONISM ON CAMPUS

Relatively few American college students challenged their universities' pursuit of friendly relations with Nazi Germany. Most students feared being drafted into an overseas conflict. They opposed any substantive U.S. actions against Nazi Germany and hoped that their university's efforts to improve relations with Berlin would help defuse tensions between the two countries. This brand of isolationism—driven by concern over how they would be personally impacted—had the effect of blunting students' interest in the persecution of Jews in Germany. Support for friendly relations between their universities and the Nazi regime and disinterest in the plight of the Jews effectively went hand in hand.

Surveys of twenty-two thousand American college students in the 1930s found that eight thousand of them considered themselves pacifists, and seven thousand said they would refuse military service. Another poll found that 63 percent of students favored unilateral American disarmament.[37] One driver of such sentiment was the economic stress of the Great Depression. One fourth of America's unemployed were fifteen to twenty-four years old; that encouraged a turning away from overseas troubles. Fear of being drafted if the United States was drawn into Europe's conflicts added a strong personal element to students' political calculations.[38]

An additional factor was the stance of their British counterparts. In 1933, the Oxford Student Union, the leading organization of university students in the United Kingdom, adopted a resolution declaring it would "under no circumstances fight for its king and country." Other British universities also adopted the Oxford Pledge, as it came to be known, and the widespread support it attracted in England had a snowball effect in the United States.[39]

A formidable coalition rooted in disparate motives thus took shape. Students who were struggling to make ends meet or who feared being drafted joined idealistic pacifists, Socialists, and Communists in declaring they would not fight for America. In 1934, twenty-five thousand students took part in a one-hour walkout from classes to demonstrate their opposition to war. An American version of the Oxford Pledge, "We will not support the U.S. government in any war it may conduct," attracted growing support on campuses. After explosive congressional hearings on World War I profiteering by banks and weapons manufacturers, the Student Strike Against War mushroomed to 175,000 participants in 1935.[40]

Participation in the annual strike peaked in 1936 at five hundred thousand, nearly half the college student population in America. But tensions were beginning to surface. The Communist students who dominated the leadership of the national American Student Union (ASU) in the 1930s took their positions based on the party line. In the early 1930s the Soviet Union preferred that America stay out of European affairs; hence their followers on U.S. college campuses secured the ASU's support for the American version of the Oxford Pledge. But when the Spanish civil war erupted in 1936 and the Kremlin decided to back the leftwing Spanish government, Communist students began clamoring for the United States to do likewise. Their sudden reversal of position left student activists deeply divided. In 1939, when the Soviets signed a nonaggression pact with the Nazis and then joined Hitler in invading Poland, their American followers reversed course again and embraced American isolationism, much to their fellow-students' confusion and dismay. The tensions exploded into public view in December 1939 following the Soviet invasion of Finland. At the ASU's annual convention, a resolution condemning the Soviet attack was defeated overwhelmingly.[41]

Communist activists also dominated the leadership of another organization, the American Youth Congress (AYC), which enjoyed crucial support from First Lady Eleanor Roosevelt because of its advocacy of New Deal–style initiatives for young people. In February 1940, the AYC held a conference in Washington DC. The 4,466 delegates were invited to a picnic on the White House lawn, during which President Roosevelt would deliver remarks. FDR took the opportunity to give the students an earful about the AYC's claim that his proposal for modest financial aid to Finland would "force America into an imperialistic war." The president said "that reasoning was unadulterated twaddle," a slap he repeated a second time for emphasis. He also called their claim "about the silliest thing that I have ever heard in my fifty-eight years of life." As for the AYC's assertion that the invasion was justified because Finland posed a threat to the USSR, "nobody with any pretense at common sense" believed that, the president said.[42]

The contrast between Roosevelt's response to his youthful critics and that of President Biden was striking. On multiple occasions when pro-Hamas hecklers shouted at Biden over Gaza, he responded by insisting that he had been doing what the hecklers demanded—pressuring Israel to cease firing at Hamas and withdraw from Gaza. By contrast, Roosevelt considered his pro-Soviet student critics to be ignoramuses, and told them so. Their positions might be "based perhaps on sincerity, but, at the same time, on 90 percent ignorance of what they were talking about," FDR said. "There is room for improvement in common-sense thinking and definite room for improvement in the art of not passing resolutions concerning things one doesn't know anything about." He characterized them as "young people [who] get a smattering of the subject from two or three speakers who have but a smattering on the subject themselves."[43]

Ignoring scattered boos from the crowd, President Roosevelt gave the students a lesson about the Soviet regime they were defending. The USSR, he said, is "run by a dictatorship, as absolute as any other dictatorship in the world." Its way of life was based on extreme "regimentation." It was responsible for "the indiscriminate killings of thousands of innocent victims" and "the banishment of religion." His own hope that Soviet Russia would "eventually become a peace-loving, popular government with free ballot" had been "shattered." He concluded by reminding the students that they were enjoying freedoms that would be denied them under the regime for which they had so much sympathy: "If we had a different kind of government, we couldn't have this meeting here on the White House lawn."[44]

FDR cut to the heart of a phenomenon that was as evident in extremist movements on campuses in the 2020s as it was in 1940s. Their most active elements tend to be ideologically driven militants—Communist Party members then, Islamist Israel-haters now. Specific social, economic, or political circumstances create opportunities for them to attract sympathetic students, not because those students are deeply acquainted with the relevant history, but precisely because they are not. Typical American college students in the 1930s had not read *Mein Kampf*; typical students today are not aware of the Palestinian Arab affinity for *Mein Kampf*. For many, highly personal factors such as the fear of being drafted or a desire to be part of a popular and seemingly idealistic cause may have influenced whether they marched against war in the 1930s or for Hamas later. Whatever their motives, the students' actions in the 1930s further contributed to the already substantial public support for remaining aloof in the face of Hitler's outrages and fascist aggression in Spain, Ethiopia, and China.

OTHER TROUBLING ECHOES

Additional similarities between then and now are also apparent. University presidents in the 1930s found it politically convenient to ignore the persecution of Jews and befriend their persecutors. In 2023–24, many college presidents likewise concluded that appeasing pro-Hamas forces on their campuses was more advantageous than siding with besieged Jewish students. Tolerating genocidal chants and the illegal occupation of swaths of campus grounds was easier than risking even greater campus turmoil. Decisive action against trespassers and anti-Jewish harassers would have meant negative publicity and, in some cases, displeasing Arab regimes that had given the school substantial financial contributions. From 2014 to 2019, Qatar, Saudi Arabia, and the United Arab Emirates contributed a combined $4.4 billion to American universities and colleges. Among the top recipients were Harvard at $894 million, MIT at $859 million, and Yale at $495 million.[45]

Today's American college students, too, share some tendencies with their pre–World War II predecessors. Ideological radicals in those days took positions based on the party line, not on a reasoned or independent analysis of facts, trends, or history; too many of today's most passionate campus protesters likewise refuse to look closely at the beliefs and actions of the Arab terrorists whose cause they champion. Many students who professed to care about the downtrodden nonetheless turned a blind eye to the suffering of Jews in Europe then; many today have turned a deaf ear to the cries of the Jewish victims of Hamas rape and torture. Even those students whose indifference to the Holocaust was shaped by convenience or a desire for social acceptance find their parallel in those whose response to October 7 was to simply follow the crowd.

The aftermath of October 7 undermined long-held assumptions among American Jews about the intellectual standards of the country's leading institutions of higher education. Traditionally, universities were the gateway to prosperity for hardworking children and grandchildren of Jewish immigrants aspiring to rise above the sweatshops and other backbreaking work that entrapped their parents or grandparents. The nation's citadels of learning offered Jews an unparalleled path to economic success and social integration. In post–World War II America, most universities opened their doors to Jews, who soon rose to prominence on faculties nationwide, in all fields, although especially in the liberal arts. Yet in the wake of October 7, many liberal-minded professors and their ostensibly liberal-minded students aligned themselves with those in the Middle East who represent values antithetical to liberalism.

The fact that universities, of all institutions, became the centers of unreason and intolerance concerning Hamas and Israel, shocked Israeli president Isaac Herzog. Himself a graduate of Cornell and New York University, Herzog expressed horror that "this is happening not on the fringes of society but in the very temples of scholarship, in halls meant to be beacons of humanism, progress, and rigorous inquiry—and it is happening not in Europe a century ago, but in the United States in 2023."[46]

The campus turmoil following October 7 also played an important part in the national debate, still unresolved, over the nature and consequences of antisemitism, to be explored in the next chapter. How has antisemitism evolved in America? Is anti-Zionism a form of antisemitism? Is it antisemitic to applaud the mass murder of Jews?

8 Antisemitism and Anti-Zionism

The United States was rocked by an unprecedented wave of antisemitism in the aftermath of October 7. More than ten thousand antisemitic incidents were recorded by the Anti-Defamation League during the first year following the Hamas attack, a 200 percent increase over the previous year and by far the largest number of incidents recorded in a one year-period during the more than four decades since the ADL began tracking them.[1] Why did October 7 trigger such an outburst? How did it differ from previous antisemitism in America? How did our nation's leaders respond?

For most of the common era—nearly two thousand years—antisemitism was primarily religious in nature. For eighteen hundred years, Christians persecuted Jews for refusing to accept Christianity. Keeping Jews in a decrepit and vulnerable state was intended to demonstrate they were being punished by God for not accepting Christianity. Meanwhile, for thirteen hundred of those years, Jews in the Muslim world were systematically persecuted for refusing to accept Islam, and kept in a degraded state because their persecutors believed it demonstrated the inferiority of the Jews' religion. In both Christian Europe and the Muslim Middle East, some periods were not quite as bad as others, due to unique local circumstances. By and large, however, religious-based antisemitism, in its various forms, kept most Jews in misery and fear for their lives.

EMERGENCE OF SECULAR ANTISEMITISM

In late nineteenth-century Europe, concurrent with the rise of secular nation-states, a number of German and French nationalists began shifting their attacks on Jews to more secular accusations: Jews are not loyal to the countries in which they live, Jews cheat non-Jews, Jews are a harmful influence on modern culture.

Secular antisemitism represented a significant departure from the old resentment of Jews for rejecting Christianity. Unlike the medieval solution of killing Jews who refused to convert, modern Jew-hatred promoted legal restrictions and other types of governmental action against Jews. To distinguish this new criticism of Jews from the medieval religious variety, the German anti-Jewish agitator Wilhelm Marr coined the term "antisemitism" in 1879.[2] His target was still the Jews; but he hoped the new, more scholarly sounding label would help legitimize Jew hatred.

The most dramatic manifestation of the new flavor of antisemitism was the Dreyfus Affair, in which trumped-up charges of treason were leveled against a French Jewish army officer in 1894. The anti-Jewish mobs rampaging through the streets of Paris were seized by a novel kind of passion. The accusation was not that Lt.-Col. Alfred Dreyfus refused to embrace Christianity; it was that because he was a Jew, he was disloyal to his country.

The most widely circulated document of the new antisemitism was the 1903 Czarist Russian fabrication *The Protocols of the Elders of Zion*. It did not blame Jews for killing Jesus; it claimed to expose their secret international conspiracy to rule the globe. Decades later, the *Protocols* would become a veritable bible for antisemites around the world, translated into numerous languages and uniting Jew-haters across national and cultural boundaries.

Secular antisemitism did not replace religion-based antisemitism; it supplemented it. Although religious hatred of Jews became less predominant in Western European countries such as France and Germany in the early twentieth century, it remained strong and occasionally flared into pogroms in East European countries where traditional Christianity still held sway during the interwar period, such as Russia and Poland. The race-focused antisemitism promulgated by the Nazis would draw support from both secular and religious haters of Jews.

ANTISEMITISM IN AMERICA

Antisemitism in the United States followed a different trajectory than its European counterpart. Until the mid-1800s, antisemitism did not constitute a major problem for American Jews. The small size of the Jewish community—numbering in the tens of thousands—made it relatively easy for Christians to accept Jews as part of American society. In addition, the United States was home to adherents of minority Christian sects who had fled Europe to escape persecution and hence were receptive to the principle of religious tolerance. The very concept of America as a land of religious liberty, with church and state separated, guaranteed—at least in theory—an equal place for Jews. It also meant that, unlike in Europe, religious institutions were never in a position to exercise control over the government and undertake state-sanctioned persecution of Jews. The absence of severe economic crises during the first century of American life also helped ensure a degree of social tranquility prior to the Civil War.

The American Jewish community grew significantly later in the century. A young and rapidly expanding nation urgently needed inexpensive labor, and opened its doors wide to immigration. Among the millions of immigrants who arrived between 1820 and 1860 were more than one hundred thousand German Jews seeking to escape political and economic turmoil as well as antisemitic discrimination. By 1877, American Jewry numbered some two hundred and fifty thousand, with the largest portion (about fifty thousand) in New York City.[3]

Some Jews achieved significant financial success as the heads of banking firms or the founders of department stores. Jewish prominence and success attracted envy. Post–Civil War literature stereotyped Jews as vulgar in their mannerisms or lifestyle and intruding in a culture where they did not belong. It was a time of struggle for social status, with former members of the middle class resenting Jewish social climbers. They established private clubs and social registers anchored in genealogical research to exclude "undesirables." For the excluded

Jews, however, ridicule and social or economic discrimination were a far cry from the anti-Jewish violence of the old world.

Unlike in Europe, antisemitism was never accepted, much less sponsored by, government authorities in the United States. From America's earliest days, federal law, at least as written, guaranteed equal rights for citizens of all religious faiths. Many state constitutions originally did specify that a citizen had to be Christian in order to vote, or hold office, and some states also required an oath upon the New Testament to take office—regulations that reflected the Protestant values dear to the new nation's majority more than a desire to disenfranchise America's then-tiny Jewish minority. By 1877, all such restrictions had been removed.

Major waves of Russian Jewish immigration to the United States began in the late 1800s. Pogroms, economic pressures, and severe residential restrictions under the czar pushed more than two million Russian Jews to seek haven in America between 1881 and 1924.[4] Backlash quickly followed. The tight restrictions imposed on immigration in the 1920s were motivated to a significant extent by anti-Jewish prejudice.

Antisemitism in America was boosted by fears arising from the 1917 Communist revolution in Russia. While traditional Church teachings reinforced old religious prejudices about Jews, new sources of anxiety emerged, such as Russian Jewish immigrants competing for jobs, introducing unwanted cultural changes, and advocating radical European ideologies. Automobile magnate Henry Ford, a national hero for his technological innovations, exploited those fears. He gave antisemitism a significant boost by serializing *The Protocols of the Elders of Zion* in his newspaper *The Dearborn Independent*—which had the largest circulation of any newspaper in the United States—in ninety installments from 1920 to 1922.[5]

The social and economic strains of the Great Depression further exacerbated antisemitism in America. During the 1930s, more than one hundred antisemitic organizations were active nationwide. Polls in the late 1930s and early 1940s found between one-third and one-half of the U.S. public perceived Jews as greedy, dishonest, and aggressive. About 15 percent of respondents said they would support "a widespread campaign against the Jews in this country" and an additional 20–25 percent indicated they would feel sympathy for such a movement; only 30 percent said they would actively oppose it.[6]

Isolationism, often laced with antisemitism, rapidly gained ground during this period. Extremist members of Congress, such as Rep. John Rankin (D-Mississippi), accused "international Jews" of trying to drag America into overseas conflicts. So did celebrity aviator Charles Lindbergh, who had become a national hero in 1927 by making the first solo transatlantic flight. He emerged as the most prominent public spokesman for the isolationist America First movement. Lindbergh publicly accused Jews of trying to involve America in a war with Germany and bemoaned "Jewish influence" in the media and government.[7] Charles E. Coughlin, a Catholic priest, used his influential radio show to promote isolationism and denounce Jews as manipulators of international finance and promoters of Communism. Tens of millions of listeners heard his message each Sunday. Beginning in 1938, excerpts from *The Protocols of the Elders of Zion* appeared in Coughlin's magazine, *Social Justice*, which had more than two hundred thousand subscribers at its peak.[8] Coughlin's Christian Front movement played a major role in waves of antisemitic assaults in New York City and Boston in 1943–44.[9] In addition, discrimination against Jews in employment and school admissions, and exclusion from clubs and resort hotels, was commonplace.

ANTI-ZIONISM, THEN AND NOW

Anti-Zionist sentiment in the United States emerged during the interwar years, in opposition to the rising tide of public sympathy for the idea of reestablishing a Jewish state in Palestine. Articulated primarily by academics, Arab Americans, and some clergy, anti-Zionism often contained a streak of thinly disguised antisemitism. The prominent educator Henry Pritchett declared in 1926 his expectation that Palestine's Jews "would develop an aggressive, egotistic national character without capacity for cooperation with the rest of the world." (Pritchett died before the establishment of the State of Israel, which became one of the leading contributors of medical, scientific and technological innovations to the international community.)[10] In the same spirit, Roger

Baldwin, executive director of the American Civil Liberties Union, claimed in 1929 that Zionist policies concerning the Arabs showed that "tolerance seems to be a stony road, even for Jews."[11]

Pritchett and other anti-Zionists sometimes weaponized passages from Jews' own sacred literature to lambast alleged Jewish shortcomings. He chastised Jewry for believing "the illusion that [they are] a chosen people."[12] Likewise, the liberal clergyman John Haynes Holmes in 1929 saw in the Zionists' arguments for Jewish statehood "war mania all over again, and once again as in ancient times, the prophets are stoned and slain." In Holmes's analogy, Jewish anti-Zionists were the prophets.[13]

A small number of American Jews strongly opposed Zionism. They were, for the most part, nineteenth-century German immigrants or their offspring who were religiously affiliated with Reform Judaism. As the modern Zionist movement began to attract attention, prominent Reform rabbis repudiated it, citing its likely negative impact on the goal of Jews integrating in the modern world. A Reform rabbinical gathering in Philadelphia in 1869 rejected "the restoration of the old Jewish state under a descendant of David" because it would involve "a second separation from the nations of the earth." Similarly, a conference of eighteen Reform rabbis in Pittsburgh in 1885 formally denounced the idea of reviving the ancient Jewish state—and other aspects of traditional Jewish beliefs and practices—as contrary to "the views and habits of modern civilization."[14]

The period in American Jewish history in which German-born Jews were the majority, which was most of the 1800s, gave way to waves of immigrants from Russia and other East European countries. Generally they were more traditional in their dress and lifestyles, and much more sympathetic to the idea of Zionism even as they themselves opted for life in America. Many of the German-American Jews looked with disdain at these Yiddish-speaking newcomers, perceiving the Russians' ethnically assertive ways as pushy, backward, and a threat to the integration of Jews in American society. "The whole Zionistic movement in this country" is made up of "ignorant people" who are determined "to show their contempt for those who try to advise them," an early American Jewish critic of Zionism charged. *The American Israelite*, an anti-Zionist newspaper, asserted that "the whole noise [in support of Jewish statehood] is made by some persons of recent immigration with which we American Jews have absolutely nothing to do."[15]

Anti-Zionism in the American Jewish community reached its point of greatest influence in the 1940s, when several dozen Reform rabbis established the American Council for Judaism, the first U.S. Jewish organization devoted to opposing the creation of a Jewish state. The council had about fourteen thousand members at its peak. That represented fewer than 1 percent of American Jewish adults, and constituted a decided minority even within the Reform movement from which it had emerged. Despite the Council's small size, the U.S. State Department treated it as a significant force in Jewish life, and the Council enjoyed ample coverage in the *New York Times*.[16] The publisher of the *Times*, Arthur Ochs Sulzberger, feared the creation of a Jewish state would undermine the status of Jews as equal American citizens and was anxious to demonstrate that he would not utilize the newspaper to promote Jewish concerns. As a result, anti-Zionists were accorded prominent space in news articles, opinion columns, and letters.[17] Despite that public relations advantage, the Council failed to win many converts to its viewpoint or to persuade the U.S. government to oppose Jewish statehood. The establishment of Israel in 1948 put an end to the Council's mission, and in effect concluded the Jewish public debate in America regarding Zionism. All the major Jewish religious denominations—Orthodox, Conservative, and Reform—rallied around the Jewish state.[18]

A new version of the debate over Zionism emerged in the aftermath of October 7, 2023. A small group of self-identified Jewish anti-Zionists participated prominently in a number of the pro-Hamas protests in major public venues, usually under the banner of the organization Jewish Voice for Peace (JVP). Established in 1996, with just "1,000 plus" members by its own accounting,[19] JVP long has faced strong criticism from the organized Jewish community; the Anti-Defamation League, for one, characterized it as "a hate group, the photo inverse of white supremacists."[20] For years, JVP had focused largely on issuing press releases and petitions. But as anti-Israel protests spread in the United States following the Hamas invasion, JVP embarked on a series of provocative, high-profile street protests to dramatize its contention that Israel should be replaced by a state of Palestine. News media coverage and social media posts attracted attention disproportionate to JVP's tiny size.

It may seem counterintuitive that the American Council for Judaism would emerge at the height of the Holocaust, and that JVP would become newly energized in response to October 7. Logically, anti-Jewish atrocities abroad should influence American Jews to become more supportive of Zionism. After all, the cause of Jewish statehood was predicated foremost on a pessimistic worldview that emphasized the inevitability of antisemitism and the vulnerability of Jewish communities throughout the Diaspora. By contrast, the optimistic worldview, embodied by both the old American Council and the new JVP, follows the vision promulgated by classical Reform Judaism in the late 1800s and early 1900s in which civilization is marching steadily toward a world of peace and progress, and Jews should become ever more integrated in the societies around them. Zionism is separatism; anti-Zionism is universalism. The mass murder of Jews in Europe in the 1940s lent credence to the Zionist view that even in countries of scientific and cultural sophistication, and where Jews are significantly assimilated, severe Jew-hatred will eventually emerge. Likewise, the murder and gang rapes of October 7, applauded by the mainstream Palestinian leadership, strengthened the argument that Palestinian Arab terrorists and their allies are intractably violent and extreme.

That being the case, the logical response of anti-Zionist Reform rabbis to news of the Holocaust in 1942 should have been either to shift away from anti-Zionism (as some did), or at least remain silent (as many others did), but certainly not to create an organization to fight Zionism—which is what a small but vocal minority of them did. To lobby against Zionism in 1942 was, in practice, to undermine the possibility of establishing a haven in Palestine for millions of Jews desperately trying to flee from the Nazis. Likewise, the logical response of the leaders and members of Jewish Voice for Peace to the atrocities of October 7 should have been to reconsider the wisdom of their anti-Israel extremism, or at least to remain silent, not to become more extreme than ever before. To lobby against Zionism after October 7 was, in practice, to take the side of the rapists and beheaders of defenseless women and children.

The explanation for this quixotic behavior, in both cases, is anchored in a particular historical precedent. For centuries, Jews in medieval Europe were restricted to ghettoes, deprived of civil rights, and subjected to oppressive discrimination that made it impossible for them to become part of the wider society, beyond limited commercial interactions. That began to change in the late 1700s, as a new era of scientific and cultural enlightenment dawned in Europe. A growing number of German Jews, feeling alienated from traditional Jewish beliefs and anxious to be part of German social and cultural life, underwent insincere conversions to Christianity. "These Jews, like most Germans of the day, believed that total conformity to the religion and culture of the majority was essential for complete loyalty to the Fatherland," a prominent scholar of the period, David Rudavsky, has written. "They considered the prize of emancipation well worth the price of apostasy. The upper stratum in German Jewry, seized with high social ambitions, commonly succumbed to this viewpoint." Conversion was their admission ticket to German society.[21]

American Jewish anti-Zionism prior to World War II followed a similar ideological trajectory. Its adherents saw Zionism as a reversal of the gains Jews had achieved in the nineteenth-century emancipation. An early document of the anti-Zionist movement, a petition by several dozen prominent American Jews to President Woodrow Wilson in 1919, charged that Zionism represented "a leap backward of 2,000 years," meaning that it would segregate Jews from non-Jews and thereby drag Jewry back to the pre-emancipation era. In the same spirit, spokesmen for the American Council of Judaism twenty-five years later regularly derided Zionism as "medieval" and "a surrender to the pre-emancipation concept." The news that reached the United States in 1942 about the mass murder of Jews in Europe did not dissuade the Council's founders from launching their movement that year. On the contrary: for them, the mass killing may well have illustrated the danger they feared Jews in America would face if their fellow-citizens turned against them the way the German public turned against European Jewry. Hating Zionism served as a kind of imaginary shield against antisemites hating them. They believed anti-Zionism would be their admission ticket to American society.[22]

Likewise, it may be that the mass murder, rape, and torture of Israeli Jews on October 7 made many Jewish anti-Zionists more, rather than less, passionate about the Palestinian cause because it pointed to what they feared might happen to them if they did not demonstrate, in the most dramatic fashion possible, their opposition to Israel's existence. Displaying intense and unwavering anti-Zionism also became the price to pay for acceptance in the social and political circles with which they most closely identify, where hatred of Israel is a cornerstone belief. Columbia University's Task Force on Antisemitism alluded to this phenomenon in its assessment, in early 2024, that Jewish students were being "asked to assure people, as the price of acceptance, that they are not 'Zionists.'" If they declined to pay that price, they could expect to be "singled out in class by their teachers and subjected to public ostracism." Some prominent Jewish anti-Zionist students acknowledged that Jews who sympathized with Israel could expect "to be ostracized on campus."[23]

POSTWAR CHANGES IN ANTISEMITISM

Antisemitism in the United States receded noticeably in the post–World War II years. The revelations of the full extent of the Holocaust, combined with the loss of so many American lives in the war against Nazi Germany, discredited everything Nazism represented. Postwar advances in civil rights shaped a more tolerant society. Federal and state antidiscrimination legislation was enacted. Antisemitism was relegated to the fringes of American society. There were exceptional incidents, such as the worldwide outbreak of swastika daubing in 1959–60 that reached many U.S. cities, but these were atypical of the era.[24]

Antisemitism began to surface more frequently in the 1960s, but from different sources. In addition to emanating from the far right, as in previous decades, increasingly it also came from the far left. The government of the Soviet Union, which initially supported the establishment of the State of Israel, soon embraced the Arab cause instead and simultaneously became a major international sponsor of antisemitic propaganda. Some of the more graphic examples of Soviet antisemitism borrowed imagery that strongly resembled *Der Sturmer*, the chief propaganda organ of the regime that tens of millions of Soviet citizens had recently died fighting against.

Such imagery became plentiful in the news media and schools throughout the Arab world, as Israeli Foreign Minister Abba Eban noted in a 1968 address. "The propaganda against Israel [in the Arab world] portrays us as a caricature, hook-nosed with tails, horns, and monstrous attributes outside the human context.," Eban declared. "Nazism is deeply embedded in the style and content of the Arab war against Israel. Last week President [Abdul] Aref of Iraq spoke about Jewish people in terms which would have done justice to the loathsome Goebbels and Streicher."[25] Palestinian Arab spokesmen in particular have often cited classic antisemitic tracts of European origin, such as *Mein Kampf* and *The Protocols of the Elders of Zion*, as proof that Israel, Zionism, and Jews are evil.[26]

A second new source of antisemitism in the late 1960s was the Black Power movement. This was especially painful to the American Jewish community because throughout the previous century, many American Jews actively assisted the advancement of African Americans. Jews played a central part in creating the NAACP (in 1909) and similar organizations. Jewish philanthropists built more than five thousand schools for rural African Americans from 1914 to 1932.[27] Thousands of Jews were active in the black civil rights movement of the 1950s and 1960s, among them a large portion of the movement's volunteer attorneys. Some African American activists resented the idea of becoming objects of charity and bristled at playing secondary organizational roles to Jewish benefactors. This was particularly true of the militant Black Panthers, whose hateful rhetoric often referred to Jews, Zionism, and Israel interchangeably.

In more recent times, high-profile expressions of anti-Jewish hostility sometimes came from more mainstream African American sources. The Rev. Jesse Jackson embraced Yasir Arafat (in 1979) and derided

Jews as "Hymies" (in 1984).[28] The Rev. Al Sharpton played a leading role in antisemitic rioting in Crown Heights, Brooklyn, in 1991.[29] Black Muslim leader Rev. Louis Farrakhan emerged as an outspoken advocate of antisemitism in the 1990s and nevertheless sometimes enjoyed friendly relations with segments of the mainstream African American community.[30] In 2016, the Black Lives Matter movement accused Israel of "genocide," and two years later, African American activists ejected Jews from the leadership of the Women's March movement.[31] The casual use of antisemitic rhetoric by several prominent black cultural celebrities in recent years added fuel to the fire.[32]

Another new variation of antisemitism in the United States, beginning in the 1980s, was to be found among some Arab-American organizations. Groups such as the American-Arab Anti-Discrimination Committee, the Muslim Public Affairs Council, and the Council on American-Islamic Relations defended the civil rights of Arab and Muslim Americans but also periodically veered into cheerleading for the PLO, Hamas, and Hezbollah, comparing Israel to the Nazis, and promulgating conspiracy theories about "Jewish power."[33]

By the early 2000s, an important new aspect of antisemitism in America was the sporadic occurrence of antisemitic terrorist attacks. Although vandalism often had been a feature of antisemitic incidents over the years, murderous violence was rare. The new wave of attackers spanned the ideological spectrum. In 2006, a Muslim extremist shot at the offices of the Seattle Jewish Federation, killing one and wounding five. In 2009, a white supremacist attacked the U.S. Holocaust Memorial Museum, killing a security guard. A neo-Nazi shot up a Jewish community center and a Jewish retirement home in Kansas in 2014, killing three. A white supremacist massacred eleven congregants in a Pittsburgh synagogue in 2018. The following year, a white supremacist fired shots at a synagogue in Poway, California, killing one and injuring three. Later that year, members of the antisemitic "Black Hebrews" cult attacked a kosher supermarket in Jersey City, New Jersey, killing six people; and an African American assailant wielding a machete murdered a rabbi and wounded four others at a Hanukkah party in Monsey, New York.

THE U.S. GOVERNMENT VS. ANTISEMITISM

Among the most significant developments concerning post–World War II antisemitism in America was the federal government's new interest in directly addressing the problem. The transformation began as a result of legislation introduced by Congressman Tom Lantos (D-California), himself a Holocaust survivor, in 2004, requiring the State Department to issue an annual report on antisemitism around the world and creating a position of U.S. envoy for monitoring and combating antisemitism abroad. President George W. Bush's State Department opposed the Lantos bill on the grounds that the U.S. government should not give "preference" to any "single religious or ethnic group," but on the eve of election-year campaign appearances in heavily Jewish areas of Florida, the president signed the bill into law.[34]

The U.S. government's involvement in monitoring or combating antisemitism worldwide risked subjecting the issue to any given administration's diplomatic or political priorities. The first antisemitism report issued under the Bush administration tread very lightly concerning Arab regimes with which it was pursuing friendly relations. The sections on Iceland and Armenia were much longer than those on the Palestinian Authority and Saudi Arabia. The antisemitism of Arab regimes likewise received sparse attention in the administration's second report. Perhaps in order to avoid future criticism over the slant of the reports, the State Department subsequently changed the reporting procedure. Instead of having the antisemitism envoy issue an annual report, as the law requires, the envoy only "provides input on anti-Semitism" in the drafting of two other annual human rights reports issued by a different division of the State Department.[35]

Another major government initiative concerning antisemitism was the Biden administration's "U.S. National Strategy to Counter Antisemitism," which was unveiled in May 2023, just five months before the United States would experience the most severe outbreak of antisemitism in recent memory. While the aforementioned U.S. envoy was tasked with monitoring antisemitism around the world, the 2023 initiative focused on combating domestic antisemitism. Its emphasis was less on new tactics than on directing existing government agencies to be on the lookout for antisemitism. The Biden plan appeared to be shaped in part by political and ideological considerations: it frequently paired antisemitism with a list of other forms of discrimination—"antisemitism, Islamophobia, online misogyny, gender-based violence" and violence against "AANHPI communities" (Asian Americans, Native Hawaiians, and Pacific Islanders). The implication was that the level of victimization of Jews was equivalent to that of the other referenced groups; in fact, anti-Jewish incidents represented 51 percent of all religion-related hate crimes during the previous year, while anti-Muslim incidents were 9.6 percent. The Biden administration's plan made reference to antisemitic incidents motivated by white supremacy, such as the 2017 Charlottesville march, but it did not specify the aggressors when mentioning that Jews had been "targeted for derision and exclusion on college campuses," or that Orthodox Jews had been "victimized while walking down the street" in racially diverse urban neighborhoods.[36] Nor did the plan acknowledge that while there are currently an estimated three thousand members of Ku Klux Klan chapters nationwide, the Rev. Louis Farrakhan's antisemitic Nation of Islam has tens of thousands of members.[37]

DEFINING ANTISEMITISM

For several years prior to October 7, a debate concerning the nature of antisemitism raged among Jewish activists, academics, and others strongly interested in the Arab-Israeli conflict. The most commonly used definition of "antisemitism" was the one drafted by the International Holocaust Remembrance Alliance (IHRA), a consortium of thirty-one countries. The U.S. State Department began using that definition in 2010, six years before the IHRA officially adopted it. In recent years, numerous local governments and nongovernmental organizations and institutions in the United States embraced it as well.[38]

Part of the IHRA definition explained antisemitism as engaging in "mendacious, dehumanizing, demonizing, or stereotypical allegations about Jews," and blaming all Jews for the acts of some Jews. But the IHRA definition also included three points that became matters of dispute. It stated that denying the Holocaust, opposing Israel's existence, and "drawing comparisons of contemporary Israeli policy to that of the Nazis" should be considered antisemitic.[39]

In early 2021, a group of academics known for their criticism of Israeli policies drafted an alternative definition of antisemitism. Their version, known as the Nexus Document, omitted any reference to Holocaust denial or Israel-Nazi analogies, and asserted that "opposition to Zionism and/or Israel does not necessarily reflect specific anti-Jewish animus." The drafters' decision to remove those items from any widely accepted definition of antisemitism was advantageous to the substantial number of academics who oppose Zionism or have compared Israel to the Nazis, and to Palestinian Arab leaders who deny or minimize the Holocaust. The labeling of those positions as antisemitic could severely discredit their advocates.[40]

What happened to this antisemitism debate in the wake of October 7? Despite the disagreements between the two definitions on some points, the two documents agreed on what arguably is the most important point of all: that statements supporting or inciting the murder of Jews are antisemitic. In effect, IHRA and Nexus agreed that the real-world consequences of certain language matters. According to the IHRA, "Calling for, aiding, or justifying the killing or harming of Jews in the name of a radical ideology or an extremist view of religion" is antisemitic. According to Nexus, "it is antisemitic to convey intense hostility toward Jews who are connected to Israel in a way that intentionally or irresponsibly (acting with disregard to potential violent consequences) provokes antisemitic violence."[41]

Even before October 7, those who publicly justified Palestinian Arab terrorist actions arguably could have been regarded as antisemitic by adherents of both the IHRA and Nexus definitions. Slandering Israel by claiming it steals Arab body parts or poisons Palestinian water sources, as many Palestinian Arab advocates did (see chapter 4), certainly qualified as irresponsibly conveying intense hostility that could provoke violence against Israeli Jews. But then the Hamas invasion thrust before the world's eyes the consequences of anti-Jewish rhetoric. After October 7, cheering for Hamas or Palestinian Islamic Jihad meant embracing those who had just slaughtered, raped, tortured, or beheaded more than 1,200 Jews in southern Israel—that is, cheering the genocide of Jews. If applauding antisemitic genocide is not antisemitic, then nothing is.

FACING THE NEW ANTISEMITISM

The ten thousand antisemitic incidents recorded by the ADL in 2023–2024 represented acts which generally were not typical of antisemitism in previous years. Many were verbal expressions of support for genocidal Hamas actions, or anti-Jewish slogans related to Israel defending itself. Some of those slurs graduated into the realm of graffiti on synagogues, or were expressed through targeted taunting, harassment, or assaults. Also noteworthy was how these haters found safety in numbers. In past years, a typical antisemitic incident would have involved an individual uttering a slur at a Jewish passerby and then quickly slinking away. The post–October 7 episodes, by contrast, frequently consisted of a number of individuals, among a large group of people, shouting anti-Jewish slogans with the protection of a likeminded crowd. Those are the kind of circumstances that help move extremist behavior from the margins to the mainstream.

What was also new was the way in which public discourse shifted in response to the declarations and actions by pro-Hamas protesters. Many elected officials and pundits, across the political spectrum, explicitly denounced their outbursts as antisemitic. The broad recognition that such behavior was antisemitic constituted a new consensus concerning the definition of antisemitism. No longer would one have to topple gravestones in a Jewish cemetery or use the words "We are against Jewish people" (to cite Rep. Ilhan Omar's preposterous formulation) to qualify as antisemitic. Cheering the murder and rape of 1,200 Israeli Jews, or calling for the murder of millions of Israeli Jews through the destruction of their state, now was widely recognized as antisemitic too.

An important contribution to this new consensus was made by then--U.S. Senate majority leader Charles Schumer (D-New York). Speaking on the Senate floor on November 29, 2023, Schumer asserted that the individuals expressing antisemitism after October 7 "are in many cases people that most liberal Jewish Americans felt previously were their ideological fellow travelers." He articulated the parameters of the new post–October 7 understanding of antisemitism. "The vitriol against Israel in the wake of October 7th is all too often crossing a line into brazen and widespread antisemitism, the likes of which we haven't seen for generations in this country—if ever."[42]

Schumer then cited four specific ways in which the new "anti-Israel vitriol" was in fact antisemitic. First, the chant "From the river to the sea"—which American anti-Zionists had adopted from the language of Hamas and other terrorist groups years before October 7—had to be considered "a violently antisemitic message" since it expresses a desire to "eradicate" Israel and thereby "to eliminate Jewish people" by the millions. Before October 7, "From the river to the sea" may have seemed theoretical, but on that day, it suddenly became very real—which in practice made it anti-Jewish, that is, antisemitic.

Second, Sen. Schumer cited "signs in the crowd[s] that read 'By Any Means Necessary.'" Again, he emphasized, the context was crucial. Before October 7, such signs seemed hypothetical and could have been interpreted as referring to a variety of "means," not all of them violent. But "after the most violent attack ever against Israeli civilians," the "casual invocation of such savagery" constituted an endorsement of the means which Hamas had employed. "While the dead bodies of Jewish Israelis were still warm," Schumer continued, "while hundreds of Jewish Israelis were being carried as hostages back to Hamas tunnels under Gaza . . . some of our fellow citizens characterize[d] a . . . vicious, bloodcurdling, premeditated massacre of innocent men, women, children, the elderly . . . as justified!" To make matters worse, "In some cases, people even celebrated what happened, describing it as the deserved fate of 'colonizers' and calling for 'glory to the martyrs' who carried out these heinous attacks." Hamas's scope and methods were genocidal, and that made them antisemitic in practice. Therefore, "this is no intellectual exercise for us. For many Jewish people, it feels like a matter of survival, informed once again by history—in this case, very personal history."[43]

As a third example of the new antisemitism, Sen. Schumer pointed to pro-Hamas demonstrators who "compare the genocide of the Holocaust equivalently to the Israeli army's actions to defeat Hamas in self-defense of their people." He was saying that two types of Israel-Nazis analogies were antisemitic: both explicit comparisons (as per the IHRA definition) and the implicit comparisons inherent in the accusation that Israel's pursuit of Hamas in Gaza was genocidal. The factual absurdity of the genocide suggested a double standard so irrational as to likely be motivated by antisemitism. Both the IHRA and Nexus definitions held that applying double standards to Israel was antisemitic, rather than a legitimate critique of Israeli policies. While pro-Hamas October 7 protesters were falsely accusing Israel of committing genocide, they were not protesting the real, ongoing genocide of the Muslim Uyghurs in China, or Arab militias' renewed genocide against Africans in Darfur in early 2024. The double standard was glaring.[44]

Sen. Schumer recalled an incident that further illustrated the double standard. When he was a Harvard undergraduate in 1970, Israel's ambassador to the United Nations, Abba Eban, addressed an audience on campus of more than two thousand, including radical-left anti-Israel activists who "sat in the gallery and hung a banner saying: 'Fight the Zionist Imperialists'" and "tried to shout him down."[45] Schumer recalled: "Eban pointed his finger up at the protesters in the gallery, and with his Etonian inflection, he calmly but strongly delivered a statement I will never forget." Eban said (Schumer paraphrased): "I am talking to you up there in the gallery. Every time a people gets their statehood, you applaud it. The Nigerians, the Pakistanis, the Zambians, you applaud their getting statehood. There's only one people, when they gain statehood, who you don't applaud, you condemn it—and that is the Jewish people. We Jews are used to that. We have lived with a double standard through the centuries. There were always things the Jews couldn't do. . . . Everyone could be a farmer, but not the Jew. Everyone could be a carpenter, but not the Jew. Everyone could move to Moscow, but not the Jew. And everyone can have their own state, but not the Jew. There is a word for that: antisemitism, and I accuse you in the gallery of it."[46]

BDS AND ANTISEMITISM

The Boycott-Divestment-Sanctions (BDS) movement had been a major component of anti-Israel activity in the United States for years before

October 7. But it gained an important boost in the aftermath of the Hamas invasion. Many of the rallies, on campuses and elsewhere, featured banners and slogans urging a worldwide boycott of Israel. The lists of demands compiled by the tent protesters invariably included calls for the universities to divest from companies doing business with Israel (see chapter 5). How to understand the nature of BDS became part of the public conversation about the post–October 7 definition of antisemitism.

The IHRA definition does not state outright that BDS advocacy is antisemitic. However, it is noteworthy that BDS promoters have not organized boycotts of other countries whose policies they oppose, meaning that the "double standard" criterion for antisemitism would seem to apply. According to the Anti-Defamation League, "at its core, BDS is an antisemitic movement" because "it is part and parcel of the larger effort to delegitimize the Jewish state," and also because if BDS achieved its goals, it "would result in the eradication of the world's only Jewish state."[47] Prominent BDS advocate Ahmed Moor wrote, "BDS does mean the end of the Jewish state," and BDS movement cofounder Omar Barghouti bluntly declared: "Definitely, most definitely, we oppose a Jewish state in any part of Palestine."[48] Moreover, the ADL noted, "Some BDS advocates and campaigns engage in antisemitic rhetoric, including allegations of Jewish power, dual loyalty, and Jewish/Israeli culpability for unrelated issues and crises." The BDS advocacy group Miftah, for one, circulated an article asserting that "the Jews used the blood of Christians in the Jewish Passover."[49] Another leading BDS voice, Electronic Intifada director Ali Abunimah, claimed that Israel turned Gaza into "a ghetto for surplus non-Jews."[50]

Some BDS activists "justify [or] express support for violence against Israelis," the ADL has pointed out. Barghouti said that Palestinian Arabs have a right to undertake "resistance by any means, including armed resistance."[51] The "end-all of BDS" is not only "to weaken Israel, to isolate Israel," but also to "support the resistance on the ground in Palestine," according to Lara Kiswani, executive director of the BDS-promoting Arab Resource and Organizing Center.[52] BDS supporter Anuradha Mittal, chair of Ben & Jerry's ice cream company, which does not sell its products in areas beyond Israel's pre-1967 armistice lines, tweeted in response to October 7: "When people are occupied, Resistance is justified!" and "From the river to the sea, Palestine will be free."[53]

BIDEN AND HARRIS BREAK NEW GROUND

In their response to the post–October 7 public debate concerning antisemitism, President Biden and Vice President Kamala Harris broke important new ground—on both sides of the debate. On the one hand, each made statements implying a measure of understanding for the anti-Israel extremists. President Biden, addressing the Democratic National Convention on August 19, 2024, said of the anti-Israel demonstrators outside the arena, "Those protesters out in the street, they have a point." The previous month, Vice President Harris told *The Nation* that the demonstrators were "showing exactly what the human emotion should be" in response to Gaza. However, in what were arguably more consequential (albeit less publicized) remarks, both Biden and Harris in effect labeled large sections of the protest movement antisemitic. Commenting on the pro-Hamas protests in Washington DC on June 8, 2024, the president tweeted that there were "horrific acts of Antisemitism" in the demonstrations, citing vandalism of Jewish homes, harassment of Jewish passersby, and "celebrating the 10/7 attack." Since celebrations of October 7 were a feature of many, if not most, of the pro-Hamas rallies, the president was essentially saying those protesters were antisemitic—and that any future celebration of the attack would constitute bigotry, not criticism of Israel. Likewise, Vice President Harris denounced as "antisemitism" the daubing of pro-Hamas, anti-Israel graffiti in a Pittsburgh Jewish neighborhood: a Hamas symbol and the words "Jews 4 Palestine" were smeared on a synagogue, and "Genocide" and "Jews hate Zionism" were painted on a sign outside the Jewish federation building.[54] For the most senior U.S. government officials to declare such expressions antisemitic—not merely vandalism or criticism of Israeli policies—has the potential to transform the public debate over the meaning of the term and its consequences in the years ahead.

Conclusion

On the day that news media outlets reported the beheading of babies at Kibbutz Kfar Aza, the Bethlehem branch of Fatah, the Palestinian Authority's ruling faction, posted a celebratory video that included a boot, adorned with the colors of the Palestinian flag, squashing a rat on an Israeli flag.

The juxtaposition of the atrocities (chapter 1) and the propaganda was painfully revealing. Dehumanizing images of Jews long have been a staple of Palestinian Arab school curricula (chapter 3) and popular culture (chapter 6). Together, for nearly three decades, the Palestinian Authority, which governed Gaza from 1994 to 2007, and Hamas, which ruled it after that, taught a generation of young Gazans that Jews are evil and deserve to be murdered; that the State of Israel must be violently destroyed; and that those Arabs who take part in the war against the Jews are heroes who are fulfilling their Islamic religious duty (chapter 3). Yet that war began many decades before the creation of the PA in 1994. Similar teachings animated the Palestinian Arab pogromists of the 1920s and 1930s, the killers and mutilators of 1948, the *fedayeen* of the 1950s, and the terrorists who filled the PLO's ranks in the 1960s and beyond (chapter 2).

Meanwhile, on a different continent, in a different language, young German children were being groomed for the same purpose: to become executioners (chapter 6). CBS news correspondent Howard K. Smith, who covered Nazi Germany on the eve of World War II, wrote in 1942 that in confronting Nazi Germany, the Allies actually were engaged in "a war to stop little twelve-year-old Hans and Fritz." The Free World was "fighting not so much for the present as for the future," because unless the Nazis were defeated and Germany was de-Nazified, the hate-filled children they were rearing would "grow up and become the rulers" of the next generation's Germany.[1]

The road to October 7 wound its way through long centuries in which young people who were nurtured on hateful religious and nationalist teachings grew up to become perpetrators of atrocities against Jews (chapter 4). In medieval times, they were called Crusaders, then Cossacks. At the turn of the twentieth century, they were Russians, then Ukrainians (chapter 6). They were succeeded by Palestinian Arabs, then the Nazis, then Palestinian Arabs again (chapter 2). The waves of anti-Jewish violence differed in scope and intensity, but their essence was the same: a deeply instilled antisemitism that could be satiated only through sadistic violence. This sentiment paved the road to October 7, 2023, just as that same sentiment lay at the heart of the many October 7s that preceded it.

It is not human nature to butcher innocent people, to rape and sexually mutilate defenseless women, or to behead children. For thousands of human beings to perpetrate such atrocities, there has to be intensive indoctrination. October 7 required a protracted and keenly focused educational process, reinforced by the surrounding society, that inculcated children with eliminationist antisemitism day after day, year after year, in their classrooms, homes, mosques, and media (chapter 3). Taught throughout their lives to view Jews as vermin, they proceeded to treat Jews as vermin when they became the willing executioners who perpetrated the horrors of October 7.

On the other hand, the history of Jewish victimization also carries within it important lessons that offer a cautionary note against despair. Just as the Jewish people have survived long centuries of antisemitic violence that sought to annihilate them, so too there is ample reason to feel optimistic that the ongoing world war against the Jews will not succeed.

While many in the international community have abandoned Israel in her darkest hour, the United States has continued to stand by the Jewish state. Every American president since the 1970s, even those who sometimes criticized or pressured Israel, provided the Jewish state with military assistance crucial to her defense. Bipartisan support for Israel in Congress and the public likewise has remained strong through the years, despite distorted media coverage of Israel and the pernicious effects of social media. Alternative media outlets are challenging the anti-Israel bias of conventional sources, exposing the extremism of Israel's enemies more quickly and adeptly than in the past, and disseminating important information about Israel that previously might have reached only minuscule audiences.

Much of the academic world has become infested with anti-Israel and antisemitic hate. In the case of some major universities, one may detect a continuity of indifference to the victimization of Jews that goes all the way back to their attempts to cultivate friendships with Nazi Germany (chapter 7). Fortunately, however, only a tiny fraction of today's college students nationwide has taken part in pro-Hamas protests. In addition, some of the university presidents who were the most timid in the face of campus extremism and antisemitism were forced by the weight of public opinion to resign, or to respond more effectively. At the same time, legal action by advocacy groups has compelled a number of universities to take appropriate steps to protect Jewish students (chapter 5).

The most important reason for some measure of optimism is the existence of a sovereign Jewish state and a powerful Jewish army that constantly confounds Israel's enemies. The statelessness and helplessness that characterized Jewish existence through centuries of crusades, pogroms, and mass murder are phenomena of bygone eras. The war against the Jews may be eternal, but that does not mean the Jews will lose that war.

Notes

INTRODUCTION

1. Stahl, "Kibbutz and Its Fullness," 5.
2. Stahl, "Kibbutz and Its Fullness," 5–6.
3. Rifkind, "In Memory of Vilna," 62.

1. IN THE CITIES OF SLAUGHTER

1. Dan Sabbagh, "Hamas Drew Detailed Attack Plans for Years with Help of Spies, Documents Suggest," *The Guardian*, December 4, 2023.
2. Six other Palestinian terrorist groups said they also took part in the October 7 attack: the Popular Resistance Committees, the Palestinian Mujahideen Movement, the Popular Front for the Liberation of Palestine (PFLP), the Popular Front for the Liberation of Palestine-General Command, the Democratic Front for the Liberation of Palestine (DFLP), and the Al-Aqsa Martyrs Brigade (a division of Fatah, headed by Palestinian Authority chairman Mahmoud Abbas). The PFLP and the DFLP are member organizations of the PA and its parent body, the Palestine Liberation Organization. The United States ceased identifying Fatah as a terrorist group following the signing of the Oslo accords in 1993, and it removed the DFLP from its official list of terrorist groups in 1999. See Tom O'Connor, "Not Only Hamas: Eight Factions at War with Israel in Gaza," *Newsweek*, November 7, 2023.
3. Schwartz, *Ghosts of a Holy War*.
4. Oren Liebermann, "Exclusive: Bodycam Video Shows Early Moments of Hamas Massacre in Israel and Tunnels under Gaza," CNN.com, November 15, 2023.
5. Georg Eckert Institute for International Textbook Research, *Report on Palestinian Textbooks*, 2021, https://www.jewishvirtuallibrary.org/jsource/anti-semitism/EU_Report_on_Palestinian_Textbooks.pdf.
6. Oren, *Six Days of War*, 108.
7. Yuval Bitton, "'I Asked Sinwar, Is It Worth 10,000 Innocent Gazans Dying? He Said, Even 100,000 Is Worth It,'" *Ha'aretz*, April 13, 2024.

8. Eden S., "We Realized the First Vehicles in the Traffic Jam Weren't Moving Because the Passengers Were Dead," October 7.org, October 17, 2023, https://www.october7.org/post/we-realized-the-first-vehicles-in-the-traffic-jam-weren-t-moving-because-the-passengers-were-dead.
9. Meir V., "People Were Crying, Injured," October 7,org, November 15, 2023, https://www.october7.org/post/people-were-crying-injured-friends-were-dying-right-in-front-of-them-and-they-couldn-t-do-anything.
10. Eden S., "We Realized the First Vehicles in the Traffic Jam Weren't Moving."
11. Einav A., "That's When I Realized That We'd Be Executed if We Didn't Run," October 7,org, October 14, 2023, https://www.october7.org/post/this-nightmare-will-never-end-but-at-least-i-m-hear-to-tell-it.
12. Roni S., "We Crouched in the Car, Heads between Our Knees, While Being Shot at in Volleys at the Car," October 7,org, January 21, 2024, https://www.october7.org/post/we-crouched-in-the-car-heads-between-our-knees-while-being-shot-at-in-volleys-at-the-car.
13. Eden S., "The Terrorists Were Meters Away from Us, Shooting and Shouting 'Jew! There's a Jew! Kill Him!,'" October7.org, November 12, 2023, https://www.october7.org/post/the-terrorists-were-meters-away-from-us-shooting-and-and-shouting-jew-there-s-a-jew-kill-him.
14. Grabowski, *Hunt for the Jews*.
15. May H, "I Smeared Blood over My Face and Lay as if I Was Dead for Three Hours," October7.org, October 12, 2023, https://www.october7.org/post/i-smeared-blood-over-my-face-and-lay-as-if-i-was-dead-for-three-hours.
16. Maya E., "I Started Preparing, as Best I Could, to Die," October 7,org, October 24, 2023, https://www.october7.org/post/we-became-silent-a-silence-which-wouldn-t-shame-anne-frank-in-the-attic.
17. Naomi H., "The Blinds Were Shut, the Doors Locked. Silence. Don't Talk. Don't Breathe. They're Here," October7.org, October 17, 2023, https://www.october7.org/post/i-text-my-inbar-that-i-love-him-and-hold-on-no-blue-check-mark-no-check-mark.
18. Gutman, *Resistance: The Warsaw Ghetto Uprising*, 224–26, 237, 244–46.
19. Rotem C., "We Realized They Want to Burn Us Alive," October7.org, January 23, 2024, https://www.october7.org/post/we-realized-they-want-to-burn-us-alive.
20. Lior Ohana, "He Planned to Propose to Her, but They Both Were Murdered by Hamas Terrorists," Ynetnews.com, October 15, 2023, https://www.ynetnews.com/magazine/article/ryry2115zp#autoplay.
21. Katy L., "I Asked the Kids to Cover Their Ears. If We Stay Alive, They Don't Need to Remember What They Hear," October 7,org, October 22, 2023,

https://www.october7.org/post/i-asked-the-kids-to-cover-their-ears-if-we-stay-alive-they-don-t-need-to-remember-what-they-hear.

22. "Israel Finds Pody of Ruth Peretz, Disabled Teen Missing since October 7," *Jerusalem Post*, November 5, 2023.
23. E. J. Dionne Jr., "Hostage's Death: 'A Shot to Forehead,'" *New York Times*, October 11, 1985.
24. "Kill, Behead, Rape: Interrogated Hamas Members Detail Atrocities against Civilians," *Times of Israel*, October 24, 2023.
25. "Handwritten Note Found on Hamas Terrorist Calls for Beheading, Removing Hearts and Livers," *Jerusalem Post*, October 25, 2023.
26. Sarit Rosenblum, "'TV Said There Were 20 Bodies, We Knew There Were 400': Healthcare Workers' Heartbreaking Accounts of October 7," Ynetnews.com, October 7, 2024.
27. Aaron Poris, "Hamas Torture Confirmed as Israeli Forensics Institute Identifies Victims," *Jerusalem Post*, October 20 and 22, 2023.
28. Ruth Marks Eglash, "IDF Tells 1 Million Gaza Residents to Evacuate Their Homes within 24 Hours," *Jewish Insider*, October 13, 2023.
29. Graves, *Experiment in Anarchy*, 157.
30. Shlomi Heller, "'They Cut Off Organs': Interrogator Reveals Hamas Terrorists' Oct. 7 Atrocities," *Jerusalem Post*, April 4, 2024.
31. Tovah Lazaroff, "Israeli Female Soldiers Shot in Crotch, Vagina, Breasts, on October 7," *Jerusalem Post*, December 5, 2023; "Hamas Terrorists 'Purposefully Obliterated Women's Faces,'" Ynetnews.com, February 1, 2024.
32. Miri Weissman, "Knesset Hears Accounts of Hamas Rape, Infanticide," *Times of Israel*, July 23, 2024.
33. Rosenblum, "'TV Said There Were 20 Bodies, We Knew There Were 400'"; "*Sefer Zekirah*, or *The Book of Remembrance*, of Rabbi Ephraim of Bonn," in Eidelberg, *Jews and the Crusaders*, 121–33.
34. Felice Friedson, "Supt. Micky Rosenfeld to TML: Palestinian Workers in Israel Aided Hamas Terrorists in Planning October 7 Infiltration," The Media Line, December 11, 2023; Joanie Margulies, "Detailed Maps Lead IDF Intelligence to Believe Spies Were Used—Report," *Jerusalem Post*, December 5, 2023.
35. Forest Rain (@frisrael), "Halil from #Gaza knew everyone in Netiv Haasara," X, October 25, 2023, https://twitter.com/frisrael/status/1717157116400541844; Hezki Baruch, "Bereaved Mother: They Abandoned Us, They Let Them Slaughter My Husband and Son," Israel National News, October 12, 2023.
36. "The Photographer Who Participated in the Coexistence Exhibition in Otef—and Was Revealed to Be an Assistant to Hamas," Israel Television Channel 13, December 7, 2023.

37. Haviv Rettig Gur and Aaron Kalman, "Among the Terrorists to Be Released, the Murderer of a Holocaust Survivor," *Times of Israel*, August 12, 2013.
38. "The 81-Year-Old Woman Who Climbed Out the Window to Escape Hamas," *Times of Israel*, February 2, 2024.
39. Andrew Tobin, "'Just as Cruel as the Terrorists': Many Ordinary Palestinians Joined in Hamas's Atrocities Against Israel," *Washington Free Beacon*, October 24, 2023.
40. Andrew Tobin, "Neflix and Kill: How a Palestinian Woman Took Over an Israeli Family's Home on Oct. 7," *Washington Free Beacon*, December 15, 2023.
41. Deborah Danan, "Oct. 7 Was Worse Than a Terror Attack. It Was a Pogrom," *Tablet*, January 24, 2024.
42. "Gazan Photographers Joined in October 7 Lynching, Raiding of Israelis—Report," *Jerusalem Post*, January 8, 2024.
43. Andrew Tobin, "Gazan 'Civilians' Involved in Every Stage of Hamas Hostage Scheme, Freed Israelis Say," *Washington Free Beacon*, January 17, 2024.
44. Tobin, "Gazan 'Civilians' Involved in Every Stage of Hamas Hostage Scheme."
45. Tobin, "'Just as Cruel as the Terrorists'"; "Avinatan and Noa Begged for Hours to Be Rescued—Until They Were Kidnapped: 'There Is a Lynching Here,'" (Hebrew), Ynetnews.com, October 7, 2023.
46. Tobin, "'Just as Cruel as the Terrorists.'"
47. Tobin, "Neflix and Kill."
48. Rachel Goldstein, "WSJ Reveals Details of Prominent Gaza Family Who Held Hostages Captive in Their Home," *Israel Hayom*, June 12, 2024.
49. Amir Tal and Stephanie Halasz, "Russian-Israeli Hostage Escaped from Hamas but Was Found and Returned by Gazans, Says Aunt," CNN.com, November 27, 2023.
50. Goldstein, "WSJ Reveals Details of Prominent Gaza Family."
51. "Released Hostage Says He Was Held by UNRWA Teacher in Gaza—Report," *Jerusalem Post*, November 30, 2023.
52. Brady Knox, "Freed Israeli Hostages Say They Were Held in UN Camp," *Washington Examiner*, January 21, 2025.
53. Gross, *Neighbors*; "Study Says Polish Neighbors Betrayed Many More Jews Than Previously Thought," Jewish Telegraphic Agency [hereafter JTA], May 11, 2018.
54. Liel Leibovitz, "Eyewitness Account of the Rave Massacre," *Tablet*, October 8, 2023; Liran Tamari, "Father of Late German Hostage: 'At Least I Know She's Not Tossed in Some Gaza Tunnel,'" Ynetnews.com, October 31, 2023.
55. Carrie Keller-Lynn, "Amid War and Urgent Need to ID Bodies, Evidence of Hamas's October 7 Rapes Slips Away," *Times of Israel*, November 9, 2023;

Itsik Saban, "'She Was Gang-raped, Then Executed': Testimonies from Oct. 7," *Israel Hayom*, November 30, 2023.

56. "Remarks by President Biden on the October 7th Terrorist Attacks and the Resilience of the State of Israel and Its People—Tel Aviv, Israel," The White House, October 18, 2023.
57. Maayan Lubell and Emily Rose, "Israeli Accounts of Sexual Violence by Hamas Rise but Justice Is Remote," Reuters, December 5, 2023; Tamari, "Father of Late German hostage."
58. "Mission Report: Official Visit of the Office of the SRSG-SVC to Israel and the Occupied West Bank, 29 January–14 February 2024," United Nations, 4–5, 12, 15, 18.
59. Klar-Chalamish, *Silent Cry*, 21.
60. "At Least 10 Freed Hostages Were Sexually Abused in Hamas Captivity, Doctor Says," *Times of Israel*, December 6, 2023.
61. Saban, "'She Was Gang-raped, Then Executed.'"
62. Klar-Chalamish, *Silent Cry*, 20, 25.
63. Klar-Chalamish, *Silent Cry*, 21.
64. Jeffrey Gettleman, Adam Sella, and Anat Schwartz, "What We Know about Sexual Violence during the Oct. 7 Attacks on Israel," *New York Times*, December 4, 2023.
65. Nina Fox, "'I Saw a Girl Who Was Raped and Set on Fire': Chilling Testimony from the Scene of the Music Festival Massacre," Ynetnews.com, January 24, 2024.
66. Klar-Chalamish, *Silent Cry*, 15.
67. Klar-Chalamish, *Silent Cry*, 24–25.
68. Gettleman, Sella, and Schwartz, "What We Know About Sexual Violence"; Shira Rubin, "Israel Investigates an Elusive, Horrific Enemy: Rape as a Weapon of War," *Washington Post*, November 25, 2023.
69. "Hamas Terrorists, Father and Son, Admit Raping before Murdering Women on Oct. 7—Daily Mail," *Jerusalem Post*, May 25, 2024.
70. Anna Schecter, "Their Bodies Tell Their Stories. They're Not Alive to Speak for Themselves," NBCNews.com, December 5, 2023.
71. "Kill, Behead, Rape: Interrogated Hamas Members Detail Atrocities against Civilians," *Times of Israel*, October 24, 2023; Schecter, "Their Bodies Tell Their Stories."
72. Schecter, "Their Bodies Tell Their Stories."
73. Schecter, "Their Bodies Tell Their Stories."
74. Lazaroff, "Israeli Female Soldiers Shot."
75. Klar-Chalamish, *Silent Cry*, 24–25, 29; Keller-Lynn, "Amid War and Urgent Need to ID Bodies"; Saban, "'She Was Gang-raped, Then Executed.'"

76. "First Survivor of 'Nova' Massacre Opens Up about Rape by Hamas Terrorists—Report," *Jerusalem Post*, July 23, 2024.
77. "At Least 10 Freed Hostages Were Sexually Abused."
78. Gettleman, Sella, and Schwartz, "What We Know About Sexual Violence"; "Graphic Report Details New Evidence of Rape, Sexual Violence during October 7 Rampage," *Times of Israel*, December 3, 2023; Rubin, "Israel Investigates an Elusive, Horrific Enemy."
79. Weissman, "Knesset Hears Accounts of Hamas Rape, Infanticide."
80. Gettleman, Sella, and Schwartz, "What We Know about Sexual Violence."
81. Klar-Chalamish, *Silent Cry*, 15, 23.
82. Christina Lamb, "First Hamas Fighters Raped Her. Then They Shot Her in the Head," *The Sunday Times*, December 2, 2023.
83. Allison Pearson, "'Not One Girl Could Be Shown to Her Parents': The Horrors of Oct 7—as Told by the Survivors," *The Telegraph*, October 7, 2024.
84. Klar-Chalamish, *Silent Cry*, 17–18.
85. Klar-Chalamish, *Silent Cry*, 30.
86. Gettleman, Sella, and Schwartz, "What We Know About Sexual Violence."
87. Brownmiller, *Against Our Will*, 49.
88. Tamar Uriel-Beeri, "Hamas Terrorists Forced Families to Watch Loved Ones Get Raped at Gunpoint," *Jerusalem Post*, February 21, 2024; Klar-Chalamish, *Silent Cry*, 26.
89. Klar-Chalamish, *Silent Cry*, 31–33. The analysis noted the reports that for the same reason, "Iranian forces also engage in practices of targeted disfigurement of detained women's faces alongside committing acts of rape."
90. Dan Diker, "The Hamas Jihad Guide for Killing, Torturing and Kidnapping Israeli Citizens," Jerusalem Center for Security and Foreign Affairs, October 16, 2024.
91. "Released Hamas Hostage on *60 Minutes*: Objecting to Anything Could Be Death Sentence," *Jerusalem Post*, December 18, 2023.
92. Tobin, "Gazan 'Civilians' Involved in Every Stage of Hamas Hostage Scheme"; Danan, "Oct. 7 Was Worse Than a Terror Attack"; "'Israel Doesn't Care about You': Former Hostage Reveals Hamas Captors' Psychological Torture," *Jerusalem Post*, March 22, 2024.
93. i24NEWS, "Hamas Moves Hostages across Gaza in Ambulances, Released Captive Reveals," Ynetnews.com, March 30, 2024.
94. David Leonhardt and Lauren Jackson, "Gaza's Vital Tunnels," *New York Times*, October 30, 2023.
95. Adam Goldman, Ronen Bergman, Patrick Kingsley, and Gal Koplewitz, "Israel Unearths More of a Subterranean Fortress Under Gaza," *New York*

Times, January 16, 2024; Isabel Kershner, "Israel Displays Tunnel System Beneath Gaza," *New York Times*, January 22, 2024.

96. "Cages, Hunger, Psychological Abuse: Reports Emerge of Testimonies from Israeli Hostages Freed Saturday from Hamas Captivity," *Haaretz*, February 2, 2025.
97. Adi Nirman, "Released Hostage Details How Hamas Keeps Captives in Caged Enclosures," *Israel Hayom*, September 12, 2024; "Freed Hostage Mia Schem Says She Was Kept in Cage with 5 Other Women Still in Gaza," *Times of Israel*, October 30, 2024.
98. "'Hamas Tore Off My Clothes, Threatened to Shoot': Gaza Hostage Tells Her Story," *Jerusalem Post*, January 31, 2024.
99. Gilad Cohen, "'One of the Girls Was Handcuffed and Beaten with a Stick,' Released Hostage Says," Ynetnews.com, February 20, 2024.
100. Shir Perets, "Starvation, Sexual Abuse, and Children Beaten: Reports Exposes Conditions of Hamas Captivity," *Jerusalem Post*, December 29, 2024.
101. Yael Ciechanover, "'We Were Crammed Together in a Tiny Room in Khan Younis, There Was No Air,' Freed Hostage Says," Ynetnews.com, January 25, 2024.
102. Cohen, "'One of the Girls was Handcuffed and Beaten.'"
103. Emanuel Fabian, "IDF Video Shows 'Horrific Conditions' in Tunnel Where 6 Hostages Were Held, Executed," *Times of Israel*, September 11, 2024.
104. Tobin, "Gazan 'Civilians' Involved in Every Stage of Hamas Hostage Scheme." There was ample additional evidence of civilian involvement. For example, under a rug in a civilian home in Gaza's Jabaliya section, Israeli soldiers found a shaft leading to the corpses of four hostages. (Lazar Berman, "Under a Rug in Gazan Home, IDF Troops Found Shaft Leading to Bodies of 4 Hostages," *Times of Israel*, May 23, 2024). Mobs of Gazans hurled rocks at the vehicles carrying Israeli hostages on their way to being released in November 2023; the hostages said they feared they would be lynched by the crowd. (Joanne Margulies, "Women Held Hostage by Hamas in Gaza Kept in Cages—Report," *Jerusalem Post*, November 28, 2023). Likewise, as Red Cross officials led Agam Goldstein-Almog out of captivity, crowds of civilians "swarmed the car and started banging on the window, shouting 'Die, die, die!'" ("'Chained Slave-Wife': Former Hostage Reveals Hamas Forced Her to Wear a Hijab, say Islamic Prayers," *Jerusalem Post*, August 22, 2024).
105. "Hostages' Stories: Gadi Mozes Paced 7km a Day in Tiny Cell, Soldiers Rationed Grains of Rice," *Times of Israel*, February 1, 2025.
106. "Released Hamas Hostage on *60 Minutes*."

107. Margulies, "Women Held Hostage by Hamas"; "Gaza Captivity Was 'Russian Roulette,' Hostage Freed from Hamas Captivity Says," *Israel Hayom*, November 12, 2023; Daniela Ginzburg and Noam Dvir, "Freed Hostage Andrey Kozlov Spent First Few Months with Hands Tied, Parents Say," *Israel Hayom*, June 13, 2024; Lahav Harkov, "Hostages Young and Old Endured Physical and Psychological Torture," *Jewish Insider*, December 4, 2023; Adi Nirman, "Hamas Starved Hostage Eden Yerushalmi to 79 Pounds," *Israel Hayom*, September 6, 2024.
108. Adir Yanko, Yael Ciechanover, and Yoav Zitun, "Rescued Hostages Say They Were Held by a Family in Rafah and 'We Were Hungry,'" Ynetnews.com, February 12, 2024; "'Hamas Treated Us Like Animals': Rescued Hostage Speaks on Gaza Captivity," *Jerusalem Post*, March 28, 2024.
109. "Hostages Had to Prepare Food but Couldn't Eat It, Mother of Hostage Says," *Jerusalem Post*, March 18, 2024.
110. "'No Showers, No Food, Cooking for Terrorists': Hostages Reveal Torment in Captivity," *Jerusalem Post*, January 25, 2025.
111. Renee Ghert-Zand, "Pediatrician Treating Freed Hostages: Reports of Their Good Condition Are Misleading," *Times of Israel*, December 4, 2023; Julia Frankel, Adam Geller, and Tim Sullivan, "After Weeks in Hamas Tunnels, Some Freed Child Hostages Still Speaking in Whispers," *Times of Israel*, December 10, 2023.
112. Debbie Weiss, "Family of Freed 12-Year-Old Boy Describes Horrific Abuse of Child Hostages by Hamas, Gazan Civilians," *The Algemeiner*, November 28, 2023; "Freed 12-Year-Old Hostage Says Captors Told Him Israel Had Been Destroyed," *Times of Israel*, December 26, 2023; Cohen, "'One of the Girls Was Handcuffed and Beaten.'"
113. Clarissa Ward, Brent Swails, and Rachel Clarke, "Father Describes How His Young Daughter Emily Hand Survived Hamas Captivity," CNN.com, November 28, 2023; Margulies, "Women Held Hostage by Hamas"; Harkov, "Hostages Young and Old Endured Physical and Psychological Torture."
114. "Top Doctor Says Freed Hostages 'Went Through Hell,'" *Times of Israel*, December 2, 2023.
115. Margulies, "Women Held Hostage by Hamas"; Jodi Rudoren, "Red Stickers for Killed, Black for Kidnapped: Bearing Witness to the Massacre at Kibbutz Nir Oz," *The Forward*, December 7, 2023; "Nurse Who Treated Elderly While in Captivity Says Hostages in 'Impossible Condition,'" *Times of Israel*, December 10, 2023.
116. "Hostages' Stories: Gadi Mozes Paced 7km a Day in Tiny Cell."
117. Ghert-Zand, "Pediatrician Treating Freed Hostages."
118. Perets, "Starvation, Sexual Abuse, and Children Beaten."

119. Lesley Stahl and David Morgan, "Doctor Who Treated Freed Hamas Hostages Describes Physical, Sexual and Psychological Abuse," CBSnews.com, December 17, 2023; Harkov, "Hostages Young and Old Endured Physical and Psychological Torture"; "Freed 12-Year-Old Hostage Says Captors Told Him Israel Had Been Destroyed."
120. Frankel, Geller, and Sullivan, "After Weeks in Hamas Tunnels, Some Freed Child Hostages Still Speaking in Whispers."
121. Stahl and Morgan, "Doctor Who Treated Freed Hamas Hostages"; Lahav Harkov, "Hostages Young and Old Endured Physical and Psychological Torture"; "Freed 12-Year-Old Hostage Says Captors Told Him Israel Had Been Destroyed"; Adir Yanko, "At Least Third of Hostages in Gaza at Immediate Risk of Death, Report," Ynetnews.com, January 9, 2024; "IDF Storms Main Hospital in Khan Younis after Prolonged Standoff," *Israel Hayom*, February 15, 2024; Perets, "Starvation, Sexual Abuse, and Children Beaten."
122. "'Shadows of Children': For the Youngest Hostages, Life Moves Forward in Whispers," *Politico*, December 9, 2023.
123. Tara John and Jennifer Griffiths, "Freed Israeli Hostage Says She Was Held in Gaza Hospital with Dozens of Others," CNN.com, January 18, 2024.
124. "Evanston Mother Held by Hamas Describes Captivity in NewsNation Interview," *Chicago Sun-Times*, March 13, 2024.
125. Debbie Weiss, "Hamas Terrorists Admit Israeli Hostages Held at Gaza's Kamal Adwan Hospital," *The Algemeiner*, January 23, 2025.
126. Perets, "Starvation, Sexual Abuse, and Children Beaten."
127. "Some Released Hostages Were Held in Tunnels with No Human Contact for Months, IDF Says," *Times of Israel*, January 27, 2025.
128. "Emily Damari's Mom: My Daughter Was Held in UNRWA Facilities, Denied Medical Treatment," *Times of Israel*, February 1, 2025.
129. "Israel Finds Boxes of Medicine Intended for Gaza Hostages in Hospital," *Jerusalem Post*, February 16, 2024.
130. "'Intense Fear, Zero Sleep': Freed Hostages Recall Captivity in Videos Shown at Rally," *Times of Israel*, December 10, 2023.
131. Perets, "Starvation, Sexual Abuse, and Children Beaten."
132. "Nurse Who Treated Elderly While in Captivity"; "Taken Captive: Oded Lifshitz, Drove Gazans to Hospitals," *Times of Israel*, October 23, 2023.
133. Farnaz Fassihi and Isabel Kershner, "U.N. Team Finds Grounds to Support Reports of Sexual Violence in Hamas Attack," *New York Times*, March 4, 2024.
134. "At Least 10 Freed Hostages Were Sexually Abused."
135. Tobin, "Gazan 'Civilians' Involved in Every Stage of Hamas Hostage Scheme."
136. Ariella Oldfield, "Terrorist 'Sexually Assaulted Hostage at Gunpoint': Freed Captive Recounts Testimony," *Times of Israel*, February 13, 2024.

137. Patrick Kingsley and Ronen Berman, "Israeli Hostage Says She Was Sexually Assaulted and Tortured in Gaza," *New York Times*, March 26, 2024. There was one ostensibly conflicting account of a sexual assault. An Israeli Army emergency medic who aided victims in multiple towns said he discovered, in a private home at Kibbutz Be'eri, "the bodies of two partially clothed teenage girls that bore signs of sexual violence." Video footage of the kibbutz later showed, in one such home, "the bodies of three female victims, fully clothed and with no apparent signs of sexual violence." The bodies in the footage may not have been the ones to which he was referring, or, given the extreme violence and trauma of October 7, he may have mistakenly thought the bodies were found at Kibbutz Be'eri, when in fact he had seen them in another location. See Adam Rasgon and Natan Odenheimer, "Israeli Soldier's Video Undercuts Medic's Account of Sexual Assault," *New York Times*, March 25, 2024.
138. Ohad Merlin, "Hamas, Al Jazeera Admit: Story of IDF Rapes in Gaza Hospital Fabricated," *Jerusalem Post*, March 25, 2024.
139. Emanuel Fabian, "IDF Spokesperson: UNRWA Staff Recordings Prove Hamas Treated Young Women 'Like Animals,'" *Times of Israel*, March 4, 2024.
140. Yaniv Voller, "The Sabaya," *Tablet*, August 2, 2024; Adi Nirman, "3 Minutes of Horror—Chilling Footage from Kidnapping of IDF Female Troops Aired," *Israel HaYom*, May 22, 2024.
141. "'Chained Slave-Wife'"; "Former Hostage Reveals Hamas Terrorists Tried to Push Her to Convert to Islam, Extorted Her Family," *Jerusalem Post*, August 27, 2024.
142. "'One Girl Was Given Ketamine': Israeli Doctor Says Hostages Abused, Drugged in Gaza," *Times of Israel*, December 12, 2023.

2. THE RISE AND STRATEGY OF HAMAS

1. Shanks, "Holy Targets."
2. Arthur James Balfour, "Balfour Declaration 1917," Yale Law School, https://avalon.law.yale.edu/20th_century/balfour.asp.
3. Eban, *Voice of Israel*, 284.
4. Morris, *Israel's Border Wars*, 337.
5. Eban, *Voice of Israel*, 279, 285–86.
6. Morris, *Israel's Border Wars*, 412, 415.
7. Israeli officials initially suspected the attackers came from Jordan, while British and UN officials believed they were either Gazans or Israeli Bedouin Arabs. In 1956, Israeli soldiers discovered identification cards from some of the victims in the possession of residents in Rafah, a Gaza Strip city, suggesting the terrorists did come from Gaza. (Morris, *Israel's Border Wars*, 297–99).

8. Morris, *Israel's Border Wars*, 298–99.
9. John Kifner, "6 Killed as Arabs Hijack Israeli Bus," *New York Times*, March 8, 1988; Dan Fisher, "'Nobody Cares,' Survivor Wrote on Hijacked Bus," *Los Angeles Times*, March 9, 1988; Bradley Burston, "The Day That the Daydream Ended," *Jerusalem Post*, March 11, 1988.
10. Morris, *Israel's Border Wars*, 345–46.
11. Morris, *Israel's Border Wars*, 373; "Sharett Protests to U.N. Head on Killing of Israelis by Egyptian Raiders," JTA, April 13, 1956.
12. Morris, *Israel's Border Wars*, 373; "Sharett Protests to U.N. Head."
13. Henriques, *100 Hours to Suez*, 194–95, 199.
14. Eban, *Voice of Israel*, 282.
15. Eban, *An Autobiography*, 453.
16. Lewis, *Multiple Identities of the Middle East*, 121–22.
17. "Arafat Compares Oslo Accords to Muhammad's Hudaybiyyah Peace Treaty, Which Led to Defeat of the Peace Partners," Palestinian Media Watch, May 10, 1994; "Yasir Arafat's Speech at the Palestinian Legislative Council" (Ramallah, May 15, 2002), *Interactive Encyclopedia of the Palestine Question*.
18. Mati Wagner, "Israeli-Palestinian Peace Process: A Clash of Narratives," *Jerusalem Post*, March 30, 2014.
19. Kressel, *"Sons of Pigs and Apes,"* 29–30.
20. Kressel, *"Sons of Pigs and Apes,"* 21.
21. Lewis, *Islam: From the Prophet Mohammed to the Capture of Constantinople*, 217–19.
22. "Abbas' Advisor on Islam: Jews Are "Humanoids . . . Apes and Pigs," Palestinian Media Watch translation of PA Television broadcast, September 30, 2022; "Fatah Spokesman: Jews Are 'Sons of Apes and Pigs,'" Palestinian Media Watch translation of PA Television broadcast, November 1, 2015.
23. Ye'or, *Dhimmi*, 167.
24. Garfinkle, "On the Origin, Meaning, Use and Abuse of a Phrase," 539–50.
25. Mandel, *Arabs and Zionism before World War I*, 35–36.
26. Porath, *Emergence of the Palestinian-Arab National Movement*, 70–73.
27. Porath, *Emergence of the Palestinian-Arab National Movement*, 70–73.
28. Golda Meir, "The Right to Self-Defense," *Jewish Frontier*, January–February 2002, 20–23, 37.
29. "Arab 'Mein Kampf' on Sale," JTA, October 31, 1938.
30. Stuart Winer and *Times of Israel*, "Herzog: Arabic Copy of 'Mein Kampf' Found on Hamas Terrorist Shows What War Is About," *Times of Israel*, November 12, 2023; "IDF Troops Find 'Mein Kampf' Copy in Nuseirat, Gaza Strip—Report," *Jerusalem Post*, June 19, 2024.

31. Itamar Marcus and Nan Jacques Zilberdik, "'Hitler's Sayings' Published by PA-Associated Youth Magazine," Palestinian Media Watch, October 21, 2013; Itamar Marcus and Nan Jacques Zilberdik, "Hitler Admired in PLO Youth Magazine Because He Murdered Jews," Palestinian Media Watch, December 20, 2011.
32. "Iktiba High School Posts Picture of Rommel with Text Praising Hitler as 'the Pinnacle of Leadership,'" Palestinian Media Watch translation of Facebook page, June 21, 2012; "Iktiba High School Posts Picture Presenting Hitler as Admirable," Palestinian Media Watch translation of Iktiba High School for Girls in Tulkarem Facebook page, May 22, 2012; "Anabta High School Posts Picture Presenting Hitler as Admirable," PMW translation of Anabta High School Facebook page, January 26, 2012.
33. Podeh, "Lie That Won't Die"; Ben-Ami, *Scars of War*, 314; Harkabi, *Arab Attitudes*, 377–78; "Abbas' Advisor: The World Established Israel as a Colonialist State to Serve Britain and the US," Palestinian Media Watch, November 19, 2023.
34. Frampton, *Muslim Brotherhood and the West*, 51; El-Awaisi, *Muslim Brothers and the Palestine Question*, 209.
35. Text of the PLO National Covenant, https://avalon.law.yale.edu/20th_century/plocov.asp. Articles 7, 8, and 9 call for "armed struggle" against Israel. Articles 10, 15, and 21 use a slight variation, "armed revolution."
36. "Hamas Covenant 1988," accessed January 28, 2025, https://avalon.law.yale.edu/20th_century/hams.asp.
37. "Our Narrative . . . Operation Al-Aqsa Flood," accessed January 28, 2025, https://www.lbcgroup.tv/uploadImages/ExtImages/Images2/Our%20Narrative-Operation%20Al-Aqsa%20Flood-Web_compressed%20(1).pdf.
38. Shlomo M. Brody, "How Israel Missed Its Chance to Eliminate the Leadership of Hamas," *Tablet*, December 4, 2023. Israel's defense minister stated in 1982 that "most of the losses we suffered [in that year's Lebanon war]—some 350 dead and 2,000 wounded—resulted from the rule we imposed on ourselves to avoid harming noncombatants." (Ariel Sharon, "Gains from the War in Lebanon," *New York Times*, August 29, 1982.)
39. Clyde Haberman, "Israel Expels 400 From Occupied Lands," *New York Times*, December 18, 1992.
40. Thomas L. Friedman, "Clinton Is Critical of the Expulsions," *New York Times*, December 18, 1992.
41. Miller, *Much Too Promised Land*, 239–40; Ross, *Missing Peace*, 96–98.
42. Laura Blumenfeld, "'The Hamas Big Fish Who Got Away," *Wall Street Journal*, November 17, 2023.

43. Steven R. Weisman, "Rice Admits U.S. Underestimated Hamas Strength," *New York Times*, January 30, 2006.
44. Murphy, "Report on Denazification" (Document no. 347), 494–98.
45. Interview with Condoleeza Rice, *Firing Line with Margaret Hoover*, PBS Television, October 12, 2024, https://x.com/FiringLineShow/status/1845173394133876942
46. "Gaza: Hamas Must End Brutal Crackdown against Protesters and Rights Defenders," Amnesty International, March 18, 2019. Given Amnesty's hostility toward Israel and strong support of the Palestinian Arab cause, its criticism of Hamas is noteworthy.
47. Dennis Ross, "Hamas Could Have Chosen Peace. Instead, It Made Gaza Suffer," *Washington Post*, August 8, 2014; Joby Warrick and Loveday Morris, "Hamas Built an Underground War Machine to Ensure Its Own Survival," *Washington Post*, October 5, 2024.
48. Ross, "Hamas Could Have Chosen Peace."
49. Ross, "Hamas Could Have Chosen Peace"; Warrick and Morris, "Hamas Built an Underground War Machine."
50. "Israel: 50 Rafah Tunnels to Egypt Unearthed," Foundation for the Defense of Democracies, May 17, 2024; Tovah Lazaroff, "'Post' in Rafah: 'No Home without a Tunnel,' says Nahal Brigade Commander," *Jerusalem Post*, June 19, 2024.
51. "Remarks by President Biden on the Terrorist Attacks in Israel," White House news release, October 10, 2023.
52. "Secretary Antony J. Blinken with Margaret Brennan of CBS's *Face the Nation*," U.S. Department of State transcript, May 12, 2024.
53. Dennis Stute, "Interview with Amos Oz: 'For Israel, It Is a Lose-Lose Situation,'" Qantara.de, January 8, 2014, https://qantara.de/en/article/interview-amos-oz-israel-it-lose-lose-situation.
54. "Article 52—General Protection of Civilian Objects," Protocol Additional to the Geneva Convention, International Humanitarian Law Database, accessed January 28, 2025, https://ihl-databases.icrc.org/en/ihl-treaties/api-1977/article-52
55. Emanuel Fabian, "Hamas Broke Temporary Truce in Gaza Minutes after It Began, Senior IDF Officer Says," *Times of Israel*, December 8, 2023.
56. Jonathan Speyer, "Driving Out Darkness with the 36th Division in Shejaia," *Jerusalem Post*, December 8, 2023.
57. News Release, "The IDF Struck an Important Hamas Operational, Political and Military Center in Gaza—the Islamic University," Office of the IDF Spokesman, October 11, 2023.

58. News Release, "Weapons Found in Al-Azhar University," Office of the IDF Spokesman, December 8, 2023.
59. Emanuel Fabian, "Troops Uncover Weapons in and around Gaza's Islamic University in Khan Younis," *Times of Israel*, January 9, 2024.
60. Julian E. Barnes, "Hamas Used Gaza Hospital as a Command Center, U.S. Intelligence Says," *New York Times*, January 2, 2024.
61. Matthew Rosenberg, Ronen Bergman, Aric Toler, and Helmuth Rosales, "How Hamas Uses Gaza's Hospitals," *New York Times*, February 12, 2024.
62. Rosenberg, Bergman, Toler, and Rosales, "How Hamas Uses Gaza's Hospitals."
63. Rosenberg, Bergman, Toler, and Rosales, "How Hamas Uses Gaza's Hospitals."
64. Rosenberg, Bergman, Toler, and Rosales, "How Hamas Uses Gaza's Hospitals."
65. "'We've Had Enough': After IDF Operation, Gazan Ambulance Driver Says Hamas Embeds in Hospitals," *Jerusalem Post*, October 28, 2024.
66. "IDF Footage Shows Hamas Terrorist Admitting to Embedding in Kamal Adwan Hospital," *Jerusalem Post*, January 7, 2025.
67. Rosenberg, Bergman, Toler, and Rosales, "How Hamas Uses Gaza's Hospitals."
68. Israel War Room (@IsraelWarRoom), "IDF interrogations of Hamas and PIJ terrorists reveal how the terrorist groups exploit Shifa Hospital for terrorist activity," X, March 26, 2024, https://x.com/IsraelWarRoom/status/1772648238815879581.
69. Emanuel Fabian, "In Interrogation, Islamic Jihad Spokesman Admits Group's Rocket Struck Gaza Hospital," *Times of Israel*, April 8, 2024.
70. "After Returning from Gaza, Kurdish Physician Says Hamas Leaders Take Shelter at Hospitals," rudaw.com, May 28, 2024, https://www.rudaw.net/english/world/28052024.
71. Daniel Greenfield, "Terrorist Murderer of 5-Year-Old Girl Caught Hiding in Shifa Maternity Ward," Israel National News, April 4, 2024.

3. KILLERS ARE MADE, NOT BORN

1. Yoav Zitun, "IDF Soldiers Find Pictures of Women and Children Holding Rifles in Gaza Home," Ynetnews.com, December 25, 2023.
2. "West Bank Kindergarten Posts TikTok Videos Showing Children Simulating Clashes with Israeli Military, Killing Soldiers, 'Martyr' Funeral," MEMRI.org, February 14, 2023.
3. Itamar Marcus and Nan Jacques Zilberdik, "PA Mocks Belgium: Names Two More Schools after Terrorist Murderer," Palestinian Media Watch, September 3, 2018.
4. Maurice Hirsch, "Immortalizing a Child Terrorist," Palestinian Media Watch, May 23, 2022.

5. Nan Jacques Zilberdik and Itamar Marcus, "Palestinian Kids Taught to Admire Escaped Terrorists," Palestinian Media Watch, September 26, 2021.
6. "Kindergarten Children Participate in Procession in Solidarity with Hunger-Striking Terrorist Prisoners," Palestinian Media Watch translation of AL-*Hayat Al-Jadida*, April 20, 2017.
7. Itamar Marcus and Nan Jacques Zilberdik, "Palestinian Girl's Hate Speech at Red Crescent Event: The Jews Kill Worshippers," Palestinian Media Watch, May 16, 2016.
8. Palestinian Media Watch translation of Al-Huda Kindergarten YouTube video, May 29, 2017.
9. "Palestinian Kindergarten Class Performs Play Called 'The Martyr's Wedding,'" Palestinian Media Watch translation of *Al-Hayat Al-Jadida*, June 2, 2011.
10. "Hamas Kindergarten Graduation Ceremony—Children Taught to Be Fighters and Suicide Bombers," Palestinian Media Watch, May 31, 2007.
11. IMPACT-se, *The 2020–21 Palestinian School Curriculum, Grades 1–12* (May 2021), 45, 17.
12. IMPACT-se, *The 2020–21 Palestinian School Curriculum, Grades 1–12* (May 2021), 65, 32.
13. IMPACT-se, *The 2020–21 Palestinian School Curriculum, Grades 1–12* (May 2021), 47, 79.
14. IMPACT-se, *The 2020–21 Palestinian School Curriculum, Grades 1–12* (May 2021), 84, 17.
15. "PA schoolbook: 'Every One of Us Wishes to Be Like . . . Dalal Mughrabi,'" Palestinian Media Watch translation of PA schoolbook, August 1, 2017.
16. IMPACT-se, *The 2020–21 Palestinian School Curriculum, Grades 1–12* (May 2021), 26–27.
17. IMPACT-se, *The 2020–21 Palestinian School Curriculum, Grades 1–12* (May 2021), 33, 72.
18. IMPACT-se, *The 2020–21 Palestinian School Curriculum, Grades 1–12* (May 2021), 27, 55.
19. IMPACT-se, *The 2020–21 Palestinian School Curriculum, Grades 1–12* (May 2021), 22.
20. "Palestinian Textbooks," November 2001, Office of the Advisor for Palestinian Affairs, Israeli Civil Administration—Judea and Samaria, https://www.jewishvirtuallibrary.org/incitement-anti-semitism-and-hatred-of-israel-in-palestinian-school-textbooks-november-2001.
21. IMPACT-se, *The 2020–21 Palestinian School Curriculum, Grades 1–12* (May 2021), 21, 29.

22. IMPACT-se, *The 2020–21 Palestinian School Curriculum, Grades 1–12* (May 2021), 58, 68.
23. IMPACT-se, *The 2020–21 Palestinian School Curriculum, Grades 1–12* (May 2021), 20, 43, 57, 41, 19.
24. IMPACT-se, *The 2020–21 Palestinian School Curriculum, Grades 1–12* (May 2021), 56, 34.
25. "Palestinian Textbooks," November 2001.
26. Arnon Grois, "Palestinian Textbooks," May 2003, https://www.jewishvirtuallibrary.org/jews-israel-and-peace-in-palestinian-textbooks-may-2003.
27. "State Department Actions to Address Problematic PA Textbook Content," April 26, 2018, https://www.jewishvirtuallibrary.org/state-department-actions-to-address-problematic-pa-textbook-content; "Breaking—UN Urges Palestinians to Stop Hate Speech against Israelis That Fuels Antisemitism," UN Watch, August 30, 2019, https://unwatch.org/breaking-un-urges-palestinians-to-stop-hate-speech-against-israelis-that-fuels-antisemitism/; "European Parliament Condemns Palestinian Authority Textbooks," May 2020, https://www.jewishvirtuallibrary.org/european-parliament-condemns-palestinian-authority-textbooks; "EU Study Confirms Incitement in Palestinian Textbooks," 2021, https://www.jewishvirtuallibrary.org/eu-study-confirms-incitement-in-palestinian-textbooks
28. "Palestinian Textbooks," February 2007, https://www.jewishvirtuallibrary.org/new-palestinian-textbooks-present-a-world-without-israel-february-2007.
29. "Senator Hillary Clinton and Palestinian Media Watch in Joint Press Conference Introducing Report on Palestinian Schoolbooks," Palestinian Media Watch, February 8, 2007; Clinton, *It Takes a Village.*
30. IMPACT-se, *UNRWA Education: Textbooks and Terror*, November 2023, 3, 101, 105.
31. Dina Rovner and Arik Agassi, "UNRWA Education: Reform or Regression? A Review of UNRWA Teachers and Schools Concerning Incitement to Hate and Violence," UN Watch and IMPACT-se, 2023, 48, 53, 63, 77.
32. "Group of 3,000 UNRWA Teachers Celebrates Hamas Massacre and Rape," UN Watch, January 10, 2024.
33. "UNRWA Confirms Terrorist Killed by IDF Who Led Re'im Shelter Massacre Was a Staffer," *Times of Israel*, October 25, 2024.
34. Patrick Kingsley and Ronen Bergman, "U.N. Agency for Palestinians Imperiled by Terrorism Charges," *New York Times*, January 29, 2024; "Eight UNRWA Employees Arrested by Israel over Hamas Ties," *Jerusalem Post*, February 22, 2024; Jeremy Sharon and Jacob Magid, "UN Says 9 UNRWA

Employees Who 'May Have Been Involved' in Oct. 7 Have Been Fired," *Jerusalem Post*, August 5, 2024.

35. Gabby Deutch, "U.S. Halts UNRWA Funding over Staffers' Involvement with Oct. 7 Terror Attacks," *Jewish Insider*, January 26, 2024.
36. Pamela Falk, "Israel Says These Photos Show How Hamas Places Weapons in and near U.N. Facilities in Gaza, Including Schools," CBSnews.com, November 8, 2023.
37. Dan Johnson and Richard Irvine-Brown, "UN Says Gunmen Were Filmed in Abandoned Rafah aid Warehouse," BBC.com, May 15, 2024.
38. Emanuel Fabian, "IDF Says It Found Hamas Command Room in UNRWA HQ, alongside Drone, Weapons Caches," *Times of Israel*, July 12, 2024; "UNRWA Confirms Terrorist Killed by IDF Who Led Re'im Shelter Massacre Was a Staffer," *Times of Israel*, October 25, 2024.
39. Lazar Berman, "In Central Gaza, Where Gunmen Lurk Underground, a Commander Sees a Long Slog Ahead," *Times of Israel*, January 18, 2023; Andrew Tobin, "UNRWA Teachers Held Israeli Boy, Elderly Woman Hostage for Hamas," *Washington Free Beacon*, February 2, 2024; Yonah Jeremy Bob and Reuters, "IDF Implicates More UNRWA Officials in October 7 Massacre Following Release of Recordings," *Jerusalem Post*, March 4, 2024; "Review of UNRWA Schools Headed by Hamas Principals," IMPACT-se, November 2024.
40. Jo Becker and Adam Rasgon, "Records Seized by Israel Show Hamas Presence in U.N. Schools," *New York Times*, December 8, 2024.
41. Becker and Rasgon, "Records Seized by Israel Show Hamas Presence in U.N. Schools."
42. Eldad J. Pardo, "Palestinian Curriculum Put to the Test: The General Certificate of High School Examination in Palestine (*Tawjihi*)," November 2019, IMPACT-se, 11, 14–15, 22.
43. "Exam Question for High School Students Encourages Violence and Death," Palestinian Media Watch translation of *Al-Ayyam* article, May 3, 2011.
44. "PA District Governor of Ramallah Praises Mothers of Teenage 'Martyrs,'" Palestinian Media Watch translation of *Al-Hayat Al-Jadida*, August 1, 2017.
45. "PA Daily about 16 Teenage Terrorists Who Never Completed Their School Exams: 'Death [of a Teenager] as a Martyr Is the Path to Excellence and Greatness,'" Palestinian Media Watch translation of *Al-Hayat Al-Jadida*, July 12, 2016.
46. "Palestinian Town Naming Street for Killer of 2 Israelis," JTA, October 28, 2015. Naming streets after terrorists is a common practice in PA and Hamas territories. The street on which the PA's headquarters are located, in the capital city of Ramallah, is named after Hamas bomb-maker Yihyeh Ayyash, who orchestrated attacks that killed at least ninety Israelis. Across the street

is "Heroic Martyr Dalal Mughrabi Square." It is an indication of how serious such symbols are regarded by Arab regimes that Egypt refused to renew diplomatic relations with Iran for more than thirty years until the Iranians changed the name of a street honoring Khaled Al-Islambuli, head of the group that assassinated Egyptian president Anwar Sadat.

47. "PA PM: Israel Is 'Waging a War against Us regarding the [PA] Curriculum' and Salaries for Terrorists and Their Families," Palestinian Media Watch translation of *Al-Hayat Al-Jadida*, December 19, 2019.
48. "PA Education Minister Denies Incitement in Palestinian Schoolbooks, Says Palestinians Won't 'Accept Conditions That Deviate from the Identity of the Palestinian Struggle' from Donors," Palestinian Media Watch translation of PA Television broadcast, November 5, 2017.
49. "School Curriculum's Role Is to Teach Kids 'Palestine Is Haifa and Acre'—Defense for Children International Palestine's Representative," Palestinian Media Watch, November 21, 2020.
50. "PA Education Ministry Accuses Israel of Forging Palestinian Schoolbooks in Jerusalem Schools," Palestinian Media Watch translation of *Al-Hayat Al-Jadida*, October 26, 2018.
51. "PA Education Minister Claims 'Zionist Websites' Fabricate Statements to Raise Issue of Incitement in PA Curriculum," Palestinian Media Watch translation of Abbas adviser Sabri Saidam's Facebook page, August 3, 2019.
52. "PA Governor: Israel Trying to Manipulate PA Schoolbooks as Part of Plan to Erase 'the Islamic and Christian Arab Culture,' Trying to Falsify History," Palestinian Media Watch translation of *Al-Hayat Al-Jadida*, April 20, 2019.
53. "PA Ambassador to UN: There Is No Incitement in PA Schoolbooks," Palestinian Media Watch translation of *Al-Hayat Al-Jadida*, March 27, 2019. PA officials also sometimes claim that criticism of their schoolbooks is "violent." See, for example, "PA Education Minister: Israel Is Carrying Out 'Brutal Incitement Campaign' against the PA Curriculum," Palestinian Media Watch translation of *Al-Hayat Al-Jadida*, February 20, 2018.
54. "76 Palestinian Authority Schools Named after Terrorists and Nazi Collaborators and Honoring Martyrs and Martyrdom," Palestinian Media Watch, September 17, 2018, 5, 2.
55. Itamar Marcus and Nan Jacques Zilberdik, "Terrorist Dalal Mughrabi Glorified in Ping Pong Tournament," Palestinian Media Watch, October 2, 2013; "Youth Karate Class Named for Terrorist Who Murdered Israeli Civilian," Palestinian Media Watch translation of *Al-Hayat Al-Jadida*, September 30, 2016; Nan Jacques Zilberdik, "PA School Names Basketball Game after Murderer," Palestinian Media Watch, March 30, 2016; Itamar Marcus and Nan Jacques Zilberdik, "PA Ministry of Education Names Sports Event for Girls

after Terrorist Murderer Who Led Killing of 37," Palestinian Media Watch, March 28, 2019; "Youth Center Tennis Tournament Named after Terrorist Abdallah Daoud," Palestinian Media Watch translation of *Al-Hayat Al-Jadida*, March 7, 2011.

56. "76 Palestinian Authority Schools Named after Terrorists," 6; "Wall Painting of Abu Jihad Inaugurated at PA School near Jenin," Palestinian Media Watch translation of *Al-Hayat Al-Jadida*, March 29, 2019.

57. Itamar Marcus and Nan Jacques Zilberdik, "PA National Security Forces Honors Arch-terrorist with Chess Tournament," Palestinian Media Watch, May 27, 2019; "Fatah Organizes Kickboxing Championship Named after Abu Jihad, Arch-terrorist," Palestinian Media Watch translation of *Al Quds*, April 18, 2016; "Martial Arts Tournament Named after Arch-terrorist: 'Prince of Martyrs Abu Jihad Festival,'" Palestinian Media Watch translation of *Al-Hayat Al-Jadida*, April 12, 2016; "Fencing Tournament Named after Arch-terrorist Abu Jihad Held under Auspices of Fatah official Jibril Rajoub," Palestinian Media Watch translation of *Al-Hayat Al-Jadida*, April 20, 2015; "Karate Championship Named after Terrorist Abdallah Daoud Sponsored by University President," Palestinian Media Watch translation of *Al-Hayat Al-Jadida*, March 30, 2011; "Tennis Tournament Named after Terrorist Halabi, Killer of 2, Was Held under Patronage of Senior Fatah Official," Palestinian Media Watch translation of *Ma'an* report, December 19, 2015; "Fatah Holds Futsal Championship Named after Arch-terrorist Abu Jihad, during which Terrorist Prisoners Were Honored," Palestinian Media Watch translation of *Al-Hayat Al-Jadida*, May 1, 2018.

58. "76 Palestinian Authority Schools Named after Terrorists," 2.

59. "76 Palestinian Authority Schools Named after Terrorists," 7; "PLO Names Youth Sports Centre after Head of Black September Terror Organization," Palestinian Media Watch translation of *Al-Hayat Al-Jadida*, October 18, 2020; "Championship in Gaza Named after Terrorist Leaders," Palestinian Media Watch translation of *Al-Hayat Al-Jadida*, January 26, 2019.

60. "76 Palestinian Authority Schools Named after Terrorists," 7–9; "Summer Camp Named after Terrorist Involved in Munich Olympics Massacre," Palestinian Media Watch translation of *Al-Hayat Al-Jadida*, July 20, 2010; "Championship in Gaza Named after Terrorist Leaders," Palestinian Media Watch translation of *Al-Hayat Al-Jadida*, January 26, 2019; "Horsejumping Competition Held in Honor of Terrorist Ali Hassan Salameh," PMW translation of *Al-Ayyam* article, January 22, 2004.

61. "76 Palestinian Authority Schools Named after Terrorists," 7–9; "Schools Named after Terrorists Abu Jihad, Abu Ali Mustafa and Ahmed Yassin," Palestinian Media Watch translation of *Al-Hayat Al-Jadida*, December 10,

2018; "Summer Camp Named after Terrorist Involved in Munich Olympics Massacre," Palestinian Media Watch translation of *Al-Hayat Al-Jadida*, July 20, 2010.

62. "76 Palestinian Authority Schools Named after Terrorists," 10–12.
63. "Sports Championship Honors Terrorist Samir Kuntar," Palestinian Media Watch translation of *Al-Hayat Al-Jadida*, May 5, 2008; Dina Kraft, "Prisoner Deal Reopens an Israeli Wound," *New York Times*, July 16, 2008. A similar method was used to murder eight-year-old Rami Haba in 1987; after dragging him to a cave, terrorists crushed his head with a rock so large, according to eyewitnesses, "that two hands were needed to lift it." The editors of the *Jerusalem Post* editorial characterized the murderer as "the bloodiest two-legged beast that nature ever suffered to crawl upon the surface of the earth." ("Murder and Retribution" [editorial], *Jerusalem Post*, May 22, 1987.)
64. Janine Zacharia, "Renaming after Terrorist Almost Cost School US Funding," *Jerusalem Post*, August 11, 2002; Itamar Marcus, "Terrorist Dalal Mughrabi's Name Still Used for USA Funded School," Palestinian Media Watch, August 18, 2002; Ian Birrell, "A Disturbing New Low for Foreign Aid," *The Sunday Mail*, March 12, 2017.
65. Shira Moshe, "Palestinian School Funded by Belgium No Longer Named for Mass-Murderer, but Keeps Logo Erasing Israel," *The Algemeiner*, September 6, 2018.
66. Itamar Marcus and Nan Jacques Zilberdik, "Abbas Supports PA's Naming Square after Terrorist Killer," Palestinian Media Watch, January 19, 2010; Itamar Marcus and Nan Jacques Zilberdik, "Fatah Officials Celebrated Popular Inauguration of Terrorist Square," Palestinian Media Watch, March 14, 2010; Itamar Marcus and Nan Jacques Zilberdik, "Palestinians Dedicate Monument to Murderer of 37," Palestinian Media Watch, March 15, 2015.
67. Itamar Marcus and Nan Jacques Zilberdik, "On Universal Children's Day—Look What the PA Teaches Its Children!," Palestinian Media Watch, November 20, 2018.
68. Marcus and Zilberdik, "On Universal Children's Day."
69. "Hamas Puppet Nassur: I Declare War on the Zionists," Palestinian Media Watch translation of Hamas Al Aqsa TV broadcast, February 13, 2009.
70. "Hamas Indoctrination of Kids: Bombs More Precious Than Children," Palestinian Media Watch translation of Hamas music video, January 8, 2009; "Hamas Children's TV: Rabbit Puppet Vows to Eat the Jews," Palestinian Media Watch translation of Hamas Al Awsa TV broadcast, February 8, 2008; "Hamas Children's TV: Puppet's Martyrdom-Death Celebrated as Wedding," Palestinian Media Watch translation of Hamas Al Awsa TV broadcast, February 1, 2008.

71. Nan Jacques Zilberdik and Itamar Marcus, "Palestinian Child Abuse! Mom Tells Her Son He Is "Ammunition," Destined for Martyrdom—in Girl's Poem," Palestinian Media Watch, November 28, 2019.
72. Itamar Marcus and Barbara Crook, "Mickey Mouse Again: Disney Images Used on PA Hate TV," Palestinian Media Watch, September 9, 2008.
73. "PA TV Glorifies Child Martyrdom: 'Martyrdom Is Bliss,'" Palestinian Media Watch translation of PA Television broadcast, September 16, 2008.
74. "Palestinian Children: Martyrdom for Allah Is Preferable to Life, Suicide Terror Is Natural," Palestinian Media Watch translation of PA Television broadcast, June 9, 2002.
75. "PA TV: Palestinian Girl Calls Upon Youth to Commit Genocide Against Jews," Palestinian Media Watch translation of PA Television broadcast, October 22, 2000.
76. Nan Jacques Zilberdik, "PA Home Videos: Children Are Taught to See Murderers as 'Heroes,'" Palestinian Media Watch, August 3, 2020.
77. "Hamas TV Music Video: Daughter of Suicide Terrorist Promises to Follow in Mother's Footsteps," Palestinian Media Watch, May 22, 2009; Donna Rachel Edmunds, "PA TV Re-Releases Pop Video Glorifying Palestinian Terrorists," *Jerusalem Post*, June 15, 2020.
78. "Former Palestinian UN Youth Ambassador Used to Promote Murderers by PA TV Live," Palestinian Media Watch translation of PA Television broadcasts on June 1, 6, 9, and 27, 2020.
79. "Children Are Taught by DFLP That Terrorists Are 'Symbols and Heroes Who Inspire Generation After Generation,'" Palestinian Media Watch translation of *Al-Hayat Al-Jadida*, November 7, 2020.
80. Itamar Marcus and Nan Jacques Zilberdik, "Palestinian Children Wear 'Suicide Belts' to Celebrate Fatah's 51 Years of Violence," Palestinian Media Watch, January 11, 2016.
81. Nan Jacques Zilberdik, "Fatah Educates Another Generation to Hate Israel," Palestinian Media Watch, October 7, 2020.
82. "Palestinian Children Taught to Believe That 'The UAE Is Not an Arab State' Following Their Peace Agreement with Israel," Palestinian Media Watch translation of Fatah Facebook page, September 15, 2020.
83. Itamar Marcus and Nan Jacques Zilberdik, "Muhammad Ordered Kids to Throw Rocks at Jews, According to PA-Funded PLO Magazine for Children," Palestinian Media Watch, November 19, 2017.
84. Itamar Marcus and Nan Jacques Zilberdik, "Fatah`s Guide to Rock Throwing for Kids," Palestinian Media Watch, December 27, 2017.
85. Three of the victims were Israeli Arabs who were attacked because they were mistaken for Israeli Jews.

86. Lange, *Paradise and Hell in Islamic Traditions*, 45; Feldner, "72 Black-Eyed Virgins?"
87. "Martyr Game Teaches Children How to be Killed," Palestinian Media Watch translations of Fatah Facebook page, March 4, 2019.
88. Palestinian Media Watch translation of Al-Jazeera TV, October 22, 2023.
89. Itamar Marcus and Nan Jacques Zilberdik, "Touch the Dead 'Martyr' and Brag to Your Friends," Palestinian Media Watch, October 15, 2018.
90. "Fatah FB Glorifies Murderer of 9: 'He Loved the Game "Jews and Arabs." . . . He Always Played the Role of the Arab Who, with His Simple Weapon, Attacked the Treacherous Jew,'" Palestinian Media Watch translation of Fatah Facebook page, January 14, 2017.
91. "Gazan Children Play 'Jews and Arabs' with Plastic Rifles, Sticks, and Hammers," Palestinian Media Watch translation of *Al-Ayyam* article, August 22, 2012; Mohammed Omer, "Give Up or . . . ! The Games Gaza's Children Play," *Washington report on Middle East Affairs*, January-February 2006, 24–25.
92. "Rock-Throwing Dolls for Palestinian Children Confiscated by Israeli Customs," Palestinian Media Watch translation of *Al-Hayat Al-Jadida*, December 9, 2015; "IDF Commando Unit Locates Weapons along with Dolls, Games Inciting Hatred," *Jerusalem Post*, January 6, 2024.
93. Ephraim D. Tepler and Itamar Marcus, "Palestinian Authority Encourages Children to Weaponize Toys Yet Enraged When Fighting Palestinian Child Soldiers," Palestinian Media Watch, January 22, 2025.
94. "Stabbing Attack Enacted by Kids in Play at PA-Funded Summer Camp," Palestinian Media Watch translation of National Committee for Summer Camps Facebook page, August 8, 2017; "Kids Enact Stabbing Attack in Play at PA-Funded Summer Camp," Palestinian Media Watch translation of National Committee for Summer Camps Facebook page, August 3, 2017; "Girls at Summer Camp Draw Map of 'Palestine' Erasing Israel," Palestinian Media Watch translation of PLO Supreme Council for Sport and Youth Affairs Facebook page, August 7, 2017; "Kids at PA-Funded Summer Camp Create Sculpture of 'Palestine' That Erases Israel," Palestinian Media Watch translation of National Committee for Summer Camps Facebook page, August 4, 2017; "PLO Youth Council Posts Image of Kids at Summer Camp Making Map of 'Palestine' with Stones," Palestinian Media Watch translation of PLO Supreme Council for Sport and Youth Affairs Facebook page, August 4, 2017; Nan Jacques Zilberdik, "The PA Summer Camps for Terror and Martyrdom," Palestinian Media Watch, August 3, 2023; Nan Jacques Zilberdik, "Fatah Summer Camp Trains Palestinian Teen Soldiers," Palestinian Media Watch, August 17, 2023; Itamar Marcus, "PA Summer Camps Teach of

a World in Which Israel No Longer Exists," Palestinian Media Watch, July 26, 2023.

95. Zilberdik, "PA Summer Camps for Terror and Martyrdom"; Zilberdik, "Fatah Summer Camp Trains Palestinian Teen Soldiers."
96. "Making Child Soldiers in PA Security Forces/Fatah Summer Camp," Palestinian Media Watch translation of Fatah TV Facebook page, August 3, 2023.
97. "PLO Supervises Summers Camps with Groups Named After Terrorists," Palestinian Media Watch translation of *Al-Hayat Al-Jadida*, August 9, 2017; Itamar Marcus and Nan Jacques Zilberdik, "PA-Fatah Summer Camp for Kids: AK-47 Automatic Weapons and Youth in Military Uniforms Dancing with Rifles," Palestinian Media Watch, June 29, 2015.
98. "Hamas Military Wing Summer Camp Trains Children with Rifles," Palestinian Media Watch translation of Facebook page of Muthanna Najjar, July 18, 2016; "Islamic Jihad Summer Camps Put Young Children through Military Drills," Palestinian Media Watch translation of Facebook page of Shehab news agency, July 12, 2016.
99. "Hamas Military Wing Summer Camp Trains Children with Rifles"; "Islamic Jihad Summer Camps Put Young Children Through Military Drills"; "Hamas Camp Teaches Military Training to Children, Including Weapons," Palestinian Media Watch translation of Wattan news agency report, August 5, 2015.
100. There are winter camps too. In the town of Al-Faria, the PA runs three camps attended by some two hundred boys and girls aged thirteen to sixteen at the Martyr Salah Khalaf Center, named after the mastermind of the Munich Olympics massacre. See "Winter Camps at Center Named after Terrorist Leader," Palestinian Media Watch translation of PA Television broadcast, January 12, 2019.
101. There was a thirty-seventh victim. When Mughrabi and her squad came ashore, they encountered Gail Rubin, an American Jewish nature photographer (and the niece of U.S. Senator Abraham Ribicoff); Mughrabi shot her to death before the terrorists proceeded to a nearby highway to hijack the bus. Following Al-Wahidi's release in a prisoner exchange, she said in an interview on PA Television on February 13, 1997: "The Jews are saying: 'The Nazis burned us in gas chambers.' That is a false tale, but at times I felt that we were those who were being burned up within the walls.
102. IMPACT-se, *Gender Inequality in Palestinian Authority Textbooks*, March 2024, 3–4.
103. "Abbas Honors Terrorist Dalal Mughrabi with Birthday Celebration," Palestinian Media Watch, December 29, 2009; "PA Names Kindergarten for

Female Terrorist Mughrabi," Palestinian Media Watch translation of *Al-Ayyam* article, May 30, 2001.

104. "5 Kids on PA TV Children's Show Praise for Mass-Murderer," Palestinian Media Watch translation of September 6, 2022, broadcast; "Girl Draws Terrorist Murderer Dalal Mughrabi Because She 'Was a Fighter Who Participated in Operations,'" Palestinian Media Watch translation of September 11, 2022, broadcast.
105. "PA Teacher Posts Schoolbook Chapter on Terrorist Murderer Dalal Mughrabi," Palestinian Media Watch, October 5, 2021, https://www.youtube.com/watch?v=yvswsyqoRow
106. Itamar Marcus and Nan Jacques Zilberdik, "PA Children Echo Adults' Terror Values," Palestinian Media Watch, June 3, 2020.
107. "Fatah Publishes Books for Kids Glorifying 'Glorious Deeds' and 'Heroism' of Terrorist 'Leaders,' including Dalal Mughrabi and Abu Jihad," Palestinian Media Watch translation of *Al-Hayat Al-Jadida*, May 13, 2019.
108. Nan Jacques Zilberdik, "Proud Mother of Terrorist Involved in Murder of 2: 'We Nursed [all of] You with the Milk of Heroism . . . You Are Heroes,'" Palestinian Media Watch, November 17, 2020.
109. Itamar Marcus, "Palestinian Children Yearn for Martyrdom, Encouraged by Parents, Schools and Friends," Palestinian Media Watch, November 30, 2000.
110. "Imprisoned Palestinian Mother Rusaila Shamasneh Launches Hunger Strike against Isolation of 14-Year-Old Daughter Sarah," *Samidoun*, February 14, 2018.
111. "Mother of Terrorist Daughter, 'All of Us, Praise Allah, Present Our Children [as Sacrifices], and We Do Not Regret a Thing," Palestinian Media Watch translation of PA Television broadcast, September 29, 2016.
112. Patrick Kingsley, "Killing of Young Gunman Highlights Shifts in Fast-Changing West Bank," *New York Times*, September 16, 2022; Anna Foster, "West Bank: Al-Aqsa Martyrs' Brigades Commander Ibrahim al-Nabulsi Killed in Nablus," BBC.com, August 9, 2022; "The Child-Martyrdom Trap of the Palestinian Authority," Palestinian Media Watch, November 22, 2019.
113. "Child-Martyrdom Trap of the Palestinian Authority."
114. "Child-Martyrdom Trap of the Palestinian Authority."
115. "Palestinian Mother Instructs Her Son How to Become a Martyr," Palestinian Media Watch translation of PA Television news broadcast, February 21, 2023.
116. Itamar Marcus, "Mothers Sing with Daughters about Being Terrorists: 'No Force in the World Can Remove the Weapon from My Hand,'" Palestinian Media Watch, June 18, 2020.

117. "Child-Martyrdom Trap of the Palestinian Authority."
118. "Teen Given Life in Prison for 'Cold-Blooded Murder' of Dafna Meir," *Times of Israel*, November 2, 2016.
119. "Father of Dead Boy: 'I'm So Happy My Son Died as a Martyr and I'm Leading Him Today as a Groom,'" Palestinian Media Watch translation of PA Television broadcast, November 6, 2021.
120. "Father of Dead Terrorist Encourages 'All the Young People to Adopt' Terror, 'the Most Correct Path,'" Palestinian Media Watch translation of PA Television news broadcast, February 11, 2023; "Child-Martyrdom Trap of the Palestinian Authority."
121. Itamar Marcus and Ephraim D. Tepler, "Can a Mother Pray for Her Son to Die as a Martyr?," Palestinian Media Watch, April 18, 2024.
122. "'My Son Wanted to Be a Martyr His Whole Life . . . Allah Be Praised,' Says Mother of 16-Year-Old Dead Child," Palestinian Media Watch translation of PA Television news broadcast, October 20, 2022.
123. Marcus and Tepler, "Can a Mother Pray for Her Son to Die as a Martyr?"
124. Marcus and Tepler, "Can a Mother Pray for Her Son to Die as a Martyr?"
125. Marcus and Tepler, "Can a Mother Pray for Her Son to Die as a Martyr?"
126. "Child-Martyrdom Trap of the Palestinian Authority."
127. Marcus and Tepler, "Can a Mother Pray for Her Son to Die as a Martyr?"
128. "Palestinian Town Naming Street for Killer of 2 Israelis."
129. "Palestinian Town Naming Street for Killer of 2 Israelis."

4. THE WAR ON THE TRUTH

1. Marc Rod, "U.S. Director of National Intelligence Says Iran Is Influencing and Funding Gaza War Protests," *Jewish Insider*, July 9, 2024.
2. National March on Washington: Free Palestine, The People's Forum, November 4, 2023, https://peoplesforum.org/events/national-march-on-washington-free-palestine/; Queers Undermining Israeli Terrorism!, Quit!, https://quitpalestine.org/contact/; The Jericho Movement, https://www.thejerichomovement.com/about; Palestinian Assembly for Liberation, https://www.palassembly.org/; Arab Americans for Syria, https://www.facebook.com/aa4syria/.
3. ADL (@ADL), "'Khaybar, Khaybar' Is a Call for the Subjugation of and Murder of Jews," X, December 29, 2024, https://x.com/ADL/status/1873421347050946851. "Khaybar" also was spray-painted in huge letters on the Hillel House at San Francisco State University. (Michael Starr, "San Francisco Hillel Building Defaced with 'Khaybar' Graffiti," *Jerusalem Post*, December 11, 2024.)

4. Niloufar Haidari, "From Yasser Arafat to Madonna: How the Palestinian Keffiyeh Became a Global Symbol," *The Guardian*, December 11, 2023; Brendan O'Neill, "The Cult of the Keffiyeh," *Spiked*, December 20, 2024.
5. Itamar Marcus and Ephraim D. Tepler, "PA Celebrates Antisemitic Campus Hate Fests," Palestinian Media Watch, May 9, 2024.
6. Charles Hilu, "Palestinian Protesters Target NYC Cancer Hospital," *Washington Free Beacon*, January 16, 2024.
7. "Anti-Israel Protesters Vandalize White House Gates, Try to Scale Fence," *Jerusalem Post*, November 5, 2023; "Thousands of Pro-Palestinians March onto the White House," *Jerusalem Post*, January 14, 2024; Keshet Neev, "'Jihad of Victory of Martyrdom': Anti-Israel Activists Protest Outside White House," *Jerusalem Post*, June 9, 2024; Patrick Reilly, "Masked Anti-Israel Protesters Take Over NYC Subway Car, Tell Zionists to Raise Their Hands: 'This Is Your Chance to Get Out,'" *New York Post*, June 11, 2024.
8. Gabe Stutman, "Pro-Palestinian Activists Take Credit for Torching UC Berkeley Police Car," *Jewish News of Northern California*, June 3, 2024; Michael Starr, "Anti-Israel Activists Allegedly Throw Firebomb at UC Berkeley Building," *Jerusalem Post*, June 14, 2024; Jashaula Pettigrew, "Portland State University's Library to Remain Closed Until Fall Due to Damage from Protest," koin.com, May 3, 2024; Alec Schemmel, "Portland PD Investigating Anarchist Group That Says It Torched Police Vehicles in Solidarity with Palestinian Protesters," *Washington Free Beacon*, May 7, 2024; Heather Knight, "Police Arrest 13 after Protesters Occupied Stanford President's Office," *New York Times*, June 5, 2024; Danielle Greyman-Kennard, "Suspected Murderer of LA Jewish Man Named," *Jerusalem Post*, November 10, 2023.
9. Shane Galvin and Carl Campanille, "NYC Anti-Israel Protesters Call for 'Intifada Revolution' Hours After ISIS Flag-Wielding Terrorists Killed at Least 14 in New Orleans," *New York Post*, January 1, 2025.
10. Noe Goldhaber, "UWPD Investigating Antisemitic Incident on Library Mall," *The Daily Cardinal*, April 30, 2024; Chuck Schiller, "Ex-L.A. Pro Soccer Player Flashes Nazi Salute at Pro-Israel Rally in Beverly Hills," *Los Angeles Times*, November 8, 2023.
11. Jackie Hajdenberg, "Hate or Just a Crime? Either Way, Jewish Restaurants Are Finding Support after Vandalism," JTA, December 8, 2023.
12. Melanie Notkin (@SavvyAuntie), "These people are chanting 'All kikes are racist' at a kosher restaurant in midtown Manhattan. Kike is an old slur for Jew," X, September 4, 2024, https://x.com/SavvyAuntie/status/1831471744445771902.
13. "All Kosher, Jewish, and Israeli-Owned Restaurants Vandalized Since Oct. 7th 2023," accessed February 25, 2025, https://yeahthatskosher.com/tracker

-all-kosher-jewish-and-israeli-owned-restaurants-vandalized-since-oct-7th-2023/.

14. Jackie Hajdenberg, "Hate, or Just a Crime? Either Way, US Jewish Restaurants Find Support after Vandalism," *Times of Israel*, December 18, 2023; Ben Sales, "Pro-Palestinian Protesters Target Philadelphia Falafel Shop Owned by Jewish Celebrity Chef Michael Solomonov," JTA, December 4, 2023.
15. "All Kosher, Jewish, and Israeli-Owned Restaurants Vandalized Since Oct. 7th 2023."
16. Aaron Sibarium, "Advocacy Workshops, Anti-Racist Audits: Inside a Top Medical School's Radical Curriculum Overhaul," *Washington Free Beacon*, November 18, 2024.
17. Ron Kampeas, "Kamala Harris Condemns Antisemitic Slogans among Protesters of Benjamin Netanyahu's Speech," JTA, July 25, 2024; Bradford Betz, "Masked Protester Hoists 'Kill Hostages Now' Sign during Israel Day Parade in NYC," FoxNews.com, June 2, 2024; Megan Paglin, "Horror as GWU Protester Carries Sign with Nazi 'Final Solution' Call for Extermination of Jews," *New York Post*, April 26, 2024. For the climate slogans, see: https://tinyurl.com/bdmst3b8.
18. "At Anti-Israel March in D.C., Explicit Expressions of Support for Terror and Antisemitism," Anti-Defamation League, November 4, 2023, https://www.adl.org/resources/article/anti-israel-march-dc-explicit-expressions-support-terror-and-antisemitism.
19. Alex Gangitano, "White House Condemns 'Death to America' Chants at Rally in Dearborn, Mich.," *The Hill*, April 9, 2024; "Police Arrest 13 after Protesters Occupied Stanford President's Office," *New York Times*, June 5, 2024.
20. Jack Elbaum, "'Honor His Last Demand': Anti-Israel Groups across US Mobilize in Support of Assassinated Terrorist Leaders," *The Algemeiner*, August 2, 2024; Chris Nesi, "Disgraceful America-hating Anti-Israel Protesters Burn US Flag on July 4th in NYC," *New York Post*, July 4, 2024; Louis Casiano and Kassy Dillon, "Massachusetts Pro-Palestinian Protestors Desecrate US Flag, Call America 'Legit Gangsters,'" FoxNews.com, October 9, 2023; https://www.youtube.com/watch?v=dwx9e56haXs.
21. "Hamas Leader Abroad Khaled Mashal Rejects Accusations of Transgressions against Civilians," MEMRI, October 19, 2023.
22. "Deputy-Chairman of Hamas's Political Bureau Saleh Al-Arouri: Hamas Did Not Target Civilians," MEMRI, October 12, 2023.
23. "Hamas Official Hisham Qasem Explains the Abduction of Thai Nationals to Gaza," MEMRI, November 26, 2023.
24. Nan Jacques Zilberdik, "PA Oct. 7 Massacre Denial: Israelis 'Killed Their Civilians, Committed All These Crimes, and Burned the Bodies,'" Palestin-

ian Media Watch, December 14, 2023; Palestinian Media Watch translation of *Donia Al-Watan article*, October 11, 2023.

25. "Our Narrative . . . Operation Al-Aqsa Flood," 7–8, https://tinyurl.com/c69tkavv; Ohad Merlin, "Hamas Releases Propaganda Doc Denying Atrocities, Blaming Israel for Civilian Deaths on Oct 7," *Jerusalem Post*, January 19, 2024.
26. "Abbas Advisor Denies Hamas' Documented Atrocities on Oct. 7 as 'Lies, Falsehoods, and Fabrications,'" Palestinian Media Watch translation of Mahmoud Al-Habbash's Facebook page, December 5, 2023.
27. Zilberdik, "PA Oct. 7 Massacre Denial."
28. Dirk-Oliver Heckmann, "Interview with Salah Abdel Shafi, Ambassador of Palestine to Austria," *Deutschlandfunk*, August 21, 2024.
29. "Despite Documentation of Hamas' Atrocities, PLO Official Denies 'Murder of Children, Rape of Women' as 'Tndentious Israeli Propaganda,'" Palestinian Media Watch translation of PA *Topic of the Day* episode, December 3, 2023.
30. "Palestinian Politician Hanan Ashrawi: Biden Just Blindly Parrots Everything He Hears from the Israeli 'Spin Machine'; Claims of Hamas Atrocities Are Lies, Nonsense, Doctored Pictures," MEMRI, October 26, 2023.
31. Palestinian Media Watch translation of PA Television broadcast, October 31, 2023.
32. Itamar Marcus, "Fatah Brags It Took Part in October 7 Slaughter," Palestinian Media Watch, November 1, 2023; Bassam Tawil, "Guess Which 'Moderate' Palestinian Terrorist Group Participated in the October 7 Massacre," Gatestone Institute, May 28, 2024.
33. Itamar Marcus, "Abbas' Response to Terror in Russia Highlights His Hypocrisy and Lies," Palestinian Media Watch, March 25, 2024.
34. Nan Jacques Zilberdik, "Abbas' Advisor Threatens Israel with More Massacres: 'Oct. 7 Can Repeat Itself 100 Times, and Perhaps Even More Seriously,'" Palestinian Media Watch, May 18, 2024.
35. Itamar Marcus and Ephraim D. Tepler, "PA's Ruling Party Continues to Celebrate and Justify October 7," Palestinian Media Watch, June 17, 2024. Prominent Jordanians also denied the atrocities. See Rafael Medoff, "Queen of the Pogrom Deniers," *Jewish Journal of Los Angeles*, October 31, 2023.
36. Jane Prinsley, "Revealed: Dozens of Palestinian Diplomats Celebrated October 7," *Jewish Chronicle of London*, August 29, 2024. The investigators were affiliated with GnasherJew, a team of British journalists who are best known for uncovering antisemitic remarks made by Jeremy Corbyn, the onetime leader of Britain's Labor Party.

37. Doha Institute, *Arab Public Opinion About the Israeli War on Gaza*, accessed on January 28, 2025, https://www.dohainstitute.org/en/News/Pages/arab-public-opinion-about-the-israeli-war-on-gaza.aspx.
38. Palestinian Center for Policy and Survey Research, "Press Release: Public Opinion Poll No 91," Palestinian Center for Policy and Survey Research, March 20, 2024.
39. Itamar Marcus, "PA's 'Pay-for-Slay' Payments to Rise by $1.3 Million Per Month," Palestinian Media Watch, January 10, 2024; Andrew Tobin, "Palestinian Authority, Key to Biden's Mideast Peace Plan, Commits to Pay $97M a Year to Hamas," *Washington Free Beacon*, March 4, 2024; Itamar Marcus and Ephraim D. Tepler, "Palestinian Authority Recognition Makes 899 Gazans Eligible for Pay-for-Slay," Palestinian Media Watch, July 23, 2024.
40. David K. Shipler, "More Schoolgirls in West Bank Fall Sick," *New York Times*, April 4, 1983.
41. Norman Kempster, "300 Arab Girls in West Bank Poisoned by Gas," *Los Angeles Times*, March 28, 1983.
42. "Israel Finds No Poison at 6 Arab Schools," *New York Times*, March 29, 1983; "16 Held on Suspicion of Faking Arab Epidemic," *Los Angeles Times*, April 8, 1983.
43. The Editors, "Poisoned Chocolates," Palestinian Media Watch, June 6, 2001.
44. Tom Gross, "Arabs Heat Up Propaganda War on Israel," Palestinian Media Watch, May 27, 2001.
45. "Israel Spreads AIDS and Other Diseases," Palestinian Media Watch translation of *Al-Hayat Al-Jadida*, February 17, 2008.
46. Nan Jacques Zilberdik, "PA Lies and Libels: 'Israel Deliberately . . . Spread(s) Lethal Epidemics and Infectious Diseases among Children in Gaza,'" Palestinian Media Watch, January 4, 2024; Itamar Marcus, "Medieval Libels in Today's PA: 'Israel Openly Murders Palestinian Children' and 'Poisons Water and Air'—in op-ed in official PA daily," Palestinian Media Watch, September 14, 2020.
47. Barton Gellman, "Pop! Went the Tale of the Bubble Gum Spiked with Sex Hormones," *Washington Post*, July 28, 1997; Raphael Israeli, "Poison: The Use of Blood Libel in the War against the Jews," Jerusalem Center for Public Affairs, April 15, 2002.
48. William A. Orme, Jr., "While Mrs. Clinton Looks On, Palestinian Officials Criticize Israel," *New York Times*, November 12, 1999.
49. Itamar Marcus and Barbara Crook, "Blood Libel: Jews Drink Muslim blood," Palestinian Media Watch, April 5, 2009.

50. "Official PA Daily: Jews' God Demands 'Passover Matzah Made from the Blood of Our Children,' as Stated in Protocols of the Elders of Zion," Palestinian Media Watch translation of *Al-Hayat Al-Jadida*, July 12, 2014.
51. Itamar Marcus and Nan Jacques Zilberdik, "Jews Make Matzah Bread from Blood, Sacrifice Humans to Satan—in Al-Aqsa Lesson," Palestinian Media Watch, June 2, 2015.
52. Subsequently, Abbas's office issued a brief statement to the foreign news media acknowledging that the reports on which Abbas based his statements were "baseless." However, Abbas himself never directly retracted the accusation. See "Abbas Walks Back Claim Rabbis Sought to 'Poison' Palestinian Wells,'" *Times of Israel*, June 25, 2016.
53. "Fatah Posts Kids` Drawings: Israel Drinks Blood of Palestinians; Israel Eats Palestinians; Yes to Violence; All of Israel Is 'Palestine' in Maps," Palestinian Media Watch translation of Fatah Facebook page, October 11, 2016.
54. HyoJin Park, "How to Be a Palestinian Supermom," *Al Jazeera*, August 23, 2017; "UN Changes Special Rapporteur Lynk's Report Following NGO Monitor Complaint," NGO Monitor, May 14, 2017. A spokesman for Amnesty International defended Mrs. Tamimi's rock-throwing rallies on the grounds that the rocks "posed little or no serious risk" to their targets.
55. Anti-Defamation League press release, November 19, 2001; Anti-Defamation League press release, June 14, 2010.
56. Palestinian Media Watch translation of PA Television broadcast, October 27, 2023.
57. Palestinian Media Watch translation of *Al-Hayat Al-Jadida*, December 29, 2023.
58. Palestinian Media Watch translation of *Al-Hayat Al-Jadida*, January 2, 2024.
59. Itamar Marcus and Ephraim D. Tepler, "PA Libel: Israel Poisoning Wells, Murdering Prisoners, and Stealing Body Parts," Palestinian Media Watch, April 15, 2024.
60. "Palestinian Terrorists Inject Mercury into Israeli Oranges; 5 Dutch Children Poisoned after Eating Them," JTA, February 2, 1978.
61. Bar-Zohar and Haber, *Quest for the Red Prince*, 55–61.
62. "76 Palestinian Authority Schools Named after Terrorists," 9–10.
63. "Hamas Used Toxic Substance to Kill Nahal Oz Troops on Oct. 7, IDF Probe Said to Show," *Times of Israel*, December 13, 2023.
64. "Unfounded Claims of 'Organ Harvesting' Reignite Embers of Decades-Old Hospital Scandal and Centuries-Old Trope," Anti-Defamation League, December 19, 2023; Mira Fox, "A Viral Post Demonizing Zionist Doctors Sounds Eerily Like a Soviet Antisemitic Conspiracy Theory," *The Forward*, January 4, 2024; "CAIR Condemns Latest Israeli Massacre of Children in

Gaza, Attempts to Lure People to Death with Fake Baby Cries, Destruction of Homes in 'Buffer Zone,'" CAIR.com, April 16, 2024.

65. Lenny Ben-David, "The Casualty Figures in Gaza Are a Scam," Jerusalem Center for Public Affairs, November 30, 2023; Lilach Shoval, "Hamas Blocks Gazans from Evacuating to Safe Zones," *Israel Hayom*, October 14, 2024.
66. Wafaa Sjhurafa and Samu Magdy, "Large-Scale Polio Vaccinations Begin in War-Ravaged Gaza after First Case in 25 Years," Associated Press, September 2, 2024; Tom Bennett, "Israel Agrees to Pauses in Fighting for Polio Vaccine Drive," bbc.com, August 30, 2024.
67. Patrick Kingsley et al, "How Hamas Is Fighting in Gaza: Tunnels, Traps and Ambushes," *New York Times*, July 13, 2024; Shirit Avitan Cohen and ILH Staff, "IDF Finds Jaw-dropping Hamas Triple-Decker Tunnels for Smuggling," *Israel Hayom*, July 9, 2024.
68. Abraham Wyner, "How the Gaza Ministry of Health Fakes Casualty Numbers," *Tablet*, March 6, 2024; Michael Oren, "The US Charge of 'Indiscriminate Bombing' Is Over the Top," *Times of Israel*, February 15, 2024.
69. UN News (@UN_News_Centre), "We are witnessing a killing of civilians that is unparalleled and unprecedented in any conflict since I have been Secretary General," X, November 20, 2023, https://x.com/un_News_Centre/status/1726609880986083685?s=20.
70. Fox, *Questionable Counting*, 6
71. "Remarks by President Biden and Prime Minister Anthony Albanese of Australia in Joint Press Conference," The White House, October 25, 2023.
72. "Pentagon 'Clarifies' Austin Cited Hamas Statistics in Testimony to Congress," *Israel Hayom*, March 1, 2024.
73. Marc Rod, "Director of National Intelligence: U.S. Does Not Take Gaza Casualty Numbers 'on Face Value,'" *Jewish Insider*, March 12, 2024.
74. Nick Robertson, "House Votes to Ban State Department from Citing Gaza Health Ministry Death Toll Statistics," *The Hill*, June 27, 2024.
75. Maayan Jaffe-Hoffman, "IDF: One in Five Gaza Rockets Misfires, Kills Palestinians," *Jerusalem Post*, October 21, 2023.
76. "Analysis Finds Flaws in Hamas Data, Drop in Rate of Gazan Women, Children Killed," *Times of Israel*, June 7, 2024.
77. Gabriel Epstein, "How Hamas Manipulates Gaza Fatality Numbers: Examining the Male Undercount and the Other Problems," Washington Institute for Near East Policy, 2024.
78. "Israel Publishes New Civilian Death Toll in Gaza," VOAnews.com, May 21, 2024.
79. Reuters, "Explainer—How Many Palestinians Has Israel's Gaza Campaign Killed?," *U.S. News & World Report*, July 10, 2024.

80. Ohad Merlin, "Hamas Document Reveals It Hides Casualties, Blames Failed Rocket Launches on Israel—IDF," *Jerusalem Post*, March 31, 2024.
81. Human Rights Watch, "Gaza: Findings on October 17 al-Ahli Hospital Explosion," November 26, 2023; Emanuel Fabian, "In Interrogation, Islamic Jihad Spokesman Admits Group's Rocket Struck Gaza Hospital," *Times of Israel*, April 8, 2024.
82. Jodi Rudoren, "Civilian or Not? New Fight in Tallying the Dead from the Gaza Conflict," *New York Times*, August 5, 2014.
83. Lenny Ben-David, "The Casualty Figures in Gaza Are a Scam," Jerusalem Center for Security and Foreign Affairs, November 30, 2023.
84. Merlin, "Hamas Document Reveals It Hides Casualties."
85. Margherita Stancati, "In Gaza, Authorities Lose Count of the Dead," *Wall Street Journal*, April 28, 2024; David Adesnik, "Gaza Health Ministry Cannot Provide Names for More Than 10,000 It Says Have Died," Foundation for the Defense of Democracies, May 2, 2024.
86. UNRWA (@UNRWA), "A child is killed every 10 minutes in the #GazaStrip," X, April 20, 2024, https://twitter.com/unrwa/status/1781731649874448394; Michelle Nichols, "A Child Killed on Average Every 10 Minutes in Gaza, Says WHO Chief," Reuters, November 10, 2023; Adam Kredo, "U.N. Cuts Gaza Death Toll Figures by Half, Confirming Hamas Is Lying about Casualties," *Washington Free Beacon*, May 13, 2024; "Daily Press Briefing by the Office of the Spokesperson for the Secretary-General," United Nations, May 10, 2024.
87. Shachar Kleiman, "Hamas Desperate for Manpower, Enlists 16-Year-Olds," *Israel Hayom*, June 18, 2024.
88. Fox, *Questionable Counting*, 6–7.
89. Nicholas Kristof (@NickKristof), "'Disturbing reports continue to emerge about mass graves in Gaza in which Palestinian victims were reportedly stripped naked with their hands tied, prompting renewed concerns about possible war crimes,'" X, April 23, 2024, https://x.com/NickKristof/status/1782766467609661671.
90. News release, "Gaza: Discovery of Mass Graves Highlights Urgent Need to Grant Access to Independent Human Rights Investigators," Amnesty International, April 24, 2024.
91. Abu Bakr Bashir, Hiba Yazek, Aric Oler, and Riley Mellen, "Gaza Authorities Say More Bodies Were Discovered in Mass Grave," *New York Times*, April 25, 2024.
92. Alexandria Ocasio-Cortez (@AOC), "How are news outlets dedicating wall-to-wall coverage to campus protests, but not the discovery of mass graves in Gaza of people with their hands tied & clothing stripped?" X, April 23, 2024, https://x.com/AOC/status/1782916332771504451.

93. Bashir, Yazek, Oler, and Mellen, "Gaza Authorities Say More Bodies Were Discovered in Mass Grave"; "Mass Graves in Gaza Show Victims' Hands Were Tied, Says UN Rights Office," UN News, April 23, 2024.
94. "Appendix to letter of July 25, 2024 re. American physicians' observations from the Gaza Strip since October 7, 2023," https://tinyurl.com/2mj2xm93; "Letter to President Biden and Vice President Harris," Gaza Healthcare Letters, October 2, 2024, https://www.gazahealthcareletters.org/usa-letter-oct-2-2024.
95. "Israel Says Gaza Has Received Almost 14,000 Trucks of Aid since Start of War," *Times of Israel*, February 23, 2024; "Nutritional Assessment of Food Aid Delivered to Gaza Via Israel During the Swords of Iron War," accessed February 2, 2025, https://biochem-food-nutrition.agri.huji.ac.il/sites/default/files/biochem-food-nutrition/files/preprint-nutritional-assessment-of-food-aid-delivered-to-gaza-via-israel-during-the-swords-of-iron-war.pdf?utm_source=substack&utm_medium=email.
96. "Nutritional Assessment of Food Aid Delivered to Gaza Via Israel During the Swords of Iron War."
97. "Hamas Has Profited from Gaza Aid 'to Tune of Half a Billion Dollars,'" *Jewish Chronicle of London*, May 20, 2024; "Hamas Warehouses in Gaza Are Overflowing with Stolen Humanitarian Aid—N12," *Jerusalem Post*, September 13, 2024; Hiba Yazbek and Erika Solomon, "Looters Strip Aid from About 100 Trucks in Gaza, U.N. Agency Says," *New York Times*, November 19, 2024.
98. Samantha Power, "Gazans are facing a catastrophic food crisis. Today from the Kerem Shalom border crossing between Israel and Gaza," X, February 28, 2024, https://x.com/Powerusaid/status/1762948968105832933; "Famine Is Imminent in North Gaza," USAID press release, March 18, 2024; Jennifer Hansler, "USAID Administrator Says It Is 'Credible' to Assess Famine Is Already Occurring in Parts of Gaza," CNN.com, April 11, 2024.
99. "Gaza Strip: Acute Food Insecurity Situation for 1 May–15 June and Projection for 16 June–30 September 2024," June 25, 2024, ipcinfo.org; Jeremy Sharon, "New Gaza Famine Report Reveals Grim March Predictions Were Vastly Exaggerated," *Times of Israel*, July 2, 2024.
100. "Statement from Former U.S. Ambassador Jacob Lew on FEWS NET Report," U.S. Embassy in Israel, December 24, 2024; Gabby Deutch, "USAID-Backed Report about Famine in Gaza Taken Down after Criticism from U.S. Ambassador to Israel," *Jewish Insider*, December 25, 2024.
101. Churchill to Roosevelt, May 7, 1944, File: Churchill to Roosevelt April–May 1944, FDRL, accessed at http://www.fdrlibrary.marist.edu/_resources/images/mr/mr0036.pdf; Roosevelt to Churchill, May 11, 1944, File: Roosevelt to

Churchill, April–May 1944, accessed at http://www.fdrlibrary.marist.edu/_resources/images/mr/mr0035.pdf.

102. Erdheim, "Could the Allies Have Bombed Auschwitz-Birkenau?"

103. Allison Brooks interview with Stuart Erdheim in *They Looked Away*; Hackett, *Buchenwald Report*, 95; Richard Davis interview with Stuart Erdheim, June 9, 2000, courtesy of Stuart Erdheim.

104. White, "'Even in Auschwitz'"; "The British Victims of Auschwitz," Auschwitz-Birkenau Memorial and Museum, accessed January 29, 2025, https://www.auschwitz.org/en/museum/news/the-british-victims-of-auschwitz,382.html.

105. Bob Drogin, "This City Was Ravaged in WWII. Why Do Few Remember the Suffering and Sacrifice?," *Los Angeles Times*, May 29, 2023.

106. Kirby and Casey, "Area Bombing of Germany."

107. Zuehlke, *Ortona*, 287, 366–67.

108. The "it happens in war" argument also was used by actor and director Mel Gibson to belittle the Holocaust. Columnist Peggy Noonan asked him in a 2004 *Reader's Digest* interview, "The Holocaust happened, right?," to which Gibson responded, "Yes, of course, atrocities happened. War is horrible. The second World War killed tens of millions of people. Some of them were Jews in concentration camps. Many people lost their lives. In the Ukraine, several million starved to death between 1932 and 1933." See Peggy Noonan, "Keeping the Faith," *Reader's Digest*, March 2004, 93.

109. Hanna Trudo, "Jayapal: Comments about Hamas Sexual Assaults 'Not Intended to Minimize Rape,'" *The Hill*, December 5, 2023.

110. UN Women, *Rape as a Tactic of War*, accessed January 29, 2025, https://www.unwomen.org/sites/default/files/Headquarters/Media/Publications/UNIFEM/EVAWkit_06_Factsheet_ConflictAndPostConflict_en.pdf.

111. UN Women (@UN_Women), "#Palestine: Hamas appoints first woman spokesperson, 23 year old Isra al-Modallal," Twitter (now X), November 8, 2013, https://twitter.com/un_Women/status/398838596561809408.

112. Jackie Hajdenberg, "Amid Outcry over Silence, UN Women Posts, Then Deletes, Condemnation of Hamas attack," JTA, November 28, 2023.

113. "UN Women Statement on the Situation in Israel and Gaza," UNwomen.org, December 1, 2023; Sam Halpern, "UN Women Finally Condemns Hamas Attacks, Sexual Violence on October 7," *Jerusalem Post*, December 2, 2023.

114. "me too International Calls for a Ceasefire," meetoomvmt.org, November 13, 2023.

115. "me too International Calls for a Ceasefire."

116. "NWSA Calls for a Ceasefire and Negotiations to End Gaza Siege and Israeli Apartheid," NWSA, October 11, 2023.

117. "AEN Section Statement on the NWSA," Academic Engagement Network, December 14, 2023, https://academicengagement.org/wp-content/uploads/2023/12/aen_Section-Statement-on-the-nwsa_12.14.23.pdf.
118. "NOW Condemns the Use of Rape as a Weapon of War," National Organization for Women, November 30, 2023.
119. "Until the Violence Stops," V-Day, December 6, 2023.
120. "Open Letter to the Israeli and U.S. Governments and Others Weaponizing the Issue of Rape," solidarity-us.org,.February 29, 2024.
121. "League of Women Voters Statement on Violence in Israel and Gaza," League of Women Voters, October 11, 2023.
122. "World YWCA Statement on Israel-Hamas War," World YWCA, October 9, 2023; "World YWCA Statement on the Genocide in Gaza and the Implications on Women and Children," World YWCA, November 9, 2023; "YWCA USA Statement on Israel-Hamas War—One Year Later," YWCA USA, October 7, 2024.
123. "Women's Media Center Condemns Hamas for Sexualized Violence," Women's Media Center, December 7, 2023, https://tinyurl.com/5fjeyyyz; Planned Parenthood (@PPFA), "Statement on violence in Israel and Gaza," X, December 5, 2023, https://twitter.com/ppfa/status/1732156756493574292?lang=en.
124. "Damning Evidence of War Crimes as Israeli Attacks Wipe Out Entire Families in Gaza," Amnesty International, October 20, 2023.
125. "Israel/OPT: Israeli Army Threats Ordering Residents of Northern Gaza to Leave May Amount to War Crimes," Amnesty International, October 25, 2023.
126. "Israel/OPT: Civilians on Both Sides Paying the Price of Unprecedented Escalation in Hostilities between Israel and Gaza as Death Toll Mounts," Amnesty International, October 7. 2023; "Israel/OPT: Israeli Army Threats"; "UN Special Rapporteur Report on Gaza Provides Crucial Evidence That Must Spur International Action to Prevent Genocide," Amnesty International, March 26, 2024; "Israel/ OPT: Hamas and Other Armed Groups Must Immediately Release Civilians Held Hostage in Gaza," Amnesty International, July 12, 2024; "Israel/OPT: One Year on from 7 October Need to Ensure a Ceasefire and Release of Hostages More Pressing Than Ever," Amnesty International, October 7, 2024.
127. Amnesty International, "*You Feel Like You Are Subhuman*," 101–2.
128. Amnesty International, "*You Feel Like You Are Subhuman*," 31, 35.
129. Amnesty International, "*You Feel Like You Are Subhuman*," 14–15, 30, 32–33.
130. Michael Starr, "Amnesty International Suspends Israel Branch for Rejecting NGO's Reports," *Jerusalem Post*, January 9, 2025.

131. "The U.N.'s Anti-Israel 'Genocide' Pledge" (editorial), *Wall Street Journal*, November 26, 2024.
132. Heather Barr, "Israel's Unlawful Blockade of Gaza Sparks Women's Rights Crisis," Human Rights Watch, October 2024; Macarena Saez, "Investigating Sexual and Gender-Based Violence in Conflict," Human Rights Watch, December 12, 2023; "'I Can't Erase All the Blood from My Mind': Palestinian Armed Groups' October 7 Assault on Israel," Human Rights Watch, July 19, 2024.
133. Haas, "Human-Rights Establishment," 100, 105.
134. Haas, "Human-Rights Establishment," 107–8.
135. Haas, "Human-Rights Establishment," 99.
136. Power, *Problem from Hell*, 11, 414, 485–86.
137. https://x.com/PowerUSAID/status/1825603130534539558, accessed September 14, 2024; https://x.com/USAIDSudan/status/1730614245522362411, accessed October 29, 2024.
138. "Israeli Forensic Teams Describe Signs of Torture, Abuse," reuters.com, October 15, 2023.
139. Emily Rose and Herbert Villarraga, "Rescue Workers Recount Horrors Found in Kibbutz Attacked by Hamas," reuters.com, October 17, 2023.
140. Emily Rose, "Israel Police Open Investigation into Sexual Violence during Oct. 7 Attack," retuers.com, November 14, 2023; Emma Farge, "Israel Seeks Recognition of Hamas Sexual Violence at UN Meeting," reuters.com, November 28, 2023; Emma Farge, "UN Commission to Investigate Hamas Sexual Violence, Appeal for Evidence," reuters.com, November 30, 2023.
141. Festinger, Riecken, and Schachter, *When Prophecy Fails*, 208.
142. David Samuels, "The Aspiring Novelist Who Became Obama's Foreign-Policy Guru," *New York Times Sunday Magazine*, May 5, 2016.

5. THE WAR ON CAMPUS

1. "Columbia Activists Had Prior Knowledge of Oct. 7, Bombshell Lawsuit Claims," University Further Hamas' Propaganda," *Newsweek*, March 25, 2025.
2. Schanzer, "Israel Imperiled," 2–8.
3. "Students for Justice in Palestine (SJP): Available Funding and Other Information," NGO Monitor, November 5, 2023.
4. "Leaked Students for Justice in Palestine Texts Show Support for Massacres of Israelis," *Jerusalem Post*, May 3, 2024.
5. "Day of Resistance Toolkit," October 2023, https://dw-wp-production.imgix.net/2023/10/day-of-resistance-toolkit.pdf.
6. "Day of Resistance Toolkit."

7. "Day of Resistance Toolkit."
8. Philologos, "Why Are Anti-Israel Chants So Dull?"
9. Philologos, "Why Are Anti-Israel Chants So Dull?"
10. Cade McAllister and Hannah Marr, "Students Project Anti-Israel, Anti-GW Messages onto Library, Sparking Outcry," *The GW Hatchet*, October 25, 2023.
11. Spencer Dalke, "National Students for Justice in Palestine Celebrates Glider Attack in 'Call to Action' Image," CampusReform.org, October 10, 2023.
12. Bradford Betz, "George Washington Statue at Namesake DC School Left Defaced for Days Now Covered Up after Dem Mayor Takes Heat," FoxNews.com, May 9, 2024.
13. Jessica Costescu, "Harvard Protesters Raise Palestinian Flags on University Building, in Spot Reserved for American Flag," *Washington Free Beacon*, April 27, 2024.
14. Sarah Rumpf-Whitten, "American Flag Torched during NYC Pro-Palestinian Demonstrations," FoxNews.com, January 26, 2024; Jack Morphet, Alex Oliveira, Reuven Fenton, and Allie Griffin, "Anti-Israel Protesters Vandalize WWI Memorial, Burn American Flag after Cops Block Group from Reaching Star-Studded Met Gala in NYC," *New York Post*, May 6, 2024; Michael Starr, "Hezbollah Flag Flies, US Flag Burns as Calls for Death to US Sound at NYC Protest," *Jerusalem Post*, April 16, 2024; Marissa Perlman, Sabrina Franza, and Todd Ferer, "After Alderman Spoke in Front of Burned American Flag, Some Colleagues Seek Formal Punishment," CBSNews.com, March 27, 2024; Alyssa Guzman, "Columbia Student Kicked and Told to 'Kill Himself' as His US Flag Is Set on Fire at NYC Pro-Palestinian Rally," *New York Post*, April 18, 2024. For the University of Washington, see https://twitter.com/choeshow/status/1789081643359322450. A May 2024 *New York Times* article about protesters taking down American flags and replacing them with PLO flags did not mention the burnings. (Nicholas Bogel-Burroughs, "The Latest Campus Battleground Is the Flagpole," *New York Times*, May 1, 2024).
15. Ofir Akunis (@Ofir_Akunis), "So, America: Is this what you want? The flag of the terrorist organization Hezbollah, a proxy of Iran, here in the heart of Manhattan?" X, June 22, 2024, https://x.com/Ofir_Akunis/status/1804600145448689971; Lawrence Richard, "Hezbollah Terror Flag Gound at Princeton's Anti-Israel Encampment, Cruz Torches the Protesters," FoxNews.com, April 26, 2024.
16. Dion J. Pierre, "Vandals Desecrate American, Israeli Flags at Northwestern University," *The Algemeiner*, May 14, 2024.
17. Michael Starr, "CUNY Prof. Threatened after Waving US Flag: 'They Want to Destroy America,'" *Jerusalem Post*, May 15, 2024.

18. Claire Thornton, "Fundraiser Celebrating Fraternities That Guarded American Flag during Protest Raises $500K," *USA Today*, May 3, 2024.
19. Ohad Merlin, "'Eradicate the US':American Student Group Publishes, Then Deletes Controversial Message," *Jerusalem Post*, September 8, 2024; Mathilda Heller, "Pro-Palestine Group Unity of Fields Calls for Police Officers to be Set on Fire," *Jerusalem Post*, May 15, 2025.
20. "More Than One-Third of Jewish College Students Are Forced to Hide Their Jewish Identity, New Hillel Poll Finds," Hillel International, November 20, 2023.
21. Eliav Breuer, "College Campuses See Disturbing Rise of Antisemitism since October 7," *Jerusalem Post*, February 20, 2024; "Antisemitism on College Campuses: Incident Tracking," accessed January 30, 2025, www.hillel.org/antisemitism-on-college-campuses-incident-tracking/.
22. Kimberly Bookman and Rob Way, "Jewish Student Speaks Out After Being Attacked on Mass Amherst Campus," www.whdh.com, November 6, 2023.
23. Sahar Tartak, "I Was Stabbed in the Eye at Yale," *The Free Press*, April 21, 2024.
24. David Swindle and Southern Jewish Life Reports, "Anti-Israel Rally at Tulane Turns Ugly with Brawl, Injuries," *Southern Jewish Life*, October 29, 2023; Written Testimony of Yasmeen S. Ohebsion, Tulane University Class of 2024—Congress of the United States House of Representatives Committee on Education & The Workforce, "Roundtable with Jewish Students Impacted by Antisemitism," February 29, 2024, https://edworkforce.house.gov/uploadedfiles/yasmeen_s._ohebsion_testimony.pdf ; "Letter to Tulane re SDS," accessed January 30, 2025, https://tinyurl.com/yrnnzsfm.
25. Rebecca Massel, "'I Am a Target': Dozens of Jewish Students Report Feeling Unsafe on Campus," *Columbia Spectator*, November 2, 2023.
26. "More Than One-Third of Jewish College Students Are Forced to Hide Their Jewish Identity."
27. Stand With Us, "Letter to City College of New York Re SJP," standwithus.com, December 12, 2023.
28. Daniel Trotta, "Two Jewish Students Attacked at Chicago's DePaul University," Reuters, November 7, 2024.
29. Foer, "Golden Age of American Jews Is Ending."
30. "More Than One-Third of Jewish College Students Are Forced to Hide Their Jewish Identity."
31. Cathryn J. Prince, "Amid Israel-Hamas War, Students Say Antisemitism Is 'New Normal' at Columbia University," *Times of Israel*, December 6, 2023; "Nearly Three Quarters of Jewish Students Experienced or Witnessed Antisemitism on Campus, New Survey Finds," Hillel International, November 29, 2023.

32. Wright et al, *In the Shadow of War*, 1–2.
33. Oliver Bok, "Karega Fired After Split Faculty Recommendations," *The Oberlin Review*, November 8, 2016; Larry Yudelson, "Rutgers to Discipline Professor Who Made Anti-Semitic Facebook Posts," *Jewish Standard of New Jersey*, December 8, 2017; Derrick Bryson Taylor, "Professor Fired after Joking That Iran Should Pick U.S. Sites to Bomb," *New York Times*, January 11, 2020.
34. Ronny Reyes, "Cornell Prof Who Called Hamas Attack 'Exhilarating' Is Back on Campus Cheering on Protests Despite Being on Leave," *New York Post*, April 29, 2024; "Cornell Prof. Who Described Oct. 7 as 'Exhilarating' Back to Teaching without Punishment," *Jerusalem Post*, September 17, 2024.
35. Andrew Lapin, "Cornell's Handling of a New Course on Gaza Could Preview Campus Israel Battles under Trump," Jewish Telegraphic Agency, November 11, 2024.
36. Stephanie Saul, "Who Are the Columbia Professors Mentioned in the House Hearing?," *New York Times*, April 17, 2024; "Columbia Hires, and Claims to Fire, Professor Who Voiced Support for Hamas Post-Oct. 7," *Times of Israel*, May 2, 2024.
37. Joseph Massad, "Just Another Battle or the Palestinian War of Liberation?," *The Electronic Intifada*, October 8, 2023.
38. Ali Abunimah, "Joseph Massad Responds to Fabrications and Lies about Him in Congress," *The Electronic Intifada*, April 17, 2024.
39. "Some U.S. Professors Praise October 7 Terror Attacks," Anti-Defamation League news release, November 8 and 21, 2023; Danielle Greyman-Kennard, "Points for Palestine: US Lecturer Offers Students Extra Credit for Anti-Israel Efforts," *Jerusalem Post*, October 26, 2023.
40. Aaron Sibarium, "UCLA Med School Requires Students to Attend Lecture Where Speaker Demands Prayer for 'Mama Earth,' Leads Chants of 'Free Palestine,'" *Washington Free Beacon*, April 2, 2024.
41. Jordan Esrig, "Stanford Suspends Africana Studies Professor Who Made Jewish Students 'Stand in the Corner' While Calling Hamas 'Freedom Fighters,'" *New York Sun*, October 14, 2023.
42. Gabby Deutch, "'It's Unspeakable': UC Berkeley Jewish Leaders Decry University's Response to Antisemitic Mob," *Jewish insider*, March 1, 2024.
43. Stand With Us, "Letter to Middlebury—October 2023," standwithus.com., October 20, 2023.
44. Amcha Initiative, *Academic Agitators: The Role of Anti-Zionist Faculty Activism in Escalating Antisemitism at the University of California After October 7, 2023*—March 2024, 2, https://amchainitiative.org/wp-content/uploads/2024/03/Academic-Agitators-Escalating-Antisemitism-Report.pdf.

45. Amcha Initiative, *Academic Agitators*, 3–4; Michael Arria, "Academics Form National Group to Advocate for Justice in Palestine," *Mondoweiss*, February 16, 2024.
46. J. Seilers Hill and Nia L. Orakwue, "Harvard Student Groups Face Intense Backlash for Statement Calling Israel 'Entirely Responsible' for Hamas Attack," *The Harvard Crimson*, October 10, 2023.
47. Anemone Hartocollis, "Internal Emails Show Harvard Leaders Debating Response to Hamas Attack," *New York Times*, October 31, 2024; "A Statement from Harvard University Leadership," October 9, 2023, https://www.harvard.edu/president/news-gay/2023/war-in-the-middle-east/.
48. "A Statement from President Claudine Gay," October 10, 2023, https://www.harvard.edu/president/news-gay/2023/war-in-the-middle-east/.
49. "A Message from President Claudine Gay: Our Choices," October 12, 2023, https://www.harvard.edu/president/news-gay/2023/our-choices/.
50. Anemona Hartocollis, "After Writing an Anti-Israel Letter, Harvard Students Are Doxxed," *New York Times*, October 18, 2023.
51. Dion J. Pierre, "Video: Jewish Student Harassed by Harvard Law Review Editor, Anti-Israel Mob on Campus," *The Algemeiner*, November 1, 2023; Alec Schemmel, "Harvard Students Captured on Film Accosting Israeli Classmate Remain in Good Standing with School, Lawsuit Alleges," *Washington Free Beacon*, January 11, 2024.
52. Spencer Dalke, "Harvard Hosts Record Number of Pro-Hamas Rallies in One Week: Report," *Campus Reform*, October 27, 2023.
53. Anemona Hartocollis, "Internal Emails Show Harvard Leaders Debating Response to Hamas Attack," *New York Times*, October 31, 2024.
54. Nick Stoico, "Harvard Students Rally in Support of Palestinians 'Under Siege in Gaza,'" *Boston Globe*, October 14, 2023; Noa Halff, "Harvard Students Hold 'Die-In' and Massive Protests in SUPPORT of Palestine Just 12 Days after Letter Sparked Outrage," *The Daily Mail*, October 19, 2023; Max Larkin, "Harvard Confronts Fear and Division a Month into Gaza Conflict," wbur.org, November 9, 2023; Kristina Rex, "Harvard Law Students Rally in Supporter of Palestinians, Accuse School of Restricting Speech," CBSnews.com, November 16, 2023;; "News by President Gay: Combating Antisemitism," November 9, 2023, https://www.harvard.edu/president/news-gay/2023/combating-antisemitism/; Anemone Hartocollis, "Internal Emails Show Harvard Leaders Debating Response to Hamas Attack," *New York Times*, October 31, 2024; Virginia Foxx, "These So-Called Elite Universities Have a Glaring Antisemitism Problem," *New York Post*, October 31, 2024.

55. Rahem D. Hamid and Elias J. Schinsgall, "More than 100 Harvard Faculty Sign Letter Criticizing President Gay's Censure of Pro-Palestine Slogan," *The Harvard Crimson*, November 15, 2023.
56. Jessica Costescu, "Chair of Harvard University History Department Belongs to Group Behind Grotesque Anti-Semitic Cartoon," *Washington Free Beacon*, February 20, 2024; Dion J. Pierre, "'Despicable': Harvard Denounces Nazi-Esque Image Shared by Anti-Zionist Faculty Group," *The Algemeiner*, February 20, 2024.
57. "Why a Rabbi Resigned from Harvard's Antisemitism Committee," Amanpour and Company, December 12, 2023, pgs.org.
58. David Wolpe (@Rabbi Wolpe), "Resigning, a Hanukkah Message," X, December 7, 2023, https://twitter.com/RabbiWolpe/status/1732847411175796747.
59. Anemone Hartocollis, "Critics Protest Harvard's Choice to Lead Antisemitism Task Force," *New York Times*, January 22, 2024; Tilly R. Robinson and Neil H. Shah, "Critics Blast, Colleagues Defend Penslar's Selection to Lead Harvard Antisemitism Task Force," *The Harvard Crimson*, January 21, 2024; Andrew Silow-Carroll, "Many Jews Criticized Harvard's Oct. 7 Response. Fewer Are Applauding President Claudine Gay's Resignation," JTA, January 5, 2024.
60. Anemona Hartocolis, "Harvard Ignored Antisemitism Advisory Group's Recommendations, House Committee Says," *New York Times*, May 16, 2024; Committee on Education & the Workforce, *Investigative Update the Antisemitism Advisory Group and Harvard's Response: Clarity and Inaction*, May 15, 2024, https://edworkforce.house.gov/uploadedfiles/5.15.24_harvard_committee_report_final.pdf.
61. Jessica Costescu, "Head of Harvard's Islamophobia Task Force Signed Statement in Support of 'Palestinian Liberation Struggle.'" *Washington Free Beacon*, May 28, 2024.
62. Harvard Jewish Alumni Alliance, *The Soil Beneath the Encampments: How Israel and Jews Became the Focus of Hate at Harvard*, May 2024, https://harvardjewishalumni.org/wp-content/uploads/2024/08/Final-hjaa-Report.The_Soil_Beneath_the_Encampments.pdf.
63. "Columbia Students for Justice in Palestine Statement of Solidarity," Institute for Palestine Studies, October 12, 2023, https://www.palestine-studies.org/en/node/1654384.
64. Isabella Ramirez et al, "Hundreds of Protesters Pack Campus Following Escalation of Violence in Israel and Gaza," *Columbia Spectator*, October 12, 2023; Amanda Woods and Olivia Land, "Israeli Student Attacked with a Stick outside Columbia University Library: Cops," *New York Post*, Octo-

ber 12, 2023; Carl Campanile, Vaughn Golden, and Anna Young, "Chuck Schumer Labeled 'Traitor' after Damning Report Reveals He Quietly Advised Columbia Leaders to Ignore Criticism of Campus Antisemitism," *New York Post*, October 31, 2024.

65. Task Force on Antisemitism, "We Hear You," *Columbia Spectator*, May 16, 2024.
66. Aaron Sibarium, "Columbia Law School Dean Gives Both Sides Treatment to Hamas's Terrorist Rampage in Israel," *Washington Free Beacon*, October 9, 2023.
67. Sibarium, "Columbia Law Dean Does Damage Control after Mealy-Mouthed Israel Statement," *Washington Free Beacon*, October 10, 2023.
68. Aaron Sibarium, "Dean of Columbia Law School Resigns Amid Anti-Semitism Scandals," *Washington Free Beacon*, November 28, 2023.
69. Haley Cohen, "Suspended Groups at Columbia University Continue to Hold Anti-Israel Campus Events," *Jewish Insider*, December 12, 2023; Yair Mohr, "Israeli Students Slam Columbia University amid Pro-Palestinian Activity," *Jewish Insider*, December 6, 2023.
70. Cohen, "Suspended Groups at Columbia University Continue to Hold Anti-Israel Campus Events"; Alana Goodman, "Columbia's Barnard College Defends Inclusion of Anti-Semitic Terror Defender in University's 'Day of Dialogue,'" *Washington Free Beacon*, January 23, 2024.
71. "Update on Campus Incidents," Office of the Provost, Columbia University, January 22, 2024, https://provost.columbia.edu/news/update-campus-incidents.
72. Chris Mendell, "Protesters Allegedly Sprayed with Hazardous Chemical at Pro-Palestinian Rally, Nearly Two Dozen Report," *Columbia Spectator*, January 22, 2024; "Update on Investigation of Reported Incidents from January 19, 2024," Columbia University Department of Public Safety, August 30, 2024; Louis Keene, "'Hazardous Chemical' Spewed at a Columbia Anti-Israel Protest Was Actually Novelty Spray, School Says," *The Forward*, September 3, 2024; Luke Tress, "Columbia Paid $395,000 in Settlement after Suspending Jewish Student for Using 'Fart Spray,'" *New York Jewish Week*, November 1, 2024.
73. *Report #1: Task Force on Antisemitism—Columbia University's Rules on Demonstrations*, March 2024, 2, 11–12, 15, https://www.columbia.edu/content/sites/default/files/content/about/Task%20Force%20on%20Antisemitism/Report_1_Columbia_University's_Rules_on_Demonstrations_March_04_2024.pdf.
74. *Report #1: Task Force on Antisemitism*, 19–21.
75. Avi Balsam, "Calls for 'Intifada' Are Traumatizing MIT's Jewish Community," *The Tech*, November 1, 2023.

76. Balsam, "Calls for 'Intifada' Are Traumatizing."
77. "Video Transcript: Our Community and the Violence in Israel and Gaza—MIT President Sally Kornbluth, October 10, 2023," Office of the President, https://president.mit.edu/writing-speeches/video-transcript-our-community-and-violence-israel-and-gaza.
78. Sally Kornbluth emails to the MIT community, November 9, 2023, http://tinyurl.com/4d997tx, and November 14, 2023, https://president.mit.edu/updates/update-events-november-9; Retsef Levi (@RetsefL), "This is the reality that MIT President wants to hide. A letter from Israeli & Jewish MIT students," X, November 10, 2023, https://twitter.com/RetsefL/status/1722852140245254559
79. Dion J. Pierre, "MIT Suspends Anti-Zionist Group for Rules Violations," *The Algemeiner*, February 14, 2024.
80. Alec Schemmel, "Speaker at MIT's 'Standing Together Against Hate' Event Endorsed Hamas Terrorism as Lawful 'Resistance,'" *Washington Free Beacon*, February 5, 2024; Alec Schemmel, "MIT Leaders Assembled a Faculty Advisory Group on Campus Anti-Semitism. Then They Ignored It," *Washington Free Beacon*, February 14, 2024.
81. "Statement from Kimberly Goff-Crews, Secretary and Vice President for University Life, on the Violent Events in Israel and Gaza," Belonging at Yale, October 9, 2023, https://belong.yale.edu/news/statement-kimberly-goff-crews-secretary-and-vice-president-university-life-violent-events.
82. "Yale Leadership Addresses the Murder of George Floyd and the Legacy of Racist Violence," Yale University, June 5, 2020, https://tinyurl.com/4996637z.
83. Peter Salovey, "War in the Middle East," Yale University, October 10, 2023, https://president.yale.edu/president/statements/war-middle-east.
84. Peter Salovey, "President's Remarks on Compassion and Civility," Yale University, November 3, 2023, https://president.yale.edu/president/speeches/presidents-remarks-compassion-and-civility.
85. Ben Raab and Kaitlyn Pohly, "Petition to Oust Pro-Palestine Professor for 'Promoting Lies and Violence' Gains 25,000 Signatures in Just over a Day," *Yale Daily News*, October 12, 2023.
86. Aaron Sibarium, "A Yale Professor Wrote an Op-Ed about Anti-Semitism on Campus. The University Spent Over a Year Investigating Him," *Washington Free Beacon*, May 9, 2024.
87. Austin Browne, "Yale Students Held Monday Rally Praising Use of 'Force' by Hamas during Horrifying Weekend Attacks," campusreform.org, October 11, 2023.
88. Micaiah Bilger, "Yale Is a 'Campus without Care' after Hosting 'Anti-Israel' Event, Jewish Students Say," *The College Fix*, November 8, 2023.

89. "University Statement on Faculty-Led Event Held on Monday, Nov. 6," Yale News, November 8, 2023, https://news.yale.edu/2023/11/08/university-statement-faculty-led-event-held-monday-nov-6
90. Esma Okutan and Tristan Hernandez, "'Doxxing Truck' Appears on Yale's Campus, Displays Student Names and Photos," *Yale Daily News*, November 17, 2023. The *News* repeatedly referred to the display as "doxxing," which it noted involves the release of "personal information"; however, the only information in the display was the students' names.
91. Beth Harpaz, "Pro-Palestinian Students Project Anti-Israel Slogans on George Washington University Library," *The Forward*, October 25, 2003; Cade McAllister and Hannah Marr, "Students Project Anti-Israel, Anti-GW Messages onto Library, Sparking Outcry," *The GW Hatchet*, October 25, 2023; "University Statement on Projections on Campus," GW Department of Media Relations, October 25, 2023.
92. Ellen M. Granberg, "Addressing the War in Israel and Gaza," GW Office of the President, October 9, 2023, https://president.gwu.edu/addressing-war-israel-and-gaza.
93. Erika Filter, "Granberg Condemns 'Celebration of Terrorism' on Campus," *The GW Hatchet*, October 12, 2023; Erika Filter, "Students Mourn Killed Palestinians in Candlelit Vigil," *The GW Hatchet*, October 12, 2023; Ellen M. Granberg to "Members of the George Washington University Community," GW Office of the President, October 11, 2023, https://president.gwu.edu/thoughts-recent-campus-events-and-war-israel-and-gaza.
94. Megan Palin, "Horror as GWU Protester Carries Sign with Nazi 'Final Solution' Call for Extermination of Jews," *New York Post*, April 26, 2024.
95. Susan Snyder, "Penn Plans to Review Policies and Training Following Controversy over Palestine Writes Festival," *Philadelphia Inquirer*, October 3, 2023; Alex Becker, "Why Is UPenn Hosting a Festival of Antisemites?," *The Hill*, September 22, 2023; Daniel Keane, "Ukrainian Authors Withdraw from Adelaide Writers' Week amid Line-Up Controversy," abc.net, February 22, 2023.
96. Snyder, "Penn Plans to Review Policies and Training"; M. Elizabeth Magill et al, "Statement on Palestine Writes Literature Festival," University of Pennsylvania, September 12, 2023, https://www.sas.upenn.edu/news/statement-palestine-writes-literature-festival; Vidya Pandiaraju and Ethan Young, "AAUP-Penn Says Academic Freedom 'Impaired' by Admin. Response to Palestine Writes, Israel-Hamas War," *The Daily Pennsylvania*, November 2, 2023.
97. Jarrad Saffren, "What Is Going on at Penn?," *Jewish Exponent*, October 24, 2023; Ramishah Maruf, "UPenn Donors Were furious about the Palestine

Writes Literature Festival. What about It Made Them Pull Their Funds?," CNN.com, October 25, 2023.

98. Liz Magill and John L. Jackson Jr., "War in the Middle East," Penn Today, October 10, 2023, https://penntoday.upenn.edu/announcements/war-middle-east; "A Message from President Magill," University of Pennsylvania Almanac, October 15, 2023, https://almanac.upenn.edu/articles/a-message-from-president-magill/; Dedepya Guthikonda, "Magill Says Penn Will Not Tolerate Hateful Speech Amid Demonstrations for Israel, Palestine," *The Daily Pennsylvanian*, October 18, 2023.
99. Sydney Freedman, "What I Heard in My Five Hours at the Walkout for Palestine," *The Daily Pennsylvanian*, October 19, 2023.
100. Hope Sheridan and Paige Rawiszer, "Penn Investigating Antisemitic Vandalism Next to AEPi House as Potential Hate Crime," *The Daily Pennsylvania*, October 26, 2023.
101. Tara Tawneh speech, Instagram, October 28, 2023, https://www.instagram.com/reel/CzijhdbOofm/.
102. Ben Binday and Sophia Liu, "Penn Denounces Projections of Messages onto Campus Buildings as 'Antisemitic,'" *The Daily Pennsylvanian*, November 16, 2023.
103. Katie Bartlett et al, "Community Members Occupy Houston Hall in Multiday 'Freedom School for Palestine,'" *The Daily Pennsylvanian*, November 16, 2023.
104. Lara Cota et al, "Penn Chavurah Screens Film Critical of Israel Despite Threats of Disciplinary Action," *The Daily Pennsylvanian*, November 30, 2023.
105. Emily Scolnick, "Pro-Palestinian Supporters Rally against War in Gaza as Penn Investigates Graffiti along March Route," *The Daily Pennsylvanian*, December 4, 2023; Johnny Diaz, "White House Condemns Protest at Israeli Restaurant in Philadelphia," *New York Times*, December 4, 2023.
106. Ethan Young, "Penn Student Appears alongside House Republican Leaders at Press Conference about Antisemitism," *The Daily Pennsylvanian*, December 6, 2023; House Republicans (@HousseGOP), "I should not be here today. . . . I should be taking in . . . my senior year of college. . . . I am because 36 hours ago, I, along with most of campus, sought refuge in our rooms as classmates and professors chanted proudly for the genocide of Jews," X, December 5, 2023, https://twitter.com/Housegop/status/1732064188980146642.
107. Jessica Costescu, "Penn Lecturer Is Behind Grotesque Anti-Semitic Cartoons," *Washington Free Beacon*, February 1, 2024; Jessica Costescu, "Penn President Will Not Act To Remove Anti-Semitic Cartoonist From Faculty, Citing 'Bedrock Commitment to Open Expression,'" *Washington Free*

Beacon, February 5, 2024; Jessica Costescu, "Penn Administrators, Professors Rally Around Anti-Semitic Cartoonist," *Washington Free Beacon*, February 15, 2024; Jessica Costescu, "Anti-Semitic Cartoonist Will Teach Fall Course at Penn, Ivy League School Announces," *Washington Free Beacon*, March 15, 2024.

108. "Transcript: What Harvard, MIT, and Penn Presidents Said at Antisemitism Hearing," Roll Call, December 13, 2023, https://rollcall.com/2023/12/13/transcript-what-harvard-mit-and-penn-presidents-said-at-antisemitism-hearing/.
109. "Transcript: What Harvard, MIT, and Penn Presidents Said at Antisemitism Hearing."
110. "Transcript: What Harvard, MIT, and Penn Presidents Said at Antisemitism Hearing."
111. "Transcript: What Harvard, MIT, and Penn Presidents Said at Antisemitism Hearing."
112. "Transcript: What Harvard, MIT, and Penn Presidents Said at Antisemitism Hearing."
113. "US Imposes Sanctions on 'Sham Charity' Fundraising for Popular Front for the Liberation of Palestine," Reuters, October 15, 2024.
114. "US Imposes Sanctions on 'Sham Charity' Fundraising."
115. Tawnell D. Hobbs, Valerie Bauerlein, and Dan Forsch, "Activist Groups Trained Students for Months Before Campus Protests," *Wall Street Journal*, May 3, 2024; "Report: Anti-Israel Campus Protesters Were Prepped for Months by Outside Activists," *Times of Israel*, May 4, 2024.
116. "Stefanik Secures Columbia University President's Commitment to Remove Antisemitic Professor from Leadership Role," stefanik.house.gov, .April 17, 2024.
117. "Ilhan Omar Grills Columbia University President Neman Shafik About Protests on Campus," YouTube, April 18, 2024, https://www.youtube.com/watch?v=d9b45or_ilq.
118. Elisabeth Buchwald, "Professor Who Columbia President Said Was 'Spoken To' for Calling Hamas Invasion 'Astounding' Says He Wasn't Disciplined," CNN.com, April 18, 2024; Jessica Costescu, "Columbia's Joseph Massad Calls BS on University President Minouche Shafik's Testimony," *Washington Free Beacon*, April 18, 2024.
119. Katherine Rosman, "Columbia Bars Student Protester Who Said 'Zionists Don't Deserve to Live,'" *New York Times*, April 26, 2024; Dion J. Pierre, "'This Is 1984': Faculty Participation in Pro-Hamas Demonstrations a 'Wake-Up Call' for Americans, Professor Says," *The Algemeiner*, April 26, 2024.

120. Isha Banerjee and Claire Cleary, "'Gaza Solidarity Encampment' Reaches Seventh Day," *Columbia Spectator*, April 24, 2024.
121. "In Focus: The First 24 Hours of the 'Gaza Solidarity Encampment,'" *Columbia Spectator*, April 18, 2024; Jessica Costescu and Jessica Schwalb, "Barnard Names New Head of Women's Center: Anti-Israel Gender Prof Who Stood Watch as Student Radicals Stormed Columbia Campus Building," *Washington Free Beacon*, January 29, 2025.
122. Pierre, "'This Is 1984.'"
123. Andrew Lapin, "Jewish Professor at Dartmouth Thrown to the Ground by Police as 90 Pro-Palestinian Protesters Are Arrested," Jewish Telegraphic Agency, May 2, 2024.
124. Anne Gray Fischer to Rafael Medoff, May 29, 2024, email communication, copy in possession of the author.
125. Jacob Magid and *Times of Israel* Staff, "Hillary Clinton: Anti-Israel Protesters 'Don't Know Very Much' about the Middle East," *Times of Israel*, May 11, 2024.
126. Ron E. Hassner, "From Which River to Which Sea?," *Wall Street Journal*, December 5, 2023.
127. Santul Nerkar, "Al Jazeera Finds Fans on Campus," *Times of Israel*, May 13, 2024; Jonathan Greenblatt, "Al Jazeera Propagates Hatred. Is It Also a Foreign Agent?," Anti-Defamation League, August 20, 2018; "ADL Voices Ongoing Concerns about Al Jazeera Following Pan-Arab Network's Acquisition of Current TV," ADL news release, January 4, 2013.
128. Santul Nerkar, "Frustrated by Gaza Coverage, Student Protesters Turn to Al Jazeera," *New York Times*, May 12, 2024
129. Sharon Otterman and Alan Binder, "Over 100 Arrested at Columbia after Pro-Palestinian Protest," *New York Times*, April 18, 2024.
130. Steven Vago and Isabel Keane, "Anti-Israel Protester Screams 'Go Back to Poland' at Demonstrators with Israeli Flag Outside Columbia, Harrowing Video Shows," *New York Post*, April 21, 2024.
131. Esha Karam et al, "'Gaza Solidarity Encampment' Enters Third Day Following Mass Arrests," *Columbia Daily Spectator*, April 19, 2024.
132. Anemone Hartocollis, "Internal Emails Show Harvard Leaders Debating Response to Hamas Attack," *New York Times*, October 31, 2024.
133. Joseph Simonson, "Anti-Israel Group Encouraged Columbia Protesters to Re-Create 'The Summer of 2020' Hours before Students Stormed a Building," *Washington Free Beacon*, May 1, 2024.
134. Francesca Block, "Exclusive: Columbia Custodian Trapped by 'Angry Mob' Speaks Out," *The Free Press*, May 6, 2024.

135. "NYPD Official: Items Found at Columbia Show Protesters Were Far from Benign," *Times of Israel*, May 4, 2024.
136. Forty-six of the Hamilton Hall occupiers were arrested, but Manhattan's district attorney did not press charges against thirty-one of them, saying there was insufficient security camera footage to convict them. He did not explain why they could not be prosecuted for trespassing or illegally wearing masks. (Chelsia Rose Marcius, "Why Bragg Dropped Charges Against Most Columbia Student Protesters," *New York Times*, June 23, 2024.)
137. Aaron Sibarium, "At Columbia, Students Who Stormed University Building Poised to Return to Campus Next Week," *Washington Free Beacon*, August 19, 2024.
138. Aaron Sibarium, "'A Huge Conflict of Interest': Two Professors on Columbia's Top Disciplinary Body Participated in Encampment, Photos Suggest," *Washington Free Beacon*, August 16, 2024.
139. Jessica Costescu, "He Sits on Columbia's Top Disciplinary Body. He Also Lauds Terrorist Plane Hijackings as 'Spectacular,'" *Washington Free Beacon*, December 12, 2024.
140. Sharon Otterman, "Most Columbia Students Arrested During Protests Will Return to Campus," *New York Times*, August 19, 2024.
141. Katie Glueck, "A Rising Democrat Leans Into the Campus Fight Over Antisemitism," *New York Times*, May 11, 2024.
142. Maya Sulkin, "Inside Columbia University's 'Museum of Terror,'" *The Free Press*, January 6, 2025.
143. Erez Linn, "Outrage after MIT Students Appear to Call for 'Death to Zionists,'" *Israel Hayom*, May 6, 2024.
144. Tani Levitt, "In the Shadow of an Anti-Israel Encampment, Jewish GWU Students Rally Against Hate," *Times of Israel*, May 4, 2024.
145. "Photo Gallery: Day One of DePaul's Divestment Encampment on the Quad," *The DePaulia*, April 30, 2024; "Police in Riot Gear Dismantle Anti-Israel Encampment at Chicago's DePaul University," *Times of Israel*, May 16, 2024.
146. Tom Norton, "Campus Protesters Spotted Wearing Hamas Headbands—What We Know," *Newsweek*, April 30, 2024.
147. Seth Mandel, "The Che Guevara of the Tentifada," commentary.org, September 4, 2024.
148. Luke Tress, "Baruch College Student Groups Protest Hillel in Rally Decried as Antisemitic," *Times of Israel*, June 7, 2024.
149. Ryan Saavedra, "Pro-Hamas Protesters at UCLA Demand 'Inhalers,' 'Vegan Food,' 'Gluten Free Food,'" *Daily Wire*, May 1, 2024.

150. Ryan Saavedra, "Pro-Hamas Protesters at University Of Chicago Demand 'HIV Tests, Dental Dams, Plan B' And More," *Daily Wire*, May 3, 2024.
151. Susanne Rust, "20 Pomona College Protesters Arrested after Storming, Occupying President's Office," *Los Angeles Times*, April 6, 2024.
152. The Post Millenial (@TPostMillennial), "Reporter grills Columbia student after she demands the university help feed protestors occupying Hamilton Hall," X, April 30, 2024, https://twitter.com/tpostMillennial/status/1785386376755900611?utm_source=substack&utm_medium=email
153. az2palestine, "Demands to the University of Arizona and the Arizona Board of Regents," Instagram, April 29, 2024, https://www.instagram.com/p/c6wk7xdlzi6/?img_index=5; cmicornell, "We Call on Cornell to Establish a Palestinian Studies Program," Instagram, April 25, 2024, https://www.instagram.com/p/c6minillxui/?img_index=6.
154. Seth Mandel, "Where's Biden's Anger at the Feckless Universities?," *Commentary* blog, May 2, 2024.
155. Foxx, "These So-Called Elite Universities Have a Glaring Antisemitism Problem."
156. Anemona Hartocollis, "U.C.L.A. Can't Let Protesters Block Jewish Students from Campus, Judge Says," *New York Times*, August 14, 2024.
157. Dion J. Pierre, "Pro-Hamas Encampment at Drexel University Pushes School into Lockdown," *The Algemeiner*, May 20, 2024; "What Do Ant-Israel Student Organizers Really Want? Examining the Extreme Demands behind the Campus Protests," Anti-Defamation League, May 15, 2024.
158. David Chang and Deanna Durante, "Drexel Professor Accused of Stealing Pro-Israel Signs from Synagogue, Home in Lower Merion," nbcphiladelphia.com, July 2, 2024.
159. "What Do Ant-Israel Student Organizers Really Want?"
160. Joseph A. Wulfsohn, "Student Demands at University of Chicago Encampment Include Defunding Police, Reparations, Cutting Emissions," FoxNews.com, May 2, 2024.
161. cuapartheiddivest, "3. Stop the Displacement," Instagram, June 1, 2024, https://www.instagram.com/p/c7rdeavopam/?utm_source=ig_web_copy_link&img_index=4.
162. Daniel Gligich, "Sonoma State Agrees to Demands from Palestinian Protesters," *The San Joaquin Valley Sun*, May 15, 2024.
163. ssu.sjp, "Community Announcement: SSU DEMANDS MET," Instagram, May 14, 2024, https://www.instagram.com/p/c6-VkZmr4zs/?img_index=1.
164. "California University President on Leave after Agreeing to Gaza Protesters' Demands," *Israel HaYom*, May 16, 2024.

165. Madison Smalstig, "Group Holds Pro-Palestinian Protest at SSU as New CSU-Wide Policies Ban Encampments, Target Face Masks," *The Press Democrat*, August 21, 2024.
166. "New School Inks Deal with Anti-Israel Protesters to Vote on Divestment," *Times of Israel*, May 21, 2024.
167. Owen Dahlkamp and Ryan Doherty, "Brown University Agrees to Hear Divestment Proposal if Encampment Is Cleared," *The Brown Daily Herald*, April 29, 2024.
168. Matt Hubbard and Dillon Mullan, "Johns Hopkins Encampment Ends after Protesters, University Come to Agreement," *Baltimore Sun*, May 13, 2024.
169. Andrew Lapin, "After Making Deals with Protesters, Universities Are Granting Hearings on Israel Divestment," Jewish Telegraphic Agency, May 10, 2024.
170. Dan Simmons, "University of Wisconsin-Milwaukee and Protesters Agree to End Encampment," *New York Times*, May 13, 2024.
171. Sarah Huddleston, Shea Vance, and Esha Karam, "Union Theological Seminary Trustees Endorse Divestment from 'Companies Profiting from the War in Palestine,'" *Columbia Spectator*, May 9, 2024.
172. "Agreement on Deering Meadow," Northwestern University, accessed February 2, 2025, https://www.northwestern.edu/leadership-notes/2024/agreement-on-deering-meadow.pdf.
173. Alana Goodman, "Northwestern Jewish Students Recount 'Scary and Shocking' Campus Anti-Semitism in Meetings with Lawmakers," *Washington Free Beacon*, May 2, 2024.
174. Alana Goodman, "Northwestern Professors Encourage Students to Skip Class to Join Anti-Israel Encampment," *Washington Free Beacon*, April 26, 2024.
175. News release, "ADL, StandWithUs, and Brandeis Center Call for the Resignation of Northwestern University President Michael Schill," Anti-Defamation League, May 1, 2024.
176. Alana Goodman, "Northwestern President Won't Commit to Excluding Anti-Semites from Anti-Semitism Task Force," *Washington Free Beacon*, May 23, 2024; "Northwestern People's Resolution," *Washington Free Beacon*, accessed February 2, 2025, https://freebeacon.com/wp-content/uploads/2024/05/Northwestern-Peoples-Resolution.pdf; Gabby Deutch, "Northwestern's Antisemitism Committee in Disarray after Jewish Members Step Down," *Jewish Insider*, May 2, 2024.
177. Gabby Deutch, "Jewish Community Members Outraged by UC-Berkeley Chancellor's Approach to Anti-Israel Protesters," *Jewish Insider*, May 17, 2024; Joe Fitzgerald Rodriguez, "Pro-Palestinian Activists Occupy Abandoned UC Berkeley Building Near People's Park," KQED.org, May 16, 2024.

178. "'No Rest Till Brown Divests': Anti-Israel Protesters Interrupt University Graduation," *Times of Israel*, May 27, 2024.
179. Andrew Lapin, "Dept. of Education Chides Brown University for Taking 'No or Little Action' in Response to Complaints of Antisemitism," JTA, July 8, 2024.
180. "Important Update on 2024 Commencement," USC Office of the Provost, April 15, 2024.
181. Susan Snyder, "Bryn Mawr Will Relocate Commencement," *Philadelphia Inquirer*, May 14, 2024.
182. Eyal Yakoby, "The Lasting Impact of the Penn Encampment," *Washington Free Beacon*, June 4, 2024.
183. Dion J. Pierre, "University of Minnesota President Admits Agreeing to Anti-Israel Terms to End Protest Despite Not Understanding Language," *The Algemeiner*, June 28, 2024.
184. Dion J. Pierre, "University Chancellor Apologizes for Caving to Pro-Hamas Protesters," *The Algemeiner*, May 22, 2024.
185. News release, "Update on Encampment in Harvard Yard," Harvard, May 14, 2024, https://www.harvard.edu/president/news/2024/update-on-encampment-in-harvard-yard/; Anemona Hartocollis, "Harvard Reaches Agreement with Protesters to End Encampment," *New York Times*, May 14, 2024; Harvard Out of Occupied Palestine (@HarvardOOP), "After Lasting Beyond Student Move-Out, the Harvard Encampment Has Concluded," X, May 14, 2024, https://x.com/HarvardOOP/status/1790359980580769956/; Alana Goodman, "Harvard Commencement Speaker Published Editorial Likening Israel to Hitler," *Washington Free Beacon*, May 3, 2024; Alana Goodman, "Harvard Graduation Marred by Anti-Semitism Controversy as Speaker Accuses Critics of Smearing Her for 'Money and Power,'" *Washington Free Beacon*, May 28, 2024.
186. Andrew Lapin, "In a Rarity, Cornell Pro-Palestinian Encampment Disbands with Neither Arrests nor Deal," JTA, May 16, 2024; Julie Senzon, "Coalition for Mutual Liberation Voluntarily Ends Encampment," *Cornell Daily Sun*, May 14, 2024; "Encampment Taken Down at Tufts University, Protest Ends 'Peacefully and Voluntarily,'" CBSNews.com/boston, May 3, 2024; "Police in Riot Gear Dismantle Anti-Israel Encampment at Chicago's DePaul University," *Times of Israel*, May 16, 2024.
187. Isabelle Taft, Alex Lemonides, Lazaro Gamio, and Anna Betts, "Campus Protests Led to More Than 3,100 Arrests, but Many Charges Have Been Dropped," *New York Times*, July 21, 2024.
188. cuapartheiddivest, "A Letter from CUAD Leadership to Khymani James and Our Comrades in Solidarity," Instagram, October 8, 2024, https://www.instagram.com/p/da3okfgoslm/?img_index=1.

189. harvadundergradpsc, "One Year of Genocide, 76 Years of Nakba," Instagram, October 7, 2024, https://www.instagram.com/p/dal8ipyp3tq/?img_index=1; Madeleine A. Hung and Joyce E. Kim, "Pro-Palestine Activists Denounce Harvard, Israel on Anniversary of Oct. 7 Attacks," *Harvard Crimson*, October 8, 2024.
190. ampaelestinect, "One Year of Genocide, One Year of Resistance," Instagram, September 25, 2024, https://www.instagram.com/p/daxaf_cmjw8/?hl=en.
191. Diamy Wang and Jasmine Ni, "Four Individuals Arrested after Pro-Palestinian March near Penn's Campus on Oct. 7 Anniversary," *The Daily Pennsylvanian*, October 7, 2024.
192. Jerry Wu and Nicole Markus, "Northwestern Will Discipline Pro-Palestinian Students Who Protested by The Rock on Oct. 7," *The Daily Northwestern*, October 7, 2024; Jeanine Yuen, "Northwestern U. Students Rally for 'Free Palestine' on Oct. 7," *The College Fix*, October 8, 2024.
193. Sierra Lopez, "Protest against Israel-Hamas War Roils UC Berkeley Campus a Day after Bay Area Jews Mourned Oct. 7 Victims," *The Mercury News*, October 9, 2024.
194. Raymond Baccari and Lauren Brill, "Pro-Palestinian Demonstration Held in Providence ahead of Oct. 7 Anniversary," wpri.com, October 5, 2024.
195. "Pro-Palestinian Protesters March throughout Lower Manhattan on Oct. 7 Anniversary," abc7ny.com, October 7, 2024; Darcie Grunblatt, "Witnessing the Intifada Calls: An Israeli's view from NYC's Pro-Palestinian Rally," *Jerusalem Post*, October 10, 2024.
196. Lexi Boccuzzi, "Anti-Israel Radicals Throw Urine-Filled Mason Jars Through University of Michigan Regent's Window," *Washington Free Beacon*, December 9, 2024.
197. Jessica Costescu and Lexi Boccuzzi, "Columbia Student Group Observes Holocaust Remembrance Day—By Noting 'Parallels' Between Auschwitz and 'Zionist Dungeons and Torture Camps,'" *Washington Free Beacon*, January 28, 2025.
198. Isha Banerjee, Rebecca Massel, and Wiann Wilson, "Protesters Vandalize University Buildings on Anniversary of Hind Rajab Killing," *Columbia Spectator*, January 30, 2025.
199. Collin Anderson, "'Death to Jews': Inside the Home of 2 SJP Leaders at George Mason University, Police Find Guns, Ammo, and Terrorist Flags," *Washington Free Beacon*, December 9, 2024; Isabelle Taft, "Virginia Student Accused of Plot to Attack Israeli Consulate in New York," *New York Times*, December 20, 2024.
200. Alexander Nazaryan, "'A Different Kind of Ivy,'" *New York Magazine*, October 6, 2024; Grace Garfoot, "UA Shuts Down Access to Mall after Pro-Palestinian Protests," *Daily Wildcat*, April 30, 2024.

201. Isabelle Taft, "How Universities Cracked Down on Pro-Palestinian Activism," *New York Times*, November 25, 2024; Jonathan Wolfe, "A Skirmish Breaks Out Near Pomona College's Graduation," *New York Times*, May 13, 2024.
202. Isabelle Taft, "How Colleges Are Changing Their Rules on Protesting," *New York Times*, September 12, 2024; Zoe Greenberg, "Penn Says It Will No Longer Respond Publicly to World Events, Unless They Directly Affect the University," *Philadelphia Inquirer*, September 10, 2024; Taft, "How Universities Cracked Down on Pro-Palestinian Activism"; Michael Starr, "University of Michigan SJP Suspended for Up to Two Years," *Jerusalem Post*, February 2, 2025.
203. Taft, "How Universities Cracked Down on Pro-Palestinian Activism."
204. Eliana Johnson, "Three Columbia Deans Placed on Leave Pending Investigation," *Washington Free Beacon*, June 20, 2024.
205. "NYU Settles Lawsuit Filed by 3 Jewish Students Who Complained of Pervasive Antisemitism," Associated Press, July 9, 2024; Surina Venkat, "Columbia Reaches Settlement in Class Action Suit Alleging Hostile Environment for Jewish Students, Establishes Additional Security Measures," *Columbia Spectator*, June 6, 2024.
206. "Joint Statement on Settlement of Suit," New York University, July 9, 2024; "Harvard and Students Against Antisemitism Announce Settlement of Lawsuit," Harvard University, January 21, 2025; "Voluntary Resolution Agreement" (with Occidental College), November 22, 2024, www.brandeiscenter.com.
207. Gwynne Hogan, Luca Goldmansour, and Melanie Marich, "CUNY City College President Laments Not Breaking Up Pro-Palestinian Encampment Sooner," *The City*, May 13, 2024.

6. HISTORICAL PARALLELS TO OCTOBER 7

1. Chazan, *God, Humanity and History*, 31.
2. Chazan, *God, Humanity and History*, 31.
3. Solomon bar Simson, "Crusades of 1096," 267; "Chronicle of Eliezer Bar Nathan," in Eidelberg, *Jews and the Crusaders*, 82, 84.
4. Solomon bar Simson, "Crusades of 1096," 271.
5. Chazan, *God, Humanity and History*, 131; Cohen, *Sanctifying the Name of God*, 107–8; Solomon bar Simson, "Crusades of 1096," 267.
6. "Chronicle of Eliezer Bar Nathan," 79–93.
7. "Sefer Zekhirah, or The Book of Remembrance, of Rabbi Ephraim of Bonn," in Eidelberg, *Jews and the Crusaders*, 121–33.
8. Carroll, *Constantine's Sword*, 272–73.

9. Rubin, *Gentile Tales*, 48–52.
10. Rubin, *Gentile Tales*, 55–57.
11. Rubin, *Gentile Tales*, 54–55, 66, 89, 116–17.
12. Rubin, *Gentile Tales*, 89–90.
13. Winkler, "Medieval Holocaust," 20–21.
14. Marcus, *Jew in the Medieval World*, 46–47.
15. Winkler, "Medieval Holocaust," 15.
16. Rubin, *Gentile Tales*, 118.
17. "Drowning of Hundreds of Jews by the Nazis in Occupied Russia Reported by Eye-witness," Jewish Telegraphic Agency, July 9, 1942.
18. Cohen, *Friars and the Jews*, 238–39.
19. Rubin, *Gentile Tales*, 135.
20. Rubin, *Gentile Tales*, 134.
21. Rubin, *Gentile Tales*, 170–71.
22. Rubin, *Gentile Tales*, 130.
23. Rubin, *Gentile Tales*, 174.
24. Rubin, *Gentile Tales*, 179–80.
25. Rubin, *Gentile Tales*, 183–84.
26. Roth, *Conversos, Inquisition, and the Expulsion of the Jews from Spain*, 230–31.
27. Roth, *Conversos, Inquisition, and the Expulsion of the Jews from Spain*, 236–37.
28. Mesch, *Abyss of Despair*, 43.
29. Mesch, *Abyss of Despair*, 43.
30. Mesch, *Abyss of Despair*, 44.
31. Mesch, *Abyss of Despair*, 44.
32. Joel Greenberg, "Palestinians Destroy Israeli Site That Was Scene of Many Clashes," *New York Times*, October 8, 2000.
33. Cowen Report, Phillip Cowen to Frank P. Sargent, December 31, 1906, and January 31, 1907, with appendices, 18, Cowen Report—European Investigation Entry No. 9; File No. 51411/056—Record Group 85, Records of the Immigration and Naturalization Service, National Archives, https://catalog.archives.gov/id/602984?objectPanel=transcription&objectPage=172.
34. Cowen Report, 9, 16–17
35. Cowen Report, 21.
36. Cowen Report, 7, Exhibit 11, 29–31.
37. Cowen Report, 35–36, 39.
38. Cowen Report, 42.
39. Shtif, *Pogroms in Ukraine*.
40. For the various estimates of the death toll, see Friedman, *Pogromchik*, 14–17.

41. Friedman, *Pogromchik*, 8–9; "Tell of Ukraine Pogroms," *New York Times*, April 7, 1919.
42. Friedman, *Pogromchik*, 10; "Jews Massacred in Ukraine," *New York Times*, March 8, 1919.
43. Friedman, *Pogromchik*, 10; "Slay Jews in Galicia," *New York Times*, April 19, 1919.
44. Friedman, *Pogromchik*, 10.
45. Friedman, *Pogromchik*, 11.
46. Friedman, *Pogromchik*, 12.
47. Astashkevich, *Gendered Violence*, xi, xiii.
48. Brownmiller, *Against Our Will*, 122–23.
49. Friedman, *Pogromchik*, 7–8; "Death Regiment in Pogrom," *New York Times*, March 28, 1919; "Sends New Report on Pogrom at Kiev," *New York Times*, January 2, 1920.
50. Friedman, *Pogromchik*, 14.
51. Friedman, *Pogromchik*, 14.
52. "The Outbreak in Jaffa," *The Maccabaean* 14, no. 4 (April 1908): 155; "The News from Zion," *The Maccabaean* 14, no. 5 (May 1908): 194; "The News from Zion," *The Maccabaean* 14, no. 6 (June 1908): 236–37; "The News from Zion," *The Maccabaean* 15, no. 6 (June 1909): 227; Dr. Benj. L. Gordon, "Ekron: A Jewish Colony in the Land of the Philistines," *The Maccabaean* 23, no. 6 (June 1913): 167; M. Bernstein and Nellie Strauss, "Yigael: A Story of Merchaviah," *The Maccabaean* 28, no. 5 (May 1916): 103–6; M. Bernstein and Nellie Strauss, "Yigael: A Story of Merchaviah (Part Two)," *The Maccabaean* 28, no. 6 (June 1916): 132–35.
53. Avneri, *Claim of Dispossession*, 12; Gottheil, "Arab Immigration," 315–24; Gottheil, "Smoking Gun," 53–64; Even if one were to exclude the areas east of the Jordan River—which would later become Transjordan and then the Kingdom of Jordan—the population of Palestine then was still less dense than that of modern-day Colorado. However, to remove those areas from the calculation would be anachronistic, since both the Arab and Jews at the time regarded the areas east of the Jordan as part of the country, and Jewish settlement was undertaken there just as it was on the western side, although in a more limited capacity, for various reasons.
54. Alroey, *Land of Refuge*, chap. 3, table 3.3.
55. Wasserstein, "Patterns of Communal Conflict in Palestine," 674.
56. Untitled editorial, *The Maccabaean* 33 (June 1920): 185; "Trouble in Jerusalem between Moslems and Jews Reported," *The Sentinel* (Chicago), April 23, 1920.
57. Jesse E. Sampter, "Passover—5680," *The Maccabaean* 33 (June 1920): 172–74.

58. Oren Kessler, "1921 Jaffa Riots 100 Years on: Mandatory Palestine's 1st 'Mass Casualty' Attack," *Times of Israel*, May 1, 1921; Sarah Honig, "Another Tack: The May Day Massacre of 1921," *Jerusalem Post*, April 30, 2009; "27 Jews Killed in Jaffa," *New York Times*, May 6, 1921.
59. "Seven Days of Bloodshed and Horror in Palestine," *Palestine Bulletin*, September 2, 1929.
60. "Seven Days of Bloodshed and Horror in Palestine."
61. Wasserstein, "Patterns of Communal Conflict in Palestine," 680.
62. Londres, *Wandering Jew*, 173.
63. Kisch, *Palestine Diary*, 280.
64. Bentwich and Bentwich, *Mandate Memories 1918–1948*, 134.
65. Van Paasen, *Days of Our Years*, 370–71.
66. "The Hebron Horror," *Palestine Bulletin*, September 22, 1929.
67. "Eye Witnesses Describe Horrors of the Moslem Arabs' Attacks at Hebron on Saturday, August 24," JTA, September 1, 1929; Auerbach, *Hebron Jews*, 69–71.
68. "Seven Days of Bloodshed and Horror in Palestine."
69. "Seven Days of Bloodshed and Horror in Palestine," *Palestine Post*, September 2, 1929; "Arabs Burn City of Safed; 22 Killed, Scores Wounded; Syrians Invade from North," *New York Times*, August 31, 1929; "Moslem Arabs Perpetrate New Attacks on Jews at Safed; 8 Jews Killed, 30 Wounded, Incomplete List," JTA, September 1, 1929; Londres, *Wandering Jew*, 175–77.
70. "Father and Two Children Murdered," *Palestine Post*, August 14, 1936, 1–2.
71. "Funeral of Safad's Road Sacrifices," *Palestine Post*, March 30, 1938; "Bechor Shichrur u'Mazal Mosseri, z"l," *Ha'aretz*, March 31, 1938; Bell, *Terror Out of Zion*, 39.
72. Carlson, *Cairo to Damascus*, 172.
73. Graves, *Experiment in Anarchy*, 157.
74. Yuval Barnea, "Gazans Tried to Sell Fallen IDF Soldier's Head for $10,000, Says Soldier's Father," *Jerusalem Post*, January 18, 2024.
75. Milstein, *History of Israel's War of Independence:—Vol. II*, 134, 189, 108–9.
76. Morris, *1948*, 361–62.
77. "Palestine: In the Hills of Hebron," *Time*, February 2, 1948; Kurzman, *Genesis 1948*, 75; Milstein, *History of Israel's War of Independence—Vol. III*, 28.
78. "Furious Fighting Continues in Hebron Hills; 17 More Jews Killed Near Kfar Etzion," JTA, January 19, 1948.
79. "Arrested 4 Found Murdered," *Palestine Post*, February 13, 1948; "Jerusalem in the War of Liberation," accessed January 31, 2025, https://www.jerusalem-love.co.il/?page_id=11457.
80. Milstein, *History of Israel's War of Independence—Vol. IV*, 142.

81. Morris, *1948*, 125.
82. Sharon, *Warrior*, 65.
83. Morris, *1948*, 293.
84. Amnon Rubinstein, "Sinai Diary: By an Israeli Soldier," *New York Times Sunday Magazine*, July 2, 1967.
85. Sam Borden, "Long-Hidden Details Reveal Cruelty of 1972 Munich Attackers," *New York Times*, December 1, 2015.
86. "Call for More Security after Golan Murders," *Jerusalem Post*, November 23, 1975.
87. Goldhagen, *Hitler's Willing Executioners*, 218.
88. Goldhagen, *Hitler's Willing Executioners*, 218.
89. Goldhagen, *Hitler's Willing Executioners*, 218.
90. Goldhagen, *Hitler's Willing Executioners*, 218.
91. Browning, *Ordinary Men*, 184.
92. Goldhagen, *Hitler's Willing Executioners*, 422–23.
93. Emanuel Fabian, "IDF: Captors Murdered Children Ariel and Kfir Bibas 'in Cold Blood' with 'Their Bare Hands,'" *Times of Israel*, February 21, 2025.
94. Gross, *Neighbors*.
95. Then-Israeli Prime Minister Yitzhak Shamir was roundly criticized in 1989 for using that same undiplomatic expression. ("Shamir's Remarks about Poland Held Up Diplomatic Relations," Jewish Telegraphic Agency, December 8, 1989).
96. Dov Segal, "The Lietukis Garage Massacre," *Jerusalem Post*, August 8, 2017
97. Segal, "Lietukis Garage Massacre."
98. Roosevelt was unwilling to say anything publicly that might damage German-American relations. See Rafael Medoff, "FDR's Secret Plea to Hitler," accessed January 31, 2025, http://new.wymaninstitute.org/2021/09/fdrs-secret-plea-to-hitler/.
99. Press Conference #142, September 7, 1934, http://www.fdrlibrary.marist.edu/_resources/images/pc/pc0011.pdf, 9–11.
100. *Education for Death: The Making of the Nazi*, October 11, 2017, YouTube, accessed January 31, 2025, https://www.youtube.com/watch?v=-u_xSDrWg68.
101. Smith, *Last Train from Berlin*, 126–28, 226.
102. Gilbert, *Holocaust*, 792–93, 806.
103. Bartoletti, *Hitler Youth*, 130.
104. Kirkpatrick, *Inner Circle*, 53.
105. Goldhagen, *Hitler's Willing Executioners*, 245–46.
106. Goldhagen, *Hitler's Willing Executioners*, 246.
107. Goldhagen, *Hitler's Willing Executioners*, 246–47.

108. Klee et al, *"Good Old Days,"* 226; "Holocaust: SS Officer's Photos Reveal Sobibor Death Camp," bbc.com, January 28, 2020.
109. Daniel Hagari (@IDFSpokesperson), "A Conversation Between a Terrorist and his Family in Which he is Proud of the Massacre of the Jews," X, October 24, 2023, https://x.com/IDFSpokesperson/status/1716867039300846031.
110. "A Hamas Terrorist Murdered Her Grandmother, Filmed It, and Posted the Clip on Facebook," *Jerusalem Post*, October 12, 2023.

7. UNIVERSITIES AND THE NAZIS

1. Beginning in 1922, Harvard adopted admissions criteria that enabled the administration to drastically reduce the number of Jewish students. (Karabel, *Chosen*, 77–108.)
2. "Render Unto Caesar" (editorial), *The Harvard Crimson*, June 13, 1934.
3. Norwood, *Third Reich in the Ivory Tower*, 50–52, 54.
4. Norwood, *Third Reich in the Ivory Tower*, 58.
5. Norwood, *Third Reich in the Ivory Tower*, 65; "Heidelberg" (editorial), *The Harvard Crimson*, March 3, 1936.
6. Norwood, "Entertaining Nazi Warriors in America, 1934–1936," 148–84.
7. Leff, *Well Worth Saving*, 53.
8. Leff, *Well Worth Saving*, 4.
9. "Nazis to Multiply Students Abroad," *New York Times*, April 25, 1936; "Nazi Students Drill on Converting World," *New York Times*, August 27, 1937; "NAZIS: Exchange Students End Training for Foreign Service," *Newsweek*, September 6, 1937.
10. Norwood, *Third Reich in the Ivory Tower*, 59.
11. Norwood, *Third Reich in the Ivory Tower*, 76–77, 85.
12. Like Harvard, Columbia University also schemed to minimize the number of Jews on campus. In the early 1900s, administrators developed a clandestine screening technique that severely limited the admission of Jewish students, faculty members, and trustees. It was more sophisticated than the methods employed by Harvard, but just as efficient. See Klingenstein, *Jews in the American Academy 1900–1940*, 146–47.
13. Norwood, *Third Reich in the Ivory Tower*, 93–98.
14. Norwood, *Third Reich in the Ivory Tower*, 94–95, 97, 98–99. Referring to Jewish students, Butler wrote to a colleague in 1934 that he was concerned about "the domination of the college in whole, or in part, by an undesirable element of the population." Butler insisted that every applicant take a test for "mental alertness" developed by the psychologist Edward Thorndike, a racist and eugenicist, in the hope it would reveal traits common to Jewish students that would make it possible to reject their applications. In 2020,

Thorndike's name was removed from a hall at Columbia Teachers College because of his racism. Nothing was done concerning the name of the Columbia president who had used Thorndike's research to suppress Jewish enrollment. See Klingenstein, *Jews in the American Academy*, 146.

15. "Protest Meeting Adopts Petition," *The Tech*, March 31, 1933.
16. "Institute Accepts German Invitation," *The Tech*, April 23, 1937 "Celebrating 'Racial' Science" (editoiral), *The Tech*, April 23, 1937; "Goettingen Protest Is Reported Signed By 300 Petitioners," *The Tech*, April 30, 1937; "More Refusals" (editorial), *The Tech*, April 30, 1937.
17. Norwood, *Third Reich in the Ivory Tower*, 71–72; Leff, *Well Worth Saving*, 106–7.
18. Wechsler, *Revolt on the Campus*, 340–41.
19. Norwood, *Third Reich in the Ivory Tower*, 15, 164–65, 57–60, 66–67, 82, 94, 32–33; Leff, *Well Worth Saving*, 60.
20. "Yale Will Not Buy Nazi-Doomed Books," *Yale Daily News*, April 27, 1938.
21. Norwood, *Third Reich in the Ivory Tower*, 125.
22. "Beer, Folk Songs, German Requisites, Says Garnett," *The GW Hatchet*, February 20, 1934.
23. "Embassy Representative Addresses German Club," *The GW Hatchet*, October 24, 1933.
24. "German Vallentine [sic] Party Features Attache Von Haften," *The GW Hatchet*, February 13, 1934.
25. "International Students Show European Films," *The GW Hatchet*, May 11, 1937.
26. Untitled photo montage, *The GW Hatchet*, April 27, 1937.
27. "Student Organizes European Tours of College Groups," *The GW Hatchet*, April 13, 1937.
28. Caute, *Fellow-Travellers*, 36.
29. Norwood, *Third Reich in the Ivory Tower*, 83, 138.
30. Gottlieb, "The American Controversy Over the Olympic Games," 181–213.
31. Favez, *Red Cross and the Holocaust*, 73–74.
32. Norwood, *Third Reich in the Ivory Tower*, 250–52.
33. "2,000 Jews Slain in Rumanian Terror; Eyewitness Tells Brutalities," Jewish Telegraphic Agency, January 30, 1941.
34. Eliade, *Autobiography—Volume 1*, 281–82; Eliade, *Autobiography—Volume 2*, 65–66; Norwood, *Third Reich in the Ivory Tower*, 255.
35. Rennie, "Diplomatic Career of Mircea Eliade," 375–92; Stigliano, "Fascism's Mythologist Mircea Eliade"; Joseph Frank, "Thinkers and Liars," *The New Republic*, November 19, 2006; Rennie and O'Cellaigh, "Mircea Eliade and Antisemitism."

36. "Honorary Degree Recipients," Office of the Provost, George Washington University; "Statement by Yale University regarding Bill Cosby's Honorary Degree," *Yale News*, May 1, 2018; "Statement on Rescinding Honorary Degree," Oberlin College, December 16, 2015.
37. Peterson, "Student Organizations and the Antiwar Movement in America," 137–38.
38. Peterson, "Student Organizations and the Antiwar Movement in America," 137.
39. Cohen, *When the Old Left Was Young*, 89–90.
40. Cohen, *When the Old Left Was Young*, 89–90.
41. Cohen, *When the Old Left Was Young*, 295–96.
42. Frank S. Adams, "Roosevelt Flays Soviet Dictatorship; Says 98% of Americans Favor Finns; Lew Proposes a Labor Peace Plan," *New York Times*, February 11, 1940; "Text of President Roosevelt's Address to the Delegates of the American Youth Congress," *New York Times*, February 11, 1940.
43. Alex Gangitano, "Biden Tells a Heckler Calling for Cease-fire: 'I Think We Need a Pause,'" *The Hill*, November 1, 2023; "Biden Tells Heckler He's Pushing for Israel to Leave Gaza," BBC.com, January 8, 2024.
44. Adams, "Roosevelt Flays Soviet Dictatorship"; "Text of President Roosevelt's Address."
45. Nathan M. Greenfield, "US Universities' Foreign Funders: How Much Do We Know?," *University World News*, December 10, 2023.
46. Isaac Herzog, "American University and College Presidents," *Times of Israel*, November 7, 2023.

8. ANTISEMITISM AND ANTI-ZIONISM

1. Anti-Defamation League, "Over 10,000 Antisemitic Incidents Recorded in the U.S. since Oct. 7, 2023, According to ADL Preliminary Data," October 6, 2024, https://www.adl.org/resources/press-release/over-10000-antisemitic-incidents-recorded-us-oct-7-2023-according-adl.
2. As the term gained currency in English, it was commonly spelled "anti-Semitism," with the hyphen and capital S, thus implying that it referred to hatred of "Semites," although most of the public always understood that it referred to hatred of Jews. In recent years, many scholars have adopted the spellings "antisemite" and "antisemitism," without the hyphen or capitalization, in order to clarify that the reference is to beliefs or actions against Jews, not against "Semites" or "Semitism." In fact, the term "Semitic" refers to languages, not a group of people or a philosophy, so the terms "anti-Semite" and "anti-Semitism" never had genuine basis.
3. Sorin, *Time for Building*, 2.
4. Sorin, *Time for Building*,, 1.

5. Woeste, *Henry Ford's War on Jews.*
6. Stember et al., *Jews in the Mind of America*, 8, 210, 215; Gartner, "Two Continuities of Antisemitism," 317–18.
7. "Edelstein Dies After Clash with Rankin in House over Anti-Jewish Speech," JTA, June 5, 1941; "Assail Lindbergh for Iowa Speech," *New York Times*, September 13, 1941.
8. Warren, *Radio Priest*, 77.
9. Norwood, "Marauding Youth," 233–67.
10. "Pritchett Reports Zionism Will Fail," *New York Times*, November 29, 1926; "Pritchett Defends Report," *New York Times*, December 5, 1926; Dr. S. Margoshes, "'Casual Impressions': An Interview with Dr. Pritchett," *New Palestine*, December 10, 1926.
11. Cohen, *Year After the Riots*, 109.
12. "Pritchett Reports Zionism Will Fail"; "Pritchett Defends Report"; Margoshes, "'Casual Impressions.'"
13. Cohen, *Year After the Riots*, 109.
14. Temkin, *New World of Reform*, 38; Polish, *Renew Our Days*, 49. In the 1930s, most Reform rabbinic leaders began moving away from the movement's old anti-Zionism stance, and in 1948, they embraced the new State of Israel.
15. Tabachnik, "American-Jewish Reaction," 60. Among Orthodox Jews in America, only a small fraction opposed Zionism, viewing it as conflicting with the idea that a Jewish state was only meant to come into being in Messianic times.
16. A core group of diehards remained active in the Council in the 1950s, in part because the State Department continued to welcome their advice. See Rafael Medoff, "The State Department's Campaign Against the 'Jewish State' Idea—in 1954," *The Algemeiner*, March 20, 2014; Kolsky, *Jews Against Zionism*, 82; Penkower, "Genesis of the American Council for Judaism," 167–94.
17. Leff, "A Tragic 'Fight in the Family,'" 3–51.
18. Jewish Voice for Peace activists occasionally engaged in disruptive behavior even before October 7, but not with the frequency or intensity displayed since then. In 2016, for example, they stormed the stage at an LGBTQ conference in Chicago to physically prevent an Israeli gay rights speaker from appearing. (Paul Miller, "LGBT Conference in Chicago Turns Violent from Anti-Israel Protesters," *Observer*, January 25, 2016.)
19. *Jewish Voice for Peace Annual Report 2023*, https://www.jewishvoiceforpeace.org/wp-content/uploads/2023/11/JVP-Annual-Report-2023.pdf.
20. Jonathan Greenblatt (@JGreenblattADL), "We long have said that these are hate groups, the photo inverse of white supremacists," X, October 18, 2023, https://x.com/jgreenblattadl/status/1714791774869487973.

21. Rudavsky, *Emancipation and Adjustment*, 74–75.
22. "Protest to Wilson Against Zionist State," *New York Times*, March 5, 1919; Kolsky, *Jews Against Zionism*, 60, 108–9, 117–18.
23. Task Force on Antisemitism, "We Hear You," *Columbia Spectator*, May 16, 2024; Ethan Fraenkel et al, "Task Force on Antisemitism, Can You Hear Us Now?," *Columbia Spectator*, June 11, 2024.
24. Alvin H. Rosenfeld, "The Return of the Swastika," *Tablet*, January 15, 2024.
25. "Eban Proposes Middle Eastern Community," *The Israel Digest*, June 28, 1968.
26. Itamar Marcus and Barbara Crook, "The Protocols of the Elders of Zion: An Authentic Document in Palestinian Authority Ideology," Palestinian Media Watch, 2005.
27. Ascoli, *Julius Rosenwald*, 372.
28. "The Reverend Jesse Jackson Embraces PLO Leader Yasser Arafat," United Press International, September 29, 1979; "PLO Claims Responsibility for Bombing Outrage in Jerusalem," JTA, September 20, 1979.
29. ADL Research Report, *Anti-Semitism of Black Demagogues and Extremists*.
30. Ron Kampeas, "What Was Louis Farrakhan Doing at That Congressional Black Caucus Meeting with Obama?," JTA, February 1, 2018.
31. Farah Stockman, "Women's March Roiled by Accusations of Anti-Semitism," *New York Times*, December 23, 2018; Ben Sales, "Author of Black Lives Matter Position on Israel Defends 'Genocide' Claim," JTA, August 9, 2016.
32. Michael Rosenberg, "Everything Isn't Kosher, but LeBron's 'Jewish Money' Post Can Be Explained," *Sports Illustrated*, December 24, 2018.
33. Lewis, "Israel's American Detractors—Back Again," 22–25.
34. The David S. Wyman Institute for Holocaust Studies undertook the mobilization of criticism. See "Congress Passes Lantos's Anti-Semitism Bill," *Jewish Community Chronicle*, October 17, 2004.
35. "About Us—Special Envoy to Monitor and Combat Antisemitism," U.S. Department of State, accessed January 31, 2025, https://www.state.gov/about-us-special-envoy-to-monitor-and-combat-antisemitism/.
36. "U.S. National Strategy to Counter Antisemitism," The White House, May 25, 2023, 9.
37. Megan Trimble, "KKK Groups Still Active in These States in 2017," *U.S. News and World Report*, August 14, 2017; "Nation of Islam," ADL.org, September 1, 2021.
38. "Defining Antisemitism," U.S. Department of State, accessed January 31, 2025, https://www.state.gov/defining-antisemitism/.
39. "The Working Definition of Antisemitism," International Holo caust Remembrance Alliance, accessed January 31, 2025, .https://www

.holocaustremembrance.com/resources/working-definitions-charters /working-definition-antisemitism.

40. "Understanding Antisemitism at Its Nexus with Israel and Zionism," The Nexus Document, accessed January 31, 2025, https://israelandantisemitism .com/the-nexus-document/.
41. "Working Definition of Antisemitism"; "Understanding Antisemitism at Its Nexus."
42. "Majority Leader Schumer Delivers Major Address on Antisemitism on the Senate Floor," Senate Democrats Office, November 29, 2023.
43. "Majority Leader Schumer Delivers Major Address on Antisemitism."
44. "Determination of the Secretary of State on Atrocities in Xinjiang," State Department news release, January 19, 2021; Nicholas Kristof, "From the Embers of an Old Genocide, a New One May Be Emerging," *New York Times*, May 15, 2024.
45. Schumer identified them as members of "the Students for a Democratic Society and the Progressive Labor Party."
46. Samuel Z. Goldhaber, "Eban Says No Israeli Withdrawal Without Prior Peace Settlement," *The Harvard Crimson*, November 10, 1970.
47. Jonathan Greenblatt, "BDS Must be Taken on With Every Measure of Seriousness," Medium, June 1, 2016; Anti-Defamation League, "The Boycott, Divestment and Sanctions Campaign (BDS)," May 24, 2022, https://www.adl.org /resources/backgrounder/boycott-divestment-and-sanctions-campaign-bds.
48. Ahmed Moor, "BDS Is a Long Term Project with Radically Transformative Potential," Mondoweiss, April 22, 2010; "Omar Barghouti: 'No Palestinian Will Ever Accept a Jewish State in Palestine,'" YouTube, May 26, 2014, https://www.youtube.com/watch?v=vYvpsGd8K4Y; Roberta P. Seid, "Omar Barghouti at UCLA: A Speaker Who Brings Hate," *Jewish Journal of Los Angeles*, January 16, 2014; Anti-Defamation League, "Boycott, Divestment and Sanctions Campaign (BDS)."
49. Gerald Steinberg, "Palestinian NGO Blood Libel, Funded by E.U. and U.S.," *Times of Israel*, April 11, 2013.
50. Ali Abunimah, "Why Israel Won't Survive," *The Electronic Intifada*, January 19, 2009.
51. Anti-Defamation League, "Boycott, Divestment and Sanctions Campaign (BDS)."
52. UAW 2865 BDS Caucus Panel Discussion, YouTube, November 12, 2014, https://www.youtube.com/watch?v=bZMp83syN40&t=840s.
53. Itamar Eichner, "Ben & Jerry's Official Posts Justification of Hamas Massacre," Ynetnews.com, December 7, 2023.

54. Ron Kampeas and Ben Sales, "Joe Biden's Critics Are Attacking Him for Saying Pro-Palestinian Protesters 'Have a Point.' His Jewish Backers Aren't Concerned," Jewish Telegraphic Agency, August 20, 2024; "Kamala Harris: Campus Protesters over Gaza War 'Showing What Human Emotion Should Be,'" *Times of Israel*, July 10, 2024; President Biden (@POTUS46archive), "The horrific acts of Antisemitism this week—including a demonstration celebrating the 10/7 attack, vandalism targeting Jewish homes, attacks on Jewish faculty at college campuses, and harassment of subway riders—are abhorrent," X, June 14, 2024, https://x.com/POTUS/status/1801609649428349193; Ron Kampeas, "Red Triangle, Symbol Associated with Hamas, Is Painted on Pittsburgh Synagogue Building," Jewish Telegraphic Agency, July 29, 2024.

CONCLUSION

1. Smith, *Last Train from Berlin*, 128.

Bibliography

ADL Research Report. *The Anti-Semitism of Black Demagogues and Extremists.* New York: Anti Defamation League, 1992.

Alroey, Gur. *Land of Refuge: Immigration to Palenstine, 1919–1927.* Bloomington: Indiana University Press, 2024.

Amnesty International. *"You Feel Like You Are Subhuman": Israel's Genocide Against Palestinians in Gaza.* London: Amnesty International, 2024.

Ascoli, Peter M. *Julius Rosenwald: The Man Who Built Sears, Roebuck and Advanced the Cause of Black Education in the American South.* Bloomington: Indiana University Press, 2006.

Astashkevich, Irina. *Gendered Violence: Jewish Women in Pogroms, 1917–1921.* Boston: Academic Studies Press, 2018.

Auerbach, Jerold S. *Hebron Jews: Memory and Conflict in the Land of Israel.* Lanham MD: Rowman & Littlefield, 2009.

Avneri, Aryeh L. *The Claim of Dispossession: Jewish Land-Settlement and the Arabs, 1878–1948.* Ramat Efal, Israel: Yad Tabenkin Institute, 1980.

Bartoletti, Susan Campbell. *Hitler Youth: Growing Up in Hitler's Shadow.* New York: Scholastic, 2005.

Bar-Zohar, Michael, and Eitan Haber. *The Quest for the Red Prince.* New York: William Morrow and Company, 1983.

Bell, J. Bowyer. *Terror Out of Zion: The Violent and Deadly Shock Troops of Israeli Independence, 1929–1949.* New York: St. Martin's, 1977.

Ben-Ami, Shlomo. *Scars of War, Wounds of Peace: The Israeli-Arab Tragedy.* New York: Oxford University Press, 2006.

Bentwich, Norman, and Helen Bentwich. *Mandate Memories 1918–1948: From the Balfour Declaration to the Establishment of Israel.* New York: Schocken, 1965.

Berg, Scott A. *Lindbergh.* New York: Putnam, 1998.

Browning, Christoper. *Ordinary Men: Reserve Police Battalion 101 and the Final Solution in Poland.* New York: HarperPerennial, 1992.

Brownmiller, Susan. *Against Our Will: Men, Women and Rape.* New York: Simon and Schuster, 1975.

Carlson, John Roy. *Cairo to Damascus.* New York: Alfred A. Knopf, 1951.

Carroll, James. *Constantine's Sword: The Church and the Jews—A History*. New York: Houghton Mifflin, 2001.

Caute, David. *The Fellow-Travellers: Intellectual Friends of Communism*. New Haven CT: Yale University Press, 1973.

Chazan, Robert. *God, Humanity and History: The Hebrew First Crusade Narratives*. Berkeley: University of California Press, 2000.

Clinton, Hilary Rodham. *It Takes a Village: And Other Lessons Children Teach Us*. New York: Simon and Schuster, 1996.

Cohen, Jeremy. *The Friars and the Jews: The Evolution of Medieval Anti-Judaism*. Ithaca NY: Cornell University Press, 1983.

———. *Sanctifying the Name of God: Jewish Martyrs and Jewish Memories of the First Crusade*. Philadelphia: University of Pennsylvania Press, 2004.

Cohen, Naomi W. *The Year After the Riots: American Responses to the Palestine Crisis of 1929–30*. Detroit: Wayne State University Press, 1988.

Cohen, Robert. *When the Old Left Was Young: Student Radicals and America's First Mass Student Movement, 1929–1941*. New York: Oxford University Press, 1993.

Dawidowicz, Lucy S. *From That Time and Place: A Memoir, 1938–1947*. New York: W. W. Norton, 1989.

———. *The War Against the Jews: 1933–1945*. New York: Random House, 1975.

Eban, Abba. *An Autobiography*. New York: Random House, 1977.

———. *Voice of Israel*. New York: Horizon Press, 1957.

Eidelberg, Shlomo, trans. and ed. *The Jews and the Crusaders*. Madison: University of Wisconsin Press, 1977.

El-Awaisi, Abd Al-Fattah Muhammad. *The Muslim Brothers and the Palestine Question 1928–1947*. London: I. B. Tauris, 1998.

Eliade, Mircea. *Autobiography—Volume 1: 1907–1937, Journey East, Journey West*. San Francisco: Harper & Row, 1981.

———. *Autobiography—Volume 2: 1937–1960, Exile's Odyssey*. Chicago: University of Chicago Press, 1988.

Erdheim, Stuart G. "Could the Allies Have Bombed Auschwitz-Birkenau?" *Holocaust and Genocide Studies* 11, no. 2 (1997): 129–70.

Favez, Jean-Claude. *The Red Cross and the Holocaust*. New York: Cambridge University Press, 1999.

Feldner, Yotam. "72 Black Eyed Virgins"? *Claremont Review of Books* 11, no.1 (Fall 2001). https://claremontreviewofbooks.com/72-black-eyed-virgins/.

Festinger, Leon, Henry W. Riecken, and Stanley Schachter. *When Prophecy Fails: A Social and Psychological Study of a Modern Group That Predicted the Destruction of the World*. New York: Harper & Row, 1956

Foer, Franklin. "The Golden Age of American Jews Is Ending." *The Atlantic*, April 2024.

Fox, Andrew. *Questionable Counting: Analysing the Death Toll from the Hamas-Run Ministry of Health in Gaza*. London: Henry M. Jackson Society, 2024.

Frampton, Martyn. *The Muslim Brotherhood and the West: A History of Enmity and Engagement*. Cambridge MA: Harvard University Press, 2018.

Friedman, Saul S. *Pogromchik: The Assassination of Simon Petlura*. New York: Hart, 1976.

Garfinkle, Adam M. "On the Origin, Meaning, Use and Abuse of a Phrase." *Middle Eastern Studies* 27, no. 4 (October 1991): 539–50.

Gartner, Lloyd. "The Two Continuities of Antisemitism." In *Antisemitism through the Ages*, edited by Shmuel Almog, 317–18. Oxford: Pergamon, 1988.

Gilbert, Martin. *The Holocaust*. New York: Holt, Reinhart & Winston, 1985.

Goldhagen, Daniel Jonah. *Hitler's Willing Executioners: Ordinary Germans and the Holocaust*. New York: Alfred A. Knopf, 1996.

Gottheil, Fred M. "Arab Immigration into Pre-State Israel: 1922–1931." *Middle Eastern Studies* 9, no. 3 (1973): 315–24.

———. "The Smoking Gun: Arab Immigration into Palestine, 1922–1931." *Middle East Quarterly* 10, no. 1 (Winter 2003): 53–64.

Gottlieb, Moshe. "The American Controversy Over the Olympic Games." *American Jewish Historical Quarterly* 61, no. 3 (March 1972): 181–213.

Grabowski, Jan. *Hunt for the Jews: Betrayal and Murder in German-Occupied Poland*. Bloomington: Indiana University Press, 2013.

Graves, R. M. *Experiment in Anarchy*. London: Victor Gollancz, 1949.

Gross, Jan T. *Neighbors: The Destruction of the Jewish Community in Jedwabne, Poland*. Princeton: Princeton University Press, 2001.

Gutman, Israel. *Resistance: The Warsaw Ghetto Uprising*. New York: Mariner Books, 1998.

Hackett, David, trans. *The Buchenwald Report*. Boulder CO: Westview Press, 1995.

Harkabi, Yehoshofat. *Arab Attitudes to Israel*. Jerusalem: Keter, 1972.

Haas, Danielle. "The Human-Rights Establishment." *Sapir* 12 (Winter 2024): 98–111.

Henriques, Robert. *100 Hours to Suez: Israel's 1956 Campaign in the Sinai Peninsula*. New York: Viking, 1957.

Karabel, Jerome. *The Chosen: The Hidden History of Admission and Exclusion at Harvard, Yale, and Princeton*. Boston: Houghton Mifflin, 2005.

Kirby, M., and R. Casey. "The Area Bombing of Germany in World War II: An Operational Research Perspective." *The Journal of the Operational Research Society* 48, no. 7 (July 1997): 661–77.

Kirkpatrick, Ivone. *The Inner Circle: Memoirs of Ivone Kirkpatrick*. London: MacMillan, 1959.

Kisch, F. M. *Palestine Diary*. London: Victor Gollancz, 1938.

Klar-Chalamish, Carmit. *Silent Cry: Sexual Violence Crimes on October 7*. Tel Aviv: Association of Rape Crisis Centers in Israel, 2024.

Klee, Ernest, Willi Dressen, and Volker Riess, eds. *"The Good Old Days": The Holocaust as Seen by Its Perpetrators and Bystanders*. New York: Free Press, 1988.

Klingenstein, Susan. *Jews in the American Academy 1900–1940*. New Haven CT: Yale University Press, 1991.

Kolsky, Thomas A. *Jews Against Zionism: The American Council for Judaism, 1942–1948*. Philadelphia: Temple University, 1990.

Kressel, Neil J. *"Sons of Pigs and Apes": Muslim Antisemitism and the Conspiracy of Silence*. Lincoln NE: Potomac Books, 2012.

Kurzman, Dan. *Genesis 1948: The First Arab-Israeli War*. New York: World Publishing, 1970.

Lange, Christian. *Paradise and Hell in Islamic Traditions*. New York: Cambridge University Press, 2015.

Leff, Laurel. "A Tragic 'Fight in the Family': The *New York Times*, Reform Judaism and the Holocaust." *American Jewish History* 88, no. 1 (March 2000): 3–51.

———. *Well Worth Saving: American Universities' Life-and-Death Decisions on Refugees from Nazi Europe*. New Haven CT: Yale University Press, 2019.

Lewis, Bernard, ed. *Islam: From the Prophet Muhammad to the Capture of Constantinople*. New York: Oxford University Press, 1987.

———. *The Multiple Identities of the Middle East*. New York: Schocken, 1998.

Lewis, Michael. "Israel's American Detractors—Back Again." *Middle East Quarterly* 4, no. 1 (Winter 1997): 22–25.

Londres, Albert. *The Wandering Jew Has Arrived*. Translated by Helga Abraham. Jerusalem: Gefen, 2017.

Mandel, Neville J. *The Arabs and Zionism Before World War I*. Berkeley: University of California Press, 1980.

Marcus, Jacob Rader. *The Jew in the Medieval World*. Cincinnati: Hebrew Union College Press, 1999.

Mesch, Abraham J., trans. and ed. *Abyss of Despair by Nathan Hanover*. New York: Transaction Books, 1950.

Miller, Aaron D. *The Much Too Promised Land: America's Elusive Search for Arab-Israeli Peace*. New York: Random House, 2008.

Milstein, Uri. *History of Israel's War of Independence—Vol. II: The First Month*. Lanham MD: University Press of America, 1997.

———. *History of Israel's War of Independence—Vol. III: The First Invasion*. Lanham MD: University Press of America, 1998.

———. *History of Israel's War of Independence—Vol. IV: Out of Crisis Came Decision*. Lanham MD: University Press of America, 1999.

Morris, Benny. *Israel's Border Wars, 1949–1956*. Oxford: Clarendon Press, 1993.

———. *1948: A History of the First Arab-Israeli War*. New Haven CT: Yale University Press, 2008.

Murphy, Robert. "Report on Denazification" (Document no. 347). In *Foreign Relations of the United States: Diplomatic Papers, The Conference of Berlin (The Potsdam Conference), 1945, Volume I*, edited by Richard Dougall et al. Washington DC: United States Government Printing Office, 1960. https://history.state.gov/historicaldocuments/frus1945Berlinv01/d347.

Norwood, Stephen H. "Entertaining Nazi Warriors in America, 1934–1936." In *From Antisemitism to Anti-Zionism the Past & Present of a Lethal Ideology*, edited by Eunice G. Pollack, 148–84. Boston: Academic Studies Press, 2017.

———. "Marauding Youth and the Christian Front: Antisemitic Violence in Boston and New York During World War II." *American Jewish History* 91, no. 2 (June 2003): 233–67.

———. *The Third Reich in the Ivory Tower: Complicity and Conflict on American Campuses*. Cambridge MA: Cambridge University Press, 2009.

Oren, Michael. *Six Days of War: June 1967 and the Making of the Modern Middle East*. Oxford: Oxford University Press, 2002.

Penkower, Monty Noam. "The Genesis of the American Council for Judaism: A Quest for Identity in World War II." *American Jewish History* 86, no. 2 (June 1998): 167–94.

Peterson, Patti McGill. "Student Organizations and the Antiwar Movement in America, 1900–1960." *American Studies* 13, no. 1 (Spring 1972): 131–47.

Philologos, "Why Are Anti-Israel Chants So Dull?," *Mosaic*, May 2, 2024.

Podeh, Elie. "The Lie That Won't Die: Collusion, 1967." *Middle East Quarterly* 11, no. 1 (Winter 2004). https://www.meforum.org/middle-east-quarterly/the-lie-that-wont-die-collusion-1967.

Polish, David. *Renew Our Days: The Zionist Issue in Reform Judaism*. Jerusalem: World Zionist Organization, 1976.

Porath, Y. *The Emergence of the Palestinian-Arab National Movement 1918–1929*. London: Frank Cass, 1974.

Power, Samantha. *"A Problem from Hell": America and the Age of Genocide*. New York: Basic Books, 2002.

Rennie, Bryan S. "The Diplomatic Career of Mircea Eliade: A Response to Adraian Berger." *Religion* 22, no. 4 (October 1992): 375–92.

Rennie, Bryan, and Philip Ó'Cellaigh. "Mircea Eliade and Antisemitism: An Exchange." *Los Angeles Review of Books*, September 13, 2018. https://lareviewofbooks.org/article/mircea-eliade-and-antisemitism-an-exchange/.

Rifkind, Donna. "In Memory of Vilna." *Commentary*, July 1989.

Ross, Dennis. *The Missing Peace: The Inside Story of the Fight for the Middle East Peace*. New York: Farrar, Straus and Giroux, 2004.

Roth, Norman. *Conversos, Inquisition, and the Expulsion of the Jews from Spain*. Madison: University of Wisconsin Press, 2002.

Rubin, Miri. *Gentile Tales: The Narrative Assault on Late Medieval Jews*. New Haven CT: Yale University Press, 2004.

Rudavsky, David. *Emancipation and Adjustment*. New York: Diplomatic Press, 1967.

Schanzer, Jonathan. "Israel Imperiled: Threats to the Jewish State." Presentation to a Joint Hearing before House Foreign Affairs Committee Subcommittee on Terrorism, Nonproliferation, and Trade and the Subcommittee on the Middle East and North Africa, Washington DC, April 19, 2016.

Schwartz, Yardena. *Ghosts of a Holy War: The 1929 Massacre in Palestine That Ignited the Arab-Israeli Conflict*. New York: Union Square, 2024.

Shanks, Hershel. "Holy Targets: Joseph's Tomb Is Just the Latest." *Biblical Archaeology Review*, January/February 2001.

Sharon, Ariel. *Warrior: An Autobiography of Ariel Sharon*. New York: Simon and Schuster, 1989.

Shtif, Nokhem. *The Pogroms in Ukraine, 1918–19: Prelude to the Holocaust*. Translated and annotated by Maurice Wolfthal. Cambridge UK: Open Book Publishers, 2019.

Smith, Howard K. *Last Train from Berlin*. New York: C. W. Morgan, 1942.

Solomon bar Simson. "Crusades of 109." In *Masterpieces of Hebrew Literature: A Treasury of 2000 Years of Jewish Creativity*, edited by Curt Leviant, 266–71. Hoboken NJ: Ktav, 1969.

Sorin, Gerald. *A Time for Building: The Third Migration*. Baltimore: Johns Hopkins University Press, 1992.

Stahl, Neta. "A Kibbutz and Its Fullness." *Jewish Review of Books*, Winter 2024.

Stember, Charles et al. *Jews in the Mind of America*. New York: Basic Books, 1966.

Stigliano, Tony. "Fascism's Mythologist Mircea Eliade and the Politics of Myth." *ReVision* 24, no. 3 (Winter 2002), link.gale.com/apps/doc/a86429838/aone?u=anon~9ddfa61&sid=googleScholar&xid=1d5e18a3.

Tabachnik, Joseph. "American-Jewish Reaction to the First Zionist Congress." In *Herzl Year Book—Volume V*, edited by Melvin Urofsky, 57–64. New York: Herzl Press, 1963.

Temkin, Sefton D. *The New World of Reform: Containing the Proceedings of the Conference of Reform Rabbis Held in Philadelphia in November 1869*. London: Leo Baeck College, 1971.

Van Paasen, Pierre. *Days of Our Years*. New York: Hillman-Curl, 1939.

Warren, Donald. *Radio Priest: Charles Coughlin, the Father of Hate Radio*. New York: Free Press, 1996.

Wasserstein, Bernard. "Patterns of Communal Conflict in Palestine." In *Essential Papers on Zionism*, edited by Jehuda Reinharz and Anita Shapira, 671–88. New York: New York University Press, 1996.

Wechsler, James P. *Revolt on the Campus*. New York: Covici Friede, 1935.

White, Joseph Robert. "'Even in Auschwitz . . . Humanity Could Prevail': British POWs and Jewish Concentration-Camp Inmates at IG Auschwitz, 1943–1945." *Holocaust and Genocide Studies* 15, no. 2 (2001): 266–95.

Winkler, Albert. "The Medieval Holocaust: The Approach of the Plague and the Destruction of Jews in Germany, 1348–1349." *Federation of East European Family History Societies* 13 (2005): 6–24.

Woeste, Victoria Saker. *Henry Ford's War on Jews and the Legal Battle Against Hate Speech*. Stanford CA: Stanford University Press, 2012.

Wright, Graham, Sasha Volodarsky, Shahar Hecht, and Leonard Saxe. *In the Shadow of War: Hotspots of Antisemitism on US College Campuses*. Waltham MA: Brandeis University, 2023.

Ye'or, Bat. *The Dhimmi: Jews and Christians Under Islam*. Teaneck NJ: Fairleigh Dickinson University, 1985.

Zuehlke, Mark. *Ortona: Canada's Epic World War II Battle*. Madeira Park BC: Douglas & McIntyre, 2004.

Index